NETWORK ARCHITECTURE AND DEVELOPMENT SERIES

The DHCP Handbook

Understanding, Deploying, and Managing Automated Configuration Services

Ralph Droms, Ph.D.
Ted Lemon

MACMILLAN
TECHNICAL
PUBLISHING
U·S·A

The DHCP Handbook: Understanding, Deploying, and Managing Automated Configuration Services

By Ralph Droms, Ph.D., and Ted Lemon

Published by:

Macmillan Technical Publishing
201 West 103rd Street
Indianapolis, IN 46290 USA

International Standard Book Number: 1-57870-137-6

Library of Congress Catalog Card Number: 99-62125

03 02 01 00 99   7 6 5 4 3 2 1

Interpretation of the printing code: The rightmost double-digit number is the year of the book's printing; the rightmost single-digit number is the number of the book's printing. For example, the printing code 99-1 shows that the first printing of the book occurred in 1999.

Printed in the United States of America

Trademark Acknowledgments

Warning and Disclaimer

Feedback Information

At Macmillan Technical Publishing, our goal is to create in-depth technical books of the highest quality and value. Each book is crafted with care and precision, undergoing rigorous development that involves the unique expertise of members from the professional technical community.

Readers' feedback is a natural continuation of this process. If you have any comments regarding how we can improve the quality of this book, or otherwise alter it to better suit your needs, you can contact us at networktech@mcp.com. Please make sure to include the book title and ISBN in your message.

We greatly appreciate your assistance.

Publisher
David Dwyer

Executive Editor
Linda Ratts Engelman

Managing Editor
Gina Brown

Acquisitions Editor
Karen Wachs

Development Editors
Shannon Leuma
Lisa Thibault

Project Editor
Laura Loveall

Copy Editor
Audrey Doyle

Indexer
Joy Dean Lee

Layout Technician
Amy Parker

Acquisitions Coordinator
Jennifer Garrett

Manufacturing Coordinator
Brook Farling

Book Designer
Gary Adair

Cover Designer
Sandra Schroeder

About the Authors

The authors of this text, Ralph Droms and Ted Lemon, bring extensive expertise and experience with DHCP and IP networking to this book. In this text, the authors combine their insights to create a unique perspective on the theory and design of the DHCP specification, and the practical aspects of implementing a DHCP server and running a DHCP service.

Ralph Droms, Ph.D., is an educator, consultant, and author. He is the chair of the IETF Dynamic Host Configuration (DHC) Working Group on automated configuration of networked computers and an Associate Professor of Computer Science at Bucknell University.

Ralph organized the DHC Working Group in 1989. He has chaired the Working Group since its inception and is a key contributor to the design and development of DHCP. Ralph is also editor of the DHCP RFCs and continues to participate in the evolution of DHCP.

Since joining the computer science department at Bucknell in 1987, Ralph has guided students through the study of TCP/IP internetworking, operating systems, and computer architecture. Previously, Ralph was a member of the computer science faculty at Pennsylvania State University. He was also on the research staff at IBM and Burroughs (Unisys).

As a consultant in network architecture and infrastructure design, Ralph works with large and small companies on a variety of TCP/IP issues including network architecture, server strategies and configurations, and the use of DHCP, DNS, and other technologies in network management. Ralph served as co-director of the computer center at Bucknell, where he supervised the design and implementation of the campus-wide, multi-protocol network.

Ralph lives with his wife and two daughters in Lewisburg, Pennsylvania. You can reach him at droms@bucknell.edu.

Ted Lemon is the author of the Internet Software Consortium DHCP Distribution, a popular Open Source distribution that includes a DHCP server, DHCP client, and relay agent. He started programming in 1977, when he decided to make a few changes to the Star Trek game, and has been working in the computer industry since 1983. He first encountered the DHCP protocol while working as a network administrator at Digital Equipment Corporation in the early 1990s and has been active in the IETF DHC Working Group since 1996. He is convinced that, while answering questions on the ISC DHCP mailing lists, he has answered roughly half of the questions that anybody has ever asked about DHCP, and he was motivated to work on this book in hopes of being able to help answer these questions more efficiently. He currently works for Internet Engines, Inc., developing the latest version of the ISC DHCP distribution.

About the Technical Reviewers

These reviewers contributed their practical, hands-on expertise to the entire development process for *The DHCP Handbook*. As the book was being written, these folks reviewed all the material for technical content, organization, and flow. Their feedback was critical to ensuring that *The DHCP Handbook* fits our readers' need for the highest-quality technical information.

Mike Carney is a Software Engineer at Sun Microsystems, Inc. Mike is a member of the Internet Engineering Group within Solaris Software, and he specializes in network configuration protocols such as DHCP. He is the author of the bundled Solaris DHCP server and has lead a successful effort to move Sun's remote booting technology away from a proprietary solution to one that uses DHCP. Mike is an active member of the IETF Dynamic Host Configuration Working Group. He leads the Futures Panel and is currently involved with helping to move the DHCPv6 specifications forward. Mike has also coordinated the DHCP interoperability testing at the Connectathon interoperability event for 4 years. Mike has more than 15 years experience in software engineering and is a graduate of the University of New Hampshire.

Richard Barr Hibbs is a Senior Systems Analyst with Pacific Bell. Richard has more than 25 years of experience in the analysis, specification, design, implementation, management, support, and marketing of internetworking and online transaction-processing systems. He is an active member of the IETF Dynamic Host Configuration (DHC) Working Group, and an observer of the Mobile-IP, Service Location, and Domain Naming System working groups. Richard holds a B.S. in Electrical Engineering from the University of Missouri and an M.S. in Electrical Engineering with a concentration in Computer Engineering from New York University. He is a California-registered professional engineer and is a member of the IEEE.

John Kemp is a UNIX Systems Engineer with Network Services at the University of Oregon. The University of Oregon is one of the leading campuses in the Northwest in the area of advanced network technologies. John holds a B.A. in English from Loyola Marymount University and a B.S. in Computer Science from the University of Nevada, Las Vegas. His primary interests are systems administration, network monitoring, and security analysis.

Dedication

To my father, who inspired me to ask questions and encouraged me to find answers.

Ralph Droms

May whatever good comes from the work I have done on this book help to bring about the enlightenment of all beings.

Ted Lemon

Acknowledgments

Thanks to everyone who contributed to this book. We had the pleasure and good fortune to work with a great team at Macmillan. Linda Engelman, Jen Garrett, Shannon Leuma, Lisa Thibault, and Karen Wachs all provided guidance and support every step along the way in the writing and production of this book.

Without the work of the DHC Working Group of the IETF, we wouldn't have DHCP to write about. We would like to thank Richard Barr Hibbs and John Kemp, our technical editors, who read the text with diligence that was above and beyond the call of duty. As a result of their efforts, we clarified some of the more difficult sections in the book. We also thank Mike Carney and Mark Sirota for their careful reading of the text and their helpful comments. We are extremely grateful to Thomas Hickman, Kim Kinnear, and Mark Stapp, all with Cisco Systems, who wrote or contributed to several chapters, as noted in the text.

From Ralph Droms:

Thanks to Bucknell University, Vint Cerf and the Corporation for National Research Initiatives, Joe D'Andrea and my other friends at Quadritek Systems (now a part of Lucent Technologies), and Mike Carney of Sun Microsystems for supporting my activities as chair of the DHC Working Group and making it possible to write this book. Doug Comer first gave me an opportunity to learn which end of a packet is up.

I thank Ted for his experience with the practice of networking that he brought to this project, for his insightful input and careful review of my writing, and for his vision about how we could make this book truly educational and useful.

My wife, Jan, improved the book with her careful editing and suggestions for organizing its content. Jan, along with our daughters Stacey and Becca, inspired me to tackle this project and see it through to completion.

From Ted Lemon:

I'd like to thank Paul Vixie for giving me the opportunity to create the ISC DHCP distribution and finding the funding that led to its development, David Conrad for his continued patience and perseverance in running the ISC, and most especially the very many users of the ISC DHCP server who have supplied me with helpful bug reports, fixes, and tales of their experiences with DHCP. Without their help, I would not have been in a position to work on this book. I'd like to thank Ralph for his thoughtful comments on the chapters I wrote, for the inspiration I obtained from him in discussing our ideas for the book, and for the chapters he wrote, without which my chapters would not have been useful.

I'd like to thank my parents for raising me with letters all around me, Martha Kitchen for her seemingly endless support, Walt Congdon for his kindness and friendship, my grandmothers for the lessons they've given me about how to live, my grandfathers for the practical spirit they both showed me, and my sister for sharing her writing experiences with me. I'd particularly like to thank Jennifer Bobbe for her patience and support while I was working on this book. I'd also like to thank the myriad other people in my life that space and poor memory have conspired to prevent me from acknowledging specifically.

Contents at a Glance

Table of Contents

Preface

Early in the development of the TCP/IP protocols, little motivation existed for automating the configuration of devices using TCP/IP. Few computers used TCP/IP, and the computers that were networked weren't very portable. Perhaps most significantly, the majority of computers were shared among many users, and had a designated administrator who managed many operational details, including TCP/IP configuration.

Today, everything is different. An organization may have thousands—in some cases, tens of thousands—of computers on its internal network. Devices ranging from mainframes, to desktop computers, to *Personal Digital Assistants (PDAs)*, to embedded processors are networked. Computers are highly mobile so that laptops, PDAs, and similar devices may move between network segments many times during the course of a single day. And today's computers are not typically managed by a trained system administrator. Most computers are set up and installed by users who aren't familiar with (and who probably don't want to know about) the arcane details of the TCP/IP protocol suite.

To meet the demands of "plug-and-play" operation through automating the configuration of networked computers, the IETF (Internet Engineering Task Force) developed DHCP (Dynamic Host Configuration Protocol). DHCP provides automated, managed configuration of computers and other devices using TCP/IP. Through DHCP, a network administrator can assign a network address and supply a subnet mask and a default router. DHCP is built around a *client-server* model in which networked computers (the clients) contact a centralized configuration server for configuration parameters. The administrator supplies the server with a description of the network infrastructure, along with rules about how to assign addresses and other configuration parameters. The server interacts directly with clients according to the rules the administrator provides. Thus, the DHCP server acts as the network administrator's agent for managing the configurations of DHCP clients.

Through the DHCP server, you can control the assignment of addresses and the configuration of other TCP/IP protocol parameters in whatever way is appropriate for your network and your organization. You can use fully dynamic address assignment, pre-assign a specific address to every computer, or use a mixed strategy in which your server computers are assigned fixed addresses and other computers are assigned addresses on demand.

The bottom line is that DHCP allows you to build a networking system that enables your users to freely add new computers, replace existing computers, and move computers between networked locations, all without explicit intervention on the part of the users or of a network administrator. In fact, this preface was written on a laptop that was connected to the campus network from Ralph Droms' home through an ADSL link, a campus office, and two campus classrooms (while he gave two final exams). Although each of these locations is serviced by a different part of the campus network, the author was able to simply turn on his laptop in each location and use the network immediately.

Objectives of this Book

As we wrote this book, we set as our goal the development of a complete resource for understanding DHCP, designing DHCP services, and debugging problems with DHCP clients and servers. We start with the background and theory of DHCP, including message exchanges between clients and server, message formats, and an introduction to the ISC DHCP server. Next, we describe the implementation and operation of DHCP servers and clients. We spend more time describing the DHCP server than the client; the DHCP server is more interesting because it is the component that the network administrator usually interacts with, whereas the DHCP client simply runs automatically and in the background. We also discuss practical aspects of DHCP—why you should use it, when to use it, and how to design and run an efficient DHCP service.

We include examples and case studies of DHCP in operation throughout the book. We drew the case studies from our experience with DHCP in real IP networks, and we constructed the examples to illustrate specific concepts and ideas. Along with these examples and case studies, we included notes, hints, remarks, and warnings based on experience with the design of DHCP, the implementation of DHCP clients and servers, and the application of DHCP to production networks. We included this material to flesh out the framework of the theory and principles of DHCP with as much information about DHCP in practice as we could.

Audience

This book is intended for network planners, implementers, and administrators; in short, anyone that must design, implement, manage, or debug a network that uses DHCP. Planners considering the use of DHCP or designing a DHCP service will find the protocol description and design guidelines of particular value. If you are not already familiar with the use and architecture of DHCP, the first three chapters introduce DHCP through an example and explain some of the details of DHCP.

The discussion of DHCP and its applications assumes some familiarity with the details of the TCP/IP protocols. In particular, we assume you understand hardware and IP addressing, subnetting, routing, and some of the application layer services such as DNS. We review some aspects of TCP/IP that are specific to understanding and using DHCP in Chapter 4, "Configuring TCP/IP Stacks." For a more comprehensive introduction to TCP/IP, we recommend either *Internetworking with TCP/IP*, by Doug Comer (1995), or *TCP/IP Illustrated* by W. Richard Stevens (1994).

Readers who are already using DHCP will find the material on configuring and tuning a DHCP server of particular interest. Anyone running a large installation will want to read about reliable DHCP service.

The later chapters are intended for anyone who is tracking and planning for future developments in DHCP. We are both participants in the IETF working group that is responsible for DHCP, and we have included material on current work within the IETF in areas such as authentication, inter-server communication, DHCP/LDAP integration, and DHCP for IPv6.

Organization

The book is written in three parts. Part I, "Introduction to DHCP," introduces DHCP through examples, and provides some background on configuring TCP/IP protocol stacks.

Part II, "DHCP Theory of Operation," focuses on the specification and operation of DHCP. This section of the book begins with an explanation of the objectives of DHCP and the motivation behind the design decisions in DHCP. Part II also includes detailed descriptions of the DHCP message formats and message exchanges between clients and servers, as well as the role of relay agents in those message exchanges.

Part III, "DHCP Servers and Clients," begins with a description of the operation of the ISC and Microsoft DHCP servers and clients. Next, we explain how to configure the ISC server with several specific examples. In the following chapters, we discuss more advanced topics in DHCP service design, such as customized client configurations, reliable DHCP service, tuning your DHCP service, and setting up DHCP in a small office or at home. Part III concludes with material on current work in DHCP, including authentication, interaction between DHCP and DNS, communication between DHCP servers, and the development of DHCP for IPv6.

Throughout the book, we give examples that use the ISC DHCP server. This server is freely available and therefore accessible even to readers whose employers may already have purchased a commercial DHCP server and, thus, are not in a position to purchase whatever commercial DHCP server we might have used in our examples. Appendix A, "Microsoft DHCP Server Examples," includes a list of examples and expository text for the Microsoft DHCP server, keyed to the examples throughout the book that use the ISC DHCP server. This server is the commercial server that a reader is most likely to have ready access to.

We would have liked to provide examples for a wider variety of DHCP servers, but unfortunately, every DHCP server has a different configuration syntax, and we simply couldn't provide examples for all of them. We believe that by showing examples presented for two DHCP servers with very different configuration mechanisms, a reader using a third DHCP server will most likely understand each example as it relates to whatever configuration mechanism that server uses.

Background on DHCP

DHCP is currently a *Draft Standard* of the IETF. It is an open, vendor-independent standard. The specifications for DHCP are written in RFC2131 and RFC2132, which are available from http://www.rfc-editor.org. DHCP clients and servers are widely available from major software vendors, as well as from the Internet Software Consortium.

DHCP is a product of the *Dynamic Host Configuration (DHC)* Working Group of the IETF. The DHC Working Group first met at the IETF meeting in Cocoa Beach, Florida, in April 1989. At that meeting, the Working Group defined the problem that it would address to be the automated configuration of TCP/IP hosts, including allocation of a network address and transmission of other parameters, such as the subnet mask and a default router.

DHCP is loosely based on BOOTP (Bootstrap Protocol) (RFC951). DHCP retains the basic message format of BOOTP and the operation of BOOTP relay agents, and it shares the UDP ports initially assigned to BOOTP (67 and 68). This backward compatibility with BOOTP allows DHCP to use the installed base of BOOTP relay agents and avoid the requirement of a DHCP server on every network segment.

DHCP is still a work in progress. The DHC Working Group has several additional functions under development for DHCP, which are described in the last few chapters of this book. For current information on the status of DHCP and the activities of the DHC Working Group, visit `http://www.dhcp.org` or `http://www.ietf.org/html.charters/dhc-charter.html`.

PART I

Introduction to DHCP

CHAPTER 1

An Introduction to DHCP

The *Dynamic Host Configuration Protocol (DHCP)* automates the process of configuring new and existing devices on TCP/IP networks. DHCP performs many of the same functions a network administrator carries out when connecting a computer to a network. DHCP enables a program to automatically manage policy decisions and bookkeeping tasks. Replacing manual configuration by a program adds flexibility, mobility, and control to networked computer configurations.

This chapter provides an overview of how network administrators allocate, manage, and configure IP addresses, and shows how they can use DHCP to accomplish these same tasks. It also introduces some of the basic terminology required to understand the capabilities that the protocol provides and examines some reasons for, and caveats about, using DHCP.

1.1 Configuring Devices on the Network

Any network administrator using TCP/IP can testify that manually configuring computers attached to a network is a time-consuming and error-prone process. Indeed, at almost any site—regardless of whether DHCP is in use—the address assignment and configuration process is automated in some way.

One of the authors of this book, Ted Lemon, worked as a network administrator at the Digital Equipment Corporation (DEC) campus in Palo Alto, California, before DHCP was available to simplify the tasks of address management and configuration. The DEC campus used a central IP address administration system, which was based on a single list, or *host table*, of computers, IP addresses, and *Domain Name System (DNS)* names for the entire network.

In order to help introduce you to the task that a DHCP server performs, we will first describe to you, from Ted's perspective, what network administrators did before DHCP became widely available.

As part of the network administration task, we updated the host table with new computers as they were added to the network and changed the entries for computers as their names and addresses changed. Periodically, we ran a shell script on the host table to update the DNS server database. We configured individual computers manually, from the entries in the host table, by physically walking up to each computer and entering the configuration information.

Users had a variety of questions about connecting their computers to the campus network. Usually, they wanted to know what IP address they could use for their computer. To respond to such questions, we asked the following:

- Who are you?

- Is this a new device, or was it connected to the network before?

- What is its old IP address?

- Where do you need to install this device?

- In what department do you work?

1.1.1 IP Address Allocation

After we obtained this information, we decided whether to give the user an IP address. It was usually easy to make this decision; if the user was an employee or contractor working in a DEC Palo Alto building, then we gave the user an address. Next we decided what IP address to assign the user. To do this, we had to know what network segments were present at the site, which segment or segments were available in the user's office, and how those network segments were configured.

If we supported a single network segment with a single IP subnet, answering these questions would have been simple, and everyone would have been allocated addresses from that subnet. However, the DEC Palo Alto campus network consisted of many network segments, routed together through a backbone network. Thus, it was a bit more difficult to assign IP addresses. In essence, each network administrator had to remember which network segments were available in which buildings, on which floors, and, in some cases, in which offices. If our memories were faulty, the address allocation was not successful, and we had to perform the process again.

After we determined the network segment to which the user's computer would be attached, we determined whether any IP addresses were available on it and chose one for the user. If not—and this was often the case—then we examined the host table for addresses that appeared to be no longer in use. Occasionally, we configured a new network segment and moved some devices to it to expand the pool of available addresses.

1.1.2 Configuration Information

In addition to choosing an IP address on the correct subnet, we also provided the user with additional information about the network, which usually consisted of:

- The addresses of the default routers for the network segment to which the device was to be connected

- The addresses of a primary and secondary domain name server that the device would use

- The subnet mask and broadcast address

If the device needed specific network services that were not used by all devices on the network, we also informed the user how to access those services and programmed that information into the device. For example, we manually configured a diskless Network File System (NFS) client's NFS mount information, and usually gave different information to each diskless NFS client.

1.1.3 Configuring Network Devices

In general, we got network configuration information into devices in two ways. When configuring a knowledgeable user's machine, we gave the information directly to that user; thus, it took a minute or two to configure a machine over the phone or via a single email message exchange. However, for users who could not configure their own machines, this process took some time. We had to determine where the user was, walk to that user's station (possibly in a different building), log in as root, type the necessary information, restart the machine, and then verify that it worked correctly.

1.1.4 Moving Devices to Different Network Segments

From time to time, a user would move from one office to another, or a user's machine would move from a lab into an office. If the network segment (or segments) to which the user's devices were attached was not available in the new location, we would de-allocate the IP addresses previously assigned to those devices and allocate them new ones on the network segment (or segments) available in the new location.

1.1.5 Moving or Adding Network Services

As organizations within DEC Palo Alto grew, it was not uncommon for us to add new facilities such as printers, name servers, and Network Time Protocol (NTP) servers to the network and then manually configure the addresses for each client. Because we did not always have time to modify the configurations of existing functioning clients, we disseminated information about new network services when new machines were installed or when users complained that, for example, they couldn't access printers closest to their cubicles.

1.1.6 Renumbering the Network

As the organization grew, we restructured the network. On one occasion, the entire DEC corporate network number changed from Class B (128.45.0.0) to Class A (16.0.0.0). This necessitated changing the IP address of every network device on the Palo Alto campus—more than 1,000 computers. Because we did not have an automatic configuration mechanism, network administrators had to renumber the machines, a process that consisted of walking to every machine and manually changing its IP address. Because people worked odd hours at DEC Palo Alto, we often forced people out of the buildings as we updated the machines. We, then, waited for problem reports indicating which machines were renumbered incorrectly.

1.1.7 Reclaiming Disused IP Addresses

Machines for which we allocated IP addresses eventually failed, moved out of our jurisdiction, or were reassigned to different users and reinstalled, at which time the machines lost their old identities. When we were aware of these transitions, we easily updated our records and reclaimed the IP addresses belonging to such machines. However, if the transfer occurred without our knowledge, then we were not aware that these IP addresses were no longer in use.

In such cases, we had no reliable way to determine whether an IP address was no longer in use. Although we often used the ping command (ICMP Echo Request/Reply protocol) to determine whether an address was still in use, no response to such a command unfortunately indicated only that the address was not in use *at that moment*. The address could have been configured in a device that was powered off. We eventually found ways of handling this problem. First, we tried to locate the person who owned the device for which the IP address was allocated. If we couldn't find the owner of the device, we pinged a suspect IP address periodically for about a month, and if we did not receive a response during that period, we reclaimed the address. Occasionally someone powered up a device that was disused for a few months, and the new device to which the old device's IP address was assigned started behaving erratically.

1.2 A First Attempt at Automating Device Configuration

In 1985, Bill Croft and John Gilmore devised a protocol called the *Bootstrap Protocol*, or *BOOTP*. The idea behind BOOTP was to automate network device configuration and, thus, eliminate the need for the system administrator to manually configure each network device.

BOOTP requires that the administrator create a table containing a list of BOOTP clients, their IP addresses, and other configuration parameters they might need. When a BOOTP client needs to configure itself, it broadcasts a request, which the BOOTP server receives. The BOOTP server looks up the client in the table, finds its parameters, and sends these parameters back.

This protocol works fairly well, except that it only configures the device—the network administrator must perform the remaining tasks. Various sites experimented with dynamic address allocation using the BOOTP protocol, but they were not very successful because the protocol was limited in what it could do; it was a simple database lookup, and it provided no means for reclaiming addresses.

DHCP is a direct descendent of BOOTP. DHCP packets and BOOTP packets look very much alike, and DHCP and BOOTP clients and servers can take advantage of the same network infrastructure. Both protocols accomplish the task of automatically configuring network devices; the difference is that DHCP can solve other problems.

1.3 The Benefits of DHCP

The tedious and time-consuming method of assigning IP addresses described in Section 1.1 was once commonplace. However, thanks to DHCP, the days when a network administrator had to manually configure each new network device before it could be used on the network are past.

With the proliferation of DHCP, network administrators can also choose the level of control they want to exercise with regard to address allocation; they can still manually assign IP addresses to DHCP clients, or they can have the DHCP server automatically allocate IP addresses for clients. They can also decide whether clients must be registered before they are assigned IP addresses.

1.3.1 Availability of DHCP Clients

The widespread availability of DHCP clients is due in large part to Microsoft Corporation's early decision to include a DHCP client in the Windows 95 distribution. Since then, most major desktop operating system vendors followed suit, and new Apple Macintosh, Windows 95, and Windows NT systems come pre-configured to use DHCP when IP networking is enabled. Most free, UNIX-like operating systems also come with DHCP clients that can be configured fairly easily, and the Internet Software Consortium (ISC) provides an open source DHCP client that runs on many commercial UNIX implementations, as well as on all free, UNIX-like operating systems.

1.3.2 DHCP on Large Networks

Using DHCP on a large network offers clear benefits. When you must allocate and then configure a great number of devices, a protocol that completely automates these processes saves a tremendous amount of time. Even if you still manually allocate IP addresses for each client, the DHCP protocol's ability to automatically reclaim IP addresses from DHCP clients saves time and hassle in the long run.

1.3.3 Mobility

One big advantage of DHCP is that it allows for mobile devices (that is, devices that are plugged in at different network locations at varying times). For example, at the University of Oregon, where DHCP is used, network connectivity is provided in the dorms, the library, teachers' offices, and classrooms. When students do homework in their dorms, they plug their laptop computers into Ethernet jacks. When these students need to go to the library to work with reference material, they unplug their laptops from the network, put them to sleep, take them to the library, and plug them back in. The laptops automatically acquire new IP addresses and continue using the network.

Teachers can work on presentations on their laptop computers in their offices but store the presentations on a file server. A teacher can then use the same laptop that is plugged into the network hookup in a classroom to access the presentation from the file server without reconfiguring the machine.

Visiting faculty and salespeople with DHCP-ready laptop computers can plug those computers into the network and immediately use the network, without requiring any intervention from a system administrator. University of Oregon faculty who go to conferences can bring their laptops, which are DHCP-ready, plug them into the terminal room network at the conference, and immediately use the network there.

1.3.4 DHCP on Small Networks

It can also be convenient to set up a DHCP server on a very small network. Even though few clients are involved in such cases, the advantages of not having to manually configure each client's IP stack can be significant. Configuring a simple DHCP server for a single subnet shouldn't take much more time than configuring the IP stack on a new machine. You must configure the IP stack on the DHCP server manually, of course, but the time you save configuring the second machine attached to the local network makes up for the time you spent configuring the DHCP server. DHCP saves time on every machine configured from the third onward.

Of course, if you are a network administrator, you will probably already know how to set up a DHCP server; if you are doing this for the first time, you may need to add five or six machines to the network before you realize any time savings. But in any case, you will have learned a valuable skill.

Another advantage of setting up DHCP on small networks is enhanced mobility. If a University of Oregon professor has a laptop computer configured to use DHCP and has a network at home, it is convenient to run DHCP on the home network. If that professor does not have DHCP service on his or her home network, then the professor must manually reconfigure the laptop computer every time he or she moves it from the home to the office or back again.

1.4 Assigning IP Addresses Using DHCP

A major difference between the ways in which the DHCP server and a network administrator allocate addresses is that DHCP enforces a limit on how long an IP address can be used. This seemingly subtle change makes many of the problems we experienced while administering the network at DEC Palo Alto much easier to solve. The rest of the protocol is analogous to what a network administrator does: A *DHCP client* (in the DHCP protocol, this refers to the device itself, not the user) requests an IP address. The server, using its knowledge of the network and a list of IP addresses and client identities it maintains, provides one. Chapter 8, "DHCP Message Exchanges," and Chapter 13, "Configuring a DHCP Server," discuss this process in detail.

1.4.1 DHCP Server as Agent

The DHCP server acts as an agent in performing address allocations. Like a network administrator, the DHCP server must have a clear, unambiguous understanding of the network's layout to assign addresses, and it must know the network's address allocation policy.

> **Note**
>
> *One of the most common errors new DHCP administrators make is thinking of the DHCP server as just another database lookup engine and, therefore, providing the DHCP server with only the information the administrator thinks it needs to know. Remember that it is just as important for the DHCP server to know what* not *to do as what to do.*

1.4.2 Address Leasing

As explained earlier, DHCP servers must operate automatically, and can't exercise judgment or ask what happened to old devices. Further differentiating between DHCP and manual address allocation is the *lease*. Rather than simply assigning each client an IP address to keep until the client is done with it, the DHCP server assigns the client an IP address with a lease; the client is allowed to use the IP address only for the duration of that lease. When the lease expires, the client is forced to stop using that IP address. To prevent a lease from expiring, which essentially shuts down all network access for the client, the client must renew its lease on its IP address from time to time.

1.4.3 Address Reclamation with DHCP

By constraining clients from using IP addresses after their leases expire, and by providing a mechanism for clients to continue renewing their leases as long as they are powered on and connected to the network, DHCP enables the reliable reclamation of disused IP addresses. If a device is left powered off for an extended period, then it must contact the DHCP server for its IP address when it is powered on again. If the address is reclaimed, it is given a new one so that there is no potential for address allocation conflict.

1.4.4 Renumbering with DHCP

The lease mechanism also facilitates renumbering. If every device on a network uses DHCP, then renumbering is a simple matter of reconfiguring the server's idea of what the network looks like. It is possible to renumber so transparently that users who do not pay close attention to their TCP/IP configuration information are unaware that the network was renumbered.

1.4.5 Describing Network Services with DHCP

In addition to providing a means for distributing IP addresses, DHCP enables configuration information to be distributed in the form of *DHCP options*. These options include:

- The default router addresses

- The domain name servers addresses

- The name of a bootfile to load (for devices that boot over the network)

- The name of the root file system and swap server (for diskless clients)

Chapter 9, "DHCP Options," provides a complete list of these options. Chapter 11 describes how to use them, and Chapter 19, "DHCP Clients," discusses options some common clients use.

1.4.6 Moving or Adding Network Services with DHCP

When a network service is added or needs to be moved, it is possible to take advantage of the regular lease renewal process to propagate this new information in a fairly timely manner. (DHCP does not allow for instant updates, however.) The administrator simply updates the DHCP server configuration as appropriate. If a service's IP address changes, then the configuration is updated to reflect this. If there is a new printer, then that printer is added to the list of printers available on the subnet (or subnets) serving the area near the printer. As DHCP clients renew their leases, they automatically acquire this new information and begin using it.

1.5 Perceived Problems of DHCP

Despite DHCP's benefits, many network administrators resist implementing the protocol because of various perceived problems, which are discussed in the following sections.

1.5.1 Excess Broadcast Traffic

Some network administrators believe that DHCP generates a large amount of broadcast traffic. While DHCP does use broadcasts early in the protocol, the amount of broadcasting is relatively minimal. In the worst case, the first two DHCP messages that a DHCP client sends must be broadcast; depending on the networking capabilities of the operating systems on the client and server, the server may also need to broadcast its responses to the client. When combined, this creates a total of four broadcast packets.

In most cases, however, the client need only send one broadcast packet on startup; most clients do not require a broadcast response. Most servers can also respond without broadcasting. Thus, in the most typical DHCP startup case, only a single packet is broadcast, not four. After a client configures its network connection, and either as long as that connection remains valid, or until the client machine is restarted, all communication with the server is unicast. Chapter 7, "Transmitting DHCP Messages," discusses these issues in greater detail.

1.5.1.1 Address Resolution Protocol

For comparison, consider the *Address Resolution Protocol*, or *ARP*. All IP broadcast networks use this protocol. When one device needs to communicate with another device that is on the same network segment, it must have the link-layer address of the second device. Because it initially knows only the other device's IP address, it must send an ARP broadcast to obtain the second device's link-layer address. After the device has that link-layer address, it periodically verifies that it still has the correct address by broadcasting another ARP request. Some ARP implementations verify the link-layer address as frequently as every 2 minutes. Because the ARP response is also broadcast, any pair of devices on a network segment that are in contact with one another using TCP/IP broadcast, on average, one ARP message every minute.

Computers tend to remain powered on for longer than 1 minute at a time; usually, computers are powered on all day. In this case, ARP generates as many as 180 broadcast packets for every packet DHCP generates. So, at four broadcast messages, DHCP is a comparatively insignificant producer of broadcast traffic.

1.5.2 Server Load

Another common assumption is that because a DHCP server is most likely serving all the DHCP clients at a site, it is difficult for a DHCP server to function at a large site. Fortunately, DHCP is comparatively undemanding. A name server for a large site might need a fairly fast machine with a good deal of memory. However, a DHCP server for the same site can usually run quite well on an old piece of junk found in the closet. It is very common to hear of people running the ISC DHCP server on an old Intel 486 machine running Linux, serving several thousand DHCP clients. Many sites serve on the order of 10,000 clients with Linux-based platforms. Although the ISC DHCP server keeps its entire client database in memory, a 10,000-client network consumes, at most, 20 megabytes of virtual memory.

Dealing with Spurious DHCP Traffic

One problem DHCP servers must deal with is broken clients that send too many requests. At Pacific Bell, a single DHCP server running on a Tandem mainframe serves more than 50,000 DHCP clients. Some of the old network hardware the company installed at some of its sites can get into a state in which it tries to obtain an IP address once every few seconds. On bad days, this means the DHCP server receives about five requests every second, with occasional sustained peaks of 50 packets per second that last for an hour or more. The DHCP server looks at all requests and decides what to do with them, even though these requests are not legitimate. Nonetheless, it handles this load without difficulty.

1.5.3 DHCP Reliability

One problem with DHCP is that if the DHCP client and the DHCP server are unable to communicate for some reason, the DHCP client's lease eventually expires, and it must stop using the network. This commonly occurs if the DHCP server goes down for longer than the duration of a lease. This can also happen if a central DHCP server is configured to serve addresses on a *wide area network (WAN)*, and one of the links in this WAN fails for a long time. In practice, temporary outages of DHCP service have little or no effect on clients because a client will try to extend the lease on its address well before the lease expires, and will continue to use its old address while attempting to contact the DHCP server.

Note

At DEC Palo Alto, we actually considered deploying DHCP very early on. We ran a fairly homogenous environment—almost every machine was a DEC station of some sort, running Ultrix. So, we could have fairly easily configured all machines to run a DHCP client on startup. However, we were afraid that if we did this, then we would experience reliability problems because of the lease mechanism, and users would complain.

Based on subsequent experiences, it is clear that this fear was unfounded. Several strategies exist for avoiding this problem, and we found that these strategies work. Clients can renew their leases, and users do not call to complain about losing network connectivity.

If you are deploying DHCP on a WAN and don't have an extremely reliable, redundant network setup, it is best to locate DHCP servers at each site rather than run one central DHCP server for the entire WAN. Some sites do run a central DHCP server for their entire WAN, but they avoid trouble by having multiple redundant links to each site so that if one link goes down, an alternate path to the DHCP server is available.

DHCP does not currently allow a backup DHCP server to serve addresses from the same range as a primary server. However, the Internet Engineering Task Force (IETF) Dynamic Host Configuration working group is working on this.

In the meantime, several strategies exist for working around this limitation:

- You can set leases to be long enough so that they do not expire before you fix a failed server.

- You can set up secondary servers that do not serve the same sets of addresses.

- If you conduct static allocation, you can actually set up completely redundant DHCP servers.

Chapter 15 discusses this in detail.

1.5.4 When Not to Use DHCP

Unlike manual network configuration, the automated DHCP process depends on the presence of a DHCP server. If you use DHCP to configure a device on a network, and if that device cannot talk to the DHCP server, it eventually stops using the network.

For this reason, using DHCP to configure network servers is not recommended. If the DHCP server fails and, as a result, the machine on which you are running your corporate name service suddenly loses its ability to communicate on the network, or your corporate SMTP (email) gateway goes down, you will quickly forget how convenient DHCP is.

Some managed hubs and other network components obtain the IP address of their management port from a vendor-supplied custom BOOTP server. It may not be a good idea in some cases to substitute a general-purpose DHCP server for the manufacturer's controller, depending on how faithfully the manufacturer adhered to the protocol and whether you have sufficient documentation to configure the server. Also, as with other network infrastructure, it may be more reliable to configure the devices manually.

1.6 Address Allocation Policies

One of the primary goals for DHCP was to design a protocol that provides a mechanism through which a network administrator can implement any desired administrative policy. The network administrator can manually configure the DHCP server with IP addresses for each machine that is connected to the network. The administrator can also simply provide a range of addresses for the DHCP server to use, and allow the DHCP server to allocate these addresses to clients automatically. It is also feasible to implement a scheme that combines both of these possibilities.

1.6.1 Static Allocation

With *static (or fixed) allocation*, the DHCP server receives a list of identification information for DHCP clients. These identifiers specifically and uniquely identify each client. Chapter 14, "Client Identification and Fixed-Address Allocation," discusses the types of identifiers that can be used.

For each identifier, the administrator gives the DHCP server an IP address to assign to that client. If the client is mobile, the administrator can assign an address for each client on each network segment to which the client is connected. A client cannot configure itself on a network segment on which the administrator has not assigned it an IP address.

1.6.2 Dynamic Allocation

With *dynamic allocation*, the DHCP server receives a range of IP addresses for each network segment on which DHCP clients are expected to be configured. When a DHCP client asks for an IP address, the DHCP server finds a free address on that network segment and supplies it to the client.

1.6.3 Automatic Allocation

The DHCP protocol specification talks about another method of address allocation called *automatic allocation*, in which the DHCP server allocates IP addresses as it does in dynamic allocation, but the addresses are allocated permanently. The DHCP servers described in this book do not actually implement automatic allocation as a specific third alternative. However, you can approximate this scenario by simply using very long lease durations.

1.6.4 Hybrid Allocation Policies

A variety of hybrid policies are also possible. With one common policy, the administrator registers a list of known client identifiers for which DHCP service is allowed, but the administrator does not assign fixed IP addresses to those clients. Those clients can then acquire IP addresses dynamically wherever they are connected. This allows the administrator to limit the use of DHCP to registered clients, but it saves the administrator the trouble of updating the DHCP server every time a client moves. With the growing popularity of portable computers, this can be a major advantage.

Some DHCP servers can assign a fixed IP address for a DHCP client on the client's home network and enable the client to acquire a dynamically assigned IP address if it roams elsewhere.

Another fairly common strategy is to assign fixed addresses to registered DHCP clients but enable unregistered DHCP clients to acquire dynamically assigned addresses. This allows users to get a specific IP address when they start up the computer but allows the network administrator to avoid keeping track of every device connecting to the network.

Which of these strategies should be adopted at a particular site is simply a policy decision. Obviously, keeping track of which DHCP clients are connected to the network is a lot of work. However, in some environments it may be worth it.

Note

Not all servers support the same set of policies. Because DHCP does not specify what policies must be supported, DHCP server implementers must choose how these policies are implemented, and the choices they make may limit the range of possible policies. For example, the Microsoft DHCP server supports a much more limited set of policies than the ISC DHCP server, even though both servers implement the same protocol.

You cannot use DHCP as a security mechanism. If a DHCP client elects not to follow the protocol, a network administrator can do little, other than track down the offending device and shut it off. A malicious user who wants to access the network can always simply make up an IP address, ARP for it, and then, if it does not get an answer, use it. Access control based on client identification can be very convenient, but it does not prevent unauthorized access to your network.

Summary

Every device that is attached to a network is configured with a unique address and with other information about the network. Historically, an administrator or a knowledgeable user manually configured each device. Addresses were allocated manually, and reclaiming addresses required a great deal of knowledge (and the process was still not very reliable).

The BOOTP protocol attempted to address this problem, but it fell short of a complete solution because it solved only the problem of configuring systems, and not the problem of allocating addresses.

The DHCP protocol automates the entire process of configuring devices to use the network. A properly configured network with a DHCP server can accommodate new devices with little or no administrator intervention, and requires no special knowledge on the part of users.

You can configure DHCP in such a way that it is reliable and consumes few network resources. Furthermore, DHCP servers can run on fairly cheap computers, and it is so easy to set them up that it is cost-effective to do so on a very small network.

If you run any sort of IP network, then you will almost certainly use DHCP on that network. DHCP will greatly simplify your work after you understand how it functions.

## CHAPTER 2

An Example of DHCP in Operation

DHCP provides a mechanism through which a computer can obtain configuration parameters for its network protocol software. This configuration information can be specific to a network segment; in particular, a DHCP server can allocate a IP address that is appropriate to the network segment to which a computer is connected. As a way of introducing the basic functions of DHCP, this chapter presents a case study of an enterprise network using DHCP to automate the configuration process.

2.1 Setting Up the GSI Intranet

This chapter discusses the use of the internal network, or *intranet*, for Generic Startup, Inc. (GSI) as the basis for an introductory example of DHCP operation. GSI has roughly 100 employees, whose offices are located in a single building. Each employee has a computer attached to the GSI network. The GSI data center includes about 20 computers providing file storage, printing, DNS, DHCP, and related services. GSI also has a connection to the Internet that is managed by the data-center staff. Figure 2.1 depicts the GSI intranet.

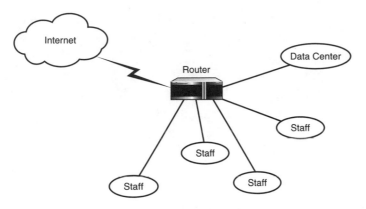

FIGURE 2.1 *Diagram of the GSI intranet.*

The network architect at GSI has organized the intranet around five network segments, all connected through a single router. The router also provides the GSI connection to the Internet. Four of the network segments connect the staff desktop computers to the router; the remaining network segment attaches all the data center computers to the router. The GSI network architect has obtained five Class C IP addresses, 192.168.11.0–192.168.15.0, for use on the GSI network and has assigned the IP addresses to the network segments, as shown in Figure 2.2.

Note

The 192.168.11.0–192.168.15.0 IP addresses are included in the block of Class C addresses reserved for private use in RFC1918 and are used here only as an example.

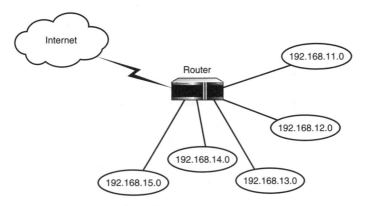

FIGURE 2.2 *IP addresses in the GSI intranet.*

So, how is DHCP used in the GSI intranet? Among the server computers on the 192.168.11.0 network is a DHCP server configured to assign IP addresses and manage the configurations of all the GSI network segments. Computers attached to the GSI intranet contact the DHCP server to obtain an IP address and other configuration information. Because the DHCP server is configured with the organization of network segments and the IP address for each segment, the server can automatically select configuration information for each computer that is appropriate for the network segment. Specifically, the DHCP server assigns an IP address to each computer without manual intervention in the selection or tracking of assigned addresses.

2.2 Using the DHCP Server to Obtain a New IP Address

In more detail, the DHCP server manages the configuration of computers attached to the GSI intranet throughout their life cycle. This section describes the interactions between a computer and the GSI DHCP server when:

- The new computer is first connected to the GSI intranet.

- The computer is restarted.

- The computer is moved to a new location within GSI.

- The computer is removed from use in GSI.

In this example, the GSI DHCP server, dhcpserve, is connected to the data-center network segment, and a new computer, desktop1, is attached to one of the staff network segments, as shown in Figure 2.3.

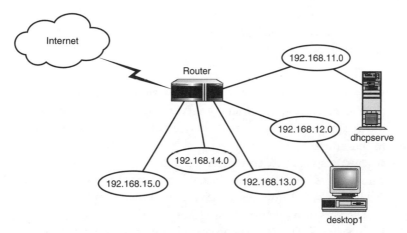

FIGURE 2.3   *desktop1 and dhcpserve connected to the GSI intranet.*

2.2.1 Locating a GSI DHCP Server

When desktop1 is first connected to the GSI intranet, it needs to contact the DHCP server to obtain an IP address and other configuration parameters. To locate a server, desktop1 broadcasts a message to locate potential DHCP servers on the GSI intranet. Then, dhcpserve receives this broadcast and replies to desktop1, identifying itself to desktop1 as a DHCP server. In this example, because desktop1 and dhcpserve are on different network segments, the router, acting as a *relay agent*, forwards messages between the two computers. Chapter 7, "Transmitting DHCP Messages," discusses relay agents in more detail. The interactions between desktop1 and dhcpserve are discussed in the following sections.

IP Address Selection

After receiving desktop1's initial message, dhcpserve selects an IP address, 192.168.12.25, which is appropriate for the 192.168.12.0 network to which desktop1 is connected. dhcpserve also chooses other configuration parameters, such as the subnet mask (255.255.255.0), the address of the router interface on the 192.168.12.0 network, and the address of the GSI DNS server. dhcpserve determines these parameters based on the DHCP client configuration rules defined by the network architect and returns an offer message containing the selected address and parameters to desktop1.

After desktop1 receives the reply from dhcpserve, it returns a message requesting for the IP address and other configuration parameters to dhcpserve. After confirming that the address is still available and all of the configuration parameters are appropriate, dhcpserve sends the parameters to desktop1 in the final message of the sequence. When the message arrives, the protocol software on desktop1 extracts the configuration parameters from the message, installs the parameters in the protocol stack, and begins network activity. The protocol software also records the configuration parameters locally in a file on desktop1 for future use.

In this example, a total of four messages have been exchanged: two messages from the client and two replies from the server. This sequence of messages may seem confusing and redundant at first. Why would desktop1 send back a request for the address and parameters that dhcpserve returned in the first offer? The short answer to this question is that the preceding sequence of messages accommodates more than one DHCP server on an intranet. This enables the DHCP client to select from responses returned by multiple servers and ensures that servers don't tie up IP addresses unnecessarily while exchanging messages with clients. This issue is discussed in more detail in Chapter 8, "DHCP Message Exchanges."

2.2.2 Restarting `desktop1`

When `desktop1` is restarted (for example, when it is first turned on in the morning) it previously obtained from `desktop1` sends the IP address and configuration parameters `dhcpserve` in a message to `dhcpserve`. As the next section explains, reconfirming its configuration gives `desktop1` the opportunity to determine if that configuration is still valid. If `desktop1` is moved to a new network segment, it needs a new IP address.

For the moment, however, `desktop1` is still attached to the 192.168.12.0 network so that when its confirmation message is received by `dhcpserve`, the server can send back an message indicating that `desktop1` can continue to use 192.168.12.25 and the other configuration parameters. After receiving the reply message from `dhcpserve`, `desktop1` can begin network activity.

Now, suppose that `desktop1` fails to contact `dhcpserve` when it restarts. This could occur if, for example, all the GSI computers are affected by a building-wide power outage, and `desktop1` has completed its restart process before `dhcpserve`. If `desktop1` receives no response to its reconfirmation message, it assumes that it is still connected to the same network segment (192.168.12.0). At this point, `desktop1` has no better information to go on, and, uses its 192.168.12.25 IP address and other parameters in the last message from `dhcpserve`.

Note

As discussed later in this chapter, `dhcpserve` *assigns a IP address to* `desktop1` *for a fixed period of time.* `desktop1` *will try to reconfirm its address and reuse its old IP address only if that configuration information has not expired. If the address has expired,* `desktop1` *will restart the DHCP process as though it never had been assigned an address.*

2.2.3 Moving `desktop1` to a New Network Segment

Now, consider the situation in which `desktop1` is moved to a new network segment. When `desktop1` is started up in the new location and sends out a confirmation request, `dhcpserve` determines that its old IP address is not valid for use on the new network segment. For example, if `desktop1` is moved to the segment with IP address 192.168.13.0, as Figure 2.4 illustrates, `dhcpserve` receives a confirmation request from `desktop1` to use its old address, 192.168.12.25, in a message that originated on network 192.168.13.0. Because the old address is not one of the valid addresses for network 192.168.13.0, `dhcpserve` determines that `desktop1` has moved to a new segment.

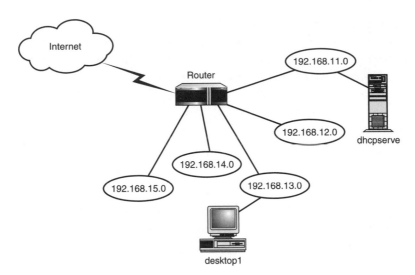

FIGURE 2.4 desktop1 *connected to the 192.168.13.0 network segment.*

When dhcpserve determines that desktop1 is now connected to a different network segment and that its IP address is no longer usable, dhcpserve sends a response to desktop1 denying use of its old address. desktop1, after receiving the negative response, marks its IP address as invalid.

Of course, desktop1 still needs an IP address from its new network segment. At this point, to obtain that address, desktop1 uses the process described in Section 2.2.1:

1. First, it broadcasts a request to obtain an address from a DHCP server.

2. After dhcpserve selects an address from the 192.168.13.0 network and sends an offer with the new address, desktop1 requests the new address.

3. dhcpserve confirms the requested address and returns that address to desktop1. In this case, dhcpserve selects 192.168.13.37 from the 192.168.13.0 network to allocate to desktop1.

4. dhcpserve and desktop1 record the new address, and desktop1 begins to use the new address immediately.

How does dhcpserve determine the network segment to which desktop1 is attached? As described in Chapter 7, when desktop1 has not yet been configured with an actual IP address, it sends its confirmation message with the source address field in the IP datagram header set to 0.0.0.0. So, in this case, dhcpserve cannot deduce the source of the message from the contents of the IP datagram header.

However, dhcpserve deduces the source of the message from desktop1 in one of two ways. If desktop1 and dhcpserve are on two different network segments, a relay agent must forward the message from desktop1 to dhcpserve. The relay agent records the information about the source of the message in the gateway address field of the message from desktop1. dhcpserve can retrieve that address from the message it receives, and determine the address of the segment to which desktop1 is currently attached.

If, on the other hand, dhcpserve receives a message with the gateway address field set to 0.0.0.0, then dhcpserve knows that the relay agent did not forward the message, and that desktop1 must be on the same subnet as dhcpserve.

2.2.4 Retiring desktop1 from Service

As additional computers are connected to the 192.168.13.0 subnet, dhcpserve allocates addresses to these new computers. Recall that 192.168.13.0 is a Class C IP address. Thus, the 192.168.13.0 subnet has addresses for only 254 computers and, eventually, dhcpserve will run out of available addresses. DHCP allows for the reallocation of addresses that are no longer in use to new computers. As computers are removed from the 192.168.13.0 subnet, dhcpserve makes those addresses available for reallocation to new computers. As long as no more than 254 computers are connected to the 192.168.13.0 subnet, dhcpserve allocates the available addresses to those connected computers.

> *Note*
>
> *Because the addresses 0 and 255 are reserved for network broadcasts and network numbering, a Class C network has 254 distinct IP addresses for hosts.*

Eventually, of course, desktop1 must go the way of all computers and be retired from service at GSI. When desktop1 is disconnected from the GSI intranet for the last time, it does not send specific notification to dhcpserve that it is being decommissioned. Instead, dhcpserve simply receives no further requests for confirmation or for new addresses from desktop1. In fact, for dhcpserve the decommissioning of desktop1 is indistinguishable from desktop1 simply not being powered on.

2.3 DHCP Address Leases

When dhcpserve allocates an address, it also specifies the length of time over which the requesting computer may use that address. This time period is called a *lease*. Much like the lease on an apartment, the lease on an address represents an agreement between the DHCP server and the DHCP client defining the time when the client will use that address. When the lease expires, the DHCP server may reallocate the address, with a new lease, to a new computer. Therefore, when the lease granted to desktop1 for the use of its address expires, dhcpserve is free to reallocate the address to a new computer.

Note

At a recent IETF meeting in Minneapolis, the meeting hosts provided a terminal room with network connections for laptops. Addresses were assigned to the laptops by using DHCP. Because far more laptops than IP addresses were available on the terminal-room network, the addresses were reassigned to newly arriving laptops as other laptops left the network. The addresses were assigned with lease times of two hours so that two hours after a laptop was disconnected from the terminal room, the DHCP server could reassign that address to another laptop.

Many more issues are related to the use of address leases than are suggested by the simple example previously described. Chapter 16, "Tuning Your DHCP Service," explains more about allocating leases, lease extension, and explicit lease termination.

It is important that DHCP servers manage IP addresses carefully because of the problems caused by allocating the same address to two different computers. Network communication with computers assigned to the same IP address may be unreliable. IP datagrams sent to the address used by both computers may be delivered to only one or the other computer. A DHCP server must take care not to reallocate to one computer an address currently in use by another computer, as this would result in both computers using the same address.

In practice, desktop1 continues to request its address for as long as it is connected to the 192.168.13.0 network segment. After it is disconnected, desktop1 makes no further requests for its address, and the lease on that address expires. At that time, dhcpserve can reallocate the address that desktop1 is no longer using to a different computer.

2.3.1 Two Alternative Mechanisms to Leasing

A lease might seem like an overly complex mechanism for the coordination of the use of IP addresses. This section describes two alternative mechanisms:

- Explicit notification from a computer to the server that an address can be reassigned

- Dynamic probing of addresses

Both of these mechanisms were considered by the working group during the development of the DHCP specification. Although both mechanisms are useful and are, in fact, recommended for use in the DHCP specification to help detect some duplicate assignments, neither can guarantee that two or more clients will not end up using the same IP address.

Explicit Departure Messages

One way in which dhcpserve might learn that a computer has left the 192.168.13.0 subnet is for that computer to send an explicit message informing dhcpserve of its departure. After receiving such a message, dhcpserve is free to reallocate the departed computer's address to another computer.

Unfortunately, it is impossible to depend on a computer to send a message when it is disconnected from the network. Computers are not always shut down gracefully, and users may not remember to send the departure message prior to disconnecting a computer. Also, if a computer has been disconnected from the segment due to a change in the network architecture— perhaps the computer has been connected to a different hub in the wiring closet—there may be no reason to have sent a message.

Dynamic Address Probing

Another strategy that might be used to determine when a IP address is no longer in use is to probe to see if a computer is already using that address. For example, dhcpserve might send an *ICMP echo request* to determine if a candidate address might already be in use. If dhcpserve receives a matching *ICMP echo reply*, a computer must be using the candidate address, and dhcpserve continues to probe for an unused address.

However, this strategy is also impractical because it cannot reliably determine if a specific address has been assigned to a computer. If dhcpserve receives an echo reply after probing an address, that address is definitely in use. However, not receiving a reply does *not* necessarily mean that the address is not in use.

A network problem may exist between dhcpserve and the computer using the candidate address, or the computer may simply be turned off. In either case, dhcpserve does not receive an echo reply, even though the address is in use.

2.3.2 Benefits of DHCP Leases

DHCP specifies the use of leases in address allocation so that a server can know reliably when it may reallocate an address. The lease constitutes an agreement between the client and the server; the server may not reallocate the address until the lease has expired, and the client may not use the address after the lease has expired. If the computer to which the address was allocated never contacts the server again, the server must wait until the lease expires before reallocating the address. Even if the computer to which the address was allocated has active network connections in place, it must terminate those connections and stop using the address as soon as the lease expires.

Summary

A computer communicates with a DHCP server in three basic ways. When the computer is first turned on, it contacts the server for a new IP address and other configuration parameters. Each time the computer is turned on after it has obtained its initial configuration information, it confirms its address and parameters with the server. If the computer is moved to a new network segment, the server notifies the computer that its address is no longer valid. The computer then contacts the server to obtain a new address and configuration parameters appropriate to the new network segment.

A DHCP server allocates a currently unused address to a computer newly attached to a network segment. As more computers are attached to a network segment, all the available addresses may be assigned. When all the addresses have been allocated, a DHCP server begins to reuse previously allocated addresses that are no longer in use. DHCP uses leases on addresses to determine when an address is no longer in use. A DHCP server does not reassign an address before its lease expires, and a computer must stop using an address as soon as the lease on that address expires.

CHAPTER 3

Configuring the DHCP Server

In managing an enterprise network, the network architect designs the network architecture and determines the configuration parameters to be assigned to hosts throughout the network. Once the network architecture has been determined, the network architect must indicate the structure of the intranet to the DHCP server. Based on that structure, the DHCP server selects configuration parameters and appropriate addresses for DHCP clients.

The examples in this chapter are based on the example GSI intranet architecture and scenarios described in Chapter 2, "An Example of DHCP in Operation." The configuration files are designed for use with the ISC DHCP server and use the syntax of the ISC DHCP server configuration files.

3.1 Specifying the Basic Intranet Architecture

The network architect models the intranet architecture within the DHCP server by identifying the IP subnets, the addresses, and the subnet masks for each of those subnets. With this information, the DHCP server associates incoming DHCP messages with subnets in the intranet. Based on the subnet from which a DHCP message was received, the server selects an appropriate IP address to assign to the client, or determines that a DHCP client has moved to a new subnet.

The ISC DHCP server configuration file is an ASCII text file that contains a series of declarations describing the intranet to be managed by the server. The server reads and parses the file when it first starts running.

> **Note**
>
> *The declarations in the file may be formatted and include extra whitespace for readability. Comments may be included in the configuration file. A comment begins with the # character and continues to the end of the line.*

3.1.1 Subnet Declarations

The basic subnet declaration in the ISC server configuration file follows the format in Example 3.1:

EXAMPLE 3.1

```
subnet subnet-address netmask subnet-mask {
        subnet declarations
        }
```

In this subnet declaration, the subnet-address is the IP address of the subnet, and the subnet-mask is the subnet mask to be used with this subnet. Both the subnet-address and the subnet-mask are written in dotted-decimal notation.

> **Note**
>
> *In this example, keywords are shown in bold, while italicized text is replaced with specific IP addresses or declarations.*

The example intranet shown in Figure 2.2 in the previous chapter is described with the configuration file shown in Example 3.2. The example configuration file includes a subnet declaration for each of the five subnets, with the IP address for each subnet and the 255.255.255.0 subnet mask.

You can include comments in the configuration file for the ISC server as lines that begin with the # character. Example 3.2 includes several comments that explain some of the details of the configuration file.

EXAMPLE 3.2

```
# Server subnet
subnet 192.168.11.0 netmask 255.255.255.0 {
    }
# Staff subnet 1
subnet 192.168.12.0 netmask 255.255.255.0 {
    }
# Staff subnet 2
subnet 192.168.13.0 netmask 255.255.255.0 {
    }
# Staff subnet 3
```

```
subnet 192.168.14.0 netmask 255.255.255.0 {
    }
# Staff subnet 4
subnet 192.168.15.0 netmask 255.255.255.0 {
    }
```

3.1.2 Subnet Address Allocation

In addition to defining the subnets, the network architect must define the range of addresses within each subnet, or *scope*, that is available for allocation by the server. Any addresses assigned to hosts or devices through some other mechanism must be excluded from the range of available addresses for each subnet. For example, in the GSI intranet, the router interface on each subnet is assigned the host address 254. Thus, on the 192.168.11.0 subnet, the router uses address 192.168.11.254.

The network architect manually configures the router interfaces, rather than using DHCP to assign the addresses. Thus, the server is configured so that the range of available addresses on each subnet does not include those addresses with host address 254.

In the ISC server configuration file, the syntax for specifying the range of available addresses in a subnet is shown in Example 3.3.

EXAMPLE 3.3

range *first-available-address last-available-address*;

Example 3.4 gives the configuration file for the GSI intranet, specifying that host addresses 1 through 29 are available in each subnet. This configuration file reserves host address 30 on each subnet for the router interface on that subnet. The server subnet declaration also reserves addresses for a DHCP server and a DNS server.

EXAMPLE 3.4

```
# Server subnet
subnet 192.168.11.0 netmask 255.255.255.0 {
    range 192.168.11.1 192.168.11.251;
    # 192.168.11.252 reserved for DHCP server
    # 192.168.11.253 reserved for DNS server
    # 192.168.11.254 reserved for router interface
    }
# Staff subnet 1
```

```
     subnet 192.168.12.0 netmask 255.255.255.0 {
         range 192.168.12.1 192.168.12.253;
         # 192.168.12.254 reserved for router interface
         }
     # Staff subnet 2
     subnet 192.168.13.0 netmask 255.255.255.0 {
         range 192.168.13.1 192.168.13.253;
         # 192.168.13.254 reserved for router interface
     }
     # Staff subnet 3
     subnet 192.168.14.0 netmask 255.255.255.0 {
         range 192.168.14.1 168.14.253;
         # 192.168.14.254 reserved for router interface
         }
     # Staff subnet 4
     subnet 192.168.15.0 netmask 255.255.255.0 {
         range 192.168.15.1 192.168.15.253;
         # 192.168.15.254 reserved for router interface
}
```

3.2 Required Configuration Parameters

DHCP provides other configuration parameters in addition to a IP address. In fact, several additional parameters must be provided to a TCP/IP host before that host can communicate with other hosts. A host must be configured with:

- Its local subnet mask

- The address of at least one router on its subnet

- The address of a Domain Name Service (DNS) server

These parameters are provided to a DHCP client through *options* in the DHCP message. Chapter 9, "DHCP Options," describes all the DHCP options in detail. A few of the most commonly used options are discussed in the following sections.

3.2.1 Configuration Options

The syntax for specifying an option is shown in Example 3.5.

EXAMPLE 3.5

option *option-name option-value*;

If the option statement appears within a subnet declaration, it is applied to any

DHCP client in that subnet. In Example 3.6, adding the option statement to the declaration for the 192.168.11.0 causes the DHCP server to send 192.168.11.254 as the default router address to any DHCP client on the 192.168.11.0 subnet.

EXAMPLE 3.6

```
# Server subnet
subnet 192.168.11.0 netmask 255.255.255.0 {
    range 192.168.11.1 192.168.11.251;
    # 192.168.11.252 reserved for DHCP server
    # 192.168.11.253 reserved for DNS server
    # 192.168.11.254 reserved for router interface
    option routers 192.168.11.254;
    }
```

The other options for configuring TCP/IP parameters are subnet-mask and domain-name-server. Recall from Figure 2.2 that GSI maintains a DNS server at 192.168.11.253. The configuration file for GSI, including default routers, subnet masks, and DNS servers, is shown in Example 3.7.

EXAMPLE 3.7

```
# Server subnet
subnet 192.168.11.0 netmask 255.255.255.0 {
    range 192.168.11.1 192.168.11.251;
    # 192.168.11.252 reserved for DHCP server
    # 192.168.11.253 reserved for DNS server
    # 192.168.11.254 reserved for router interface
    option routers 192.168.11.254;
    option subnet-mask 255.255.255.0;
    option domain-name-servers 192.168.11.253;
    }
# Staff subnet 1
subnet 192.168.12.0 netmask 255.255.255.0 {
    range 192.168.12.1 192.168.12.253;
    # 192.168.12.254 reserved for router interface
    option routers 192.168.12.254;
    option subnet-mask 255.255.255.0;
    option domain-name-servers 192.168.11.253;
}
# Staff subnet 2
subnet 192.168.13.0 netmask 255.255.255.0 {
    range 192.168.13.1 192.168.13.253;
    # 192.168.13.254 reserved for router interface
    option routers 192.168.13.254;
    option subnet-mask 255.255.255.0;
    option domain-name-servers 192.168.11.253;
}
# Staff subnet 3
```

```
subnet 192.168.14.0 netmask 255.255.255.0 {
    range 192.168.14.1 168.14.253;
    # 192.168.14.254 reserved for router interface
    option routers 192.168.14.254;
    option subnet-mask 255.255.255.0;
    option domain-name-servers 192.168.11.253;
}
# Staff subnet 4
subnet 192.168.15.0 netmask 255.255.255.0 {
    range 192.168.15.1 192.168.15.253;
    # 192.168.15.254 reserved for router interface
    option routers 192.168.15.254;
    option subnet-mask 255.255.255.0;
    option domain-name-servers 192.168.11.253;
}
```

3.3 Specifying Leases

Chapter 2 describes the use of leases as a mechanism through which a DHCP server knows when a host will stop using an IP address. The DHCP specification allows a lease to be up to $2^{32} -2$ seconds (49,710 days, or about 135 years).

> **Note**
>
> $2^{32} -2$ is expressed as $FFFFFFFE_{16}$. This is the largest number that can be stored in the 32-bit lease field in a DHCP message. (This does not include $FFFFFFFF_{16}$, which represents an infinite lease.)

Considerations in choosing lease times for DHCP clients are discussed later in this section.

3.3.1 Lease Durations

A DHCP client may request a particular lease duration, but the network architect may choose to configure the DHCP server to ignore that request. The DHCP specification does not include rules or requirements for lease allocation or duration; those policies are defined by the network architect and are implemented by the DHCP server.

Default and Maximum Lease Lengths

The ISC server allows the network architect to specify both a default lease length and a maximum lease length. The default lease is used if the client does not request a specific lease, and the maximum lease length defines the longest lease that the server will allocate. If a client requests a lease longer than the maximum lease length, then the server simply issues a lease equal to the maximum lease length.

The syntax for defining the default lease and maximum lease lengths is shown in Example 3.8, and *time* is expressed in seconds.

EXAMPLE 3.8

```
default-lease-time time
max-lease-time time
```

Subnet Lease Lengths

Choosing appropriate lease times for a subnet depends on the types of hosts
that will connect to that subnet. Table 3.1 lists some types of subnets and example lease times.

TABLE 3.1 EXAMPLE LEASE TIMES

Type of Subnet	Primary Use	Default Lease
University computer lab	Students with laptops	2 hours
"Hotel" office	Daily use by staff	12 hours
Staff offices	Permanent staff	30 days
Central servers	Organization servers	3 months

Note

*"Hotelling" means the temporary use of offices by staff on a daily basis. The "hotel" offices are
equipped with a wall jack through which a laptop is connected to the GSI intranet. As a different
person may use these offices each day, the intranet must accommodate dynamic allocation of an IP
address to the computer or computers in those offices on a daily basis.*

Chapter 16, "Tuning Your DHCP Service," includes a more detailed discussion
of lease times for specific scenarios.

3.3.2 GSI Subnet Leases

In the GSI intranet, the 192.168.11.0 subnet is used for servers, which have a
default lease of 90 days. The 192.168.12.0, 192.168.13.0, and 192.168.14.0 subnets
are used for staff offices, and the computers connected to those subnets have a
default lease of 30 days. The remaining subnet, 192.168.15.0, is used for
"hotelling," and computers connected to that subnet have a default lease of 12
hours.

The configuration file for these lease times is shown in Example 3.9.

EXAMPLE 3.9

```
# Server subnet
subnet 192.168.11.0 netmask 255.255.255.0 {
    range 192.168.11.1 192.168.11.251;
    # 192.168.11.252 reserved for DHCP server
    # 192.168.11.253 reserved for DNS server
    # 192.168.11.254 reserved for router interface
    option routers 192.168.11.254;
    option subnet-mask 255.255.255.0;
    option domain-name-servers 192.168.11.253;
    # default lease = 90 days, max lease = 120 days
    default-lease-time 7776000;
    max-lease-time 10368000;
    }
# Staff subnet 1
subnet 192.168.12.0 netmask 255.255.255.0 {
    range 192.168.12.1 192.168.12.253;
    # 192.168.12.254 reserved for router interface
    option routers 192.168.12.254;
    option subnet-mask 255.255.255.0;
    option domain-name-servers 192.168.11.253;
    # default lease = 30 days, max lease = 45 days
    default-lease-time 2592000;
    max-lease-time 3888000;
}
# Staff subnet 2
subnet 192.168.13.0 netmask 255.255.255.0 {
    range 192.168.13.1 192.168.13.253;
    # 192.168.13.254 reserved for router interface
    option routers 192.168.13.254;
    option subnet-mask 255.255.255.0;
    option domain-name-servers 192.168.11.253;
    # default lease = 30 days, max lease = 45 days
    default-lease-time 2592000;
    max-lease-time 3888000;
}
# Staff subnet 3
subnet 192.168.14.0 netmask 255.255.255.0 {
    range 192.168.14.1 168.14.253;
    # 192.168.14.254 reserved for router interface
    option routers 192.168.14.254;
    option subnet-mask 255.255.255.0;
    option domain-name-servers 192.168.11.253;
    # default lease = 30 days, max lease = 45 days
    default-lease-time 2592000;
    max-lease-time 3888000;
}
# Staff subnet 4
subnet 192.168.15.0 netmask 255.255.255.0 {
    range 192.168.15.1 192.168.15.253;
    # 192.168.15.254 reserved for router interface
```

```
    option routers 192.168.15.254;
    option subnet-mask 255.255.255.0;
    option domain-name-servers 192.168.11.253;
    # default lease = 12 hrs, max lease = 24 hrs
    default-lease-time 43200;
    max-lease-time 86400;
}
```

3.4 Other DHCP Options

The configuration file in Example 3.9 specifies the configuration parameters that the network architect must define to the DHCP server. Many other options (RFC2132) can be provided to a DHCP client. Some of these options, such as *domain name*, are widely used, while others, such as *Impress server*, are rarely used.

Note

The Impress server option specifies a list of Imagen Impress servers (a type of networked printer that is no longer manufactured) that the DHCP client can use. This option was originally defined as a BOOTP (RFC1048, RFC951) vendor extension and is included as a DHCP option for backward compatibility.

However, all these DHCP options are specified in the configuration file for an ISC DHCP server using the syntax illustrated in Example 3.10.

EXAMPLE 3.10

```
option option-name option-value;
```

Appendix B includes a complete list of options that can be specified to the ISC server.

3.4.1 Subnet Options

Some options should apply to all subnets, while others are specific to certain subnets. In the GSI intranet, all hosts use the same DNS server, although each subnet uses a different default router.

In an ISC DHCP server configuration file, global options are defined at the beginning of the file. These global options then apply to each defined subnet so that the definitions need not be repeated in each subnet definition. The configuration file in Example 3.11 specifies that *dns.genstart.com* should be used by all the hosts in the GSI network, and that those hosts should use *genstart.com* as their DNS domain. The default routers are still specified for each subnet.

EXAMPLE 3.11

```
    option domain-name-servers "dns1.genstart.com", "dns2.genstart.com";
    option domain-name "genstart.com";
    # default lease = 30 days, max lease = 45 days
    default-lease-time 2592000;
    max-lease-time 3888000;
# Server subnet
    subnet 192.168.11.0 netmask 255.255.255.0 {
        range 192.168.11.1 192.168.11.251;
        # 192.168.11.252 reserved for DHCP server
        # 192.168.11.253 reserved for DNS server
        # 192.168.11.254 reserved for router interface
        option routers 192.168.11.254;
        option subnet-mask 255.255.255.0;
        # default lease = 90 days, max lease = 120 days
        default-lease-time 7776000;
        max-lease-time 10368000;
        }
    # Staff subnet 1
    subnet 192.168.12.0 netmask 255.255.255.0 {
        range 192.168.12.1 192.168.12.253;
        # 192.168.12.254 reserved for router interface
        option routers 192.168.12.254;
        option subnet-mask 255.255.255.0;
        }
    # Staff subnet 2
    subnet 192.168.13.0 netmask 255.255.255.0 {
        range 192.168.13.1 192.168.13.253;
        # 192.168.13.254 reserved for router interface
        option routers 192.168.13.254;
        option subnet-mask 255.255.255.0;
    }
    # Staff subnet 3
    subnet 192.168.14.0 netmask 255.255.255.0 {
        range 192.168.14.1 168.14.253;
        # 192.168.14.254 reserved for router interface
        option routers 192.168.14.254;
        option subnet-mask 255.255.255.0;
    }
    # Staff subnet 4
    subnet 192.168.15.0 netmask 255.255.255.0 {
        range 192.168.15.1 192.168.15.253;
        # 192.168.15.254 reserved for router interface
        option routers 192.168.15.254;
        option subnet-mask 255.255.255.0;
        # default lease = 12 hrs, max-lease-time = 24 hrs
        default-lease-time 43200;
        max-lease-time 86400;
    }
```

3.4.2 Global Values for Options

Example 3.11 demonstrates that options can be specified as DNS names as well as IP addresses. The ISC server resolves any DNS names in the configuration file and uses the corresponding IP address as the value for the associated option. Also, Example 3.11 illustrates that global values for options can be overridden with new values for specific subnets. The global values for default lease time and maximum lease time values are set to 30 days and 45 days, respectively; those values are set to 90 days and 120 days, respectively, within the server subnet declaration.

3.5 Extending a Lease and Moving Between Subnets

Using the configuration file in Example 3.11, here is a closer look at some of the examples from Chapter 2. Section 2.2 describes the steps in the configuration of a GSI client, desktop1, when it is first connected to the 192.168.12.0 subnet of the GSI intranet. When the DHCP server, dhcpserve, receives the initial broadcast message from desktop1, the server determines that desktop1 is connected to the 192.168.12.0 subnet. This subnet is labeled *Staff subnet 1* in Example 3.11. From the configuration file, the DHCP server determines that desktop1 should receive an address in the range 192.168.12.1-192.168.12.253. To accompany that selected address, the DHCP server selects the subnet-specific values for the subnet mask and default router, and global values for domain name and domain name servers. Because desktop1 did not request a specific lease time, the DHCP server chooses a lease time of 30 days, and the server returns the parameters in Table 3.2 to desktop1. At the same time, the server records the information about the allocated address and lease time on disk.

TABLE 3.2 INITIAL PARAMETERS FOR DESKTOP1

Option name	Option value
IP address	192.168.12.25
Subnet mask	255.255.255.0
Default router	192.168.12.254
Domain name	"genstart.com"
Domain name servers	"dns.genstart.com,"
Lease time	30 days (25,920,000 seconds)

3.5.1 Extending a GSI Lease

Section 2.2.2 of Chapter 2 describes the sequence of events that occur when desktop1 restarts while it is still connected to the 192.168.12.0 subnet. In that situation, desktop1 broadcasts a DHCP message to confirm its address, 192.168.12.25. The DHCP server on dhcpserve receives the confirmation request, and consults its configuration and lease data. Based on the entry for Staff subnet 1, the server confirms that 192.168.12.25 is a valid address for the network segment to which desktop1 is currently connected. The server then consults the lease data and confirms that desktop1 has a valid lease on 192.168.12.25. Having established the validity of the requested address, the DHCP server extends the lease on the address to the default value of 30 days and returns an acknowledgment. After receiving the acknowledgment, desktop1 records the new lease time and continues to use its old address.

3.5.2 Moving Between GSI Subnets

Suppose, now, that desktop1 is relocated to a new subnet, as described in Section 2.2.3. As in the previous example, desktop1 first broadcasts a message to confirm its address. But in this case, the DHCP server determines that 192.168.12.25 is not a valid address for the segment to which it is attached. The server examines the address recorded in the DHCP message by the relay agent, 192.168.13.254, and identifies Staff subnet 2 as the source of the message. Because 192.168.12.25 is not in the range of addresses on Staff subnet 2, the server returns a message denying desktop1 the use of the requested address.

After receiving the negative reply from the DHCP server, desktop1 restarts the DHCP process as it would if it had no valid address. It broadcasts an initial message to locate dhcpserve, which allocates a IP address, 192.168.12.37, from the range of addresses available on the new network to which desktop1 is now attached. desktop1 records the new address and begins using the network with its newly assigned address.

3.6 Other Configuration Information

The file in Example 3.11 is a complete, although minimal, configuration file for the GSI intranet. In practice, the configuration file would likely include additional information, such as global parameters for other GSI servers and statically assigned addresses, as described in Chapter 13, "Configuring a DHCP Server."

Summary

Network architects can use DHCP to automate the management of IP host configuration. The network architect's role is to define the intranet architecture and rules for IP host configuration. The DHCP server then uses that architecture and ruleset to determine specific configuration parameters for each host.

The network architect describes the architecture and host configuration rules to the server through a configuration mechanism, such as a file or an interactive user interface.

The ISC DHCP server uses a file, which is read when the server first starts up. The network architect defines global and network-specific configuration parameters within the configuration file. As the ISC server receives DHCP messages, it consults the network description from the configuration file and determines the specific parameters to be passed to the IP host. This chapter introduced some of the more widely used features of the ISC server configuration file. Chapter 8 describes the DHCP options in more detail, while Chapter 13 elaborates on the format and use of the configuration file.

CHAPTER 4

Configuring TCP/IP Stacks

Correctly operating and maintaining a network that uses DHCP requires an understanding of the fundamentals of TCP/IP networking. The following pages provide an overview of the TCP/IP Internet protocol suite and a summary of the parts of the TCP/IP protocols that are relevant to DHCP. If you are experienced with the use and design of TCP/IP, then you may want to skim this chapter. On the other hand, if you want a comprehensive review of TCP/IP, you may want to consider reading the *Internetworking with TCP/IP* series (Comer, 1995) or *TCP/IP Illustrated* (Stevens, 1994).

The following sections of this chapter look at each of the layers of the TCP/IP suite and describe some of the characteristics and features of each layer individually. One of the important functions of DHCP is to transmit TCP/IP software configuration parameters, and this chapter identifies some of those parameters.

4.1 The TCP/IP Protocol Suite

The TCP/IP protocol suite is a collection of related computer communication protocols that, when used together, provide network communication services among applications. TCP/IP is the protocol suite used on the Internet. Because TCP/IP is vendor-independent and can be used on many hardware/software platforms, it has also become to be the most widely used protocol suite on corporate intranets.

TCP/IP is designed around the five-layer protocol shown in Figure 4.1. Each layer includes configuration parameters that control the functions of the protocols in that layer. Many of these configuration parameters have default values that allow the protocol to function in most cases. Other parameters, such as the IP address and subnet mask, must be set to specific values for each computer and have no valid default values. In any case, even one incorrectly set parameter may cause the entire stack to perform poorly, experience intermittent failures, or simply not work at all.

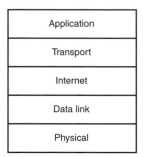

| Application |
| Transport |
| Internet |
| Data link |
| Physical |

FIGURE 4.1   *The five layers of the TCP/IP suite.*

4.2 The Physical Layer

The *physical layer*, also known as the *hardware layer*, delivers data encoded in a physical representation such as electrical current, radio waves, or light. The data is carried through a *medium* such as copper wire or optical fiber. In addition to *unicast delivery* of data, in which data is transmitted from a source to one specific destination, some types of network hardware support *broadcast delivery* of one message to every station on the network.

The destination of a message, or *frame*, is identified by the message's *hardware address*. Each station on a *network segment* (or a distinct physical network) must have a unique hardware address for messages to be delivered reliably to their intended destinations. Some network technologies, such as Ethernet, encode a hardware address in the *network interface card (NIC)* that connects a station to the network. Each Ethernet NIC is given a unique hardware address when it is manufactured so that no two Ethernet NICs ever have the same hardware address.

4.3 The Data Link Layer

The *data link layer* is responsible for delivering IP messages, or *datagrams*, across a network segment to the next hop on the path to the datagrams' destination. The IP software passes an IP datagram as well as the IP address of the next hop to the data link layer, which translates that address into a hardware address and transmits the datagram. This translation may be accomplished in several ways, including static translation tables and dynamic mechanisms that obtain the hardware address through the network itself.

4.3.1 Encapsulation

IP datagrams are *encapsulated*, which means they are carried as the data in a hardware frame. For Ethernet hardware, two alternative forms of encapsulation exist: *DIX* (named for the original developers of Ethernet, Digital Equipment Corporation, Intel, and Xerox) and IEEE 802.3. DIX encoding uses a 16-bit field in the Ethernet header to identify the protocol (IP, ARP, etc.) carried in the frame, while IEEE 802.3 encodes the protocol in the data area itself. DHCP specifies to the data link layer implementation which encapsulation form to use.

4.3.2 ARP

The most widely used translation mechanism is *Address Resolution Protocol (ARP)*. With ARP, a computer uses the network to find the hardware address of a destination based on its IP address. To use ARP, the data link layer first broadcasts a request to find the next hop destination. The destination replies with its hardware address, which the source then uses to send the datagram to the destination. The source also records the destination hardware address in a local cache for future use. The contents of this cache must be deleted periodically to ensure that the hardware addresses are updated, and the lifetime of an ARP cache entry can be specified through DHCP.

4.4 The Internet Layer

The *internet layer* is responsible for end-to-end delivery of protocol messages between computers. The *Internet Protocol (IP)* is the protocol from the TCP/IP suite that implements the internet layer. Logically, an internet can be thought of as a collection of independent network segments or physical networks, interconnected by *routers* that are attached to two or more network segments. *Hosts* connected to the network segments communicate by exchanging network messages through the interconnecting routers.

The *IP datagram* is the basic message unit for data delivered by IP; a host forms an IP datagram and identifies the destination to which the datagram should be delivered, and the IP software on the host and routers cooperates to deliver the datagram to the destination.

4.4.1 Network (IP) Addresses

Each computer that uses IP is assigned an *IP address*. This IP address actually performs two functions:

- It uniquely identifies the computer.

- It specifies the network segment to which the computer is connected.

In contrast, other forms of addresses, such as an Ethernet address, provide unique identification only and give no information about location.

As Figure 4.2 shows, an IP address includes a *network part* and a *host part*. As a special case, each network segment in an internet has its own *network number*, with a unique network part and a host part of zero. The IP address for a computer is composed of the network number from the network segment to which it is attached, and a host part unique among all the computers on that segment.

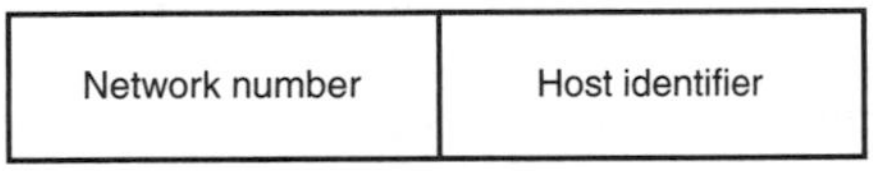

Network number	Host identifier

FIGURE 4.2 *The structure of an IP address.*

Composing the IP address from a network number and a host address produces some interesting features. First, it means IP datagrams can be forwarded to their destination by examining only the network part and not the entire IP address. The amount of information needed to forward datagrams depends on the number of network segments in the internet, not on the number of attached computers.

The second interesting property of IP addresses is that a computer's IP address depends on the network segment to which it is attached. Thus, when a computer is first attached to an internet, it must be given an address from the network segment to which it is attached. If that computer is then moved to a different network segment, it must be given a new IP address.

Third, the host part of a computer's IP address must be unique among all the computers on its network segment. If two computers from the same network use the same host identifier, they will both use the same IP address and their network connections will be unreliable or unusable.

These related problems—correctly configuring a computer with an address that depends on its location within the network, and avoiding simultaneous use of the same address by different computers—were the initial motivation for DHCP. Prior to the development of DHCP, a network architect might have had to walk around with a slip of paper or a spreadsheet listing available addresses. To add a new computer to the network without DHCP, he or she would have to consult the list of available addresses, select an unused address, carefully mark the address as "in use," and manually configure the computer with that address using a stack configuration tool.

Not only is this procedure time-consuming and error-prone, it doesn't scale well. Imagine the potential for conflict in a large organization where multiple network administrators try to assign IP addresses simultaneously from the same spreadsheet or sheet of paper.

4.4.2 Subnetting

The original IP specification defines three major *address classes*, which identify the ways in which an IP address is split into a IP address and a host identifier (RFC790). The format of each address class determines the number of networks available in that class, and the number of hosts that can be attached to each network. RFC988 defines an additional address class, D, which is used for multicast (described later in this chapter). The format of the four address classes and the number of networks and hosts for each class are shown in Figure 4.3.

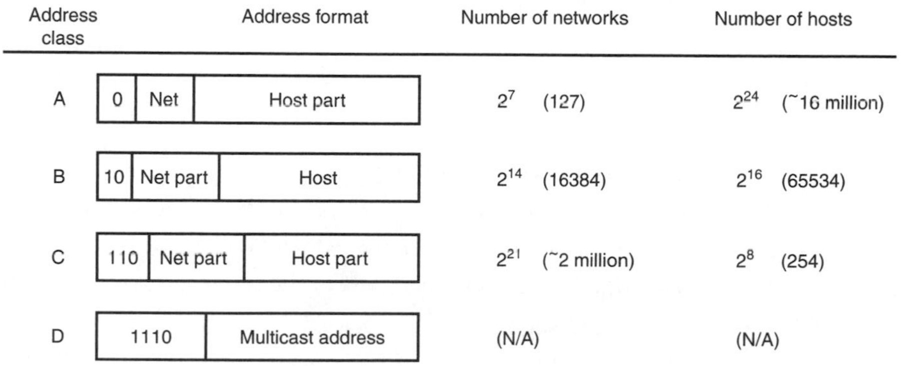

Address class	Address format	Number of networks	Number of hosts
A	0 | Net | Host part	2^7 (127)	2^{24} (~16 million)
B	10 | Net part | Host	2^{14} (16384)	2^{16} (65534)
C	110 | Net part | Host part	2^{21} (~2 million)	2^8 (254)
D	1110 | Multicast address	(N/A)	(N/A)

FIGURE 4.3 *The structure of Class A, B, and C addresses.*

In many situations, the IP address classes aren't a good match with a particular network architecture. For example, a network segment with 400 computers needs a Class B address that can accommodate more than 65,000 computers. This wastes more than 99 percent of the available addresses.

Subnetting (RFC950, RFC1878, RFC1519) is a technique for dividing Class A, B, or C addresses into smaller groups of IP addresses that more closely match the addressing requirements for network segments. In a subnetted intranet, the host identifier part of a IP address is split into a subnet address and a host address. The subnet address locates the network segment within the collection of segments that share the same network number, and the host address identifies the specific host on that network segment. Figure 4.4 illustrates the format of a subnetted IP address.

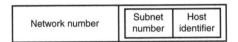

FIGURE 4.4 *The structure of a subnetted IP address.*

In the original IP addressing scheme, the division between the IP address and the host identifier is defined by the first three bits of an IP address. How is the format of a subnetted IP address defined? Each subnetted address must have an associated *subnet mask*, which identifies which bits of the address make up the subnet address and which are used as the host address. A subnet mask is a 32-bit number with a "1" in every bit from the IP address that is to be used as the IP address or the subnet address, and a "0" in every bit from the IP address that is to be used as the host address.

Note

The subnet bits in a subnet are contiguous, and are located just to the right of the network number field. Thus, a notation such as /24 indicates that the most significant 24 bits of the subnet mask are set to 1.

The subnet mask is applied to IP addresses to determine if two IP addresses are part of the same or different subnets. The subnet address can be extracted from an IP address by computing the bitwise logical AND of the address and the subnet mask. Two IP addresses are then part of the same subnet if the resulting subnet addresses are equal.

As discussed in the next section, computers using IP as part of the IP datagram delivery process employ this equality test. The subnet mask is, therefore, just as important to the correct operation of IP as the IP address; if a computer has an incorrect subnet mask, it may be unable to correctly process some IP datagrams.

4.4.3 Datagram Delivery

Hosts and routers cooperate to deliver datagrams from the source host to the destination host. The original source of a datagram and each router along the datagram's path to its destination examine the datagram to determine its destination and then forward the datagram to the next router on the way to the destination. The computer that creates the datagram must make an initial decision about delivery: Is the destination of this datagram on the same network segment? If so, the source can deliver the datagram directly to the destination. Otherwise, the source must deliver the datagram to a router for forwarding to the destination.

The source determines if the destination is on the same network segment by applying its subnet mask to both its own address and the destination address. If the resulting IP addresses match, the destination is on the same network segment. Otherwise, the source must forward the datagram to a router. Thus, a computer using TCP/IP must be configured with the address of at least one router in order to deliver datagrams to destinations on different network segments.

A computer uses a *routing table* that contains the addresses of routers to be used for specific destinations. Often, a computer has one or more entries in its routing table and uses these entries if no specific router for a destination exists. These entries, called *default routes*, identify *default routers* and must be inserted into the routing table manually or automatically through DHCP, or by another mechanism such as *router discovery* (RFC1256).

4.4.4 Multiple IP Networks on a Network Segment

Although the discussion of IP addressing and datagram delivery in the previous sections described a network segment as having a single IP IP address, it is possible to assign multiple IP networks to a physical network segment. These IP networks, sometimes referred to as *shared* or *overlay* segments, function as though they are assigned to independent network segments. Datagrams that are sent from a computer on one IP network to a computer on the other network on the same segment must be forwarded through a router, even though both computers are on the same physical network. Routers attached to the network segment have separate routing table entries for each IP network that point to the same network interface.

Assigning multiple IP networks to a single network segment complicates the management of DHCP servers because the server must know which IP networks are associated with a common network segment. In addition, the network architect may have rules about which IP network on a network segment a computer should use, and the server must follow those rules.

4.4.5 Multicast

IP includes a form of datagram delivery called *multicast*, in which a datagram is delivered to more than one destination. Multicast differs from broadcast in that a multicast datagram may be delivered to a subset of the computers on an internet, rather than to all the computers on a single IP network.

Multicast is used in applications in which many hosts want to receive copies of datagrams sent by a source without the overhead of sending a separate copy of the data to each destination. Examples of applications that use multicast include digitized audio/video conferencing, other collaborative applications, and routing protocols.

4.4.6 Other Internet Layer Parameters

Several other IP functions have operational parameters that must be correctly configured.

TTL

One of these functions is the IP datagram *time to live (TTL)*. Each datagram has a TTL field that is used to detect situations such as a datagram caught in a routing loop. The TTL may be explicitly specified to the IP software. If it is not, the IP software uses a default value for the TTL field in datagrams. The default value may be changed to accommodate, for example, a larger internet.

MTU

Another function that can be configured is the *maximum transfer unit (MTU)*, which is used for frames transmitted on the network segment to which a computer is attached. The MTU is the largest data payload that can be carried in a frame on the local network. Usually, the MTU can be determined from the network interface and from the type of hardware used in the local network. In some circumstances—for example, in the case of a bridged network with dissimilar hardware technologies—computers may need to use a smaller MTU than is allowed by the local hardware. This MTU value can be configured in the IP software.

PMTU

The *path maximum transfer unit (PMTU)* is used to control the size of segments transmitted by TCP. The PMTU value is selected to avoid fragmentation of datagrams carrying TCP segments. The IP software determines the PMTU dynamically by monitoring reports of datagram fragmentation. When the IP software detects that datagrams are being fragmented, it reduces the PMTU value until fragmentation no longer occurs. To ensure that the largest possible PMTU value is discovered, the IP software periodically probes with larger datagrams and watches for fragmentation. The details of the PMTU mechanism are controlled through configuration parameters in the IP software.

4.4.7 Summary of IP Software Parameters

Table 4.1 lists all the parameters that can be configured in the IP software. This list was derived from several sources, including the Host Requirements documents (RFC1122, RFC1123, and RFC1127) and the protocol specifications for path MTU discovery (RFC1191) and router discovery (RFC1256).

> **Note**
>
> *The Host Requirements documents (RFC1122, RFC1123, and RFC1127) summarize and analyze all the protocols in the TCP/IP suite. They include clarifications to protocol specifications from other RFCs, "best practices" and hints to implementers, summaries of important information about protocols, and interactions among protocols. Anyone implementing stacks, evaluating products, building applications, or otherwise using TCP/IP in nontrivial ways should read the Host Requirements documents.*

TABLE 4.1 CONFIGURABLE IP LAYER PARAMETERS

Parameter Name	Values
IP Layer Parameters, Per Host	
Be a router	on/off
Nonlocal source routing	on/off
Policy filters for nonlocal source routing	list of filters
Maximum datagram reassembly size	integer
Default TTL	integer
PMTU aging timeout	integer
MTU plateau table	list of integers
IP Layer Parameters, Per Interface	
IP address	32-bit integer
Subnet mask	32-bit integer
MTU	integer

continues

TABLE 4.1 CONTINUED

Parameter Name	Values
IP Layer Parameters, Per Interface	
All-subnets-MTU	on/off
Broadcast address type	0.0.0.0/255.255.255.255
Perform mask discovery	on/off
Be a mask supplier	on/off
Perform router discovery	on/off
Router solicitation address	32-bit integer
Default routers	list of 32-bit integers
Static routes, list of:	
destination	32-bit integer
destination mask	32-bit integer
type-of-service	integer
first-hop router	32-bit integer
Ignore redirects	on/off
PMTU	integer
Perform PMTU discovery	integer

4.5 The Transport Layer

The two protocols in the *transport layer* deliver data between applications through an internet, using the IP datagram delivery service. The *User Datagram Protocol (UDP)* provides best-effort, connectionless delivery of discrete messages, and the *Transmission Control Protocol (TCP)* provides reliable, connection-oriented delivery of arbitrarily long messages or streams of data. While TCP is, by far, more widely used, each protocol is appropriate for certain types of applications.

4.5.1 UDP

UDP provides independent delivery of individual messages. The UDP software accepts outgoing messages from the application layer and adds a header containing the destination port, the source port, and a checksum. The UDP software then passes the message to the IP software, along with the IP address of the destination. The IP software delivers the datagram to the destination computer. At the destination, the UDP software uses the destination port number to deliver the datagram to the receiving program.

Because UDP does not guarantee reliable delivery, the destination sends no acknowledgments or other indications of successful receipt of UDP messages. Reliability in applications that use UDP is the responsibility of the application layer protocol. For example, the *Trivial File Transfer Protocol (TFTP)*, which uses UDP, employs a *send-and-wait* mechanism in which the receiver sends a reply message to the sender to acknowledge receipt of each message from the sender.

DHCP uses UDP to deliver protocol messages between clients and hosts. UDP has two specific features that are used by DHCP:

- UDP messages can be *broadcast* and delivered to every computer on a network segment rather than to just a single destination computer.

- UDP messages can be transmitted with a source IP address of 0.0.0.0 if the source computer has not yet been assigned an IP address.

These two features, as described in more detail in Chapter 7, "Transmitting DHCP Messages," allow a computer to use UDP to locate and communicate with a DHCP server before the computer has an IP address.

4.5.2 TCP

In contrast to the best-effort message delivery provided by UDP, TCP uses acknowledgments and retransmission to provide reliable delivery of data that is guaranteed to be correct and in the correct order, without loss or duplication. An application hands outgoing data to the TCP software, which splits the data into *segments*. TCP then uses IP to deliver these segments to the destination. The TCP software at the destination reconstructs the original message from the individual segments and passes the data to the receiving application.

A TCP receiver sends acknowledgment messages to inform the sender of data that has been successfully delivered to the receiver. If the sender fails to receive an acknowledgment, it retransmits the data until the data is successfully delivered and the sender receives the acknowledgment.

TCP also includes a form of *flow control* that enables a receiver to slow down the rate at which the sender transmits data. The receiver defines a *receive window*, and the sender only transmits data within that window. The receiver informs the sender of the size of its receive window through a field in the TCP header. If the receiver wants to pause the transmission without shutting down the connection, it sets the receive window to zero. Later, to resume transmission, the receiver sets the receive window to a nonzero number.

4.6 The Application Layer

The *application layer* includes specific protocols that define interactions between application programs. These application protocols use the transport layer to exchange messages, which are formatted according to the rules of the application protocol. Most application layer protocols are specific to that application; only a few application protocols are shared among different applications.

Some protocols that are required or crucial to the operation of a TCP/IP intranet are actually application protocols. The *Domain Name System (DNS)*, through which human-friendly names such as *desktop1.gsi.com* are translated into IP addresses, uses an application protocol that is carried by either UDP or TCP. As mentioned in Section 4.5.1, TFTP, which is used to transmit software to diskless systems, is an application protocol that uses UDP. Routing protocols, such as *Routing Information Protocol (RIP)* and *Open Shortest Path First (OSPF)*, are carried in UDP and TCP, respectively.

4.6.1 Client-Server Model

Most protocols in the application layer are based on the *client–server model*, in which client applications contact a server to perform application-specific functions. The server application starts first, and waits for incoming messages from client applications. Clients then send messages to the server with requests for some function or data. DHCP is based on this client-server model.

In a client-server system, the client is configured with the IP address of the server and contacts the server through that address when required by the application. A DHCP server can inform a DHCP client of the addresses of servers for many different application protocols, including DNS, *Network Time Protocol (NTP)*, *Simple Mail Transport Protocol (SMTP)*, *Post Office Protocol (POP)*, and *Network News Transport Protocol (NNTP)*.

Summary

The TCP/IP protocol suite is the basis for network communications in the Internet. TCP/IP includes several layers of protocols, each of which implements specific services and which, taken together, provide communications between application programs. Two major styles of communication exist: best-effort datagram delivery through UDP, and reliable, data-stream delivery through TCP. Both TCP and UDP depend on IP for end-to-end message delivery through an internet.

To accommodate the widest possible variety of network hardware and computer systems, the protocols in the TCP/IP suite are set up with configuration parameters. Some of these parameters are required for correct operation of the protocols, while others enhance the performance of applications using TCP/IP. Configuration of the most fundamental of these parameters, the IP address, is crucial because incorrect assignment to one computer may affect the operation of other computers as well.

PART II

DHCP Theory of Operation

## CHAPTER 5

DHCP Client-Server Model

Whereas previous chapters give specific examples of DHCP in operation, this chapter summarizes DHCP theory and principles and explains why some DHCP features are included in the specification in their current form. This chapter describes:

- Some of the goals and constraints within which DHCP was designed

- The relationship between DHCP and other, related protocols

- The client-server architecture DHCP uses

5.1 DHCP Goals and Design Decisions

As earlier chapters explain, DHCP's primary goal is to automatically configure networked computers that use TCP/IP. Because TCP/IP is used in such diverse environments, the TCP/IP stack includes several parameters that may be configured for a specific computer and network (RFC1122). After using DHCP to obtain this TCP/IP stack configuration information, a networked computer can exchange packets with other computers on the Internet.

5.1.1 Administrative Control, Correctness, and Reliability

A network administrator can use DHCP to control the configuration of individual computers according to a set of particular requirements. That is, DHCP provides a way to convey configuration parameters to the computers being managed without dictating policies about how those computers should be configured.

For example, a DHCP server is not required to respond to every DHCP message it receives. In this case, if the network policy does not enable automatic configuration of computers not previously connected to the network, the network administrator can simply configure the DHCP server to ignore DHCPDISCOVER messages. This design goal enables the network administrator to use DHCP in a variety of situations and to implement a range of IP address and configuration policies. In this way, a DHCP server acts as an "administrative assistant," interpreting the configuration policies the network administrator develops and passing along specific parameters to individual computers based on those policies.

Assigning IP addresses Dynamically

The most obvious policy a network administrator develops for a DHCP server is one that controls the assignment of IP addresses to computers. Dynamic assignment of IP addresses enables new computers to join a network and obtain configuration parameters without manual intervention. The danger in dynamic address assignment is that two computers may obtain the same IP address, which prevents both computers from using the network. Meanwhile, such duplicate address assignment can be *very* difficult to find. Therefore, DHCP is designed to eliminate any possibility of assigning the same IP address to two computers at the same time.

In conjunction with dynamic address allocation, DHCP enables automatic address reuse. Because only a limited number of IP addresses are available in any IP subnet, the DHCP server eventually runs out of addresses to allocate, unless it can recover addresses that are no longer in use. The solution to address reuse in DHCP is to assign addresses for a finite period of time, known as a *lease*. At the end of the lease on a IP address, the DHCP server can safely reassign that address to a different client. In this way, a server can recycle the IP addresses in an IP subnet from computers that have left the network to new computers.

When Servers Are Unavailable

Because access to DHCP services is critical to the operation of an organization's computers (and, therefore, to the function of the organization as a whole), the DHCP specification enables the use of redundant DHCP servers. Computers using DHCP broadcast an initial message to locate DHCP servers and must be prepared to receive responses from more than one server. Likewise, when extending a lease on an address, a computer broadcasts its request to find any available DHCP server if the original server doesn't respond.

The DHCP specification even anticipates the possibility that no DHCP servers are available. In this situation, a computer can use its old address if it can't find a server when restarting. In the common case, when it has not moved to a new network segment and still has time left on its address lease, a computer can start using the network even if the DHCP server is down.

Relay Agents

An architectural design decision that increases the manageability and feasibility of deploying DHCP servers is the mechanism through which relay agents pass DHCP messages between clients and servers. Without relay agents, the network administrator has to set up a DHCP server on every network segment in the organization, a configuration that is difficult to implement and manage. Relay agents enable DHCP service to be provided by just a few servers in a centrally managed location.

5.1.2 Avoiding Manual Configuration and Reducing Changes to Configuration

DHCP is an effective tool for managing thousands of computers, in part because it provides automated configuration services for new computers that were not previously connected to the network. That is, a computer can use DHCP with no manual configuration on the part of the user or the network administrator. A computer equipped with a DHCP client can find a DHCP server, exchange DHCP messages with that server, and use the information from the DHCP server to configure its TCP/IP stack. All this occurs as soon as the machine is started, without the network administrator taking special action for individual computers.

At the same time, DHCP does not require manual configuration of DHCP servers to function with a new computer. DHCP servers can determine configuration parameters for new computers that were not previously connected to the network and respond to those computers when they first contact the DHCP server. Network administrators retain control over the configuration of new computers through policies set up on the DHCP server.

Finally, DHCP minimizes the changes to a client's configuration by retaining that configuration across client and server restarts. Servers must record assigned addresses and leases to permanent storage before responding to the DHCP client so that a reliable record exists that is consistent with the address assignments recorded by clients. Servers then use this record to confirm the address assignments when clients restart the computer. The DHCP specification also recommends that servers archive address assignment information so that the address is reassigned to the same client, even after the lease expires.

Clients with local permanent storage record their configuration information for reconfirmation when they restart the computer.

5.1.3 Identifying Clients

A server must be able to identify the source of incoming DHCP messages so that it can match those requests with existing entries in its database of assigned addresses. Ideally, each computer's identifier is unique among all computers and does not require manual initialization, but this is often not the case. One candidate for an identifier is the hardware, or *link-layer*, address of the interface to which the IP address is assigned. The link-layer address is unique among the devices on a network segment—in fact, for most network technologies, the link-layer address is unique among all computers using that same technology. The link-layer address is automatically configured and available without requiring user intervention.

The link-layer address has some limitations as a DHCP identifier, however. It lacks flexibility, and using it as a DHCP identifier also overloads its use as a mechanism for message delivery. For clients who want to use a different tag to identify a computer, DHCP includes the `client identifier` option. This option tells the server to use the value in the option as its identifier for the client, rather than the client's hardware address. Some sites, for example, configure computers to use the computer's fully qualified domain name as the client identifier.

Whether the server uses the client's hardware address or a client identifier to identify the DHCP client, the value of the identifier is assumed to be unique only on the network segment to which the client is attached. The server uses the combination of the network segment address and the client identifier to look up the client's information in the server's database of assigned addresses and configurations.

5.1.4 Functions Not Included in DHCP

Several functions or features were not incorporated into the protocol specification. The DHC working group is developing designs to add some of these functions, such as an open-standard inter-server protocol, to the DHCP specification. However, the working group has decided not to include certain other functions that do not comply with the group's design goals.

One IP address per Interface

The DHCP specification restricts the use of DHCP to a single IP address for each network interface on a device. When DHCP was designed, few TCP/IP stacks were configured with more than one IP address on a single interface, and it was not necessary to assign more than one IP address to an interface.

> ### Note
>
> Obtaining multiple IP addresses for a single interface can be done using a different `client iden-tifier` option for each IP address. A DHCP server will treat messages with different client identifiers as though they came from distinct DHCP clients, even though the hardware addresses in those messages might be identical. So, to assign multiple addresses to an interface, arrange for the DHCP client to make multiple requests to the server, each with a different client identifier.
>
> DHCPv6, the version of DHCP under development for IPv6, enables the assignment of multiple IP addresses to a single interface. This feature of DHCPv6 is discussed in more detail in Chapter 27, "DHCP for IPv6."

Server-Initiated Messages

The DHC working group decided early on in the design of DHCP not to include messages the server initiates—for example, a message from a server to a client informing the client of new configuration parameters. Such a function is useful if a new router is attached to a network segment, or if a network service such as DNS or LPR is moved to a different computer. However, when this option was considered, the working group decided that it was not feasible to implement in the client and it was too complex to specify and implement in servers. DHCP is designed around the model that the client is the active participant and the server is the active aprticipant, which maximizes scalability. Therefore, the proposal for server-initiated messages was not adopted.

Communication Between Servers

Although the DHCP specification enables the existence of multiple servers, it doesn't include protocol for communication among DHCP servers. As later chapters discuss in more detail, DHCP servers must exchange information if a network administrator is to take full advantage of redundant servers. The DHC working group has been working on the development of an inter-server protocol for some time. Chapter 25, "Inter-Server Communication," describes the most recent inter-server protocol, which provides a hot-backup, redundant server that automatically takes over primary DHCP server responsibility if the normal server fails.

Automatic DNS Updates

A natural link exists between DHCP and DNS; when a server assigns a new IP address to a DHCP client, DNS entries for that client must be added or upgraded. But, when DHCP was first designed, the DNS database could be updated only through manual entries. No protocol existed through which the DNS database could be updated automatically. The DHC working group decided this problem was outside the scope of its charter and declined to develop a solution. Now that dynamic DNS updates are defined in RFC2136, the working group is developing a formal definition of the interactions between DHCP and DNS.

Router Configuration

The DHCP specification clearly states that the protocol is not intended to configure routers. The working group adopted that restriction on the scope of DHCP early on, to avoid the potential of added complexity in support of router configuration. As routers are typically static, and because it is critical to the operation of a network that routers are correctly configured, interest in expanding DHCP to support router configuration is minimal.

Note

Walt Lazear of Mitre Corporation has done some research into what he calls "self-discovering" networks. The way this works is that a self-configuring router is connected between a network segment that already has DHCP service and routing, and one or more network segments that do not. The router has no preconfigured knowledge of its configuration—it uses the DHCP protocol to contact a DHCP server, which provides it with configuration information. Using this information, it configures all of its interfaces and begins routing. At the same time, it configures its own DHCP server, which can then be used by the next router in the chain to configure itself. By deploying these routers in a lattice, network configuration information can propagate from a central server out to the edges of the network without requiring any intervention on the part of a knowledgeable user—the ultimate in plug-and-play networking.

5.2 Related TCP/IP Protocols

Clients can also use other TCP/IP protocols to obtain some of the configuration information DHCP provides, including:

Protocol	Function
Bootstrap Protocol (BOOTP)	Static IP address, some stack parameters and addresses of some servers. DHCP is based on BOOTP, and DHCP servers are easily extended to provide service to BOOTP clients.
Reverse Address Resolution Protocol (RARP) Dynamic RARP (DRARP)	Static IP address (RARP) and automatic assignment of IP address (DRARP).
Internet Control Message Protocol (ICMP)	Provides subnet mask and default router.
Service Location Protocol (SLP)	Dynamic directory for identifying and locating network services; can provide flexible and dynamic configuration of services also provided through DHCP options.

The *RARP* (RFC903) and *DRARP* (RFC1931) provide a computer with its IP address, based on its link-layer address. Both RARP and DRARP use the same message format as Address Resolution Protocol (ARP) (RFC826), and return the IP address assigned to a link-layer address. A computer using RARP or DRARP to obtain its IP address broadcasts a request message containing its link-layer address on its network segment. A server, which must be connected to the same network segment, determines the computer's IP address based on its link-layer address, and returns that address in a reply message.

RARP and DRARP differ in the way in which they determine the IP address to return to a requesting computer. RARP uses a table of link-layer addresses and IP addresses, which the network administrator creates and edits manually. DRARP assigns addresses to new clients automatically, without direct intervention by the network administrator.

Although RARP and DRARP provide only a IP address, many computers use TFTP to obtain further configuration information from the server that answered the RARP or DRARP request. For example, Sun diskless workstations use TFTP to download an appropriately configured UNIX kernel after obtaining a IP address from the RARP or DRARP server. Note that at this writing, newer Sun systems can use DHCP rather than RARP.

The *ICMP* (RFC792) includes two mechanisms that a computer can use to obtain protocol stack parameters. A local authority, such as a router, uses the subnet mask message (RFC950) to inform a computer of the appropriate subnet mask. A computer uses the ICMP router discovery messages (RFC1256) to learn about routers on its local network segment. Two types of router discovery messages exist: the first, which the computer broadcasts, asks for a response from routers on the network segment. The second, which routers broadcast, announces that the router on the network segment is available. A computer uses a router discovered through the router discovery mechanism as its default router.

A computer can find network services, such as DNS and printers, using the *SLP* (RFC2165). SLP is configured either with a central server or as a distributed service. In either case, a computer looking for a particular service formulates a request for the service and submits the request through SLP. The response, from either the SLP server or the computers providing the requested service, returns information to the requesting computer describing the service and the address of the computer providing the service.

Note

*Taken together, RARP/DRARP, the ICMP subnet mask and router discovery messages, and SLP pro-
vide most of the important configuration information a TCP/IP host requires. As explained in
Chapter 2, "An Example of DHCP in Operation," a computer needs a IP address, the subnet mask, the
address of at least one default router, and the address of a DNS server before it can effectively use
TCP/IP.*

*A network administrator may find that DHCP is a better choice than these other protocols for com-
puter configuration management. Most importantly, DHCP provides all these configuration functions through a single service. A network administrator manages only one DHCP server, rather than
separate RARP/DRARP, ICMP, and SLP servers. Another advantage of using DHCP is that it includes
the leasing mechanism for automated recovery and reliable reassignment of IP addresses. Finally,
DHCP can provide other TCP/IP stack parameters in addition to an IP address, subnet mask, and
default router, and DHCP does not require a server on every network segment.*

5.3 DHCP Client-Server Architecture

In the DHCP client-server model, the clients are the computers using DHCP
services to obtain IP addresses and parameters, and the DHCP servers, which
network administrators manage, hand out the configuration information.
DHCP clients initiate all client-server transactions and are responsible for handling all the details of each transaction, including generating transaction identifiers and retransmitting lost protocol messages.

In one sense, clients are more complicated than servers are, in that clients must
maintain internal state information and generate the appropriate sequences of
messages for client-server transactions. Servers do not have to maintain state
information for clients (although they must, of course, keep track of address
assignments and leases); they can simply respond whenever they receive a
request from the client.

In another sense, servers are complex in their own way. A server must read and
parse a configuration file describing the network architecture and the local
DHCP policies, as well as store the information about assigned addresses on
disk. Most importantly, a server must be implemented carefully so that it
responds quickly to client messages.

The DHCP model of centralized administration came about for at least two
reasons:

- To minimize client configuration before the client uses DHCP

- To give network administrators full control over the configuration of networked computers

5.3.1 BOOTP Architecture Influence

BOOTP also heavily influences DHCP architecture and details. The client-server organization in DHCP is identical to the BOOTP model. The DHCP message formats, including the fixed-format header area and the individual option formats, are almost identical to those in BOOTP. DHCP also uses relay agents in the same way as BOOTP to forward DHCP messages from clients to servers, avoiding the need for a DHCP server on every network segment.

Note

Compatibility with BOOTP relay agents was the deciding factor in reusing the BOOTP message formats for DHCP. When DHCP was designed, router vendors were just beginning to include BOOTP message forwarding in their products. Rather than delay DHCP deployment until a new type of relay agent was developed and integrated into routers, the DHC working group decided to retain the BOOTP message format so that DHCP could use the installed base of BOOTP relay agents.

Summary

DHCP provides hands-off configuration of networked computers through network messages the computer exchanges with a centralized server. The server manages the client's configuration, assigning it a IP address, and determining other configuration parameters as specified by the network administrator's policies.

The client-server model in DHCP assigns all responsibility for initiating transactions to the client. Servers are essentially stateless, and can respond to individual client messages independently. A server does maintain pertinent information about the addresses assigned to clients, but it need not track the state of each client as it obtains and uses its configuration.

Other protocols, including RARP/DRARP, ICMP, and SLP, also provide some of the services DHCP provides. DHCP has the advantage of providing configuration management through a single service, reducing administrative overhead.

There are several functions that the DHC working group considered for DHCP but decided to leave out of the final design for various reasons. As this book was written, the working group is also working on several new functions, including authentication, more flexibility in computer identification, and a protocol through which DHCP servers can exchange information about clients.

CHAPTER **6**

The Format of DHCP Messages

DHCP clients and servers communicate through the exchange of messages described in the protocol specification. All DHCP messages share a common format, illustrated in this chapter. Future chapters describe how DHCP messages are transmitted using UDP, and the specific options that can be carried in a DHCP message.

DHCP was developed from BOOTP (RFC951) and uses a message format based on the BOOTP specification. Because DHCP also shares UDP ports 67 and 68 with BOOTP, DHCP messages include a special option in the option field that differentiates them from BOOTP messages.

6.1 Format Overview

All DHCP messages include a fixed-format section and a variable-format option section. The variable-format section holds options, which carry additional configuration parameters. The contents of the fixed-format section and the format of the options section vary according to the type of DHCP message.

The fixed-format section is divided into several fields that carry information such as:

- The network and hardware addresses of the client

- The IP address of the server

- Control information about the message itself

These fields appear in every DHCP message, although not all fields are used in every type of message.

The type of DHCP message being carried is specified in the options section of the variable-format section. The options section carries one or more DHCP options whose length is variable and whose contents and format depend on the option type. Some options carry control information about the DHCP message, such as the message type and an identifier for the client. Other options carry parameters that control the client's protocol configuration. Only those options required in a particular DHCP message need to appear in that message, which helps to minimize the length of DHCP messages.

By default, DHCP messages contain 576 or fewer bytes. However, a client may indicate to a server that it is prepared to accept messages larger than 576 bytes. If the server's response requires more than 576 bytes and the server can send a larger message, it may take advantage of the client's willingness to accept a larger message. In such cases, each message is carried in a single UDP datagram.

6.2 Fixed-Format Section

The fixed-format section, illustrated in Figure 6.1, appears in every DHCP message. In the figure, each row represents 32 bits of the fixed-format section. Individual fields are delimited by vertical bars and are labeled with the name of the field. Some of the larger fields are summarized in the figure, and their lengths are given explicitly. The fields in the fixed-format section are summarized in Table 6.1.

TABLE 6.1 SUMMARY OF DHCP MESSAGE FIELDS

Field	Description
op	Message operation code; set to 1 in messages sent by a client and 2 in messages sent by a server. The two possible values for op are carried forward from BOOTP for backward compatibility and are sometimes called BOOTREQUEST and BOOTREPLY, respectively.
htype	Hardware address type; definitions are taken from the IANA list of ARP hardware types (RFC1700). For example, Ethernet type is specified by htype set to 1.
hlen	Hardware address length (in bytes); defines length of hardware address in chaddr field.
hops	Number of relay agents that have forwarded this message.
xid	Transaction identifier; used by clients to match responses from servers with previously transmitted requests.
secs	Elapsed time (in seconds) since client began DHCP process.

Field	Description
flags	Flags field; the leftmost fit, called the *broadcast bit*, may be set to 1 to indicate that messages to the client must be broadcast(see Section 7.1 for details).
ciaddr	Client's IP address; set by client when client has confirmed that its IP address is valid.
yiaddr	Client's IP address; set by server to inform client of client's IP address; that is, "your" IP address.
siaddr	IP address of next server for client to use in configuration process; for example, server to contact for TFTP download of operating system kernel.
giaddr	Relay agent (or gateway) IP address; filled in by relay agent with address of interface through which DHCP message was received.
chaddr	Client's hardware address.
sname	Name of next server for client to use in configuration process.
file	Name of file for client to request from next server; for example, name of file containing operating system for this client.

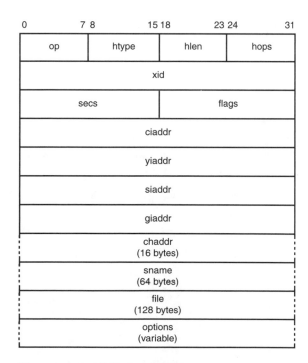

FIGURE 6.1 *Fields in a DHCP message.*

6.3 options **Section**

The options section of a DHCP message carries a sequence of options, which convey additional configuration information between the client and the server. Each option includes an *option code,* an *option length,* and *option data,* as illustrated in Figure 6.2. The option code identifies the specific option and the information carried in the option. The option data field is the actual information, and the option length gives the length, in bytes, of the option data field.

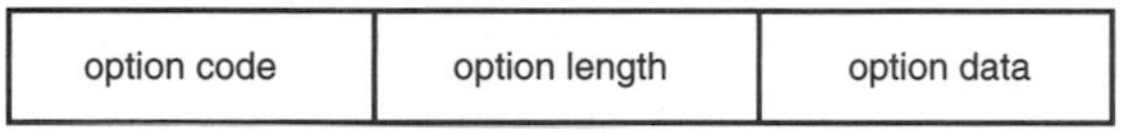

option code	option length	option data

FIGURE 6.2   *Format of DHCP options.*

The first four bytes in the options section define the format of the remainder of the section. The four bytes are set to the decimal values 99, 130, 83, 99 (or 63, 82, 53, 63 in hexadecimal). These values are referred to as a *magic number* in the BOOTP specification (RFC951) and a *magic cookie* in the DHCP options and BOOTP extensions (originally defined in RFC1048 and included in RFC2132).

Note

This format specification enables the development of new formats for the options *field. In fact, as this book is being written, the DHC working group is developing a new format that addresses some problems in the current format, such as the limited number of available option codes. This chapter explains the current format for the* options *section; details of the new options are discussed in Chapter 26, "Guiding the Evolution of DHCP."*

The options are stored sequentially in the options section, without word alignment or other formatting restrictions. The option data is formatted according to the specification of the particular option. Example data formats include a single IP address, a list of IP addresses, and a character string.

The remainder of Section 6.3 describes some example options, and Section 6.4 illustrates the use of DHCP message fields and options in messages exchanged between a client and a server. The options described in the remainder of this section illustrate some specific option data formats.

Option Origin

One of the reasons to use a `variable format option` section is to allow the definition of new options as new configuration requirements are defined. Many of the options in RFC2132 carry the addresses of servers for applications and services that hadn't been invented when the first version of DHCP was published as a standard in 1993. Today, new options are being developed to add security features to DHCP, to adapt DHCP to new technologies, such as xDSL and cable modems, and to allow DHCP to operate with other protocols such as DNS.

The IETF defines new options through a process described in RFC2132 and subsequently modified in RFC2489 (also BCP 29). Each new option (or group of related options) is described in a separate document and considered for adoption independently. In the review process, which is based on the IETF standards process for new Internet protocols, a new option is first defined in an Internet draft. The draft is then reviewed by the DHC working group of the IETF and is revised based on input from the working group. Once the draft has passed the working group review, it is submitted to the IESG for acceptance as an Internet Standard. When the new option is accepted as a standard, it is assigned an option number.

6.3.1 `DHCP message type` Option

The first example option is the `DHCP message type`. DHCP client-server message exchanges are composed of messages of different types, representing the steps in the transaction. DHCP messages are often referred to by their type; for example, the client in Section 2 first broadcast a `DHCPDISCOVER` message (or just `DISCOVER`), and the server replied with a `DHCPOFFER` message.

The `DHCP message type` option is included in every DHCP message and identifies the type of DHCP message being sent. The `DHCP message type` option includes the DHCP message type option code (53), the length of the `data` field (1), and the message type, encoded as a single byte with one of the following values:

Message Type	Option Value
DHCPDISCOVER	1
DHCPOFFER	2
DHCPREQUEST	3
DHCPDECLINE	4
DHCPACK	5
DHCPNAK	6
DHCPRELEASE	7
DHCPINFORM	8

Figure 6.3 illustrates the format of the DHCP message type option.

| 53 | 1 | Message type |

F IGURE 6.3 *Format of* DHCP message type *option.*

Note

The DHCP message type *option also differentiates DHCP messages from BOOTP messages. Because DHCP and BOOTP employ different messages and semantics, a server must be able to distinguish between DHCP messages and BOOTP messages, and process each appropriately. Although both DHCP and BOOTP messages share the same format and are delivered to the same UDP port, only DHCP messages include a* DHCP message type *option. Thus, a server can use the presence of the* DHCP message type *option to determine that a message is a DHCP message.*

6.3.2 subnet mask **Option**

The subnet mask option carries the subnet mask that the client should use for its local network segment. While the client's IP address appears in the ciaddr field in the fixed-format section of the DHCP message, the subnet mask is carried in an option. It is unnecessary for a DHCP server to send a subnet mask to every DHCP client. If the server does not send a subnet mask to the client, the client assumes that subnetting is not in use.

Note

The allocation of a field in the fixed-format *section of the message to the client's IP address while using an option for the* subnet mask *was first employed in BOOTP and carried over to DHCP. The reason for this design decision is unclear. It might have been made because subnetting was developed after the first specification of BOOTP was written. Or it could be because the BOOTP/DHCP message must carry the client's IP address, while the* subnet mask *is not always required.*

The subnet mask option includes an option code of 1, a length of 4, and a subnet mask encoded as a 32-bit IP address. The subnet mask is encoded in network byte ordering, with the most significant byte immediately following the length field. Figure 6.4 illustrates the format of the subnet mask option.

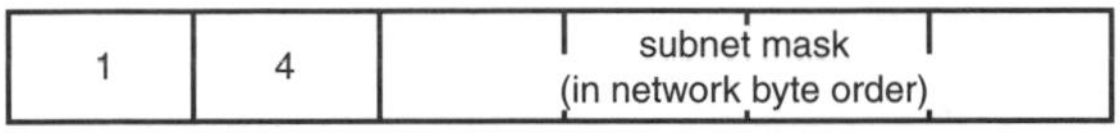

1	4	subnet mask (in network byte order)

FIGURE 6.4   *Format of the DHCP* subnet mask *option.*

6.3.3 router **Option**

Before a host can exchange IP datagrams with other hosts on different network segments, it must know the address of at least one router on its network segment. The router option carries a list of routers, sometimes known as *default routers*, which are connected to the same network segment as the client. The router option may carry the addresses of more than one router, so as to provide backup routers that a client can use in case one router fails. The router option includes an option code of 2, a length that is four times the number of routers listed in the option, and the addresses of the routers.

Figure 6.5 provides an example of the router option. In the figure, the option includes two router addresses; more router addresses can be carried if desired. Although the routers are listed in order of preference, in practice it is up to the client to decide how to choose among the specified routers.

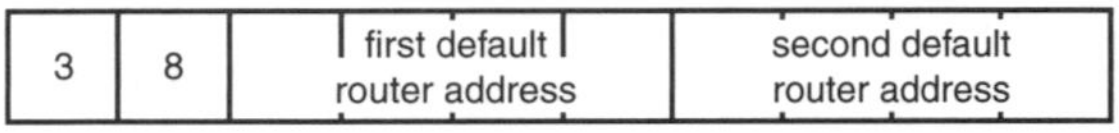

3	8	first default router address	second default router address

FIGURE 6.5   *Format of the* router *option.*

6.3.4 DNS server **Option**

If a host is to support the translation of Domain Name System (DNS) names into IP addresses, it must know the address of a DNS server to which it can send name resolution requests. The DNS server option carries a list of addresses of DNS servers that the client can use, in the same format as the router option. The DNS server option includes the option code 6, the length (four times the number of DNS server addresses carried in the option), and the addresses of the DNS servers.

Figure 6.6 gives the format of the DNS server option carrying the address of one DNS server. Like the router option, the DNS server option can carry more than one server address.

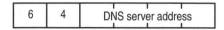

FIGURE 6.6 *Format of the DNS server option.*

6.3.5 requested IP address **Option**

When a DHCP client is allocated an IP address, it must check that address every time it starts or connects to a network. As described in the example in Section 2.3, the client contacts the DHCP server with a DHCP message containing the address assigned to the client. The address is carried in the requested IP address option. The format of this option includes the option code (50), the length (4) and the client's requested address, as shown in Figure 6.7.

FIGURE 6.7 *Format of the requested IP address option.*

6.3.6 end **Option**

The last option described in this section is the end option. It indicates the end of the options in the options section of a DHCP message. The end option is formatted in a slightly different manner from the other options described in this section; the end option is a fixed length and includes neither a length field nor data. The format, as shown in Figure 6.8, is a single byte set to the value 255.

Note

The end option is not required by the DHCP specification, and it might not appear in the options section of every DHCP message. DHCP clients and servers must be prepared to correctly process DHCP messages that do not include an end option.

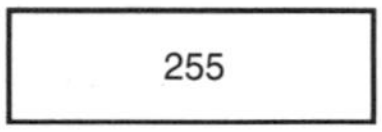

```
           255
```

FIGURE 6.8 *Format of the end option.*

6.4 Example Message Formats

To illustrate the format of DHCP messages, this section uses the example in Section 2.3 and presents the details of the DHCPREQUEST message sent from the client to the server, and the details of the DHCPACK message sent in reply from the server to the client. While the DHCPREQUEST message does not begin the protocol exchange between client and server (that is the purpose of the DHCPDISCOVER message), it is the most frequently observed DHCP message type, as is made clear later in discussions of the protocol exchange.

6.4.1 DHCPREQUEST **Message Format**

The client constructs its DHCPREQUEST message with its hardware address in the chaddr field and its IP address in the requested IP address option. The resulting message is depicted in Figure 6.9.

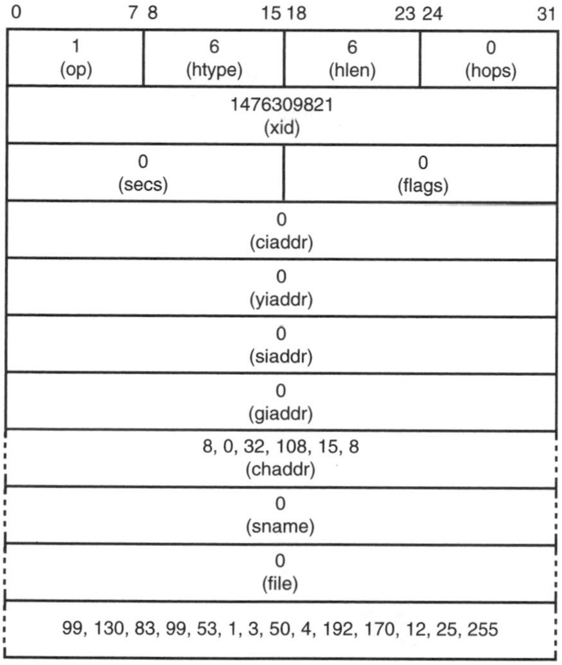

FIGURE 6.9 *Example* DHCPREQUEST *message.*

In this message, the client has filled in the following fields and options:

TABLE 6.2 FIELDS IN AN EXAMPLE DHCPREQUEST MESSAGE

Field or Option Name	Value	Comments
op	1	A message from a client.
htype	1	Indicates Ethernet address.
hlen	6	Length (in bytes) of hardware address.

continues

TABLE 6.2 CONTINUED

Field or Option Name	Value	Comments
hops	0	Indicates that message has not been forwarded by relay agents.
xid	1476309821	Random number chosen by client to identify this request.
secs	0	Time elapsed (in seconds) since client began sending DHCP requests.
flags	0	Indicates no flags are set.
ciaddr	0	(unused in this message)
yiaddr	0	(unused in DHCPREQUEST)
siaddr	0	(unused in DHCPREQUEST)
giaddr	0	Contains address of relay agent if forwarded by relay agent.
chaddr	8:00:20:76:0f:08	Client's hardware address.
sname	0	(unused in DHCPREQUEST)
file	0	(unused in this message)
DHCP message type	3	DHCPREQUEST message.
requested IP address	192.170.12.25	Address for which client has a lease.
end	255	End of options in option section.

Here is the DHCPREQUEST message as it is transmitted to the server, in hexa-decimal format:

	00	01	02	03	04	05	06	07	08	09	0A	0B	0C	0D	0E	0F
010	01	06	06	00	57	FE	B3	3D	00	00	00	00	00	00	00	00
020	00	00	00	00	00	00	00	00	00	00	00	00	08	00	20	76
030	0F	08	00	00	00	00	00	00	00	00	00	00	00	00	00	00
...																
0E0	00	00	00	00	00	00	00	00	00	00	00	00	63	82	53	63
0F0	35	01	03	32	04	C0	AA	0C	19	FF	00	00	00	00	00	00

6.4.2 DHCPACK Message Format

In response to the DHCPREQUEST message described previously, the server constructs a DHCPACK message confirming that the client's IP address is appropriate for the network segment to which it is attached. In this example, the server also includes other configuration parameters: the subnet mask, the address of a default router, and the address of a DNS server. Figure 6.10 illustrates the contents of the DHCPACK message.

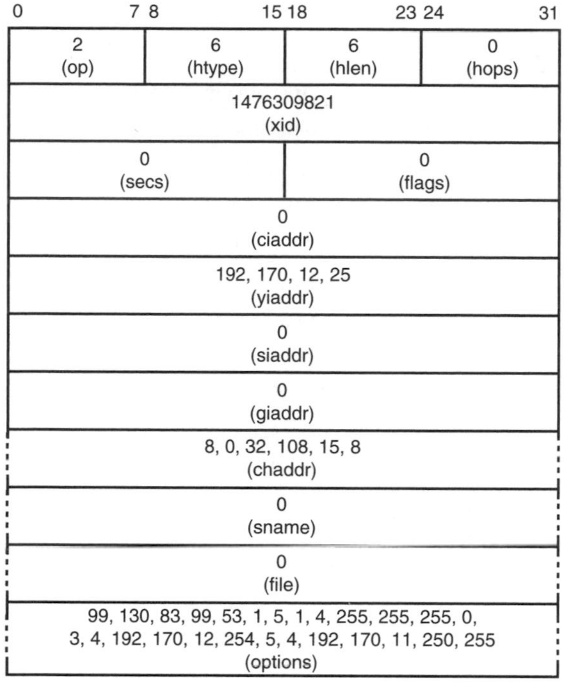

0 7 8	15 18	23 24	31
2 (op)	6 (htype)	6 (hlen)	0 (hops)
1476309821 (xid)			
0 (secs)		0 (flags)	
0 (ciaddr)			
192, 170, 12, 25 (yiaddr)			
0 (siaddr)			
0 (giaddr)			
8, 0, 32, 108, 15, 8 (chaddr)			
0 (sname)			
0 (file)			
99, 130, 83, 99, 53, 1, 5, 1, 4, 255, 255, 255, 0, 3, 4, 192, 170, 12, 254, 5, 4, 192, 170, 11, 250, 255 (options)			

FIGURE 6.10   *Example* DHCPACK *message.*

The fields and options the server sends in a DHCPACK message are as follows:

TABLE 6.3 FIELDS IN AN EXAMPLE DHCPACK MESSAGE

Field or Option Name	Value	Comments
op	2	A message from a server.
htype	1	Indicates Ethernet address.
hlen	6	Length (in bytes) of hardware address.
hops	0	Indicates that message has not been forwarded by relay agents.
xid	1476309821	Copied from the client's DHCPREQUEST message.
secs	0	(unused in DHCPACK)
flags	0	Indicates that no flags are set.
ciaddr	0	(unused in DHCPACK)
yiaddr	192.170.12.25	Address confirmed by server.
siaddr	0	(unused in DHCPACK)

continues

TABLE 6.3 CONTINUED

Field or Option Name	Value	Comments
giaddr	0	(unused in DHCPACK)
chaddr	8:00:20:76:0f:08	Client's hardware address.
sname	0	(unused in DHCPACK)
file	0	(unused in DHCPACK)
DHCP message type	5	DHCPACK message.
subnet mask	255.255.255.0	Subnet mask for client.
router	192.17.12.254	Default router for client.
DNS server	192.17.11.250	DNS server for client.
end	255	End of options in option section.

Here is the DHCPACK message in hexadecimal format:

	00	01	02	03	04	05	06	07	08	09	0A	0B	0C	0D	0E	0F
010	02	06	06	00	57	FE	B3	3D	00	00	00	00	00	00	00	00
020	00	00	00	00	00	00	00	00	00	00	00	00	08	00	20	76
030	0F	08	00	00	00	00	00	00	00	00	00	00	00	00	00	00
...																
0E0	00	00	00	00	00	00	00	00	00	00	00	00	63	82	53	63
0F0	35	01	03	32	04	C0	AA	0C	19	FF	00	00	00	00	00	00

Special Cases

A couple of special cases affect the format of options in a DHCP message. The first occurs when multiple instances of the same option appear in the options area. The motivation for allowing multiple instances of an option comes from the limitation on the data carried in an option. Because the size of the data must be specified in a single byte, an option carries, at most, 255 bytes of data. A few options that can carry a list of data items might conceivably exceed this limitation. Therefore, multiple instances of those options—for example, the DNS server option—are allowed in a single message. The protocol specifies that the data from instances of a single option are concatenated and interpreted as a single instance of the option. Thus, a list of 70

DNS servers can be split into two DNS server options, each carrying the addresses of 35 servers in 140 bytes.

The situation in which long lists of items are carried in an option leads to the second special case. Suppose the collection of options being sent in a DHCP message exceeds the default maximum options section size of 312 bytes. In anticipation of this problem, the protocol enables redefinition of the sname and file fields from the fixed-format section of the DHCP message to hold options rather than a server name and configuration file name. Using the two fields from the fixed format allows for 192 additional bytes of options, an increase of more than 60 percent.

6.5 Design Constraints

One might look at the format of a DHCP message and ask, "How did anyone come up with *this* format?" In the right situation, Ralph Droms, who is one of the authors of this book and was part of the initial DHCP design process, might be persuaded to admit that the DHCP message format is, indeed, arcane and bordering on ugly. The primary constraint around which the DHCP message format was designed is backward compatibility with BOOTP messages. When the design choices were made (1990-1991), some router vendors were including BOOTP relay agents in their products. The DHCP designers retained the original BOOTP format for DHCP to leverage the availability of these BOOTP relay agents to allow for easy DHCP deployment. To ensure that the BOOTP relay agents would correctly forward DHCP messages, the BOOTP format was retained. Rather than encode new DHCP functions in the op field (which might have caused deployed BOOTP relay agents to reject the message), the DHCP functions were encoded as options (which BOOTP relay agents never touch). In retrospect, it might have been better to design a new message format for DHCP and persuade the router vendors to implement DHCP-specific relay agents.

DHCP messages differ from BOOTP messages in four important ways:

- DHCP messages include a flags field, which is in an area defined as "unused" by the BOOTP specification. The definition of the flags came about as an engineering solution (or workaround) for certain TCP/IP stacks; Chapter 7, "Transmitting DHCP Messages," explains the details of the flags field.

- DHCP allows the options section (called the vendor extensions field in BOOTP) to be at least 312 bytes long, while BOOTP allows only 64 bytes of options.

- The DHCP message type option identifies DHCP messages.

- The sname and file fields in a DHCP message can be used to hold additional options.

DHCP also retains the format of options, originally defined in RFC1048, and the convention of reserving option codes 128–254 for local use. As such, a network architect can safely use the local-use options without conflicting with standard options, which use option codes 1–127. However, this numbering convention is becoming problematic because the option codes are being exhausted.

When BOOTP first adopted the convention 10 years ago, only a handful of options existed. Therefore, reserving only the first 127 for globally defined options seemed appropriate.

> **Note**
>
> *Although option codes 128–254 are supposed to be reserved for definition and local use by network administrators, some vendors of DHCP clients use those option codes for options specific to their particular clients. When vendors use option codes 128–254 for their own clients, they create a potential conflict with local use of those option codes. Rather than using option codes 128–254 for their clients, vendors should use vendor-specific options, a procedure discussed in more detail in Chapter 8, "DHCP Message Exchanges."*

Today, however, more than 80 percent of those global option codes have been used, and it is possible that all of the option codes will soon be exhausted. The DHC working group is considering this problem and expects to have a solution before the option codes are depleted.

Summary

DHCP messages include a `fixed-format` section and a `variable-format` section. The message format is based on the message format used by BOOTP, primarily to ensure backward compatibility with BOOTP relay agents. Several different DHCP messages exist, and all share the same format. The `fixed-format` section of a DHCP message carries information that identifies the client to the server and conveys some configuration information from the server to the client. The `variable-format` section holds *options*, which carry additional configuration parameters.

The type of DHCP message is determined by the `DHCP message type` option. The appearance of this option also differentiates DHCP from BOOTP messages. If a DHCP/BOOTP format message includes a `DHCP message type` option, it is a DHCP message; otherwise, it is interpreted as a BOOTP message. Other options carry protocol stack configuration parameters, the addresses of application servers, and other configuration information.

CHAPTER 7

Transmitting DHCP Messages

When transmitting DHCP messages, the client sends datagrams to UDP port 67, and the server sends datagrams to UDP port 68. Use of these ports is derived from Bootstrap Protocol (BOOTP), where the ports were originally defined as BOOTPS and BOOTPC, respectively. Port 67 is sometimes called the *DHCP Server port*, while port 68 is known as the *DHCP Client port*.

Use of UDP raises an interesting question: How can a DHCP client use UDP before the client has a valid IP address? DHCP solves the problem of IP addressing within UDP by specifying in DHCP messages the limited broadcast IP address, 255.255.255.255, as the destination IP address and the "this host" address, 0.0.0.0, as the source IP address.

Use of the limited broadcast IP address limits the delivery of messages from a client to servers that are connected to the same network segment as the client. DHCP uses relay agents, often running in routers, to forward broadcast messages from clients to servers and replies from servers back to clients.

This chapter explains DHCP message delivery, including the use of UDP and broadcast, relay agents, and retransmission of lost DHCP messages.

7.1 Using UDP for DHCP

The client sends all DHCP messages to UDP port 67 (the DHCP Server port). The client broadcasts messages if it does not yet have an address. If the client knows the address of a DHCP server and has an IP address of its own, it sends DHCP messages directly to the server.

7.1.1 Broadcast Messages

If the client doesn't yet have an IP address it knows is valid, it broadcasts messages to the limited broadcast IP address, 255.255.255.255, and to the appropriate link-layer broadcast address. The client uses port 68 (the DHCP client port) as the UDP source port, 0.0.0.0 as the IP source address, and its own link-layer address as the frame source address. This use of IP and link-layer addresses complies with RFC1122.

> **Note**
>
> DHCP assumes the use of a hardware technology that supports broadcast media. Use of DHCP over nonbroadcast media has been proposed, but standards have not been developed to date.

In the DHCP message header, the client puts its link-layer address in the `chaddr` field and sets the `ciaddr` field to 0. The `ciaddr` field is used only if the client has confirmed that its IP address is usable on its local network. The client also sets the `op` field to `BOOTREQUEST`.

Figure 7.1 shows a DHCP message broadcast by the client `desktop1`.

7.1.2 Unicast Messages

When the client has a valid IP address, it sends DHCP messages to the DHCP server using IP unicast, using its own IP address as the IP source address. The client then fills in the `chaddr` field with its link-layer address and the `ciaddr` field with its IP address.

The client uses IP unicast when it is extending the lease on an address or asking for configuration information with `DHCPINFORM`.

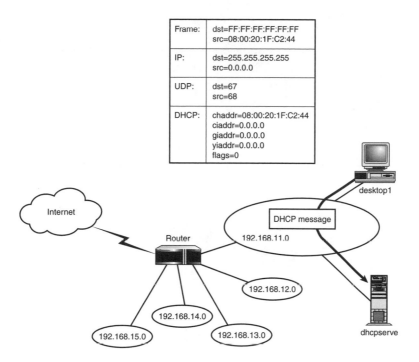

FIGURE 7.1 *A DHCP message broadcast by client* desktop1.

7.1.3 Server Response Messages

Servers send DHCP messages to clients with:

- The UDP destination port 68

- The UDP source port 67

- The IP destination address set to the client's IP address

- The link-layer destination address set to the client's link-layer address

Servers also set the op field to BOOTREPLY.

Figure 7.2 shows a DHCP message sent by a server in response to the message from the DHCP client in Figure 7.1.

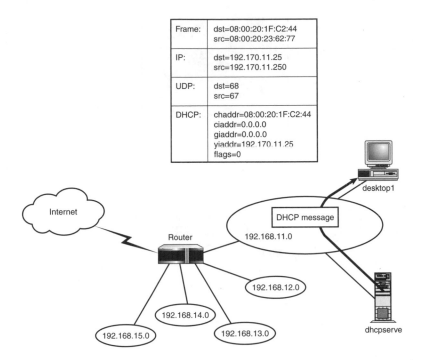

FIGURE 7.2 *A DHCP message sent by* dhcpserve *in response to a message from* desktop1.

Note

If the server sends a DHCP message to a client before the client has confirmed its IP address, the client will not respond to link-layer address resolution protocols such as ARP. As an implementation detail, the DHCP server may have to explicitly create an entry in the ARP table for the computer on which the server is running so that the link layer implementation can determine the link-layer address for the client.

7.1.4 Using Broadcast for Delivery to Clients

Some TCP/IP implementations do not accept incoming IP datagrams with a unicast destination address before the IP address has been configured. For such implementations, the server sends DHCP messages to the IP broadcast address, 255.255.255.255, and to the local hardware broadcast address. The client can still determine the IP address the server assigned to it from the DHCP message itself.

> **Note**
>
> *The Internet Software Consortium (ISC) DHCP server cheats when it can by setting the IP destination address to 255.255.255.255 and the link layer destination address to the client's link-layer address. This is technically incorrect, but it works well and reduces the amount of broadcast traffic generated by the DHCP server.*

7.1.5 Using the Broadcast Flag

Sending DHCP messages to the client's IP address is the preferred delivery mechanism because it avoids interrupting other clients with a broadcast message. Therefore, servers use unicast for DHCP messages unless a client explicitly requests the use of broadcast.

A client can specify that servers use broadcast by setting the *broadcast flag* in the flags field of the DHCP message header. If a server receives a DHCP message with the broadcast flag set to 1, the server broadcasts responses to the client. Some networking APIs do not provide a mechanism whereby the DHCP server creates entries in the ARP table or sets the link layer destination address of a packet. In such cases, the DHCP server must broadcast messages to clients that do not have confirmed IP addresses, regardless of whether the client has set the broadcast flag.

7.2 Relay Agents

Relay agents forward DHCP messages from clients to servers without special processing on the part of the client. That is, a DHCP client sends messages without knowing whether a DHCP server or relay agent is on the network segment to which it is connected. A relay agent listens to UDP port 67 and receives broadcast messages from DHCP clients. When the relay agent receives a client message, the relay agent:

1. Inserts into the giaddr field the address of the network interface on which the message was received

2. Increments the hop count

3. Forwards the message to the list of DHCP servers configured by the network administrator

Figure 7.3 shows the original message broadcast by the DHCP client and the message forwarded by the relay agent to the DHCP server. In this example, the DHCP message on network segment 192.170.12.0 is essentially the same as the message in Figure 7.1. The contents of the message from the relay agent to the DHCP server illustrate the details of the forwarded message.

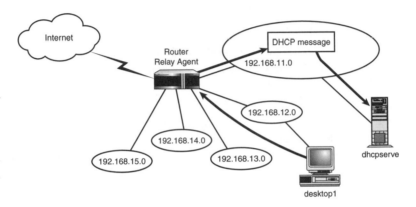

Frame:	dst=08:00:20:23:62:77 src=08:00:20:A3:99:4C
IP:	dst=192.170.11.250 src=192.170.12.254
UDP:	dst=67 src=68
DHCP:	chaddr=08:00:20:1F:C2:44 ciaddr=0.0.0.0 giaddr=192.170.12.254 yiaddr=0.0.0.0 flags=0

FIGURE 7.3 *A DHCP message forwarded from* desktop1 *to* dhcpserve *by relay agent in router.*

7.2.1 Forwarding Destinations

The destination to which a relay agent forwards DHCP messages must be explicitly configured for the relay agent. Many relay agents can be configured with more than one forwarding destination. This enables the relay agent to forward separate copies of the client DHCP message to multiple DHCP servers. Also, the forwarding address need not be a unicast address identifying a specific DHCP server. The address can be a broadcast address or the address of another relay agent.

These alternative addresses may provide additional flexibility in developing a DHCP server architecture. For example, using a subnet-directed broadcast address allows the relay agent to forward DHCP messages to a network segment to which DHCP servers are connected, without knowing the specific addresses of those servers.

7.2.2 Response Delivery

DHCP servers also use relay agents to deliver responses to DHCP clients. However, a DHCP server must explicitly forward DHCP messages to the appropriate relay agent. To determine how to deliver responses, a server examines the giaddr field in the message from the client. If the giaddr field is set to 0, a relay agent did not forward the message and the client must be connected to the same network segment as the server. In this case, the server delivers the message directly to the client. If the giaddr field is not set to 0, the server sends the response to the IP address in the giaddr field—which is the address of the relay agent that originally forwarded the client's DHCP message to the server.

Figure 7.4 shows the message the server sent to the relay agent, and the message the relay agent delivered to the client in response to the example message in Figure 7.3.

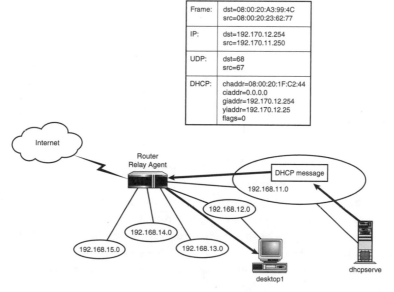

FIGURE 7.4 *Response from* dhcpserve *forwarded by relay agent in router to* desktop1.

Messages from a server to a relay agent are sent to UDP port 67. A relay agent forwards to the appropriate client messages it receives through port 67, with the op field set to BOOTREPLY. The relay agent forwards the server message to the client on the network segment identified by the address in the giaddr field. Because this field contains the IP address of the interface on which the client's message was originally received, the relay agent can deliver the response to the client through the same interface. The relay agent must also honor the broadcast flag and broadcast the response to the client if the broadcast flag is set to 1.

7.2.3 Multiple Relay Agents

A DHCP message can be forwarded through more than one relay agent. In this case, the second relay agent will find that the giaddr field in the message already contains the address of the first relay agent. If a relay agent receives a DHCP message with a nonzero giaddr field, it forwards the message as usual but does not modify the contents of the giaddr field. When a DHCP server receives a message that has been forwarded by multiple relay agents, the giaddr field contains the address of the relay agent that first received the message. The server sends its response directly to the address specified in the giaddr field, bypassing the intermediate relay agents.

7.2.4 Relay Agent Implementation

A relay agent does not have to keep track of information about specific DHCP messages it forwards. However, it must be configured with the address or addresses to which the client messages should be forwarded. Otherwise, all the information the relay agent needs is contained in the DHCP messages. This stateless operation means that a relay agent is simple to implement, doesn't consume many resources, and supports any number of DHCP clients without scaling problems.

Most commercial routers provide a relay agent function; while it is not necessary that a router perform this function, relay agents in dedicated routers are probably the most common configuration.

7.3 Reliable Delivery of DHCP Messages

Because UDP does not guarantee delivery, DHCP must include some provision for reliable delivery. DHCP clients, not servers, are responsible for managing message delivery. A client uses the response from a server as an implicit acknowledgment of receipt of the original message from the client. If the client does not receive a response to a message, the client retransmits the message as necessary until the server receives a response, or until the client decides that the server is not responding to messages.

The DHCP specification defines the amount of time a client must wait before retransmitting a message. The client waits 4 seconds before the first retransmission. It then doubling the waiting time between retransmissions, up to a maximum of 64 seconds. The particular implementation determines how many retransmissions to send before deciding to give up on the transmission of a message.

7.3.1 Avoiding Message Collisions

Under some circumstances, clients may experience collisions when sending DHCP messages over a network medium such as Ethernet. It is easy to imagine a scenario in which this might happen: Two identical machines on a network segment, which restart at the same time due to a power failure, initiate their DHCP protocol exchanges at almost the same time. A network segment with many identical or similar machines has a higher probability of collisions due to simultaneous transmission of DHCP messages. DHCP includes two mechanisms to decrease the likelihood of collisions. First, a client is required to delay its initial DHCP message by a random time between 0 and 10 seconds. Second, a DHCP client adjusts the delay time between transmissions with a random value in the range of –1 to +1.

7.3.2 Transaction IDs

A DHCP client inserts a 32-bit identification number, or *transaction ID,* in the `fixed-format` section of every DHCP message. The DHCP specification gives the client significant freedom in choosing transaction IDs; the goal is to minimize the chance that two DHCP clients use the same transaction ID simultaneously. The client may reuse the same transaction ID when it retransmits a DHCP message, or it may choose a different transaction ID for retransmissions. Similarly, the client may choose subsequent transaction IDs sequentially, starting with an initial random transaction ID, or it may choose each transaction ID at random.

The server copies the transaction ID from incoming DHCP messages into the corresponding responses. A client then matches the transaction ID in a server response to the transaction ID from the client's most recently transmitted message. If the transaction IDs match, the client accepts the response to its previous message; otherwise, the client discards the message and continues waiting for the correct response. Inappropriate delivery of a server response to a client may occur, for example, if a client sets the broadcast flag to 1, requesting that responses be broadcast. These responses will be delivered to every DHCP client on the network segment and must be filtered out by the clients that did not send the original message.

> **Note**
>
> The ISC DHCP client and other DHCP clients check the returned client hardware address and the
> xid to further reduce the likelihood of a collision.

7.4 Other Transmission Methods

A DHCP client uses broadcast and relay agents to send messages to DHCP servers when the client does not have a IP address. Once the client has an address and knows the address of a DHCP server, it uses unicast and transmits messages directly to servers through the normal IP datagram delivery service. This section discusses how DHCPREQUEST, DHCPINFORM, and DHCPRELEASE messages are delivered using unicast. The use of these messages is discussed in more detail in Chapter 8, "DHCP Message Exchanges."

7.4.1 DHCPREQUEST Messages

The protocol uses DHCPREQUEST messages at four stages of a lease's lifetime:

- During the initial selection of the lease

- When confirming the validity of an IP address after a restart

- When the lease is renewed at specific points during its lifetime

- When the lease is rebound near the end of its lifetime

The DHCPREQUEST message, sent during the initial selection phase, indicates which lease offer the client has accepted and implicitly indicates that offers from servers the client has not selected may be offered again at a later time. This DHCPREQUEST message is broadcast and must use the server identifier option to indicate which server it has selected. It may also include other options specifying desired configuration values. The requested IP address option must be set to the value of yiaddr in the DHCPOFFER message from the server.

This broadcast DHCPREQUEST message is relayed through DHCP/BOOTP relay agents. It is important that BOOTP relay agents forward the DHCPREQUEST message to the same set of DHCP servers that received the original DHCPDISCOVER message. To help ensure that they do, the DHCPREQUEST message uses the same value in the DHCP message header's secs field and is sent to the same IP broadcast address as the original DHCPDISCOVER message. A DHCP client broadcasts a DHCPREQUEST message when it restarts or reconnects to the network. This message contains the client's current IP address to be confirmed by the DHCP server.

> **Note**
>
> *Some relay agents take advantage of the ability to use more than one DHCP server to provide backup reliability and load balancing by selectively forwarding DHCP messages to different servers. For example, a relay agent might forward messages with the* secs *field set to 0 to a primary server, and other messages to a backup server. To ensure that messages are forwarded to the correct server, the client must set the* secs *field in the* DHCPREQUEST *message to the same value used in the* DHCPDISCOVER *message.*

The DHCPREQUEST message sent to request an extension of a client's lease on an address is unicast rather than broadcast. The client sends the extension request to the server from which the address was originally obtained (the client records the server's IP address when it first receives it). It then uses the client's own valid IP address as the source address in the message.

If the server from which the client requests a lease extension has moved to a new network or is temporarily shut down, the client does not receive a response from the server. In this case, the client sends a DHCPREQUEST message to 255.255.255.255 so that the message is delivered to any available local servers and relay agents can forward it to other servers. Because the client still has a valid IP address at this time, it uses that address as the source address in the message. The server uses unicast to send responses to DHCPREQUEST messages that request a lease extension directly to the requesting client.

7.4.2 DHCPINFORM Messages

A client that does not need to obtain an address through DHCP uses the DHCPINFORM message. Computers with manually configured IP addresses, such as large systems or mission-critical servers, can use DHCPINFORM to learn of other information, such as the location of printer, time, mail, or other servers. The client can use either unicast to send a message to a server known by the client, or broadcast to find any available server. In either case, the client uses its own valid IP address as the source address in the message.

7.4.3 DHCPRELEASE Messages

Clients also use unicast to deliver DHCPRELEASE messages to the server from which the address was originally obtained. The client puts the address it is returning to the server in the ciaddr field. However, because the DHCP specification defines that the client terminates its lease on an address when it first transmits the DHCPRELEASE message, the server cannot deliver a response to the client (as it no longer has a valid IP address). Thus, servers do not respond to DHCPRELEASE messages, and clients do not wait for a response to DHCPRELEASE messages.

Summary

DHCP uses UDP to transmit protocol messages. To deliver messages from a client that doesn't have a IP address, DHCP specifies the use of the limited broadcast IP address, 255.255.255.255, and the "this host" IP address, 0.0.0.0, in DHCP messages. When a client has a IP address and knows the address of a server, it uses unicast to transmit messages to the server.

Broadcast messages from a DHCP client can be delivered only to servers on the same network segment. DHCP uses relay agents to forward messages between clients and servers on different network segments. Relay agents are often implemented in routers. DHCP's design ensures that the relay agent is essentially stateless because it need not store information about messages it forwards.

DHCP clients are responsible for reliable delivery of protocol messages. Clients use responses from servers as acknowledgments of receipt, and retransmit messages for which responses are not received. Clients use randomized exponential backoff to determine how long to wait before retransmitting a lost message. This retransmission strategy reduces network congestion if many DHCP clients are on a network segment, and smoothes the load on a server serving a large network with a heavy client load.

CHAPTER 8

DHCP Message Exchanges

Chapter 2, "An Example of DHCP in Operation," and Chapter 3, "Configuring the DHCP Server," explain how DHCP clients and servers communicate. Chapter 7, "Transmitting DHCP Messages," describes how DHCP messages are transmitted using UDP. This chapter takes a detailed look at the DHCP messages the protocol exchanges with clients and servers. It covers the typical lifecycle of a client: from initial configuration, restarting, and reconfiguring after moving to a new network segment, to notifying the server it is leaving the network.

The examples in this chapter are based on the GSI network established in Chapter 2, which includes one DHCP server and several DHCP clients. The message exchange explanation includes packet traces of the messages. The packet traces were generated with the network analysis tool *snoop*, available with Sun's Solaris operating system, and were edited to delete extraneous information and to focus on the parts of the messages relevant to DHCP.

This chapter concentrates on the messages themselves, simply describing the decisions that a DHCP server makes when interacting with a DHCP client. DHCP server address, leasing, and configuration policies are covered in Chapter 13, "Configuring a DHCP Server," and Chapter 14, "Client Identification and Fixed Address Allocation."

8.1 Client States

DHCP client operation is modeled in RFC2131 by a *state machine*, and DHCP client behavior is described by a *state transition diagram*. This section introduces the various states. A closer look at the way a client behaves, along with details regarding state transitions, is provided later in this chapter.

When a client does not have a valid IP address, it is said to be in INIT state. Figure 8.1 illustrates the client states and state transitions. During the initial configuration process, the client normally moves to SELECTING state; when it is successfully configured with an IP address, it moves to BOUND state. When the client restarts, it goes to INIT-REBOOT state, and after it confirms its IP address is still valid, it moves to BOUND state. If a server sends a DHCPNAK message to the client because the client moved to a new network, the client reverts to INIT state.

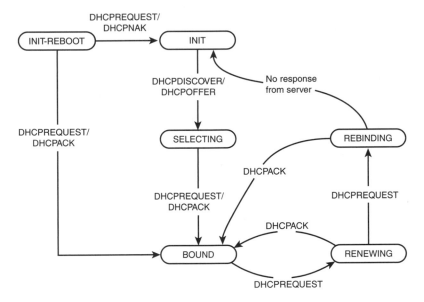

FIGURE 8.1   *A finite state machine for a DHCP client.*

Note

The DHCP specification in RFC2131 does not explicitly describe the behavior of a client that restarts with an expired lease on its most recent IP address. RFC2131 simply states that a client goes to INIT-REBOOT state if it restarts with a previously assigned address. It does not specifically require that the lease on the address has expired.

Section 3.2 of RFC2131 (on page 20) specifies that a client may use a previously assigned address if it doesn't receive a confirming DHCPACK message from a DHCP server in response to its DHCPREQUEST *message. This behavior implies that the lease on the previously unassigned address has not expired.*

Some clients go to INIT-REBOOT *state with a previously assigned address, regardless of the state of the lease on that address. A client implementing this behavior sends an initial* DHCPREQUEST *and proceeds to* BOUND *state if it receives a* DHCPACK *in response. If the client does not receive a* DHCPACK *and the lease has not expired, then it uses its previously assigned address. If the lease has expired, the client either reverts to* INIT *state or abandons DHCP initialization.*

Some time before the client's lease on the IP address expires, the client enters the RENEWING state and attempts to extend its lease by unicasting a message to the server from which it obtained its IP address. If the client receives no response to its unicast renewal request, at a later time it will enter the REBINDING state and broadcast a message to extend its lease from any available server. If the lease expires without the client successfully renewing its lease, it reverts to the INIT state.

8.1.1 Obtaining an Initial Configuration

When a computer configured to use DHCP is connected to a network, it determines whether it has a valid IP address. A client may be without a valid address because it is new and has not had a IP address assigned to it, the lease on its previous address expired, or a server told the client its IP address is invalid. In these cases, the client is in INIT state because it does not have a valid address.

DHCPDISCOVER **Message**

To obtain a IP address and other configuration parameters, the client finds a DHCP server or servers. The client sends a broadcast DHCPDISCOVER message, and the message is delivered to all the DHCP servers on the same network segment as the client. The DHCPDISCOVER message is also received by relay agents on the client's network segment and forwarded to other DHCP servers on other networks. Example 8.1 is based on the network configuration in Figure 2.3 in Chapter 2. The client and server are on the same network segment, which has the network number 192.168.11.0.

Example 8.1 shows the output from *snoop* looking at the DHCPDISCOVER message from *desktop1*.

E X A M P L E 8.1

```
ETHER:  ----- Ether Header -----
ETHER:  Destination = ff:ff:ff:ff:ff:ff, (broadcast)
ETHER:  Source      = 8:0:20:7c:fb:89, Sun
IP:     ----- IP Header -----
IP:     Protocol = 17 (UDP)
IP:     Source address = 0.0.0.0, OLD-BROADCAST
```

```
IP:    Destination address = 255.255.255.255, BROADCAST
UDP:   ----- UDP Header -----
UDP:   Source port = 68
UDP:   Destination port = 67 (BOOTPS)
DHCP: ----- Dynamic Host Configuration Protocol -----
DHCP: Transaction ID = 0xc8206f1c
DHCP: Client address (ciaddr) = 0.0.0.0
DHCP: Your client address (yiaddr) = 0.0.0.0
DHCP: Client hardware address (chaddr) = 08:00:20:7C:FB:89
DHCP: ----- (Options) field options -----
DHCP: Message type = DHCPDISCOVER
```

As described in Chapter 7, this message is broadcast to the Ethernet broadcast
address FF:FF:FF:FF:FF:FF and to the IP limited broadcast address
255.255.255.255. The client uses the IP address 0.0.0.0 as the UDP source
address and in the ciaddr address. The DHCP message type option identifies this
message as a DHCPDISCOVER message, and the client does not include additional
DHCP options.

DHCPOFFER **Message**

After the server receives the DHCPDISCOVER message from the client, it finds an
address to assign to the client and puts it in a DHCPOFFER message. The server
also includes in the DHCPOFFER message other configuration parameters for the
client, as defined by the server's configuration file. After the server has completed the DHCPOFFER message, it sends the message back to the client.

Example 8.2 shows the DHCPOFFER message sent in response to the previous
DHCPDISCOVER message.

EXAMPLE 8.2

```
ETHER:    ----- Ether Header -----
ETHER:  Destination = ff:ff:ff:ff:ff:ff, (broadcast)
ETHER:  Source      = 8:0:20:76:f:8, Sun
IP:    ----- IP Header -----
IP:    Protocol = 17 (UDP)
IP:    Source address = 192.168.11.60, 192.168.11.60
IP:    Destination address = 255.255.255.255, BROADCAST
UDP:   ----- UDP Header -----
UDP:   Source port = 67
UDP:   Destination port = 68 (BOOTPC)
DHCP: ----- Dynamic Host Configuration Protocol -----
DHCP: Transaction ID = 0xc8206f1c
DHCP: Client address (ciaddr) = 0.0.0.0
DHCP: Your client address (yiaddr) = 192.168.11.25
DHCP: Client hardware address (chaddr) = 08:00:20:7C:FB:89
DHCP: ----- (Options) field options -----
DHCP: Message type = DHCPOFFER
```

```
DHCP: DHCP Server Identifier = 192.168.11.60
DHCP: IP Address Lease Time = 120 seconds
DHCP: Renewal (T1) Time Value = 60 seconds
DHCP: Rebinding (T2) Time Value = 105 seconds
DHCP: Subnet Mask = 255.255.255.0
```

This message is sent to desktop1's hardware address, 08:00:20:76:fb:89, and to the newly assigned IP address, 192.168.11.25. The server copies the transaction identifier, c8206f1c$_{16}$, from desktop1's DHCPDISCOVER message, so the client can identify the DHCPOFFER response. The server gives the client a lease time of 120 seconds and indicates that the client should try to extend its lease after 60 seconds.

Note

Note that these times are artificially short to illustrate the lease extension message exchange. It is more common for a server to set lease time to be several hours or days.

DHCPREQUEST **Message**

After desktop1 receives the DHCPOFFER from dhcpserve, it sends a DHCPREQUEST message asking for the configuration information from dhcpserve. The DHCPREQUEST message is shown in Example 8.3.

EXAMPLE 8.3

```
ETHER:  ----- Ether Header -----
ETHER:  Destination = ff:ff:ff:ff:ff:ff, (broadcast)
ETHER:  Source      = 8:0:20:7c:fb:89, Sun
IP:     ----- IP Header -----
IP:     Protocol = 17 (UDP)
IP:     Source address = 0.0.0.0, OLD-BROADCAST
IP:     Destination address = 255.255.255.255, BROADCAST
UDP:    ----- UDP Header -----
UDP:    Source port = 68
UDP:    Destination port = 67 (BOOTPS)
DHCP:   ----- Dynamic Host Configuration Protocol -----
DHCP:   Transaction ID = 0xc8206f1d
DHCP:   Client address (ciaddr) = 0.0.0.0
DHCP:   Your client address (yiaddr) = 192.168.11.25
DHCP:   Client hardware address (chaddr) = 08:00:20:7C:FB:89
DHCP:   ----- (Options) field options -----
DHCP:   DHCP Server Identifier = 192.168.11.60
DHCP:   IP Address Lease Time = 120 seconds
DHCP:   Renewal (T1) Time Value = 60 seconds
DHCP:   Rebinding (T2) Time Value = 105 seconds
DHCP:   Subnet Mask = 255.255.255.0
DHCP:   Message type = DHCPREQUEST
DHCP:   Requested IP Address = 192.168.11.25
```

In this DHCPREQUEST message, desktop1 asks for the address and other configuration parameters dhcpserve supplied in the DHCPOFFER message. desktop1 uses a new transaction identifier, and broadcasts the message using the FF:FF:FF:FF:FF:FF and 255.255.255.255 broadcast addresses.

DHCPACK **Message**

After receiving the DHCPREQUEST message, dhcpserve checks the requested address and configuration parameters to ensure that the address is still available and the parameters are correct. dhcpserve records the assigned address and sends the following DHCPACK message to desktop1.

EXAMPLE 8.4

```
ETHER:    ----- Ether Header -----
ETHER:    Destination = ff:ff:ff:ff:ff:ff, (broadcast)
ETHER:    Source      = 8:0:20:76:f:8, Sun
IP:     ----- IP Header -----
IP:     Source address = 192.168.11.60, 192.168.11.60
IP:     Destination address = 255.255.255.255, BROADCAST
UDP:    ----- UDP Header -----
UDP:    Source port = 67
UDP:    Destination port = 68 (BOOTPC)
DHCP: ----- Dynamic Host Configuration Protocol -----
DHCP: Transaction ID = 0xc8206f1d
DHCP: Client address (ciaddr) = 0.0.0.0
DHCP: Your client address (yiaddr) = 192.168.11.25
DHCP: Client hardware address (chaddr) = 08:00:20:7C:FB:89
DHCP: ----- (Options) field options -----
DHCP: Message type = DHCPACK
DHCP: DHCP Server Identifier = 134.82.56.108
DHCP: IP Address Lease Time = 120 seconds
DHCP: Renewal (T1) Time Value = 60 seconds
DHCP: Rebinding (T2) Time Value = 105 seconds
DHCP: Subnet Mask = 255.255.255.0
```

Figure 8.2 shows a timeline of the messages exchanged by desktop1 and dhcpserve as the client obtains its initial address.

When desktop1 receives this DHCPACK message, it records the assignment information and configures its TCP/IP protocol software with the IP address and other parameters. Now, desktop1 can begin using TCP/IP.

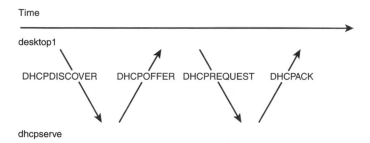

FIGURE 8.2 *Timeline of messages exchanged between client and server to assign an initial address.*

8.1.2 Confirming an IP Address when Restarting

Every time desktop1 restarts—for example, after power cycling—it checks whether it recorded an address with a lease that has not expired. After desktop1 is installed and assigned its initial address, it typically has an address it can reuse. Most organizations configure their DHCP servers to assign addresses with leases long enough to span periods of time, such as evenings and weekends, when computers are usually turned off. If desktop1 finds an address with a lease that has not expired, it goes into INIT-REBOOT state and attempts to confirm that its address is still valid.

INIT-REBOOT DHCPREQUEST **Message**

The client sends the IP address to be confirmed in a DHCPREQUEST message, which is received and checked by all DHCP servers configured for the network segment to which the client is attached. Example 8.5 shows a DHCPREQUEST message sent by a client in INIT-REBOOT state.

EXAMPLE 8.5

```
ETHER:   ----- Ether Header -----
ETHER:   Destination = ff:ff:ff:ff:ff:ff, (broadcast)
ETHER:   Source      = 8:0:20:7c:fb:89, Sun
IP:      ----- IP Header -----
IP:      Protocol = 17 (UDP)
IP:      Source address = 0.0.0.0, OLD-BROADCAST
IP:      Destination address = 255.255.255.255, BROADCAST
UDP:     ----- UDP Header -----
UDP:     Source port = 68
UDP:     Destination port = 67 (BOOTPS)
DHCP:    ----- Dynamic Host Configuration Protocol -----
DHCP:    Transaction ID = 0xc8206f1f
DHCP:    Client address (ciaddr) = 0.0.0.0
DHCP:    Your client address (yiaddr) = 0.0.0.0
DHCP:    Client hardware address (chaddr) = 08:00:20:7C:FB:89
```

```
DHCP: ----- (Options) field options -----
DHCP: IP Address Lease Time = 120 seconds
DHCP: Renewal (T1) Time Value = 60 seconds
DHCP: Rebinding (T2) Time Value = 105 seconds
DHCP: Subnet Mask = 255.255.255.0
DHCP: Message type = DHCPREQUEST
DHCP: Requested IP Address = 192.168.11.25
```

This message is broadcast because desktop1's address may be invalid, even if the lease on that address has not expired. For example, if desktop1 moves to a new office, or if the network architect assigns a new address to the network to which desktop1 is attached, desktop1 has an address that does not match the local IP address.

When dhcpserve receives desktop1's DHCPREQUEST message, it extracts desktop1's requested address from the options section, and ensures that the address is from an IP subnet assigned to the network segment to which desktop1 is attached. Unless desktop1 is in an environment where computers are frequently moved between offices, the address usually checks out and desktop1 can use it.

DHCPACK Message

dhcpserve replies to desktop1 at this point with a DHCPACK message. dhcpserve puts all the configuration parameters in the response message and returns the message to desktop1. Example 8.6 shows the details of a DHCPACK message.

EXAMPLE 8.6

```
ETHER:  ----- Ether Header -----
ETHER:  Destination = ff:ff:ff:ff:ff:ff, (broadcast)
ETHER:  Source      = 8:0:20:76:f:8, Sun
IP:    ----- IP Header -----
IP:    Source address = 192.168.11.60, 192.168.11.60
IP:    Destination address = 255.255.255.255, BROADCAST
UDP:   ----- UDP Header -----
UDP:   Source port = 67
UDP:   Destination port = 68 (BOOTPC)
DHCP: ----- Dynamic Host Configuration Protocol -----
DHCP: Transaction ID = 0xc8206f1f
DHCP: Client address (ciaddr) = 0.0.0.0
DHCP: Your client address (yiaddr) = 192.168.11.25
DHCP: Client hardware address (chaddr) = 08:00:20:7C:FB:89
DHCP: ----- (Options) field options -----
DHCP: Message type = DHCPACK
DHCP: DHCP Server Identifier = 134.82.56.108
DHCP: IP Address Lease Time = 120 seconds
DHCP: Renewal (T1) Time Value = 60 seconds
DHCP: Rebinding (T2) Time Value = 105 seconds
DHCP: Subnet Mask = 255.255.255.0
```

When desktop1 receives the DHCPACK, it uses the parameters from the message to set its IP address and protocol software configuration. Then, it is ready to use the network. Figure 8.3 gives a timeline of the messages exchanged between desktop1 and dhcpserve as the client rechecks its IP address when restarting.

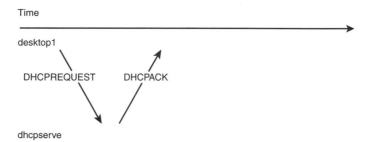

FIGURE 8.3 *Timeline of messages exchanged between client and server when client restarts.*

If desktop1 receives no response to its broadcast message when it first starts up, then it may be that DHCP servers are inaccessible due to a power outage or a temporary network problem. Rather than keep DHCP clients from using the network if the servers do not respond, a client can use its previous address if the lease on that address is still valid.

8.1.3 Extending a Lease

Suppose desktop1 continues running without being turned off or restarting. Eventually, the lease on the address assigned to desktop1 will run out. The leasing mechanism is designed to give DHCP servers a reliable way to reclaim unused addresses, not to take away addresses from computers still in use. So, DHCP includes a way for a computer to extend the lease on its address without interrupting network use.

A DHCP client extends its lease by sending a message to a server requesting more time on the lease. The request for an extension is sent in a DHCPREQUEST message, and the client can ask for whatever length lease it chooses. At this point, the DHCP server decides how long an extension to grant and returns the new lease duration to the client in a DHCPACK message.

The choice of lease length is up to the server. In fact, the server can choose not to extend the lease or can ignore lease extension requests altogether.

Lease Extension Request

A DHCP client is said to be in RENEWING state when it begins asking for a lease extension. Example 8.7 shows an example of a DHCPREQUEST message from desktop1, asking for an extension of its current lease on 192.170.11.0. Note that the message is sent directly to dhcpserve, and includes the length of the extension desktop1 wants as well as the other protocol parameters desktop1 is using.

EXAMPLE 8.7

```
ETHER:   ----- Ether Header -----
ETHER:  Destination = 8:0:20:76:f:8, Sun
ETHER:  Source      = 8:0:20:7c:fb:89, Sun
IP:     ----- IP Header -----
IP:     Protocol = 17 (UDP)
IP:     Source address = 192.170.11.25, 192.170.11.25
IP:     Destination address = 192.170.11.60, 192.170.11.60
UDP:    ----- UDP Header -----
UDP:    Source port = 68
UDP:    Destination port = 67 (BOOTPS)
DHCP:   ----- Dynamic Host Configuration Protocol -----
DHCP: Transaction ID = 0xc8206f1c
DHCP: Client address (ciaddr) = 192.170.11.25
DHCP: Your client address (yiaddr) = 192.170.11.25
DHCP: Client hardware address (chaddr) = 08:00:20:7C:FB:89
DHCP:   ----- (Options) field options -----
DHCP: DHCP Server Identifier = 192.170.11.60
DHCP: IP Address Lease Time = 120 seconds
DHCP: Renewal (T1) Time Value = 60 seconds
DHCP: Rebinding (T2) Time Value = 105 seconds
DHCP: Subnet Mask = 255.255.255.0
DHCP: Message type = DHCPREQUEST
```

Lease Extension Response

Example 8.8 shows dhcpserve's response.

EXAMPLE 8.8

```
ETHER:   ----- Ether Header -----
ETHER:  Destination = 8:0:20:7c:fb:89, Sun
ETHER:  Source      = 8:0:20:76:f:8, Sun
IP:     Protocol = 17 (UDP)
IP:     Source address = 192.170.11.60, 192.170.11.60
IP:     Destination address = 192.170.11.25, 192.170.11.25
UDP:    ----- UDP Header -----
UDP:    Source port = 67
UDP:    Destination port = 68 (BOOTPC)
DHCP:   ----- Dynamic Host Configuration Protocol -----
DHCP: Transaction ID = 0xc8206f1c
DHCP: Client address (ciaddr) = 192.170.11.25
```

```
DHCP: Your client address (yiaddr) = 192.170.11.25
DHCP: Client hardware address (chaddr) = 08:00:20:7C:FB:89
DHCP: ----- (Options) field options -----
DHCP: Message type = DHCPACK
DHCP: DHCP Server Identifier = 192.170.11.60
DHCP: IP Address Lease Time = 120 seconds
DHCP: Renewal (T1) Time Value = 60 seconds
DHCP: Rebinding (T2) Time Value = 105 seconds
DHCP: Subnet Mask = 255.255.255.0
```

In this response, dhcpserve agrees to desktop1's request for an extension of 120 seconds. When desktop1 receives the DHCPACK from dhcpserve, it records the lease duration and other parameters from the message. Figure 8.4 shows the timeline of these messages.

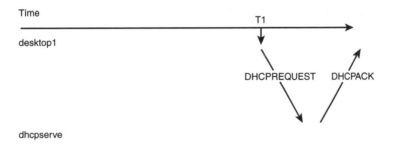

FIGURE 8.4 *Timeline of messages exchanged by client and server to extend a lease.*

The message exchange and lease extension happen in the background, without interrupting other applications. This process does not affect the user; as long as a DHCP server is available, a DHCP client can run without limits imposed by the DHCP leasing mechanism.

T1

The time at which desktop1 begins asking to extend its lease is called (not terribly imaginatively) *T1*. The DHCP server explicitly tells a client when to extend its lease by configuring T1, which is also known as the *renewal time*. If the server does not give the client a value for T1, it defaults to one-half the original lease.

In the previous example, if desktop1 does not receive a response to its lease extension request, it retransmits the request according to the rules described in Chapter 7. As long as the lease extension is received before the lease expires, desktop1 can continue using the network.

8.1.4 Extending a Lease from a Different Server

If a client in the RENEWING state fails to contact its original DHCP server, the client enters the REBINDING state at a later time, called *T2*.

After T2 is reached, the client begins broadcasting its DHCPREQUEST messages rather than unicasting them to the server that gave it its current lease. At this point, if another server receives the DHCPREQUEST message and can extend the lease, it does so, and the client can continue operating with its lease.

Note

This mechanism for finding alternate servers for extending a lease was included in DHCP to enhance reliability. If the server from which a DHCP client received its lease is unavailable for an extended period, the client automatically locates another server. In the same way, a primary DHCP server may be moved to a new computer system, with a new IP address, and the deployed clients automatically find the server when they cannot contact it at its old address.

Using alternate DHCP servers implies that the servers can coordinate the information about clients and leases. If dhcpserve gives an address to desktop1, other servers must learn about that address and its lease before they can extend the lease. The DHCP specification does not define a standard way for servers to exchange lease information. Chapter 15, "Setting Up a Reliable DHCP Service," discusses some alternatives for using multiple DHCP servers.

In the REBINDING state, except when using broadcast instead of unicast, the client and server exchange a DHCPREQUEST and DHCPACK message as described in the previous section. When the client receives a DHCPACK, it records the new lease and the responding server's address. The next time the client extends its lease, it uses this new server.

8.1.5 When a Lease Expires

If a client fails to contact a server and renew its lease before the lease expires, the client must stop using its IP address and go back to the INIT state. When the client's lease on an address expires while the client is using the network, open TCP connections are lost, and the user might have to reconnect to network applications that were in use. Data (and tempers!) can be lost when the client's lease expires. So, it is important for the client to extend the lease before it expires. Ways of preventing lease expiration are discussed in Chapter 15.

8.1.6 Moving to a New Network

If desktop1 moves to a new network segment while it is powered off, it sends a DHCPREQUEST with the old address the next time it starts up. When it receives the DHCPREQUEST, dhcpserve matches the network segment with the requested address, and determines that the address does not work on that network segment. For example, if desktop1 moves from the 192.168.12.0 subnet to the

192.168.11.0 subnet, it sends its previous address—say, 192.168.12.25—in a message that the server receives directly from the 192.168.11.0 subnet. The server checks its configuration information and finds that the 192.168.12.0 subnet is on a different network segment so that desktop1's address is invalid.

dhcpserve notifies desktop1 that its address is invalid by sending a DHCPNAK message. After desktop1 receives the DHCPNAK message, it discards its old address and enters the INIT state. At that point, the client tries obtaining a new, valid address as though it just started up with no IP address. So, desktop1 goes through the process described in Section 8.1.1 to locate a server and obtain an address that works on its new subnet. Figure 8.5 illustrates this sequence of messages.

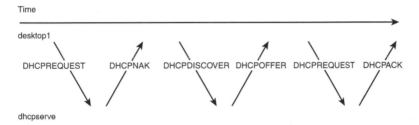

FIGURE 8.5 *Messages used by a DHCP client to obtain an address from a new subnet.*

8.2 Working with Multiple Servers

Although the examples thus far focus on the messages exchanged between a client and a single server, the DHCP specification is, in fact, written to accommodate the use of more than one server. More than one server may be involved in all client-server exchanges—not just as alternate servers for lease extensions, as described in Section 8.1.3. The model of operation described in RFC2131 enables multiple, independent DHCP servers on an organization's network, and requires that a DHCP client is prepared to receive multiple responses to its broadcast messages.

8.2.1 Obtaining an Initial Address

When a DHCP client broadcasts a DHCPDISCOVER message, it may receive responses from more than one server. Each responding server has an address and other configuration information for the client. The client listens for these responses after sending the DHCPDISCOVER and selects one of the responding servers as the source of its address. The client uses whatever criteria it wants to select a server. In practice, however, most clients simply choose the first server to respond.

What about the servers and the offered addresses that are not selected? The client indicates which server it has selected in its DHCPREQUEST message by including the server's IP address in the server identifier option. The DHCPREQUEST is then broadcast and delivered to all DHCP servers. The selected server responds to the client, while the other servers return the offered addresses to their pools of available addresses. Figure 8.6 illustrates this sequence of messages.

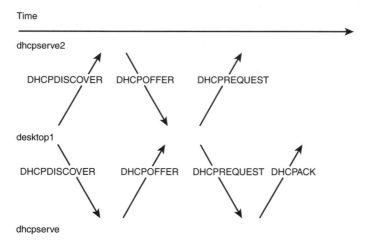

FIGURE 8.6 *Timeline of messages exchanged between a client and multiple servers when the client restarts.*

Of course, the broadcast DHCPREQUEST message may not reach all the DHCP servers. How long should a server reserve an offered address, waiting for the message from the client? Reserving the address forever is, of course, a bad idea. If only a relatively small number of addresses are available, the server will eventually run out of addresses.

In fact, the DHCP specification enables the server to decide whether to reserve an address. If, for some reason, it assigns an address to client B that it previously offered to client A before client A requested the address, the server sends a DHCPNAK in response to client A's request. When the client receives the DHCPNAK, it restarts its configuration process.

> **Note**
>
> *The Internet Software Consortium DHCP server does not attempt to handle DHCPREQUEST messages intended for other servers. Instead, it reserves leases offered to clients for 2 minutes. The server also returns addresses offered but not subsequently requested to the end of the list of available addresses. As long as enough addresses are available on the network, even a DHCPREQUEST from the client more than two minutes after the address was offered will probably be honored.*

8.2.2 Restarting

A client may also receive replies from multiple servers in response to its DHCPREQUEST message when restarting. In this case, the client's job is easier—it simply records the lease and configuration parameters from the first response and discards subsequent responses.

A potential problem exists with the consistency of the lease information after servers extend a client's lease. Because the client does not respond to the servers' DHCPACK messages, the servers don't know which response the client accepted. If the servers offer different leases, they will have different information about when the client's lease expires. This problem can occur when the client restarts and when it broadcasts a request to extend its lease. This problem is discussed as part of the larger issue of exchanging DHCP information among servers in Chapter 25, "Inter-Server Communication."

8.2.3 Broadcasting to Extend a Lease

A broadcast DHCPREQUEST message a client sends to find an alternate server to extend its lease may also trigger replies from multiple servers. The client's response is much the same as if it receives multiple responses to its initial message when restarting; the client simply records the lease and server identifier from the first reply it receives, and discards the rest.

8.3 Other Message Exchanges

Two additional message sequences remain for discussion:

- The sequence used by a client that is configured with an IP address through another mechanism

- The sequence used by a client to terminate its lease before the lease expires

These messages are used less frequently than the messages described earlier in this chapter.

8.3.1 Obtaining Configuration Information with an IP Address Not Obtained Through DHCP

Some network devices are manually configured with an IP address or they obtain their addresses through another protocol such as *Point to Point Protocol (PPP)* (RFC1661).

A network administrator might want to provide other configuration parameters to these devices through DHCP. Using DHCP for configuration parameters such as DNS servers and NTP servers enables the administrator to change the addresses of those servers automatically on all managed computers, minimizing manual configuration and assuring consistency.

A client with an IP address sends a DHCPINFORM message to a server to obtain other configuration parameters. When the server receives the DHCPINFORM message, it determines all the appropriate parameters, using the same policies it employs for computers using dynamic address assignment. The server returns those parameters to the client in a DHCPACK message.

> **Note**
>
> DHCPINFORM *doesn't have an automatic update mechanism. If the DHCP server administrator changes network configuration parameters, but the client does not use* DHCPINFORM *to obtain the new parameters, the client may be using the old, incorrect parameters until the next time it is restarted (which could be quite a long time).*

8.3.2 Terminating a Lease

A client gives up its lease on an address before the lease expires by sending a DHCPRELEASE message. A user may want to send a DHCPRELEASE message from a computer that is about to be moved from one subnet to another, so the server knows that the computer's old address is immediately available for reassignment. Some DHCP clients can be configured to send a DHCPRELEASE each time the computer is shut down.

The client sends its current address in the DHCPRELEASE message and does not wait for a response. The client stops using its old address as soon as it sends the DHCPRELEASE, so the server cannot send a response to the client. And, as a practical matter, a user won't want to wait for the server to respond while the computer is shutting down.

Summary

Several interactions between DHCP clients and servers involve specific sequences of messages. These interactions are designed to allow the clients to operate without prior knowledge of the location of DHCP servers, and to accommodate responses from more than one server. The interactions also minimize the effect of network and server failures on the client. The goal is to provide a robust protocol that enables clients to function in the event of network problems.

DHCP clients typically use four message exchanges. When a client does not have a IP address, it uses a two-step process to locate a DHCP server and obtain an initial address. After the client has obtained an address, it confirms that its address is still valid whenever the client restarts. A client can contact the server and extend the lease on its address while the client is still running.

Two other message sequences are less frequently used. A client sends a DHCPRELEASE message to terminate its lease on an address before the lease expires. If the client already has an IP address, it uses DHCPINFORM to obtain other configuration information such as server addresses.

Both this chapter and Chapter 7 describe the mechanisms through which clients and servers communicate in DHCP. The next chapter looks at the specific information that clients and servers exchange in the options section of DHCP messages.

CHAPTER **9**

DHCP Options

Chapter 6, "The Format of DHCP Messages," introduced *options* as the mechanism through which a DHCP message type is identified and configuration parameters are transmitted between DHCP servers and clients. This chapter describes DHCP options, as defined by RFC2132. The next few chapters explain how options are used in DHCP messages.

The options described in this chapter are organized into several sections. The first section illustrates the options specific to DHCP. Options providing configuration parameters for the DHCP client are explained in Section 9.2, and options carrying TCP/IP stack parameters are explained in Section 9.3. Application and service parameter options are defined in Section 9.4.

As illustrated in the previous chapter, all DHCP options, except for END and PAD, share the same three-part format: a 1-byte option code, a 1-byte length field, and the data carried by the option. Options carry data in different formats, including IP addresses, character strings, and integers. The descriptions in this chapter give the option code, the acceptable length field values, and the format of the data in each option.

NOTE

The DHCP options listing servers or other network devices identify servers by their IP addresses rather than domain names. Thus, if the servers are relocated or are for some other reason renumbered, the DHCP server databases must be updated to reflect those new addresses. Also, DHCP clients will not have the valid addresses for the servers until the clients re-contact the DHCP servers when they restart or extend their leases.

continues

The DHC Working Group has received proposals to extend DHCP options to accommodate domain names as well as IP addresses. As this book was being written, the working group was considering a new format for DHCP options that enables the use of domain names in options.

9.1 DHCP-Specific Options

Although both DHCP and BOOTP clients and servers can use the other options described in this chapter, the options in this section are specific to DHCP operation.

NOTE

The description of each option in this chapter includes a table giving the option code, the range of values of the length *field, and the interpretation of data values, along with a short textual description of the option.*

9.1.1 DHCP message type

Option code:	53
Length:	1
Data:	

DHCPDISCOVER	1
DHCPOFFER	2
DHCPREQUEST	3
DHCPDECLINE	4
DHCPACK	5
DHCPNAK	6
DHCPRELEASE	7
DHCPINFORM	8

DHCP client-server transactions use several different message types. The DHCP message type option identifies a specific type of DHCP message. Chapter 7, "Transmitting DHCP Messages," explains how the different message types are used.

9.1.2 client identifier

Option code:	61
Length:	n
Data:	identifier (n bytes)

The client identifier option carries a value DHCP servers use to distinguish a DHCP client. If the client identifier option is present, the DHCP server uses it; otherwise, the server uses the contents of the chaddr field. A DHCP client's identifier must be unique among all the identifiers on the IP network to which the client is attached. The server treats a DHCP client identifier as an opaque value and does not interpret it in any way.

RFC2132 suggests client identifiers be composed of a 1-byte type field, followed by the identifier itself, similar to the combination of htype and haddr fields in the fixed-format section of a DHCP message. If this format is employed, the type value in the client identifier is either selected from the ARP hardware address types defined in STD2, or is set to 0. In the latter case, the client identifier is an arbitrary string, such as a domain name, rather than a hardware address.

NOTE

Although RFC2132 suggests the typed format for client identifiers, many DHCP clients simply send a text string with no type identifier.

9.1.3 server identifier

Option code:	54
Length:	4
Data:	IP address

The server identifier option gives the IP address of the server involved in the DHCP transaction. If the server has more than one network interface, it uses the address of the interface through which the client in the server identifier option received the message.

The server identifier option differs from the siaddr field in the DHCP message header section. A client uses the server identifier to determine the source of a DHCP message delivered to the client, and to select the server to which a broadcast DHCP message is directed. The siaddr field holds the IP address of the server willing to provide additional bootstrap services, such as additional configuration information or an operating system kernel, through a network protocol such as TFTP.

9.1.4 requested address

Option code:	50
Length:	4
Data:	IP address

The requested IP address option contains the IP address the client requests when it does not have explicit confirmation that its current address is valid. A client includes its previous IP address in a requested IP address option when sending a DHCPREQUEST message during restart.

9.1.5 lease time

Option code:	51
Length:	4
Data:	lease time

The lease time is the duration of the lease for an address assigned to a client. The lease time is an unsigned 32-bit number representing the length of the lease in seconds. The reserved value $FFFFFFFF_{16}$ indicates a lease that never expires (in other words, a lease that is of infinite duration).

When a server sends a message to a client, the lease time represents the length of the lease the server selected according to the network's policies. When a client sends a message to a server, the lease time represents the length of the lease the client is requesting from the server. The lease time the server supplies is authoritative, and the client must honor it, regardless of the lease time it requests.

9.1.6 lease renewal time (T1)

Option code:	58
Length:	4
Data:	T1

T1 represents the point in time when a client begins extending the lease on its address. Beginning at time T1, the client unicasts DHCPREQUEST messages to the server from which the lease on the address was obtained. This option specifies the value of T1 to the client as a 32-bit unsigned integer representing T1 in seconds. If the server does not use this option to specify T1 to the client, the client uses half the initial lease duration for T1.

9.1.7 lease renewal time (T2)

Option code:	59
Length:	4
Data:	T2

T2 represents the point in time when a client begins finding a new server through which it can extend the lease on its address. Beginning at time T2, the client broadcasts DHCPREQUEST messages to locate a server willing to extend its lease. This option specifies the T2 value to the client as a 32-bit unsigned integer representing T2 in seconds. If the server does not use this option to specify T2 to the client, the client uses seven-eighths of the initial lease duration for T2.

9.1.8 vendor class identifier

Option code:	60
Length:	n
Data:	vendor class identifier

A DHCP client uses the vendor class identifier option to pass information about the client's vendor type and configuration. The server uses this option to interpret the contents of the vendor-specific options field, and (optionally) to select specific configuration parameters for a client. The identifier is a string of opaque byte values that is not terminated with a null character.

9.1.9 vendor-specific information

Option code:	43
Length:	n
Data:	vendor-specific information

The vendor-specific information option carries information interpreted according to the client vendor type, as specified in the vendor class identifier. This option enables a vendor to define new options used only by its clients, without going through the standards process or consuming limited option code space.

Note

Although the vendor-specific information *option appears in Section 8 of RFC2132, "Application and Service Parameters," it is really a DHCP-specific option and should appear in Section 9 of the RFC.*

If more than one option is carried in the vendor-specific information option, then the options are encoded in the same way as DHCP options and encapsulated in the vendor-specific information option data area. For example, if a vendor defines two options with option codes 125 and 126, a vendor-specific information option carrying those vendor codes is encoded as:

43	9	125	4	192	168	7	4	126	1	1

In this example, the option code is 43, specifying the vendor-specific information option. The length is 9, giving the length of all the data for the option. The first encapsulated option is the vendor's option 125, with a length of 4 and data 192.168.7.4. The second encapsulated option is 126, with a length of 1 and data 1.

9.1.10 parameter request list

Option code:	55
Length:	n
Data:	n option codes

A DHCP client uses the parameter request list option to request specific parameter values from a server. Each byte in the parameter request list is a DHCP option code the client wants the server to provide. The server includes values for the requested option, along with other options required by the protocol, in its response to the client.

9.1.11 message

Option code:	56
Length:	n
Data:	n characters

DHCP servers and clients use the message option to transmit an error message to a DHCP message recipient. The format of the contents of the message option is unspecified and is typically a character-string message displayed to a user or recorded in a log file.

Note

The DHCP specification calls for the use of 7-bit USASCII characters as used by the NVT (Network Virtual Terminal) and defined in the TELNET protocol (RFC854). The DHCP RFCs refer to NVT ASCII characters and NVT ASCII strings. This chapter simply uses characters and strings.

9.1.12 maximum DHCP message size

Option code:	57
Length:	2
Data:	length

A client or server uses the maximum DHCP message size option to advertise that it will accept incoming messages larger than the default maximum size DHCP message of 576 bytes. The length is stored as an unsigned 16-bit integer and must not be less than 576.

9.1.13 option overload

Option code:	52	
Length:	1	
Data:	1	file field holds options
	2	sname field holds options
	3	both fields hold options

If the option overload option is present in a DHCP message, the message recipient concatenates the specified fields with the options field and interprets the options in the resulting list. See Section 6.4 for a more detailed explanation.

9.1.14 TFTP server name

Option code:	66
Length:	n
Data:	n characters

The TFTP server name option identifies a TFTP server for the client to use in the next phase of its bootstrap process, when the sname field in the DHCP header has been used for DHCP options. The name is a string that is not terminated with a null character.

9.1.15 bootfile name

Option code:	66
Length:	n
Data:	n characters

The bootfile name option identifies a bootfile name for the client to use when the file field in the DHCP header is used for DHCP options. The name is a string that is not terminated with a null character.

9.1.16 pad

Option code: 0

The pad option carries no information and is skipped when the options field is interpreted. It can be used, for example, to pad the options section to the BOOTP standard of 64 bytes.

9.1.17 end

Option code: 255

The end option indicates the end of the options carried in the options field.

> **Note**
>
> Only the pad and end options do not include a length or data field.

9.2 Host Configuration Parameters Options

These options provide configuration parameters applying to the host.

9.2.1 host name

Option code: 12

Length: n

Data: n characters

The host name option gives the client's name. This name can be only the client's name or the name qualified with the local domain name. The name is a string that is not terminated with a null character.

A client uses the host name option to inform the DHCP server of the name the client is using. A server uses the host name option to inform the client of the name it should use for itself. RFCs 2131 and 2132 are unclear as to how clients and servers should react if they disagree on the name the client should use.

> **Note**
>
> RFC2132 recommends that the host name option carry the client's name and that the domain name option carry the client's domain.

9.2.2 domain name

Option code: 15

Length: n

Data: n characters

The domain name option specifies the name of the client's domain for resolving names in the Domain Name System (DNS). The name is a string of characters that is not terminated with a null character.

Note

The domain name option specifies only a single domain for name resolution. At the time of this writing, the DHC working group was developing a new option that specifies a list of domain names used in name resolution.

9.2.3 time offset

Option code:	2
Length:	4
Data:	32-bit signed integer

The time offset option specifies which time zone offset from Universal Time Coordinated (UTC) the client should use. The offset is a signed 32-bit integer expressing the offset in seconds. A positive offset indicates a location east of the zero meridian, and a negative offset indicates a location west of the zero meridian.

9.2.4 bootfile size

Option code:	13
Length:	2
Data:	16-bit unsigned integer

The bootfile size option gives the size of the client's bootfile. The size is an unsigned 16-bit integer specifying the number of 512 byte blocks in the bootfile.

9.2.5 root path

Option code:	17
Length:	n
Data:	n characters

The root path option gives the filename (full path name) of the directory being used as the client's root disk partition. Diskless clients use it to mount a network disk from the server identified in the siaddr or sname fields.

9.2.6 extensions path

Option code:	18
Length:	n
Data:	n characters

The extensions path option gives the filename (full path name) of a file containing additional options for the client. The name is a string that is not terminated with a null character. The client obtains a copy of the file identified in the extensions path option using TFTP from the server identified in the siaddr or sname fields. After retrieving the file, the client interprets the contents of the file using the same syntax as the contents of the options field.

9.2.7 merit dump file

Option code:	14
Length:	n
Data:	n characters

The merit dump file option gives the name of a file where the client should dump a core image if the client crashes. The name is a string that is not terminated with a null character.

9.3 TCP/IP Stack Configuration Parameters

The next sections describe several types of TCP/IP stack configuration parameters. Most of the parameters apply to the IP layer—either to all IP traffic on the client, or to the traffic on a specific interface. Other parameters configure the link layer and the TCP layer.

9.3.1 IP Layer Parameters for the Client

Each of the options in this section supplies a configuration parameter applying to all IP traffic on the client.

router

Option code:	3
Length:	n
Data:	list of IP addresses

The router option lists the addresses of default routers for the client to add to its routing table. The routers are listed by their IP addresses in order of preference. The length field gives the total length of the list of routers and must be a multiple of 4; if the list contains *r* routers, the length is 4*r*.

```
default IP time to live
```
Option code:	23
Length:	1
Data:	1 byte

The default IP time to live option gives the default value for the TTL (time to live) field in the IP header of datagrams the client transmits.

```
IP forwarding enable/disable
```
Option code:	19	
Length:	1	
Data:	0	disable forwarding
	1	enable forwarding

The IP forwarding enable/disable option controls whether a client with more than one interface should forward IP datagrams between its interfaces.

```
maximum datagram reassembly size
```
Option code:	22
Length:	2
Data:	16-bit integer

The maximum datagram reassembly size option specifies the largest fragmented IP datagram the client is prepared to reassemble.

Nonlocal Source Routing Options

The next two options control the forwarding of IP datagrams with nonlocal source routes (RFC1122, Section 3.3.5).

```
nonlocal source route enable/disable
```
Option code:	20	
Length:	1	
Data:	0	disable forwarding of datagrams with nonlocal source routes
	1	enable forwarding of datagrams with non-local source routes

The `nonlocal source route enable/disable` option controls whether the client forwards such datagrams.

`policy filter`

Option code:	21
Length:	n
Data:	list of filters

The `policy filter` option controls the filters applied to those datagrams. Each filter includes a IP address and a subnet mask. The client discards an IP datagram with a source route whose next hop does not match one of the addresses (with its associated subnet mask applied) given in the `policy filter` option. The `length` field for the `policy filter` option must be a multiple of 8; if f filters exist, the length is $8f$.

Path Maximum Transmission Unit (PMTU) Options

These options control the PMTU mechanism in the client.

`PMTU aging timeout`

Option code:	24
Length:	4
Data:	32-bit integer

The `PMTU aging timeout` option specifies the timeout to be used when aging PMTU values. The option gives the timeout value in seconds.

`PMTU plateau table`

Option code:	21
Length:	n
Data:	list of 16-bit integers

The `PMTU plateau table` option specifies a table of MTU sizes for use in the PMTU mechanism. Each MTU size is an unsigned 16-bit integer. The MTU sizes are listed in order from smallest to largest. The minimum MTU value must be at least 68. The length of the PMTU plateau table list must be a multiple of 2; if p plateau values exist, the length is $2p$.

9.3.2 IP Layer Parameters for an Interface Options

These options give configuration parameters applying to the IP traffic through a specific interface. Because a DHCP client with multiple network interfaces must use DHCP separately for each interface, it can receive customized configuration parameters for each interface.

subnet mask

Option code:	1
Length:	4
Data:	subnet mask

The subnet mask option carries the subnet mask for the interface to which the DHCP message is delivered. The subnet mask is represented as a 32-bit integer in "native" format, with bits set to 1, corresponding to each bit in the address to be used in a network or subnet number.

broadcast address

Option code:	28
Length:	4
Data:	IP address

The broadcast address option specifies the IP broadcast address for the network to which the configured interface is attached. The address is represented as a 32-bit IP address. Example broadcast addresses include all 1s (255.255.255.255), 0, or a network broadcast address such as 192.1.1.255 or 192.1.1.0.

static routes

Option code:	33
Length:	n
Data:	list of IP address pairs

The static routes option lists static routes for the client to install in its routing table. Each static route is listed as the address of the destination and the address of the router to use for that destination. If duplicate static routes for a destination exist, the routes are listed in decreasing order of priority. The length of this option must be a multiple of 8. If s static routes exist, the length is $8s$.

Router Discovery Options

The next two options control the use of *router discovery* (RFC1256).

perform router discovery

Option code:	31	
Length:	1	
Data:	0	do not perform router discovery
	1	perform router discovery

The perform router discovery option specifies whether the client should initiate the router discovery protocol in RFC1256.

router solicitation address

Option code:	32
Length:	4
Data:	IP address

The router solicitation address option gives the address the client should use to transmit router discovery protocol messages.

9.3.3 Link Layer Parameters Options

A few options affect the configuration of link layer parameters. These options apply only to the link layer software for the interface over which the DHCP message is received.

ARP cache timeout

Option code:	35
Length:	4
Data:	32-bit integer

The ARP cache timeout option specifies the lifetime for entries in the ARP cache. The timeout value is represented in seconds.

Ethernet encapsulation

Option code:	36	
Length:	1	
Data:	0	Ethernet version 2 encapsulation
	1	IEEE 802.3 encapsulation

The Ethernet encapsulation option selects either Ethernet version 2 (RFC894) or IEEE 802.3 (RFC1042) encapsulation for IP datagrams.

trailer encapsulation

Option code:	34	
Length:	1	
Data:	0	do not use trailers
	1	attempt to use trailers

The trailer encapsulation option controls whether the client should negotiate the use of trailers (RFC893) by using the ARP protocol.

9.3.4 TCP Parameters Options

The options described in this section give values for TCP software configuration parameters. These options affect the parameters for all TCP traffic on the client.

TCP default TTL

Option code:	37
Length:	1
Data:	8-bit integer

The TCP default TTL option sets the TTL (time to live) that the TCP layer should use when sending TCP segments.

TCP Keepalive Parameters Options

These two options control the operation of the TCP keepalive mechanism.

TCP keepalive interval

Option code:	38	
Length:	4	
Data:	0	do not use keepalive
	nonzero integer	keepalive interval

The TCP keepalive interval option specifies the time the client should wait before a keepalive segment. The interval is given in seconds. If the data value is zero, the client should not use keepalive segments unless an application specifically requests it.

```
TCP keepalive garbage
```
Option code:	39
Length:	1
Data:	0 do not send garbage byte
	1 send garbage byte

The `TCP keepalive garbage` option specifies whether the client should send a garbage byte in keepalive segments.

9.4 Service Parameters Options

The remaining options provide parameters for a variety of services. Most of these options provide the address of a server or servers for a specific service. Some options give additional information about a service, such as the `NIS` or `NIS+ domain`.

9.4.1 `SMTP server`

Option code:	69
Length:	n
Data:	list of IP addresses

The `SMTP server` option lists addresses of Simple Mail Transport Protocol (SMTP[RFC821]) servers available to the client. The length must be a multiple of 4; if s SMTP servers are in the option, the length is $4s$.

9.4.2 `POP server`

Option code:	70
Length:	n
Data:	list of IP addresses

The `POP server` option lists addresses of Post Office Protocol version 3 (POP3 [RFC1939]) servers available to the client. If more than one address is in the list, the POP3 servers are listed in order of preference. The length must be a multiple of 4; if p POP3 servers are in the option, the length is $4p$.

9.4.3 `NTP server`

Option code:	42
Length:	n
Data:	list of IP addresses

The NTP server option lists addresses of Network Time Protocol (NTP) (RFC1305) servers available to the client. If more than one address is in the list, the NTP servers are listed in order of preference. The length must be a multiple of 4; if n NTP servers are in the option, the length is $4n$.

9.4.4 finger server

Option code:	73
Length:	n
Data:	list of IP addresses

The finger server option lists addresses of finger protocol (RFC1288) servers available to the client. If more than one address is in the list, the finger servers are listed in order of preference. The length must be a multiple of 4; if f finger servers are in the option, the length is $4f$.

9.4.5 WWW server

Option code:	72
Length:	n
Data:	list of IP addresses

The WWW server option lists addresses of World Wide Web (HTTP [RFC1945]) servers available to the client. If more than one address is in the list, the WWW servers are listed in order of preference. The length must be a multiple of 4; if w WWW servers are in the option, the length is $4w$.

9.4.6 NNTP server

Option code:	71
Length:	n
Data:	list of IP addresses

The NNTP server option lists addresses of Network News Transport Protocol (NNTP[RFC977]), or NetNews, servers available to the client. If more than one address is in the list, the NNTP servers are listed in order of preference. The length must be a multiple of 4; if n NNTP servers are in the option, the length is $4n$.

9.4.7 IRC server

Option code:	74
Length:	n
Data:	list of IP addresses

The IRC server option lists addresses of Internet Relay Chat (IRC[RFC1459]) servers available to the client. If more than one address is in the list, the IRC servers are listed in order of preference. The length must be a multiple of 4; if i IRC servers are in the option, the length is $4i$.

9.4.8 X Window System Options

Two options provide information to the client about X Window System resources.

X Window System Font Server

Option code:	48
Length:	n
Data:	list of IP addresses

The X Window System Font Server option lists addresses of font servers available to the client. If more than one address is in the list, the font servers are listed in order of preference. The length must be a multiple of 4; if f font servers are in the list, the length is $4f$.

X Window System Display Manager

Option code:	49
Length:	n
Data:	list of IP addresses

The X Window System Display Manager option lists systems running the X display manager available to the client. If more than one address is in the list, the display manager systems are listed in order of preference. The length must be a multiple of 4; if d display manager systems are in the list, the length is $4d$.

9.4.9 mobile IP home agent

Option code:	68	
Length:	0	no agents are available
	n	length of list
Data:		list of IP addresses

The mobile IP home agent option is used with the mobile IP protocol (RFC2002). The option lists addresses of home agents available to the client. If the length is 0, no home agents are available. Otherwise, the length must be a multiple of 4; if h home agents exist, the length is $4h$.

9.4.10 NIS, NIS+ Options

Several options pass information to the client about *Network Information Service (NIS)* and *Network Information Service+ (NIS+)*.

NIS/NIS+ addresses

Option code:	41
Length:	n
Data:	list of IP addresses
Option code:	65
Length:	n
Data:	list of IP addresses

The first two options list addresses of NIS and NIS+ servers, respectively. If more than one address is in the list, the servers are listed in order of preference. The length must be a multiple of 4; if n servers are in the list, the length is $4n$.

NIS/NIS+ domain

Option code:	40
Length:	n
Data:	NIS domain
Option code:	64
Length:	n
Data:	NIS+ domain

The second two options give the client its NIS and NIS+ domain, respectively. The name in each option is a string that is not terminated with a null character.

9.4.11 NetBIOS over TCP/IP Options

These options inform the client as to the use of NetBIOS over TCP/IP, as described in RFC1001 and RFC1002.

NetBIOS address over TCP/IP name servers

Option code:	44
Length:	n
Data:	list of IP addresses

The NetBIOS address over TCP/IP name servers option lists the addresses of NetBIOS over TCP/IP name servers available to the client. If more than one address is in the list, the servers are listed in order of preference. The length must be a multiple of 4; if n servers are in the list, the length is $4n$.

NetBIOS address over TCP/IP datagram distribution server

Option code:	45
Length:	n
Data:	list of IP addresses

The NetBIOS address over TCP/IP datagram distribution (NBDD) server option lists the addresses of NetBIOS over TCP/IP datagram distribution (NBDD) servers available to the client. If more than one address is in the list, the servers are listed in order of preference. The length must be a multiple of 4; if n servers are in the list, the length is 4n.

NetBIOS address over TCP/IP node type

Option code:	46	
Length:	1	
Data:	1	B-node: Broadcast - no WINS
	2	P-node: Peer - WINS only
	4	M-node: Mixed - broadcast, then WINS
	8	H-node: Hybrid - WINS, then broadcast

The NetBIOS address over TCP/IP node type option specifies the type of node to which the client should configure itself. The data in the option encodes the node type.

NetBIOS address over TCP/IP scope

Option code:	47
Length:	n
Data:	NetBIOS over TCP/IP scope

The NetBIOS address over TCP/IP scope option specifies the NetBIOS over TCP/IP scope for the client. The scope is encoded as a string of characters, which must be selected according to the restrictions in RFC1002, RFC1002, and RFC1035. The scope character string is not terminated with a null character.

9.4.12 StreetTalk Options

These two options give information on StreetTalk servers available to the client.

StreetTalk server

Option code:	74
Length:	n
Data:	list of IP addresses

The StreetTalk server option lists the addresses of StreetTalk servers for the client. If more than one address is in the list, the servers are listed in order of preference. The length must be a multiple of 4; if s servers are in the list, the length is $4s$.

StreetTalk Directory Assistance server

Option code:	75
Length:	n
Data:	list of IP addresses

The second option, the StreetTalk Directory Assistance server option, lists the addresses of StreetTalk Directory Assistance (STDA) servers available to the client. If more than one address is in the list, the servers are listed in order of preference. The length must be a multiple of 4; if s servers are in the list, the length is $4s$.

9.4.13 NDS Options

The three options described in this section inform the client about the use of *NetWare Directory Services (NDS)*.

Note

All the options described earlier in this section are specified in RFC2132. The NDS options described in this section were defined after RFC2132 was published, and are specified in RFC2241. The Netware/IP options in the next section were also defined after RFC2132 was published, and are specified in RFC2242.

NDS servers

    Option code: 85

    Length: n

    Data: list of IP addresses

The NDS servers option lists the addresses of NDS servers available to the client. If more than one address is in the list, the servers are listed in order of preference. The length must be a multiple of 4; if *s* servers are in the list, the length is 4*s*.

NDS Tree Name

    Option code: 86

    Length: n

    Data: UTF-8-byte string

The NDS Tree Name option provides the name of the NDS tree available to the client. The names of NDS trees are normally specified as 16-bit Unicode strings. When carried in an NDS Tree Name option, an NDS tree name is encoded using *UTF-8 (UCS Transformation Format-8)*. The resulting byte string is not terminated with a null character.

Note

ISO/IEC 10646-1 defines a multi-octet character set called the Universal Character Set (UCS), which incorporates the characters from most of the writing systems existing today. UCS also defines an encoding representing each of those characters as a 16-bit number. A string composed of these 16-bit UCS values is called an UCS string.

The UCS standard also defines UCS Transformation Format (UTF-8) encoding, which represents 7-bit ASCII values in a single byte, and then uses multibyte values to represent other characters from the Unicode Standard. UTF-8 is useful because text using simple 7-bit values is left unchanged when converted to UTF-8, providing backward compatibility.

NDS context

    Option code: 87

    Length: n

    Data: UTF-8-byte string

The third option, the NDS context option, gives the initial NDS context for the client. NDS contexts are normally specified as 16-bit Unicode strings. When carried in an NDS context option, an NDS context is encoded using UTF-8. The resulting byte string is not terminated with a null character.

> **Note**
>
> *Because of restrictions in the DHCP option format in which the* length *field is encoded as a single byte, a DHCP option can carry only 255 data bytes. However, an NDS context name can be longer than 255 bytes. To accommodate longer NDS context names, the sender splits the context name among multiple occurrences of the* NDS context *option. The receiver then concatenates the* data *fields of the* NDS context *options to reconstruct the complete NDS context name.*

9.4.14 NetWare/IP Options

Two options provide information about the client's configuration for NetWare/IP.

NetWare/IP Domain Name

      Option code: 62

      Length: n

      Data: n characters

The NetWare/IP Domain Name option provides the name of the NetWare/IP Domain for the client. The name is a string of characters that is not terminated with a null character.

NetWare/IP Information

      Option code: 63

      Length: n

      Data: NetWare/IP information

The second NetWare/IP option is the NetWare/IP Information option. This option carries additional NetWare/IP information for the client.

NetWare/IP Suboptions

The data area of the NetWare/IP option is composed of one or more suboptions. The suboptions are encoded in the same way as DHCP options; each suboption includes a suboption code, a length, and the data.

The first four suboptions define how the NetWare/IP information is carried. The NetWare/IP Information option must include one of these suboptions as the first suboption in the option's information area.

NWIP_DOES_NOT_EXIST

      Suboption code: 1

      Length: 0

      Data: N/A

In this option, the DHCP server does not have NetWare/IP information for the client.

NWIP_EXIST_IN_OPTIONS_AREA

    Suboption code: 2

    Length: 0

    Data: N/A

The NetWare/IP information is contained in the NetWare/IP Information option's options field. The remainder of the data in the NetWare/IP Information option contains additional suboptions, defined later in this section.

NWIP_EXIST_BUT_TOO_BIG

    Suboption code: 4

    Length: 0

    Data: N/A

The DHCP server has NetWare/IP configuration information for the client, but the server cannot fit the information in the DHCP message.

NWIP_EXIST_IN_SNAME_FILE

    Suboption code: 3

    Length: 0

    Data: N/A

The NetWare/IP configuration information is in the sname field and, if necessary, in the file field in the fixed-format section of the DHCP message. If this method of transmitting the NetWare/IP configuration information is used, the NetWare/IP Information option appears in the options section, containing only the NWIP_EXIST_IN_SNAME_FILE suboption. The sname and file fields then contain (optionally) a NetWare/IP Domain Name option and a NetWare/IP Information option. The NetWare/IP Information option in the sname and file fields contains the NetWare/IP information in the suboptions described later in this section, but does not include one of these first four suboptions.

The remaining suboptions carry the NetWare/IP configuration information itself.

NSQ_BROADCAST

Suboption code:	5		
Length:	1		
Data:	0	client should not use a NetWare Nearest Server Query	
	1	client should use a NetWare Nearest Server Query	

NSQ_BROADCAST specifies whether the client should use a NetWare Nearest Server Query to locate a NetWare/IP server.

PREFERRED_DSS

Suboption code:	6
Length:	n
Data:	list of IP addresses

PREFERRED_DSS lists the addresses of NetWare Domain SAP/RIP Servers (DSS). The maximum number of addresses carried in the PREFERRED_DSS option is 5. If s servers are in the list, the length field is $4s$.

NEAREST_NWIP_SERVER

Suboption code:	7
Length:	n
Data:	list of IP addresses

NEAREST_NWIP_SERVER lists the addresses of Nearest NetWare/IP Servers. The maximum number of addresses carried in the NEAREST_NWIP_SERVER option is 5. If s servers are in the list, the length field is $4s$.

AUTORETRIES

Suboption code:	8
Length:	1
Data:	1 byte

AUTORETRIES specifies the number of times a client should attempt to contact a DSS server initially. The number of retries is encoded as an unsigned 1-byte integer.

AUTORETRY_SECS

>   Suboption code: 9

>   Length: 1

>   Data: 1 byte

AUTORETRY_SECS specifies the number of seconds a client should wait between attempts to contact a DSS server. The number of seconds is encoded as an unsigned 1-byte integer.

NWIP_1_1

>   Suboption code: 10

>   Length: 0

>   Data: 0   client should not use NetWare/IP Version 1.1 compatibility

>   1   client should use NetWare/IP Version 1.1 compatibility

NWIP_1_1 specifies whether the client should employ NetWare/IP Version 1.1 compatibility, to contact a NetWare/IP Version 1.1 server.

PRIMARY_DSS

>   Suboption code: 11

>   Length: 4

>   Data: IP address

PRIMARY_DSS specifies the address of the Primary Domain SAP/RIP Service server for the client.

Summary

The options section of a DHCP message carries values for most configuration parameters. These parameters are carried in options, whose formats are described in this chapter. Each option carries a separate configuration parameter, as defined by the option's *option code*. The data formats for each option are defined in RFC2132. One group of options carries information specific to the operation of DHCP, identifying the type of each DHCP message and the server to which the message is directed. Other options carry information for the DHCP client, parameters for the client's TCP/IP software, and addresses of servers such as SMTP, NTP, and NIS.

Options range in complexity, from the `TCP Default TTL` option to the `NetWare/IP Information` option. The `subnet mask` option, the `default routers` option, and the `DNS server` option are the most commonly used options.

Some options, such as the `Impress server` option, refer to services that are no longer available. Those options are still in the protocol specification for backward compatibility with earlier versions of DHCP and BOOTP.

## CHAPTER 10

Theory of Operation of a DHCP Server

This chapter describes the actual operation of a DHCP server. It uses as an example the operation of version 3.0 of the ISC DHCP server because the source code is readily available; interested readers can follow along and see how it is implemented. In addition, one of the authors is intimately familiar with version 3.0's operation. Although the operation of some of the features of the DHCP server is ISC-specific, this discussion should also be meaningful to users of other DHCP servers.

When properly configured and running, the DHCP server normally runs continuously in the background, as a daemon. It listens for DHCP and BOOTP requests on UDP port 67. Whenever such a request is received, the server first examines the request to see what network it came from. It then looks to see what kind of request it is. The server responds to BOOTREQUEST packets in the BOOTP protocol, and DHCPDISCOVER, DHCPREQUEST, DHCPDECLINE, DHCPRELEASE, and DHCPINFORM messages in the DHCP protocol.

10.1 Address Allocation Strategy

Addresses are allocated out of *address pools*, or they are statically allocated to specific clients using host declarations. An address pool is simply a set of one or more addresses, which are declared using range statements. Address pools can have permit lists that enable some clients to be allocated addresses from the pool. All the addresses in any pool declaration must be on the same network segment, but they may be on more than one subnet, and more than one pool declaration can exist for a given network segment.

When the server receives a DHCPDISCOVER or BOOTREQUEST message, it attempts to allocate an IP address for the client sending the message. It first looks for a host declaration that matches the client and contains a fixed-address declaration for an IP address that is valid on the network segment to which the client is connected. If it finds such an entry, that IP address is always assigned to the client.

Otherwise, it looks to see whether the client has an existing lease that is either still valid or hasn't been reused since it expired. If it finds such a lease, it checks to see whether the client can still use the address. If the client specified an old address to try, and that address is on the network segment to which the client is connected, the server also tries to allocate that address for the client. Usually the client's former address and the address it requests are the same.

10.1.1 Address Use Denied

The client may not be able to continue using its old address for a variety of reasons. If the client is connected to a different network segment than it was when the address it is requesting was allocated, it is not able to continue using the address. Addresses are allocated from pools, and pools have permit lists that permit or deny certain clients from using the addresses in the pool. If the permit list on the pool from which the client's old address was allocated changed so that the client is no longer able to use the address, or if the information the client sends changed so that the result of checking the permit list is different, the client cannot use the address.

For example, suppose a subnet has two address pool declarations, as shown in Example 10.1.

EXAMPLE 10.1

```
pool {
  range 10.0.0.10 10.0.0.99;
}

pool {
  range 10.0.0.100 10.0.0.199;
}
```

In addition, suppose that when a particular client first acquires its address, it is assigned the IP address 10.0.0.10. After the client acquires this address, the administrator decides to move all clients out of the 10.0.0.10–10.0.0.99 address range. The administrator modifies the pool configuration as shown in Example 10.2 and then restarts the DHCP server.

EXAMPLE 10.2

```
pool {
  deny all;
  range 10.0.0.10 10.0.0.99;
}

pool {
  range 10.0.0.100 10.0.0.199;
}
```

When the client tries to renew its lease on the IP address 10.0.0.10, the server checks the permit list for the range from which the address is allocated and finds that the client can no longer use the address. If the client has an old address and can still use it, the DHCP server assigns that address. If the client has an old address it can no longer use for reasons other than the fact that it is on a different network segment and the address is still considered in use by the client, the address is freed.

If the client isn't assigned an old address because there isn't one or because the client is unable to, the server searches through the pool declarations for the network segment to which the client is connected for an address that is available and that the client can have.

All the range declarations for a given network segment that are not contained in explicit pool declarations are grouped into one or two implicit pool declarations. All the range declarations with the dynamic-bootp flag (see Appendix B, "ISC DHCP Server Configuration File Reference") are grouped into one pool that enables addresses in the pool to be allocated to BOOTP clients. All the range declarations that do not contain the dynamic-bootp flag are grouped into a separate pool. The pool declarations for a given network segment are sorted in the order in which they are declared in the configuration file, and they are searched in that order.

In searching each pool, the server first looks for an address that has never been associated with a client, and then, if it doesn't find one, it looks for a previously assigned address that is now available. The server continues to search through all the address pools for the network segment to which the client is attached for an address that has never been associated with a client, until it finds one or runs out of pools. If it finds one, that address is allocated to the client. If not, the first available address that it finds is assigned to the client. If no addresses are available in any pool for the network segment, the server logs a message to that effect and no response is sent to the client.

10.1.2 Address Assignment

After the server allocates an address, it sends an ICMP echo request to that address to see whether it is already in use. It waits for about 1 second for the response, and if it doesn't receive one, it sends a DHCPOFFER message to the client with the address that was allocated. If the client is a BOOTP client, the server records the allocated address in the lease database, confirms that it is written to disk, and then sends a BOOTREPLY message with the client's new address. This is the end of the transaction for a BOOTP client. If the address is assigned in a fixed-address declaration, the server writes no information into the lease database.

If the server receives an ICMP echo reply message in response to its ICMP echo request, it marks the address as abandoned and logs a message indicating that this has occurred so that an administrator can take action. A permanent lease is assigned to that IP address, and it is marked as abandoned. The abandoned lease immediately is written to the lease database so that the server does not attempt to allocate the address again later.

10.2 Address Renewal Strategy

After a DHCP client receives a DHCPOFFER, if it chooses to select the address the server offered, it responds with a DHCPREQUEST message requesting the offered address. Clients with leases also send DHCPREQUEST messages from time to time to renew their leases. When the server receives a DHCPREQUEST message, it has three choices:

- It can ignore the message.
- It can respond with a DHCPNAK.
- It can respond with a DHCPACK.

If the server recognizes the address the client is requesting as its own—that is, if it is in an address pool declaration or a static address assignment—and the address is valid for the network segment to which the client is attached, the server checks whether the client has permission to continue using the address. If the client does not have permission to continue using the address, the server sends the client a DHCPNAK message.

10.2.1 Errant DHCPNAK Messages

Sometimes the server sends the client a DHCPNAK message when it is not strictly allowed by the protocol. For example, if the client is in the RENEWING state, a DHCPNAK message is unexpected, but the server can't reliably tell that a client is in the RENEWING state, so it may send a DHCPNAK message to the client anyway. Sending a DHCPNAK in this situation does not cause problems.

If the server recognizes the IP address being requested as its own and if it recognizes the network segment to which the client is attached and the address the client is requesting is not valid for that subnet, the server responds with a DHCPNAK message. If the server is declared *authoritative* for the network segment to which the client is connected and the client is requesting an IP address that is not valid on that network segment, the server always responds with a DHCPNAK, even if the address is not its own.

If the address is valid for the network segment to which the client is connected, but the server does not recognize the address, the server does not respond, even if the client specifies the server's address in the dhcp-server-identifier option.

10.2.2 Lease Extensions

If the address the client is requesting is valid for the network segment to which the client is attached and is an address the server can assign, and if the client may use it, the server computes the new expiration time for the lease. If the client requests a particular lease duration, the server makes sure the requested lease time is within a range specified by the min-lease-time and max-lease-time parameters. If it is not, it is set to the value of min-lease-time if it is too short, and to the value of max-lease-time if it is too long.

If the client does not request a specific lease duration, the lease duration specified by the default-lease-time is used, and the same limits are applied.

After the server computes the duration of the lease, it records the lease on disk and waits for the operating system to confirm that the data was written to disk. It then sends a DHCPACK to the client with the computed lease duration and writes a log message.

10.3 DHCP Message Handling

DHCP clients respond to a variety of messages during operation, including DHCPDECLINE, DHCPRELEASE, and DHCPINFORM. The following sections discuss message handling.

10.3.1 DHCPDECLINE **Handling**

DHCP clients can send DHCPDECLINE messages if they receive an IP address that another client is using. The client detects this by sending an ARP request for the IP address it is assigned when it receives a DHCPACK message while in the REQUESTING state. If it receives a response to this ARP message, the client knows the address it received is in use, so it sends a DHCPDECLINE, indicating to the DHCP server that the client cannot use the address.

The ISC DHCP server honors DHCPDECLINE messages from clients, creating permanent leases for such addresses, marking them as abandoned, and logging a message indicating this happened. If a client is sending DHCPDECLINE messages as a denial of service attack, the server reclaims abandoned leases according to a strategy described later in this chapter. This prevents such denial of service attacks from causing great harm, although they still place an additional load on the DHCP server.

10.3.2 DHCPRELEASE **Handling**

When the server receives a DHCPRELEASE message from a client, it changes the expiration time of the lease to the current time and records the lease. A message is logged indicating this happened.

10.3.3 DHCPINFORM **Handling**

Version 3.0 of the ISC DHCP server supports the DHCPINFORM message. When the server receives a DHCPINFORM message, it collects the parameters that are appropriate for the network segment that the client claims to be connected and sends them to the client in a DHCPACK message. No address allocation is performed. The server prints log messages indicating that the DHCPINFORM message was received and the DHCPACK was sent.

10.4 Abandoned Lease Address Reclaimation

The DHCP server makes some attempt to reclaim abandoned leases in situations where it appears that the lease is abandoned due to an implementation error in the DHCP client. If a DHCP client sends a DHCPREQUEST message requesting an abandoned IP address, the server removes the flag indicating that the lease is abandoned and enables the client to renew the lease. The DHCP server also attempts to reclaim abandoned leases if no free and unabandoned leases exist on a network segment, and one is needed.

Summary

The DHCP server runs continuously as a background process, processing client requests as they arrive. When a client request for a new IP address arrives, the server must attempt to allocate an address, either from the dynamic pool or using a prearranged static assignment. If an address is found for the client, the server ensures that it is not in use and then offers it to the client.

When clients try to renew a lease, the server must decide whether the IP address a client is renewing is appropriate for the client. It must tell the client to stop using it, tell the client it can continue using it, or assume that some other server will respond if it seems valid but is not an address the DHCP server is managing, and therefore remain silent.

If the server finds an IP address that should be available but is nonetheless in use, it does not assign the address to a client but marks it as abandoned. The server does not attempt to use addresses marked as abandoned unless a shortage of IP addresses occurs during some subsequent address allocation attempt. If such a shortage occurs, the server again attempts to allocate the abandoned address.

The server maintains a persistent database of leases that are confirmed to DHCP clients and does not confirm a lease until it is written to the persistent database.

CHAPTER 11

The Microsoft DHCP Server

The Microsoft DHCP server is distributed as part of the Windows NT server. The Microsoft server includes two components: the DHCP server and the DHCP manager. The DHCP server is responsible for all interactions with DHCP clients, and the DHCP manager provides a user interface for controlling and configuring the server.

This section describes how to install, configure, and manage the Microsoft server. Appendix A, "Microsoft DHCP Server Examples," includes additional examples and screen shots of Microsoft server use.

11.1 Server Installation

You install the Microsoft DHCP server on Windows NT with the Network control panel. To bring up the Network control panel, select the Control Panels entry from the Settings entry in the Start menu, as shown in Figure 11.1. Open the Network control panel, and then select the Services tab.

Next select Microsoft DHCP Server from the Network Service list, and click the Add button. This process loads both the DHCP server and DHCP manager.

FIGURE 11.1 *Starting the Network control panel.*

FIGURE 11.2 *Installing the Microsoft DHCP service from the Network control panel.*

Note

The most recent version of the Microsoft DHCP service, from Windows NT 4.0 Service Pack 4 (SP4), is substantially different from previous versions. This chapter describes the SP4 version of the Microsoft service. If you reload the DHCP service from the original CD-ROM, you must reinstall SP4 to guarantee that you have the most recent version of the DHCP service. One way to check that you have the SP4 version of the service is to verify that the DHCP Manager includes an entry for Superscopes *in the Scopes menu.*

After installation, the server is configured to start automatically (along with other services) when you start Windows NT. However, the server doesn't respond to incoming client requests until you configure and activate the scopes, as described in the next section of this chapter. You can control the operation of the server with the Service control panel, which is described in more detail later in this chapter.

You must fully configure the Microsoft server before activating any scopes; otherwise, your server may respond to client requests with incomplete or incorrect configuration information. Your server may also interfere with the operation of clients that are managed by other servers, by inappropriately sending DHCPNAK messages for requests from network segments that are not yet included in the server's configuration.

11.2 Managing DHCP Servers

The Microsoft DHCP service can include multiple DHCP servers, which are controlled through the DHCP Manager. The installation process configures the DHCP Manager for a DHCP server running on the same computer as the DHCP Manager. If you plan to use other DHCP servers, you must configure the DHCP Manager for the additional servers.

Start the DHCP Manager by selecting its entry from Administrative Tools in the Start menu, as shown in Figure 11.3.

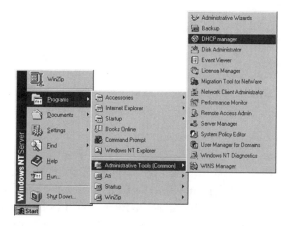

FIGURE 11.3   *Starting the DHCP Manager.*

To add a new server, select Add from the Server menu. The DHCP Manager displays the window shown in Figure 11.4. Enter the name or IP address of the new server and click OK. The DHCP Manager contacts the new server and adds it to its list of available servers.

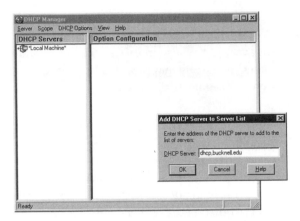

FIGURE 11.4 *Adding a new DHCP server.*

11.3 Configuring a DHCP Server

The Microsoft server configuration is defined around *scopes*, which are similar to the *subnet* declarations for the ISC server. Each scope defines a network segment, the addresses available for assignment within that network segment, and the subnet mask for the segment. The definition of a scope in the Microsoft server performs the same function as the subnet and range in the ISC configuration file and is unrelated to the concept of scopes and scoping in the ISC DHCP server.

11.3.1 Scopes

To configure the Microsoft server, start by configuring the scopes the server will manage. Scopes and options are configured through the DHCP Manager. Start the DHCP Manager and select the entry for the DHCP server you want to configure. This section uses the Local Server entry, which identifies the DHCP server running on your computer, as an example. Select Create Entry from the Scope menu. The DHCP Manager displays a configuration window, in which you enter the available addresses, the subnet mask, the name, and an optional comment for this scope. Figure 11.5 shows the window used to create a new scope.

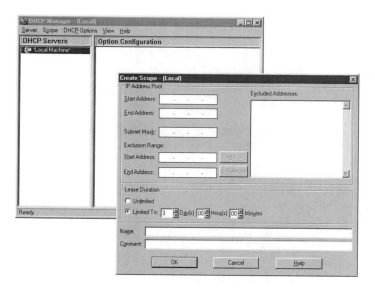

FIGURE 11.5   *Creating a new scope in the DHCP Manager.*

Available and Excluded Addresses in a Scope

Within a scope, you can designate a list of *excluded addresses* the DHCP server
should not assign. You can define the list of available addresses so that it contains just those addresses in the scope that are available for the server to assign.
However, each scope definition can contain only one list of available addresses;
each scope definition must be contiguous and specified by the first and last
addresses in the list. So, if you want the list of available addresses to include
noncontiguous addresses, you must declare the list of available addresses to
span all the available addresses, and then specifically exclude some addresses.

To illustrate the definition of available addresses to the Microsoft server, suppose a network segment is defined to have IP address 192.168.11.0 and subnet
mask 255.255.255.0, and the DHCP server is to assign addresses 192.168.11.10-
192.168.11.19 and 192.168.11.30-192.168.11.39.

The declaration in the configuration file for the ISC server is shown in
Example 11.1.

EXAMPLE 11.1

```
subnet 192.168.11.0 subnet-mask 255.255.255.0 {
  range 192.168.11.10-192.168.11.19;
  range 192.168.11.30-192.168.11.39;
}
```

Figure 11.6 illustrates the same configuration defined through the DHCP Manager.

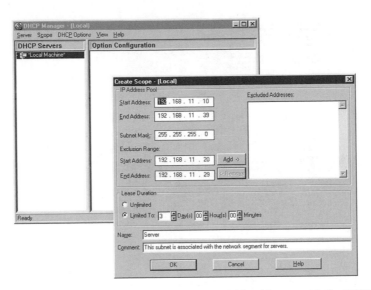

FIGURE 11.6 *Defining a scope and available addresses with the DHCP Manager.*

You can configure the Microsoft server for the same range of available addresses by setting the range to 192.168.11.10-192.168.11.39 and then putting the range 192.168.11.20-192.168.11.29 in the list of excluded addresses.

A more general configuration of the Microsoft server in this case is to declare the entire range of addresses in the subnet, 192.168.11.1 - 192.168.11.254, as available addresses, and then explicitly add all the addresses not available for DHCP to the list of excluded addresses. With this configuration for the scope, you can change the list of available addresses by modifying the list of excluded addresses, without changing the range of available addresses in the scope. The list of excluded addresses in this example is:

192.168.11.1-192.168.11.9

192.168.11.20-192.168.11.29

192.168.11.40-192.168.11.254

Naming Scopes

Each scope defined for the Microsoft server may have an associated name. You use this name to identify the scope in the list of available scopes displayed by the DHCP Manager. Select the names for your scopes carefully because you must locate scopes by name in the DHCP Manager. The DHCP Manager displays the scopes in alphabetical order. You might, for example, want to define a naming convention that groups related scopes together in the list of scopes by assigning names with the same prefix to those related scopes.

11.3.2 Superscopes

The Microsoft DHCP service SP4 release includes the ability to define *super-scopes*, through which you can associate multiple scopes with a single network segment. Superscopes are equivalent to the shared-network declaration in the ISC server configuration file. You use a superscope when you've assigned multiple IP subnets to a single network segment.

The primary function of superscopes is address assignment. The DHCP server groups together all the available addresses from the scopes in a superscope into a single pool of available addresses for the network segment. It finds an unassigned address from one of the scopes in the superscope to assign to a client that needs an address from the superscope.

Client options are managed through the separate scopes in a superscope. The DHCP Manager does not include a mechanism for defining options that are common to all scopes in a superscope, nor does it give you a way to examine the list of available addresses across the superscope.

Note

The DHCP administrator must make sure that options are defined consistently across the scopes within a superscope. Options such as the DNS server or NTP server should usually be defined uniformly across the superscope. Some options, such as the default routers, should be configured differently for each scope.

Superscopes are managed through the DHCP Manager. To create a superscope, select a DHCP server and then select the Superscope entry in the Scope menu. The DHCP Manager displays a window for managing superscopes, which is shown in Figure 11.7.

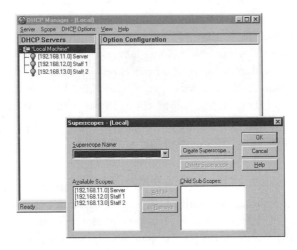

FIGURE 11.7   *Superscope management in the DHCP Manager.*

Click the Create Superscope button and type the name of the new superscope. A list of scopes that you can add to your new superscope appears. Add the desired scopes to the superscope and click OK.

To change the scopes in a superscope, first select the superscope in the DHCP Manager, which displays a window showing the scopes in the superscope and any available scopes. Figure 11.8 illustrates the window for editing superscopes. Click the Add button to change the membership of the superscope.

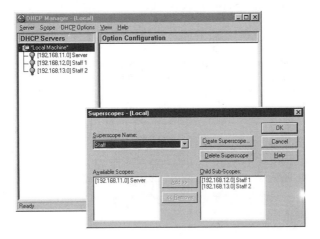

FIGURE 11.8   *Changing the scopes in a superscope.*

11.3.3 Reservations

You can permanently assign a specific address to a client by establishing a *reservation*. A reservation is appropriate for a client that should always use the same IP address, such as a computer providing a service like DNS. A reservation is established as part of the scope to which the reserved address belongs. The address assigned through a reservation must be in the range of available addresses for the scope.

The DHCP server manager creates, changes, and deletes reservations. To create a reservation, select Add Reservations from the Scopes menu. The Server Manager displays a window requesting the following information:

IP Address	The address to be reserved; it must be an unassigned address within the range of addresses for a scope.
Unique Identifier	The value the DHCP client sends in the client identifier option. For Microsoft DHCP clients, this is always the numeric code for the hardware type, followed by the link-layer address, as described in Chapter 14, "Client Identification and Fixed-Address Allocation."
Client Name	A name for this client, which is used only to identify the reservation by the server manager and does not set the host name of the client.
Client Comment	Optional text to describe the client and reservation.

After filling in the values for the requested fields, click the Add button to add the reservation to the DHCP configuration database. Figure 11.9 demonstrates the definition of a reservation.

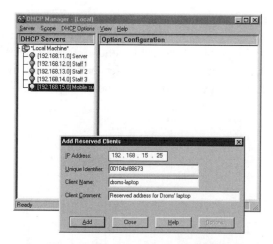

FIGURE 11.9 *Defining a reservation for a DHCP client.*

11.3.4 Configuring Options

As with the ISC server, you can configure the Microsoft server with rules to govern the values for options the server passes to DHCP clients. However, you can configure the Microsoft server with only three types of rules:

- Values for options defined to apply to clients in a specific scope

- Values for options defined to apply to specific clients that are pre-assigned specific addresses

- Values to be applied to every client the server manages

Note

Although you can assign individual clients specific option values through pre-assigned address entries in the server configuration database, no general mechanism enables the definition of sub-groups of clients or the assignment of option values to clients that have dynamically assigned addresses.

To select a specific option for configuration, the DHCP Manager displays a pull-down menu with a list of all available DHCP options. In this list, the options are identified by both option number and name. Table D.1 in Appendix D, "DHCP Options Summary," gives a list of all DHCP options and the Microsoft server's name for each option.

Local Options

Local options specify values for options to be returned to any client within the scope for which the local option is defined. That is, a client receives the option values from the scope to which the client belongs.

To configure a local option, select a scope in the DHCP Server Manager and click Scope in the Options menu. The manager displays a window in which you can choose an option and the value to be returned to clients in that scope. After you've selected an option for a scope, it appears in the server manager's main window when the scope is selected. Figure 11.10 shows the configuration of the Routers option for a single scope.

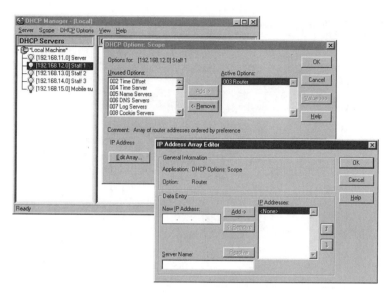

FIGURE 11.10 *Configuring* Routers *as a local option.*

Global Options

You may also define *global options*, which are returned to clients from any scope managed by the server. Global options are configured through the Global option of the Options menu, and are displayed with the list of local options when a scope is selected in the Server Manager's main window. Figure 11.11 shows the configuration of the DNS Servers option as a global option.

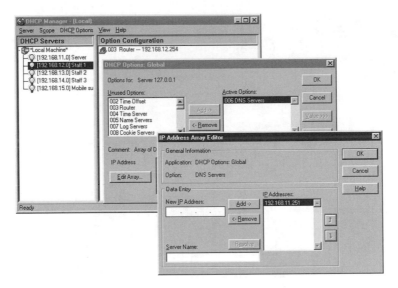

FIGURE 11.11   *Configuring* DNS *servers as a global option.*

11.3.5 Client Differentiation

The DHCP server manager allows you to specify options for a host that has a reserved address. Through the Active Leases entry of the Scope menu, you can add options and values, and override scope and global options. Select the reservation you want to change, click Properties, and then click Options to specify the options associated with the reservation.

No mechanism exists in the Microsoft server to differentiate among clients within a scope. That is, any client assigned a dynamic address from a scope is given the local options for the scope and for the global options. You can't return specific options to an individual host within a scope that is assigned a dynamic address; therefore, if you want to return customized options to a specific host, you must give that host a reserved address and specify the options in the reservation.

11.3.6 Defining New Options

The Microsoft server comes configured with all the options defined in RFC2132. You can define new options in the server through the Defaults selection in the Options menu. Click the New button, which displays an interactive window for the new option. The Name field defines the name, and the Identifier field defines the option code for the new option. The option code and name are displayed in the list of options (for example, 03 Routers) in the Scope and Global definition windows, as shown in Figure 11.12.

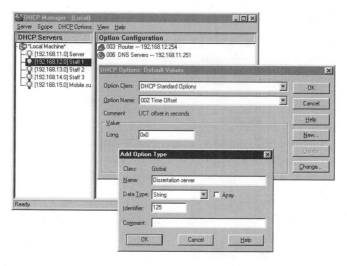

FIGURE 11.12   *Defining a new option.*

The `Data Type` menu selects the type of data that can be carried in the newly
defined option. The following data types are allowed:

Byte	8-bit integer
Word	16-bit integer
Long	32-bit integer
IP address	32-bit IP address
String	String of ASCII characters

Selecting the `Array` checkbox defines the option to carry a list of data values in
the way that the `Routers` option carries a list of IP addresses. Additional data
types are available in the `Data Type` menu. These other data types are not currently implemented in the Microsoft DHCP service.

When a new option is defined, it appears in the `Option Name` menu when defining scope or global options. Clicking the `Value` button on the scope or global
definition window displays the current value of the option and enables you to
change the value. If the option carries a list of data values, you can add, delete,
or reorder the list of values through the `Value` window.

11.4 Server Control

You can control the DHCP service through three different Windows management applications. Each control function is covered in the next sections of this chapter.

11.4.1 Scope Activation

The server can activate or deactivate individual scopes. You should completely configure each scope before activating it. When you first create a new scope, the DHCP server manager asks whether it should be activated; answer No and configure any options and reserved addresses before activating the scope.

After you configure the scope, highlight the scope in the main server manager window and select Activate from the Scope menu, as shown in Figure 11.13.

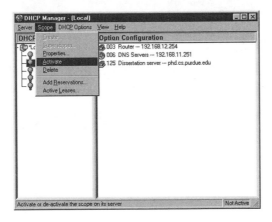

FIGURE 11.13   *Activating a scope.*

11.4.2 Starting the DHCP Server Automatically and Manually

The Services control panel enables you to start and stop the DHCP server, and to arrange for the server to start automatically when Windows NT is started. To control these server functions, start the Services control panel and select Microsoft DHCP Server from the list of services. Click the Stop or Start button, shown in Figure 11.14, to stop or start the DHCP service manually. Click the Startup button to display a window through which you can disable or enable automatic initiation of the DHCP service at system startup.

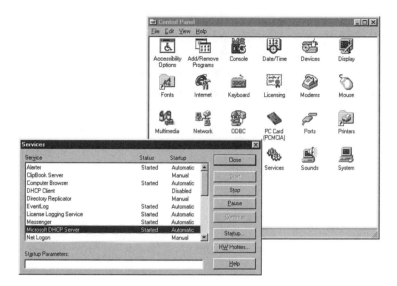

FIGURE 11.14 *Controlling the DHCP server.*

11.4.3 Uninstalling the DHCP Service

You can uninstall the DHCP service by using the Network control panel. Select Services, select Microsoft DHCP Server from the list of services, and click the Delete button. The DHCP server and DHCP server manager are removed from your system.

Summary

The Microsoft Windows NT Server 4 standard distribution includes a DHCP server. The Microsoft DHCP software includes two components: a DHCP server and a DHCP manager. The server runs as an independent process and is responsible for all interactions with DHCP clients. The manager provides a GUI for configuration and management of DHCP servers.

You specify the configuration of your network to the DHCP server through the DHCP manager. Each range of available addresses is defined as a *scope*. The definition for a scope may include option values for that scope; any client assigned an address from that scope also receives the option values defined for the scope. Options may also be defined as *global* to apply to all scopes managed by a server. The Microsoft DHCP manager can assign values to most of the options defined in Appendix D, and you can define your own options to accommodate newly standardized DHCP options or your own locally defined options.

The Microsoft DHCP manager uses *superscopes* to define the configuration of network segments that are assigned more than one IP subnet. Each superscope consists of a set of scopes, which are then assumed to be assigned to a common network segment. The Microsoft DHCP server may choose from the available addresses of any of the scopes in a superscope when assigning a new address to a DHCP client.

## CHAPTER 12

The ISC DHCP Server

This chapter discusses how the ISC DHCP server operates. Specifically, it describes:

- how to get it

- how to configure it

- what you need to do before you can start it

- how you can configure it to run in a production environment

The complete set of DHC server configuration commands is documented in Appendix B, "ISC DHCP Server Configuration File Reference." Although this chapter briefly describes what you must do to configure the ISC DHCP server, you should also read the other chapters in this book that describe in detail the theory behind setting up a successful DHCP service on a production network.

12.1 Obtaining the ISC DHCP Server

The ISC DHCP server is one of three components that compose the ISC DHCP distribution. The other two components are a DHCP client and a DHCP relay agent. If you install the ISC DHCP distribution, you actually get all three components. The instructions on acquiring and installing the server also apply to acquiring and installing the client and relay agent. Chapter 13, "Configuring a DHCP Server," provides an example of how to use the ISC DHCP relay agent, and Chapter 19, "DHCP Clients," describes in detail how to use the ISC DHCP client.

The ISC DHCP distribution is an open source product; that is, the source is provided for free, and you are free to modify it. The ISC sells support packages and encourages donations, but it does not charge to use the software. Because the software is normally provided in source form, this is the form described in this chapter.

The ISC DHCP distribution is available from the ISC Web site at `http://www.isc.org/dhcp.html`. You can also find it at `ftp://ftp.isc.org/isc/dhcp`. The DHCP distribution is updated from time to time, and the version number is encoded in the name of the file you download. The format of the filename depends on whether a released version is available or is in alpha or beta testing. Released versions have filenames similar to `dhcp-1.0pl2.tar.gz`, in which 1.0 is the version number, pl2 is patchlevel 2, and tar.gz is appended because the distribution is a UNIX Tape Archive ("tar") file compressed with the GNU zip utility (gzip).

Beta releases have filenames similar to `dhcp-2.0b1pl27.tar.gz`, in which 2.0 is the version to be used when the software is released from beta, b1 stands for the first beta, and pl27 stands for patchlevel 27. Alpha releases have filenames similar to `dhcp-3.0-alpha-19990425`, in which 3.0 is the version number under which the software will eventually be released, and 19990425 is the date of the snapshot. The first four digits represent the year, the next two digits represent the month, and the final two digits represent the day of the month.

12.1.1 Support for the ISC DHCP Server

Support for the ISC DHCP server is provided free of charge (as time allows, of course) on the ISC DHCP server mailing list; information about the mailing list is available at `http://www.isc.org/dhcp.html`. To get help, just send an email to the mailing list describing your problem in detail and asking for help with it.

Note

You can also purchase a commercial support contract from the ISC.

Although the email address of the author of the ISC DHCP distribution is readily available, he would appreciate it if you would not contact him directly for support, or even to ask about the appropriateness of asking for support. If you need help with the ISC DHCP server, ask for help on the ISC DHCP server mailing list. Information about an archive of the mailing list and a FAQ is also available at `http://www.isc.org/dhcp.html`.

Bug Reports

When reporting bugs, be sure to provide complete information to the ISC support team. Following is a list of the information to include in your initial bug report:

- the specific operating system name and version of the machine on which the DHCP server or client is running

- the specific operating system name and version of the machine on which the client is running, if you have trouble getting a client working with the server

- if you're running Linux, the version of the kernel, C library, and distribution (for example, Linux 2.0.35, libc 2, Red Hat 5.1)

- the specific version of the DHCP distribution you're running (for example, 2.0b1pl19, not 2.0)

- a detailed explanation of the problem that assumes the recipient will have absolutely no knowledge of your situation

- your dhcpd.conf and dhcpd.leases files if they're not huge (if they are huge, the support team may need them anyway, but don't send them until you're asked)

- a log of your server or client running until it encounters the problem (for example, if you have trouble getting a client to acquire an address, restart the server with the -d flag and then restart the client, and send the resulting output to the support team)

- if the server is dumping core, run the debugger and get a stack trace. For example, if your debugger is gdb, perform the following:

```
gdb dhcpd dhcpd.core
(gdb) where
        [...]
(gdb) quit
```

This assumes you're debugging the DHCP server and the core file is in dhcpd.core.

12.1.2 Installing the ISC DHCP Distribution

To use the ISC DHCP distribution, you must unpack the distribution, configure it for your system, build it, and install it.

Unpacking

To unpack the ISC DHCP distribution, you must connect to a directory on a filesystem with about 12 megabytes of free space. Then you must use the `gunzip` command to uncompress the tar file and use the `tar` command to extract its contents, as shown in Example 12.1.

EXAMPLE **12.1**

```
% gunzip <dhcp-3.0-alpha-19990425.tar.gz ¦tar xf -
%
```

The `tar` command extracts the distribution into a directory with the name of the distribution you are building. In the preceding example, this is `dhcp-3.0-alpha-1990425`.

Configuring

You must then connect to that directory and use the `configure` command to configure the distribution, as shown in Example 12.2.

EXAMPLE **12.2**

```
% cd dhcp-3.0-alpha-19990425
% ./configure
System Type: netbsd
%
```

If the `configure` command indicates it is unfamiliar with the system you are using, you must configure the DHCP distribution yourself or ask for help on the ISC DHCP server mailing list.

Building

After you unpack the distribution, you must build it. To build it, simply type `make`, as shown in Example 12.3. In this example, many lines of output were deleted and replaced with ellipses to save space. However, it does show part of the output of the make to give you an idea of what to expect.

EXAMPLE **12.3**

```
% make
Making all in common
cc -g  -I.. -I../includes -Wall -Wstrict-prototypes -Wno-unused -Wno-implicit -W
no-comment  -Wno-uninitialized -Werror -Wno-switch -pipe  -c raw.c
[...]
```

```
rm -f libdhcp.a
ar cruv libdhcp.a raw.o parse.o nit.o icmp.o dispatch.o conflex.o upf.o bpf.o so
cket.o  lpf.o dlpi.o packet.o memory.o print.o options.o inet.o convert.o tree.
o tables.o hash.o alloc.o errwarn.o inet_addr.o dns.o  resolv.o execute.o discov
er.o auth.o
[...]
ranlib libdhcp.a
Making all in server
cc -g  -I.. -I../includes -Wall -Wstrict-prototypes -Wno-unused -Wno-implicit -W
no-comment  -Wno-uninitialized -Werror -Wno-switch -pipe   -c dhcpd.c
[...]
cc  -o dhcpd dhcpd.o dhcp.o bootp.o confpars.o db.o class.o failover.o ../common
/libdhcp.a
Making all in client
cc -g  -I.. -I../includes -Wall -Wstrict-prototypes -Wno-unused -Wno-implicit -W
no-comment  -Wno-uninitialized -Werror -Wno-switch -pipe   -c dhclient.c
cc  -o dhclient dhclient.o clparse.o ../common/libdhcp.a
Making all in relay
cc -g  -I.. -I../includes -Wall -Wstrict-prototypes -Wno-unused -Wno-implicit -W
no-comment  -Wno-uninitialized -Werror -Wno-switch -pipe   -c dhcrelay.c
cc  -o dhcrelay dhcrelay.o ../common/libdhcp.a
%
```

Note

The make should complete without errors, but some operating systems may give warning messages. This may occur because of differences between the vendor's C library and the POSIX and ANSI standards, or, more likely, because of differences in areas not covered by the standards. For operating systems the ISC DHCP distribution currently supports, warnings you may see generally do not represent actual problems about which you should be concerned. If you do have concerns, you can raise them on the ISC mailing list. The ISC's goal is for warnings to be eliminated in all compiles on all architectures.

If the make fails with an error, it could be because the version of the DHCP distribution you are using wasn't tested on the architecture on which you are compiling, or it may be because you have a nonstandard compiler setup. Make sure the problem is not with your installation before asking for help on the mailing list. You should also make sure you are using the most recent distribution of the release cycle you're trying to build. For example, don't ask for help compiling 2.0b1pl27 (a beta test snapshot) when 2.0pl2 (that is, two patchlevels after the end of the beta test) is available. However, if you are sure you are using the most recent distribution and you can't get it to compile, you are encouraged to ask for help.

Installing

After you build the distribution, you can install it on your system using the make install command. This installs the entire distribution: the client, the server, and the relay agent, as well as all the documentation. If you want to install only the server, or if you want to install in a special location, you can locate the executables within the build tree and copy them into place yourself. Example 12.4 shows a sample installation.

Example 12.4

```
% su
Password:
# make install
Installing in common
for dir in /usr/share/man/cat5; do  foo="";  for bar in `echo ${dir} ¦tr / ' '`;
 do foo=${foo}/$bar;  if [ ! -d $foo ]; then  mkdir $foo;  chmod 755 $foo;  fi;
  done;  done
install -c  dhcp-options.cat5   /usr/share/man/cat5/dhcp-options.0
install -c  dhcp-eval.cat5   /usr/share/man/cat5/dhcp-eval.0
install -c  dhcp-contrib.cat5   /usr/share/man/cat5/dhcp-contrib.0
Installing in server
for dir in /usr/sbin /usr/share/man/cat8 /usr/share/man/cat5 /var/db; do foo=""
;  for bar in `echo ${dir} ¦tr / ' '`; do  foo=${foo}/$bar; if [ ! -d $foo ]; t
hen  mkdir $foo;  chmod 755 $foo;  fi;  done;  done
install -c -m 444 dhcpd /usr/sbin
chmod 755 /usr/sbin/dhcpd
install -c  dhcpd.cat8   /usr/share/man/cat8/dhcpd.0
install -c  dhcpd.conf.cat5   /usr/share/man/cat5/dhcpd.conf.0
install -c  dhcpd.leases.cat5   /usr/share/man/cat5/dhcpd.leases.0
Installing in client
nroff -man dhclient.man8 >dhclient.man8
for dir in /sbin /etc /usr/share/man/cat5 /usr/share/man/cat8 /var/db;  do foo=
"";  for bar in `echo ${dir} ¦tr / ' '`; do  foo=${foo}/$bar;  if [ ! -d $foo ];
 then  mkdir $foo;  chmod 755 $foo;  fi;  done;  done
install -c -m 444 dhclient /sbin
chmod 755 /sbin/dhclient
if [ xnetbsd = xnone ]; then  echo "No client script available.";  else install
-c -m 444 scripts/netbsd /etc/dhclient-script;  chmod 700 /etc/dhclient-script;
 fi
install -c  dhclient.cat8   /usr/share/man/cat8/dhclient.0
install -c  dhclient-script.cat8   /usr/share/man/cat8/dhclient-script.0
install -c  dhclient.conf.cat5   /usr/share/man/cat5/dhclient.conf.0
install -c  dhclient.leases.cat5   /usr/share/man/cat5/dhclient.leases.0
Installing in relay
for dir in /usr/sbin /usr/share/man/cat8; do  foo="";  for bar in `echo ${dir} ¦
tr / ' '`; do  foo=${foo}/$bar;  if [ ! -d $foo ]; then  mkdir $foo; chmod 755
$foo;  fi;  done;  done
install -c -m 444 dhcrelay /usr/sbin
chmod 755 /usr/sbin/dhcrelay
install -c  dhcrelay.cat8   /usr/share/man/cat8/dhcrelay.0
# exit
%
```

Vendor-Supplied Versions of the ISC DHCP Distribution

Ideally, your operating system vendor supplies a version of the ISC DHCP server in its distribution, and you don't have to go through the steps described previously. Unfortunately, even vendors that do include the ISC DHCP distribution with their operating systems typically do not include the most recent version, for the simple reason that the most recent stable version when they cut their operating system distribution was since superseded by a new version.

In particular, Red Hat Software kindly included version 2.0b1pl6 of the ISC DHCP Distribution with version 5.1 of its Linux distribution. It did exactly the right thing: pl6 was the official stable release for several months when Red Hat included it. Unfortunately, about three months after it released its distribution, a new flurry of activity started on the ISC DHCP server, partially in response to the release of Linux version 2.2. This activity resulted in the resolution of quite a few bugs in 2.0b1pl6, and in the addition of a number of features that were in high demand. This situation persists in Red Hat Linux version 6.0. At the time of the Red Hat 6.0 release, the ISC DHCP distribution was in a phase of rapid development, and Red Hat probably felt it was a bad time to try to update their distribution.

Sometime in the year 2000, the ISC DHCP distribution is expected to be sufficiently mature. Further significant development will be unnecessary, and only bug fixes and the like will be required. If this actually happens, the version of the DHCP server that OS vendors ship will probably be stable enough for you to use. For now, before you use the vendor's version of the DHCP server, it's best to go straight to the ISC and see that the version the vendor is shipping doesn't have known bugs. The ISC Web page for any given version of the DHCP distribution includes a complete history of the changes that were made. You can follow that history back to the version you have from your OS vendor and see whether any significant changes were made.

Example 12.5 shows how you can tell what version of the DHCP server you currently have installed. The version number is printed at the end of the first line of output (if you don't have a configuration file yet, this command prints an error message after it gives you the release information, but you can ignore the error message for now).

EXAMPLE 12.5

```
% dhcpd -t
Internet Software Consortium DHCP Server V3.0-alpha 980424
Copyright 1995, 1996, 1997, 1998, 1999 The Internet Software Consortium.
All rights reserved.
%
```

12.1.3 Logging

The DHCP server logs quite a bit of information using the *syslog Application Programming Interface (API)*. The syslog API provides a way for UNIX server programs running as daemons to log events to a centralized event logging daemon, `syslogd`. This daemon is configured through the `/etc/syslog.conf` file. The syslog API enables each information provider to specify a facility code, indicating a rough category into which it falls. The ISC DHCP server normally classifies itself in the daemon category, as do such other daemons as the name server and the Network Time Protocol (NTP) server.

Some sites prefer to keep the DHCP logs separate. If you want to do this, you can change the facility that the DHCP server reports by editing the file so that it includes `site.h` in the distribution, and defining `DHCPD_LOG_FACILITY` to be something other than `LOG_DAEMON`. After making this change, you must type `make clean` to remove the old version of the server, and then redo the build and install procedure mentioned previously.

12.2 Prerequisites to Operation of the ISC DHCP Server

The DHCP server is implemented so that if it detects something inconsistent about its configuration, it refuses to operate. This is because a misconfigured DHCP server can potentially cause more harm to your network than simply having no DHCP server at all. Version 3 of the server also requires that you explicitly enable any features that can potentially cause problems when enabled in situations where it is not appropriate.

12.2.1 Lease Database

Before invoking the DHCP server, you must create an empty lease database file for it. On a UNIX or UNIX-like machine, you can do this by typing `touch file`, in which `file` is the full path and name of the lease database file. Chapter 24, "The DHCP Database," describes how to determine the pathname for the lease database file on your operating system.

The DHCP server stores its lease database as an ASCII text file, much like its configuration file. This file contains the DHCP server's entire knowledge of what it promised to its clients, and thus is *very* important. The DHCP server does not operate if it detects conditions that suggest that by doing so it will lose information from the lease file.

When the DHCP server rewrites the lease database to remove obsolete entries, it does so by creating a temporary file, writing a complete lease database into that file, renaming the old lease file with the backup filename `dhcpd.leases~`, and renaming the new database with the old name.

If the system crashes just as this renaming operation occurs, some of the filesystem directory information may update prior to the crash, but some may not. This can result in a new lease database called dhcpd.leases.*pid* (in which *pid* is the process ID of the DHCP server when it wrote the new file) and an old database called dhcpd.leases~, but no lease file called dhcpd.leases.

To the DHCP server, this condition can't be safely distinguished from the situation in which you have just installed the DHCP server and do not yet have a lease. As a result, the DHCP server *never* creates a lease database file on its own. It always insists that you do it. If you try to start the server without first creating a lease database file, it displays the error message shown in Example 12.6.

EXAMPLE 12.6

```
Can't open lease database /tmp/dhcpd.leases: No such file or directory
Check for failed database rewrite attempt!
Please read the dhcpd.leases manual page if you don't know what to do
about this.
```

12.2.2 Configuration File

The DHCP configuration file is described in this chapter and previous chapters. You must include the following in the DHCP server's configuration file, or the server will not operate:

- complete subnet declarations for all network segments on which the server provides service

- IP addresses for all clients for which the server provides service

- complete subnet declarations for all network segments to which the server computer's network interfaces are connected

- statements as to whether the server is authoritative for any given subnet

You must declare every network segment to which clients served by the DHCP are attached. Even if every client you are serving has a fixed-address statement, the server still needs to know the configuration of the network segments: the subnet number of each segment, and each segment's subnet mask. If more than one subnet exists on a given network segment, every subnet on that network segment must be explicitly declared, not just the subnet or subnets you are serving. All subnets on a given network segment should be enclosed within a shared-network statement. This is explained in greater detail in Chapter 13.

IP Addresses

You must provide IP addresses for the server to assign for all clients you want to serve. If you are providing static IP address assignments, you must have a host declaration for every client on every network segment to which the client might ever be connected. Static assignments are described in detail in Chapter 14, "Client Identification and Fixed-Address Allocation."

If you are providing pools of addresses from which the server dynamically allocates addresses to clients, you must declare these pools using range statements within subnet declarations, or pool declarations within subnet or shared-network declarations. Dynamic allocation is covered in Chapter 13. Address pools are covered in Chapter 17, "Conditional Behavior."

Network Segment Declaration

DHCP servers are commonly deployed in such a way that the network segment or segments to which they are connected may not require DHCP service, or may receive DHCP service from other servers. The configurations of these network segments must still be declared; otherwise the DHCP server can't behave correctly.

If the network to which the DHCP server is connected is a machine room network on which no DHCP service is provided, it is sufficient to provide complete declarations for the network segment. These may be an empty subnet declaration or, if the network segment is configured with more than one subnet, a shared-network declaration containing empty subnet declarations for all the subnets configured on the network segment.

If one or more network segments to which the server is connected are in different administrative domains, the server should still have complete subnet and/or shared-network declarations for those networks. However, because the server is not authoritative, if you are operating a version 2 server, each shared-network or subnet declaration should contain a not authoritative statement to indicate that the DHCP server should be completely silent on that subnet.

Statements of Authority

As the final requirement, the server configuration file should have statements of authority for each subnet or shared-network declaration for which the default authority is incorrect. If the server's authority is the same on all configured network segments, it can be stated in the global scope.

Version 2 of the ISC DHCP server is authoritative by default; that is, it assumes it knows everything about any network segment it serves and sends DHCPNAK packets to clients it believes are misconfigured on all network segments of which it is aware.

Version 3 assumes the opposite: It does not have complete information about the configurations of the subnets it is serving or about other subnets of which it is aware but on which it is not providing service. This means that if a client is moved from one network segment to another and sends a DHCPREQUEST for an address on its former subnet, the server does not send a DHCPNAK, so the client continues to use the incorrect address until it can no longer renew its lease. DHCP servers deployed in production environments should simply state that they are authoritative in the global scope so that proper DHCPNAK behavior occurs. DHCP servers that are authoritative for some network segments and not for others should state they are authoritative in those scopes.

This change in behavior may seem very inconvenient, but the reason it does this is good and one that network administrators in production environments should appreciate. If a user on a network you support decides to deploy his or her authoritative but misconfigured DHCP server on that network, it can cause a disruption of service for all users on the network. You can configure Version 2 of the ISC DHCP server to do this accidentally, but Version 3 must be explicitly configured this way so that misconfiguration is much less likely to happen.

12.3 Configuring the ISC DHCP Server

The DHCP server configuration is stored in the /etc/dhcpd.conf file. This file is a free-form ASCII text file containing a sequence of declarations and statements, similar to a C or Perl program. A complete reference to the DHCP server's configuration statements is provided in Appendix B. This section introduces the concepts involved in writing configuration files and shows some examples.

The configuration file performs five basic functions:

- It describes the layout of the network being served.

- It sets parameters that control how the DHCP server behaves.

- It defines options and parameters that are sent to clients.

- It defines ways of sending different parameters to different clients, based on what they send or to what part of the network they are connected.

- It provides IP addresses for DHCP clients.

12.3.1 Server Control Parameters

Parameters that control the DHCP server's behavior define the following:

- the duration of leases the server provides

- whether the server assigns an address to a client

- whether the server responds to a client's first request

Example 12.6 shows a typical set of server parameters.

EXAMPLE 12.6

```
default-lease-time 86400;
max-lease-time 86400;
min-lease-time 300;
allow-bootp no;
authoritative;
```

In this example, the default and maximum lease times are set to 86,400 seconds, or one day. The minimum lease time is set to 300 seconds, or 5 minutes. BOOTP requests are disabled, and the server is declared to be authoritative for the networks it serves. The complete meaning of all these parameters is described in Appendix B.

12.3.2 Client Options and Parameters

The DHCP server sends *options* to clients. These are described in greater detail in other chapters, but essentially options contain information about the network to which the client is connected or about network services that are available to the client. The DHCP server can also send three parameters that are not technically options but that are treated in the same way: the `filename`, `server-name`, and `next-server` parameters.

Options are specified with the `option` keyword, followed by the option name, followed by the option data. Example 12.7 shows a typical option that might be sent to a client.

EXAMPLE 12.7

```
option domain-name "example.org";
```

Client parameters are specified in the same way as server parameters, with the name of the parameter followed by its value, as shown in Example 12.8.

EXAMPLE **12.8**

```
filename "netbsd-alpha";
```

All options defined by the DHCP server are documented in Appendix B.

User-Defined Options

In addition to the predefined options listed in Appendix B, the ISC DHCP server also provides the ability to define new options. These include new options standardized after the version of the server you are running was shipped, experimental options, site-local options, or vendor-specific options.

New options are defined by specifying an option name, a code, and a format. Example 12.9 shows an option called `acme-config-file`, with a code of `129`, whose format is a simple string of ASCII text.

EXAMPLE **12.9**

```
option acme-config-file code 129 = text;
```

Options can be more complex. You can define options that encode a set of values of different types, an array of values, or an array of sets of values. Example 12.10 shows an option definition that encodes one or more IP addresses, an option definition that encodes one or more sets of IP addresses and 16-bit numbers, and an option that encodes an IP address, a 32-bit number, and an ASCII text string.

EXAMPLE **12.10**

```
option acme-font-servers code 130 = array of ip-address;
option acme-registrars = array of { ip-address, integer 16 };
option acme-license-info = { ip-address, integer 32, text };
```

Note

The DHCP server currently supports only data types defined in RFC2132. You cannot encode some things that might be desirable—for example, you cannot send more than one text string.

Appendix B gives a complete list of data types that you can express.

Option Spaces

In addition to defining new options that are used just like regular DHCP options, you can also declare new *option spaces*. An option space is simply a separate collection of options, with a separate numbering system. The standard set of DHCP options is numbered from zero to 255, with all option numbers greater than 128 reserved for site-local use. If you define a new option space, it has its own numbering system, probably also from zero to 255, with different options corresponding to each number.

Three predefined option spaces exist: the *dhcp option space*, the *server option space*, and the *agent option space*. You may not define new option spaces with these names. You can use the agent option space in conditional expressions to refer to sub-options of the `relay agent information` option; the other two option space names are used internally by the DHCP server and are not intended to be referred to directly by the user.

A network administrator might define new option spaces for two reasons. For example, some DHCP clients use vendor-specific options, which are numbered from zero to 255 and do not coincide with the standard set of DHCP options because they are encapsulated in their own DHCP option. Vendor-specific options are described in detail in Chapter 17.

The second reason to define a new option space is so that overlapping site-specific option codes can be defined. This may be necessary because some vendors of DHCP and BOOTP clients (for example, NCD and Hewlett-Packard) used the site-specific code range (128-254) to define their own vendor-specific option codes before it was reserved for site-specific options and before the vendor-specific encapsulated option was defined.

`site-option-space` Parameter

Some of the option codes for these vendors may overlap, yet you may want to provide different global values for different vendors. You can do this by defining option spaces and then using the `site-option-space` parameter to determine which option code is actually sent to the client.

Example 12.11 shows a configuration that provides different global values for a site-specific option to two different devices that are identified using host declarations. This example makes practical sense only if many host declarations exist, not just two.

EXAMPLE 12.11

```
option space acme;
option acme.toast-color = integer 16;
option acme.toast-color 4096;

option space ypl;
option ypl.ot-modulation = array of integer 32;
option ypl.ot-modulation 10, 188277, 423119, 9188271;

host acme1 {
  hardware ethernet 99:aa:bb:0c:ad:e2;
  site-option-space acme;
}

host ypl1 {
  hardware ethernet aa:ee:ee:1c:a2:29;
  site-option-space ypl;
}
```

The site-option-space parameter tells the DHCP server that for all options whose codes are between 128 and 254, the server should use the values declared in the specified option space instead of the values from the default option space.

12.3.3 Network Configuration Information

Network configuration information describes to the DHCP server the physical layout of the network. The DHCP server actually doesn't need to know how network segments are interconnected; the network infrastructure—routers, bridges, Ethernet switches, and so on—takes care of this. It does need to know what subnets are assigned to each network segment, and what network segments are present in the network.

Even network segments that don't get DHCP service may need to be described to the server, either so that it can behave appropriately in response to requests from those networks, or so that it can be told not to respond to requests on those networks. The ISC DHCP server is actually quite insistent about this. If you do not describe the networks to which the DHCP server machine is attached, it refuses to operate.

Configuration File Declarations

The two declarations in the DHCP server configuration file that pertain to the network configuration are the *shared network* and *subnet declarations*. The shared-network declaration describes a network segment: a single network on which any connected node receives all link-layer broadcasts sent by any other connected node. The subnet declaration declares an IP subnet: a single network on which any connected node receives all IP-layer broadcasts sent by any other connected node. You can configure more than one subnet on a network segment. In this case, you must enclose the subnet declarations for those subnets in a shared-network declaration. If only one IP subnet is configured on a particular network segment, you don't have to write an explicit shared-network declaration.

Chapter 13 describes subnet and shared-network declarations in detail. Example 12.12 shows an example of a subnet declaration for the subnet whose network number is 10.117.22.0 and whose subnet mask is 255.255.255.0.

EXAMPLE 12.12

```
subnet 10.117.22.0 netmask 255.255.255.0 {
}
```

12.3.4 Scopes

The ISC DHCP server derives the parameters used to control its behavior with respect to a certain client, and the parameters and options it sends the client, from the *scopes* in which the client appears. Scopes do *not* control the choice of address assigned to a client; this is controlled by the network segment to which the client is connected and the address allocation rules that apply for whatever addresses are available on that network segment.

Global options work through scoping. An option that appears in the global scope (that is, outside of any declaration with its own scope) applies to all clients. Options in scopes other than the global scope apply only to those clients that appear within those scopes and the scopes outside of them. For example, if a client matches a host declaration, the client appears in the host declaration scope and all the scopes outside of it.

Example 12.13 shows a configuration that uses scoping heavily. Every declaration in the DHCP server configuration file that has enclosing braces automatically comes with its own scope. In addition, scopes can be explicitly declared using the group statement. Example 12.13 uses the group statement to provide the same parameters to a group of host declarations for NCD X terminals that otherwise have no common scope.

EXAMPLE 12.13

```
option domain-name "example.org";
option domain-name-servers ns1.example.org, ns2.example.org;

subnet 10.0.17.0 netmask 255.255.255.0 {
    option broadcast-address 10.0.17.255;
    option routers 10.0.17.254;
    range 10.0.17.10 10.0.17.253;
}

subnet 10.0.16.0 netmask 255.255.255.0 {
    option broadcast-address 10.0.16.255;
    option routers 10.0.16.254;
    range 10.0.16.10 10.0.16.253;
}

# NCD X terminals
group {
    filename "/tftpboot/Xncd19c";
    host ncd1 { hardware ethernet 00:00:a7:09:21:ac; }
    host ncd2 { hardware ethernet 00:00:a7:1c:33:90; }
    host ncd3 { hardware ethernet 00:00:a7:2a:04:17; }
}
```

If a client connected to the 10.0.16.0 subnet sends a DHCPDISCOVER message, the DHCP server considers that client to be in the scope of the 10.0.16.0 subnet. It finds the broadcast-address and routers options in that scope, and then it moves to the scope that is outside the subnet scope—in this case the global scope—and finds the domain-name and domain-name-servers options. The complete set of explicitly specified options it finds for the client, then, is the broadcast-address, routers, domain-name, and domain-name-servers options.

Clients can appear in more than one scope at the same time. Figure 12.1 shows a diagram of the scopes declared in Example 12.13. As you can see, each host declaration has a scope. When a client matches a host declaration, the DHCP server considers that client to be in the scope of the host declaration. It *also* considers the client to be in the scope of the subnet declaration for the subnet from which the client is assigned an IP address. If, for example, the client matching the ncd1 host declaration is assigned an address on the 10.0.16.0 subnet, it appears in that subnet's scope, in the host declaration scope, and in all the scopes containing them.

The DHCP server processes scopes by cycling through each specific scope in which the client appears, in reverse order of specificity—in this case the subnet scope and then the host scope.

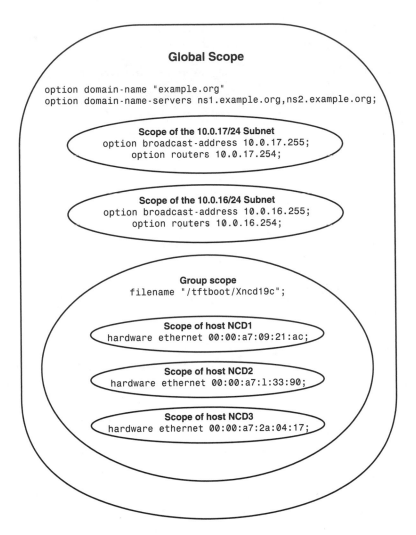

FIGURE 12.1 *A diagram of the scopes in Example 12.13.*

Specific Scopes

A *specific scope* is a scope the client specifically matched, not the scopes containing such a scope. For example, a client never matches the global scope; it gets parameters from the global scope because the global scope contains some scope that it did match.

The *specificity* of a scope that a client matches is dependent on the type of declaration with which the scope is associated. The fewer clients a particular type
of declaration may match, the more specific its scope is considered to be. This
ordering is somewhat arbitrary; classes are considered more specific than subnets, for example, so a *subnet* declaration that can match only 10 clients can be
considered less specific than a *class* declaration that happens to match hun-
dreds of clients throughout the network.

The exact ordering of specificity of declarations starts with the most specific
declaration, the *host* declaration, and continues through the *subclass, class, subnet*, and *pool* scopes, to the least specific scope, which is the *shared-network*
scope. Scopes that don't match clients (for example, group scopes and the
global scope) do not have an inherent specificity. For each *specific* scope that the
server considers, it also considers the scopes outside of that scope, all the way
to the global scope. The outermost scope is actually considered first so that
inner scopes can override parameters that appear in outer scopes.

The server never considers the same scope twice. If the same outer scope contains two specific scopes that the client matched, that scope is considered in the
process of evaluating the more specific of the two specific scopes, and is
skipped when processing the other specific scope.

The scopes considered for the client ncd1 in Example 12.13 are, in order, the
global scope, the scope of subnet 10.0.16.0, the scope for the group declaration
that surrounds the ncd1 host declaration, and the scope for the ncd1 host declaration.

An additional complication is that different values for the same parameter or
option can be specified in different scopes. The scoping rules described previously are intended to ensure that the option or parameter that applies to a particular client is predictable. The result of these rules is that the parameter or
option that appears in the most specific scope is always the one that is used. If
a parameter within a *host* declaration is different from the same parameter
within a *subnet* declaration, the parameter in the host declaration is used. If an
option declared within a *subnet* declaration is different from the value declared
for that option in the global scope, the value in the subnet declaration applies
to all clients connected to that subnet, and the value in the global scope applies
to all other clients (assuming it isn't overridden in other inner scopes).

12.3.5 IP Address Assignments

You can provide IP addresses for clients in three ways: through static IP address assignments, *pool* declarations, or *range* statements. Pool declarations actually contain range statements, but they are handled somewhat differently.

Static IP address assignments are performed through host declarations. Chapter 14 goes through static IP address assignment in detail. Briefly, for each client that receives a static assignment, there must be a host declaration with information that the server can use to match the declaration to the client, and that declaration must also contain a fixed-address declaration containing the IP address to assign. When a fixed mapping exists for a client, the client is assigned only its fixed address if it is connected to the network segment on which that address is valid. If it is connected to some network for which it has no fixed-address declaration, it is dynamically assigned an address, or it receives no address at all, depending on how the server is configured.

Addresses are assigned dynamically out of address pools. Address pools can be declared with range statements, or with pool declarations containing range statements. Enclosing range statements within pool statements provides some additional control over address assignment. Chapter 17 describes how to put permit lists on pool statements. Chapter 13 describes simple range statements not enclosed in pool statements.

12.4 Invoking the ISC DHCP Server

After you have produced a configuration for your DHCP server, you must know how to invoke it. Invoking the DHCP server involves two aspects: command-line arguments, and getting it to work right for a particular operating system.

12.4.1 Command-Line Arguments

The server takes command-line switches that determine:

- the UDP port on which it listens
- whether it runs in the background as a daemon
- whether debugging output is logged to stdout
- what filename to use for the configuration file, lease database file, and process ID file
- whether to merely test the configuration
- whether to be verbose on startup

You can also specify the names of interfaces on which to operate, although this is not necessarily a good idea, as discussed in Section 12.4.2.

Switches

The -p switch indicates the UDP port on which the server should listen. If this flag is specified, the server uses the next higher port number as its source port. The DHCP protocol specifies that the server should always listen on port 67 and transmit on port 68. If the -p 67 switch is given (or if no -p switch is given), this is what happens. In general use, it is never appropriate to use the -p -1 switch, but it can be very useful for debugging or benchmarking.

The -f switch indicates that the server should operate normally but should not fork a subprocess and exit to the invoking process. Normally, if you just type dhcpd, the DHCP server prints a startup message and then appears to exit, at which point you receive a shell prompt. However, what actually happens is that the server started a child process that then detaches itself from the terminal and runs in the background, while the parent process (the one you started when you typed the command) exits. The -t flag prevents this, and is useful in situations in which you are invoking the DHCP server from an /etc/inittab (this is a UNIX System V concept, and may or may not even be possible on the version of the operating system you are running).

The -d switch tells the server to run in the foreground, as with the -f switch, but in addition the server logs all its output to the terminal, instead of just logging it to the syslog daemon. This can be very useful when you are debugging the server; you simply invoke it from the command line and watch as it configures (or fails to configure) a client. If you are reporting a bug on the dhcp-server mailing list, you are always asked for the server output, and this is the easiest way to get it.

The DHCP server normally looks for its configuration file in /etc/dhcpd.conf. If you are testing, or simply don't want your configuration file to be stored in /etc, you can override this using the -cf switch, followed by the filename that you prefer.

The server normally stores its lease database in a specific directory that varies from system to system. You can use the -lf switch to specify a different filename and location for the lease database. All temporary filenames are also based on the specified name and directory.

When the server runs in the background as a daemon, it creates a file into which it saves its process ID. This file is normally stored in the /var/run or /etc directory, again depending on the operating system. You can use the -pf switch to specify a different filename and directory.

The DHCP server does not continue to operate if it finds errors in the configuration file because any errors could result in it badly misconfiguring clients on the network. Therefore, after making changes to the configuration file, it's a very good idea to make sure that it's correct before installing it. You can do this with the -t switch; the server tests the specified configuration file and prints error messages if it finds errors. The exit status is zero if no errors exist, and nonzero if errors exist. Thus, shell scripts and human users can use this.

The server normally prints a startup message with the version number, the copyright information, and some information on how to contact the ISC. After you see this information once, you probably don't need to see it again (besides, it can make the system startup messages look messy). To prevent this message from printing, use the -q switch.

12.4.2 Specifying Interfaces

On some operating systems, you can specify on which network interface or interfaces the DHCP server should respond to requests. This works correctly only on operating systems on which the DHCP distribution supports more than one network interface. If the operating system doesn't support a mechanism by which the server can tell on which interface a packet arrived, or determine on which interface one will be sent, you can't do this.

The usual reason for specifying interfaces on the command line is that you are installing a DHCP server on a machine that is directly connected to networks in two different administrative domains. For example, in a home-office configuration where you have an ADSL connection to the Internet, you may set up a Linux or NetBSD system as a router between your Internet service provider's (ISP's) network and your home-office network. Both of these networks appear to be broadcast networks, but the ADSL network is in your ISP's administrative domain, and your ISP will probably become very upset if you begin providing DHCP service on its network. By specifying on the command line the interface attached to your home-office network, you can prevent the DHCP server from operating on the other network.

Another reason to specify interface names on the command line is that the DHCP server may sometimes incorrectly identify a network interface as a broadcast interface when it is not. It may then attempt to use this interface, and it may be unable to operate as a result. If this happens, explicitly list all your computers' broadcast interfaces on the command line, and the server should ignore the misidentified interface.

12.5 Server Operation

After the server is installed, the server administrator may need to do a variety of things. The first task is to make sure the server is started automatically whenever the server machine is started so that DHCP service isn't stopped by restarts. The server administrator may subsequently need to restart the server to install a new configuration, or may need to modify the lease database.

12.5.1 Starting the Server Automatically

After you configure the DHCP server to your satisfaction, you must arrange for it to start automatically. On UNIX and UNIX-like operating systems, servers are normally started by the *init* daemon. The init daemon starts in one of three ways, depending on the operating system: from an /etc/inittab file, an /etc/rc shell script, or a separate script in the /etc/rc.d directory.

You may be able to determine which of these three methods is used on your operating system by reading the manual page for the init program. If that doesn't help, look for an /etc/inittab file; if one exists, that's how servers are started. There should be a manual page for the /etc/inittab file. If you invoke the server from inittab, make sure to give it the -f switch because versions of init that use inittab automatically start a new instance of a daemon when the old one exits. Without the -f flag, the DHCP server always appears to have exited from the perspective of the process that started it.

If no /etc/inittab exists, look for an /etc/rc file. If such a file exists, it is probably a shell script that invokes various daemons on startup. Most operating systems that provide /etc/rc scripts expect you to make local modifications in a local file, called /etc/rc.local. Your entry in /etc/rc.local should look something like the one in Example 12.14.

EXAMPLE 12.14

```
if [ -f /etc/dhcpd.conf ]; then
  echo -n ' dhcpd'; dhcpd >/dev/console 2>&1
fi
```

Shell Scripts

If no /etc/rc exists, or if an /etc/rc.d exists in addition to an /etc/rc, you should add a shell script to /etc/rc.d that invokes the DHCP server and then exits with a zero status. The /etc/rc.d startup method works by having a complete set of startup files in /etc/rc.d that start and stop any server. You may want to look through one of the scripts there for an example because these scripts operate differently on different operating systems, but Example 12.15 provides one possible example of a startup script.

EXAMPLE 12.15

```
#!/bin/sh

if [ x$1 = xstart ]; then
  dhcpd >/dev/console 2>&1
fi

if [ x$1 = xstop ]; then
  kill `cat /var/run/dhcpd.pid`
fi

exit $?
```

Start-Up Files

After you add your shell script to /etc/rc.d, you must configure it to run. Systems that use /etc/rc.d generally order their startup with a set of /etc/rcn.d directories, in which n is a number representing a runlevel. Runlevel numbers aren't standardized. So, if you don't know it and your documentation doesn't say, you must look through these directories to find the one where network daemons are set up. When you find that directory, you must create a symbolic link from the startup file you just created into the directory.

The system startup script sorts the names of the files in this directory and executes them in the sort order. Therefore, the filename you choose must appear later in the sorted list of files than any scripts that must be executed before the server can start (for example, the script that configures the network). Filenames in these directories usually start with a letter, followed by a two-digit number. Use the same letter, a number that's higher than the number of any network startup scripts your script depends on (for example, the one that starts the name server), and then the name of the real script file. So, for example, if you name your script *dhcpstart*, and your rcN.d directory for network startup is rc3.d, you might type ln -s /etc/rc.d/dhcpstart /etc/rc3.d/S57dhcpstart.

12.5.2 Updating the Server Configuration

When the server is running, you can freely update the configuration file without disturbing it. After you update the file, stop the server using the UNIX `kill` command. If you are running it out of `/etc/inittab`, it should restart automatically. If not, you must restart it yourself by invoking it with the same arguments specified in the system startup script.

You do not risk data loss when sending a `SIGTERM` signal to the server; the server never sends updates to the client for information that isn't confirmed as written to disk by the operating system.

12.5.3 Modifying the Lease Database

If, for some reason, you must make changes to the lease database, you *must* stop the server before any such changes are made; otherwise, data loss is not only possible but also likely. After you make the changes, you can restart the server, and it immediately picks up any changes that you made to the file.

Summary

The ISC DHCP server is an open source software product from the Internet Software Consortium. Support is available in a variety of ways, depending on a particular user's needs. Before you can use the DHCP server, you must create a lease database and a configuration file. The configuration file should define IP addresses to assign to clients, set any required local configuration parameters, and provide options that are correct for the clients on all network segments on which IP addresses may be assigned.

The server runs continuously as a background daemon. When the configuration file is updated, the server must be restarted for the changes to take effect. If the lease database is to be modified other than by the DHCP server, the DHCP server must be stopped prior to modification and restarted afterward. If the server is being used in production, it should be started automatically when the system on which it is configured to run is powered on.

## CHAPTER 13

Configuring a DHCP Server

This chapter demonstrates how to configure a DHCP server to provide basic DHCP service, using the ISC DHCP server for illustration. This includes:

- Describing the network topology

- Setting up pools of addresses from which the server can dynamically assign addresses to new clients

- Setting up basic services, some of which may vary according to the topology

Chapter 14, "Client Identification and Fixed-Address Allocation," covers static address assignment and client identification.

This chapter presupposes an understanding of the basic server configuration file format the ISC DHCP server uses as described in Chapter 3, "Configuring the DHCP Server." It also presupposes an understanding of IP subnetting as described in Chapter 4, "Configuring TCP/IP Stacks," and an understanding of DHCP message passing as described in Chapter 7, "Transmitting DHCP Messages."

13.1 The Configuration of an Individual Subnet

Even if a network is small, it always includes at least one subnet. This section uses an example based on Ted Lemon's home network. Ted's network consists of a single Ethernet segment behind a router connecting it to the Internet. One subnet is on the Ethernet, which was assigned a network number of 10.0.0.0 and a subnet mask of 255.255.255.0. To define this subnet for the server, Ted writes a *subnet declaration* as shown in Example 13.1.

EXAMPLE 13.1

```
subnet 10.0.0.0 netmask 255.255.255.0 {
}
```

This declaration simply informs the server that the 10.0.0.0 subnet exists; it does not configure the server to answer requests for addresses on the 10.0.0.0 subnet. With this information, the server has enough knowledge about the network so that it can respond with a DHCPNAK message to a request for an invalid address. For example, if a DHCP client broadcasts a DHCPREQUEST message on the 10.0.0.0 subnet asking for an IP address of 10.20.0.15, which is a different subnet, the DHCP server can respond with a DHCPNAK message, informing the client that the requested address does not work.

Subnet Declarations

Some DHCP servers do not require written subnet declarations in all cases. These servers derive network topology information by looking at the IP addresses and subnet masks of the interfaces connected to the DHCP server machine and then requiring the network administrator to specify more information for networks to which they are not directly connected.

This may seem like a convenience at first. However, as a network grows, and the DHCP server configuration file grows with it, the subnet configuration information the network administrator included implicitly when creating the configuration file may change. If the administrator copies the configuration file for use on a machine connected to a different subnet, the assumptions being depended on are no longer true.

For this reason, the ISC DHCP server requires that all subnets supported in the configuration file be explicitly declared. The file is, thus, completely portable, and all assumptions about the network topology are visible to other network administrators who may need to adjust the configuration. Even if the DHCP server you are using does not require that all assumptions about network topology be made explicit, it is strongly recommended that you do so if the server allows it.

13.1.1 Address Allocation

To enable the server to assign addresses to clients, the network administrator must define which addresses in the subnet are available for dynamic allocation. The address range for this subnet includes the addresses 10.0.0.0 through 10.0.0.255—a total of 256 addresses. Of these, 10.0.0.0 and 10.0.0.255 are reserved as broadcast addresses, so 254 actual IP addresses can be allocated.

The first step in setting up a subnet for dynamic allocation is to determine which of these addresses the DHCP server should make available. At this time, it is also important to decide which addresses should be reserved for computers, whose addresses must not change and should not be configured using DHCP. You may also want to reserve some addresses for later use.

Reserved Addresses

On the example network, two fixed addresses are not allocated by DHCP: the router's address, 10.0.0.1, and the DHCP server's address, 10.0.0.2. The DHCP server does not necessarily need to know about these addresses, but it is important to remember to exclude these addresses from the list of addresses allocated by the server.

Dynamic Address Pool

If you are confident that there will never be more permanently assigned IP addresses on the network, you can allocate all the remaining 252 IP addresses to the DHCP server in a dynamic pool. However, prudence suggests reserving some of the addresses in the event that new servers are added. Therefore, it is better to reserve addresses 10.0.0.1 through 10.0.0.9 for servers and to enable the DHCP server to assign addresses from the remaining pool. To provide addresses to the DHCP server for assignment, use the range statement shown in Example 13.2.

EXAMPLE 13.2

```
range 10.0.0.10 10.0.0.254;
```

The client that received a DHCPNAK message earlier will now get a response when it sends a DHCPDISCOVER message. Assuming it is the first DHCP client to try to connect to the network, it will most likely be offered an IP address of 10.0.0.10, which is the first available address for dynamic allocation.

13.1.2 Client Configuration Information

At this point, the DHCP server has received only enough information to assign the client an IP address. However, as mentioned in Chapter 1, "An Introduction to DHCP," and Chapter 9, "DHCP Options," this is not enough information to enable the client to do anything useful. At a minimum, the client must know the IP address of a router that can serve as its default route, and it probably needs the IP address of at least one name server. This is shown in Example 13.3.

EXAMPLE 13.3

```
option domain-name-servers ns.nyc.fugue.com;
option routers gw.nyc.fugue.com;
```

> **Note**
>
> *In this example, the values of the* domain name servers *and* routers *options are declared using the domain names corresponding to those servers. The DHCP server translates these domain names into IP addresses and sends the IP addresses to the DHCP client. By doing this, the network administrator avoids editing the configuration file when the IP addresses assigned to the routers and servers change.*
>
> *The only drawback to this is that it takes time to look up a domain name. If a client sends a request and the DHCP server finds it has to look up one or more names to satisfy that request, it will have to send its own request to the DNS server for each name, wait for the responses, and then send its reply to the client.*
>
> *To take advantage of this feature, it is a good idea to have a DNS server running either on the same machine as your DHCP server, or locally on the same network segment that is either a primary or secondary server for all domain names mentioned in your DHCP server configuration file.*

Some clients also require the broadcast address option, although many will compute it themselves from the IP address and subnet mask. Example 13.4 shows how to send this option explicitly.

EXAMPLE 13.4

```
option broadcast-address 10.0.0.255;
```

If the network administrator does not specify the subnet-mask option, the DHCP server uses the subnet mask value from the subnet declaration. To simplify maintenance, however, do not explicitly write a subnet mask declaration. Example 13.5 shows an example of a subnet-mask option declaration.

EXAMPLE 13.5

```
option subnet-mask 255.255.255.0;
```

13.1.3 A Complete Subnet Configuration

Described thus far is the minimal set of options needed to enable most DHCP clients to use a simple network, such as the one at Ted Lemon's home. In practice, it is likely that more options must be specified in a configuration. Chapter 9 gives a complete list of DHCP options.

Example 13.6 shows the complete DHCP server configuration file with the option declarations that were shown in the previous examples.

EXAMPLE 13.6

```
subnet 10.0.0.0 netmask 255.255.255.0 {
        range 10.0.0.10 10.0.0.254;
```

```
        option domain-name-servers ns.nyc.fugue.com;
        option routers gw.nyc.fugue.com;
        option broadcast-address 10.0.0.255;
    }
```

13.2 Supporting Multiple Network Segments

Many DHCP installations require that DHCP servers provide service on more than one subnet. For example, at the DEC Palo Alto campus, five separate business units were located in four buildings, and each business unit had from one to four network segments of its own.

When servicing more than one network segment, the network administrator must

- Write a subnet declaration for each network segment

- Define a range of addresses for each subnet that the DHCP server can allocate

- Write option declarations for all the options that are different on some subnets

- Make sure DHCP packets from all network segments can get to the DHCP server

Each additional subnet declaration is written in the way described in Section 13.1. This section describes ways of arranging for the DHCP server to receive DHCP broadcasts from each of the network segments that it supports.

13.2.1 Multiple Network Interfaces

One way to support more than one network segment from a single DHCP server is to directly connect to every network segment you want to support the computer on which the DHCP server program is running. The machine, therefore, must be installed in a location where all network segments are available, and a network interface must be installed in the server computer for each network segment. Figure 13.1 shows an example of such a configuration.

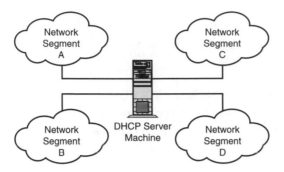

FIGURE 13.1 *Connecting the DHCP server directly to all network segments.*

13.2.2 Using DHCP Relay Agents

The more common way to enable a DHCP server to provide service on more than one network segment is to set up relay agents on each network segment being served. Relay agents are configured with a list of one or more DHCP servers. When a relay agent receives a message from a DHCP client on a particular network segment, it relays that message to the server after storing the IP address of the interface on which it received the request in the giaddr field of the message.

The server uses the giaddr field to determine what network segment the client is attached to. When it has a reply for the client, it sends the reply back to the relay agent using the IP address the relay agent stored in the giaddr field. The DHCP relay agent then sends the message back to the DHCP client. Chapter 7 describes this process in greater technical detail.

Note

Chapter 7 mentions that a DHCP relay agent can forward DHCP messages to a broadcast address. Although this is a legal configuration, and it should work, there are good reasons to avoid it. Every DHCP message relayed to the server will have been broadcast twice—once by the client and once by the relay agent. If you want to minimize broadcast traffic on a network, this is obviously not a good idea. Also, if a DHCP server is unintentionally enabled on a network segment on which the relay agent will be broadcasting, that server will receive all relayed packets and possibly respond incorrectly to them.

If the relay agent unicasts its messages, such incorrect responses cannot occur because the relay agent is configured to relay messages only to servers the network administrator intends to use.

Finally, the network administrator has a great deal of control over the network, determining what IP address the DHCP server will be assigned. As long as the server IP address does not change, relay agents do not have to be reconfigured. The only reason that its IP address would change is if the server moves to a different subnet. Setting up a relay agent to broadcast does not help in this case; if the network administrator moves the server to a different subnet, the relay agent still must be reconfigured. It is not convenient to have the relay agent broadcast the packets it relays, and it is best avoided.

Relay Agent Types

Two common kinds of DHCP relay agents exist: those that run in IP routers, and those that run on general-purpose computers. Relay agents are not routers; they are network server programs that pass packets from clients to servers and from servers to clients.

One possible configuration is to have a server machine on every network segment on which DHCP services will be provided and to have one of the services on that computer be a relay agent that relays DHCP requests back to a central DHCP server. The drawback to this setup, which is illustrated in Figure 13.2, is that a server is then needed on every supported network segment.

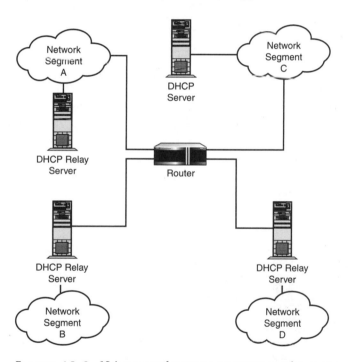

FIGURE 13.2 *Using general-purpose computers as relay agents.*

If you use dedicated routers to route on the network, and if the router software includes a DHCP relay agent, it may be convenient to use the embedded relay agent. A router must be connected to every network segment anyway, so in this case you do not incur an additional equipment overhead for providing DHCP service. Figure 13.3 shows an example of this sort of configuration.

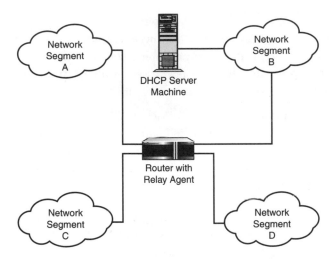

FIGURE 13.3   *Using a dedicated router with its own DHCP relay agent.*

If a general-purpose computer does the routing, you can likewise run a DHCP relay agent program on each of your routers. It is becoming popular at some cost-sensitive sites to set up inexpensive Linux or NetBSD-based computers that start from a floppy or very small hard drive to act as dedicated routers. Starting up a DHCP relay agent on such a machine takes little additional effort and serves the same purpose as a built-in DHCP relay agent on a dedicated router. Figure 13.4 shows such a configuration.

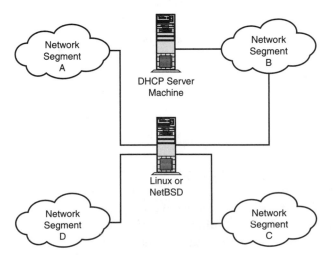

FIGURE 13.4   *Using an inexpensive PC running Linux or NetBSD for routing and DHCP relay.*

The Internet Software Consortium DHCP Relay Agent

The *Internet Software Consortium (ISC) DHCP relay agent* is a widely available relay agent that works on general-purpose computers. This program typically runs automatically at system startup. The IP addresses or domain names of the DHCP server or DHCP servers to which the relay agent should forward DHCP messages are specified on the command line as shown in Example 13.7.

EXAMPLE 13.7

```
dhcrelay dhcp.rc.isc.org
```

The Cisco DHCP Relay Agent

Most dedicated routers contain built-in DHCP relay agents, and each router must be configured differently. It is difficult to document every possible embedded router; for this book, Cisco routers are used as an example.

Cisco routers running Cisco IOS version 10.0 and later support DHCP relaying as part of a general mechanism for forwarding UDP broadcasts. Every interface on a Cisco router is declared using an interface declaration. Following the interface declaration for the interface connected to each network segment for which the network administrator wants to provide DHCP relaying, one or more IP helper-address statements must be written—one for each DHCP server to which DHCP packets will be relayed.

The Cisco IP helper-address statement unfortunately enables relaying of a number of UDP-based protocols by default. These include the Time Server (port 37), TACACS (port 49), DNS (port 53), DHCP/BOOTP (port 67 and 68), TFTP (port 69), NetBIOS Name Service (port 137), and NetBIOS Datagram Service (Port 138) protocols. It is a good idea to disable relaying of these protocols unless you want them relayed. The Cisco IP forward-protocol statement controls the relaying of UDP broadcast packets.

Example 13.8 shows how relaying is enabled on two interfaces to a single DHCP server at IP address 10.20.11.7 and how all UDP ports except for the DHCP ports are disabled.

EXAMPLE 13.8

```
no ip forward-protocol udp 37
no ip forward-protocol udp 49
no ip forward-protocol udp 53
no ip forward-protocol udp 69
no ip forward-protocol udp 137
no ip forward-protocol udp 138
```

```
ip forward-protocol udp 67
ip forward-protocol udp 68
interface ethernet 0
     ip address 10.20.11.1 255.255.255.0
interface ethernet 1
     ip address 10.20.12.1 255.255.255.0
     ip helper-address 10.20.11.7
interface ethernet 2
     ip address 10.20.13.1 255.255.255.0
     ip helper-address 10.20.11.7
```

In this example, three Ethernet interfaces are defined. The first is connected to subnet 10.20.11/24, which is the subnet that the DHCP server is also connected to. No IP helper-address statement exists for this interface because the DHCP server does not need relaying for its own subnet. The other two interfaces are connected to subnets 10.20.12/24 and 10.20.13/24, and both of these interface definitions include IP helper-address statements pointing to the DHCP server. The IP forward-protocol statements are outside of the interface definitions because they apply globally.

Other Embedded Relay Agents

Most dedicated routers come with DHCP relay agents. The documentation that comes with a router should state what is needed to configure it. If the documentation is not sufficient, contact the support group for the DHCP server. In all likelihood, someone else who is using that server is also using the same router and knows how to make it work. It is beyond the scope of this book to provide a complete list of such support groups; information on obtaining support can be found in the documentation accompanying most DHCP servers.

A DHCP Configuration for the ISC Office

The Internet Software Consortium (ISC) office is a modest affair—a small building with perhaps 20 offices, a machine room, and a testing lab hosted by Vixie Enterprises. Two network segments exist: the office network and the lab network. The DHCP server runs on a server on the office network, and a small, dedicated router with a built-in relay agent relays DHCP traffic from the lab network.

The isc.org domain is actually used only for publicly published machines—all the internal machines are in the rc.vix.com domain for the Redwood City, California, offices of Vixie Enterprises. Figure 13.5 shows a diagram of the network.

The ISC office has a pair of name servers: one running on bb.rc.vix.com, and one running on ib.rc.vix.com. These servers provide name service for the entire office—every DHCP client uses them, regardless of the network segment to which it is connected. The domain name for the entire office is rc.vix.com. Network Time Protocol (NTP) is also used quite heavily. The ISC's standard NTP server is clock.isc.org.

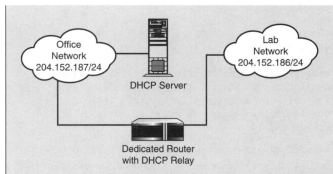

FIGURE 13.5 *The ISC office network.*

Because these options are the same regardless of the network segment to which a DHCP client is connected, they can be defined globally for all network segments. The global options are specified at the beginning of the file, before any subnet declarations, as Example 13.9 shows.

EXAMPLE 13.9

```
option domain-name-servers bb.rc.vix.com,
                           ib.rc.vix.com;
option domain-name "rc.vix.com";
option ntp-servers clock.isc.org;
```

The office network has a network number of 204.152.187.0 and a subnet mask of 255.255.255.0. The Cisco router, which routes to both the build lab network and the Internet, is connected at IP address 204.152.187.254. Example 13.10 shows the subnet declaration for the office network.

EXAMPLE 13.10

```
subnet 204.152.187.0 netmask 255.255.255.0 {
        range 204.152.187.200 204.152.187.239;
        option routers 204.152.187.254;
        option broadcast-address 204.152.187.255;
}
```

You may notice that for a subnet with 254 possible IP addresses, only 40 addresses are available to the DHCP server for dynamic allocation. This is because many computers with fixed addresses are on this network, and only relatively few computers—mostly laptops and desktops—are configured with DHCP.

The build lab network has a network number of 204.152.186.0 and a subnet mask of 255.255.255.0. It is routed through the same Cisco router, at IP address 204.152.186.254. Example 13.11 shows the subnet declaration, which looks very much like the one for the office network.

continues

continued

EXAMPLE 13.11

```
subnet 204.152.186.0 netmask 255.255.255.0 {
        range 204.152.186.20 204.152.186.30;
        option routers 204.152.186.254;
        option broadcast-address 204.152.186.255;
}
```

The difference in the address ranges reflects the fact that the build lab network contains many computers with fixed IP addresses running a variety of different operating systems. Unfortunately, none of them provide a DHCP client, and all of them must have permanently assigned IP addresses. It is quite rare for somebody to plug a DHCP-aware computer into the network, but a few addresses are kept available just in case.

A Cisco router connects the two networks. The router is configured using the Cisco IP helper-address and IP forward-protocol statements. Example 13.12 shows the relevant sections of the Cisco configuration file.

EXAMPLE 13.12

```
no ip forward-protocol udp 37
no ip forward-protocol udp 49
no ip forward-protocol udp 53
no ip forward-protocol udp 69
no ip forward-protocol udp 137
no ip forward-protocol udp 138
ip forward-protocol udp 67
ip forward-protocol udp 68
interface ethernet 0
        ip address 204.152.187.0 255.255.255.0
interface ethernet 1
        ip address 204.152.186.0 255.255.255.0
        ip helper-address 204.152.187.11
```

Example 13.13 shows the complete DHCP configuration file for the ISC Redwood City office.

EXAMPLE 13.13

```
option domain-name-servers bb.rc.vix.com,
                           ib.rc.vix.com;
option domain-name "rc.vix.com";
option ntp-servers clock.isc.org;
```

```
subnet 204.152.187.0 netmask 255.255.255.0 {
        range 204.152.187.200 204.152.187.239;
        option routers 204.152.187.254;
        option broadcast-address 204.152.187.255;
}

subnet 204.152.186.0 netmask 255.255.255.0 {
        range 204.152.186.20 204.152.186.30;
        option routers 204.152.186.254;
        option broadcast-address 204.152.186.255;
}
```

13.3 Multiple IP Subnets per Network Segment

It is very common to use the term *subnet* interchangeably with the term *network segment*. Both terms are defined as any set of network connections such that a computer plugged into any one connection can send packets to a computer plugged into any other connection without requiring the help of a router.

In fact, subnets are an artifact of the way IP addressing works. In order for IP routing to work, all machines on a given subnet must be on a single network segment. However, it is not required that only one subnet be configured on a single network segment.

Some sites take advantage of this as a way of allocating address space; when a network segment is first deployed, a single IP subnet is allocated for it. When all (or really most) IP addresses on that network segment have been consumed, the site administrator may allocate a second IP subnet to run on the same network segment.

The ISC DHCP server documentation refers to this kind of configuration as a *shared network* because one network segment is shared by two IP subnets. Another common term for this configuration is an *overlay network*. In the Microsoft DHCP server, subnets are referred to as *scopes*, and network segments with more than one subnet are referred to as *superscopes*.

Note

Except when referring specifically to Microsoft DHCP server menu options, the word scope is never used in this way in this book because it conflicts with the usual computer science meaning of the word scope, which is used quite heavily.

Such configurations exhibit some unexpected behaviors. For example, two computers connected to the same network segment but with IP addresses on different subnets cannot normally send packets to one another without the help of a router. In theory, the two machines should be able to transmit packets directly to each other at the physical network layer, but the IP protocol does not allow it

13.3.1 Address Allocation on Shared Networks

Because the network administrator defines IP subnets and assigns them to network segments, a client's subnet cannot be determined just by its network connection. The client is connected to a network segment on which any number of IP subnets may be configured.

Thus, when a request arrives from a client, the DHCP server must first determine the network segment from which the message was sent. If the client is requesting an existing address, the DHCP server can check the requested address to determine whether it is from any of the IP subnets assigned to the client's network segment. If so, and if the address is available for the client, the server can assign the client that address.

If a client is asking for a new address on its network segment, however, and there is more than one subnet from which to choose, nothing tells the DHCP server which subnet to use. The ISC DHCP server will normally pick the first available IP address from the list of available IP addresses for that network segment. That list could well contain addresses for any number of IP subnets. So, the choice of the subnet within a shared network on which the client gets its IP address is essentially arbitrary.

This can be inconvenient. If clients on different subnets must communicate through routers, then it is good to ensure that clients that might often communicate with one another wind up on the same subnet.

For instance, consider three departments (for example, accounting, sales, and marketing) using the same network segment. If you have allocated three IP subnets to that network segment, you would most likely want all the clients from sales to be located on the first subnet, all the clients from marketing to be on the second subnet, and all the clients from accounting on the third subnet. Chapter 17, "Conditional Behavior," discusses ways this can be done, but in general, it is so difficult to accomplish that it may simply not be worth it.

You can declare a shared network by enclosing a set of subnet statements within a shared-network statement, as Example 13.14 shows.

EXAMPLE 13.14

```
shared-network FLOOR1 {
        subnet 204.152.188.0 netmask 255.255.255.240 {
        }
        subnet 10.0.0.0 netmask 255.255.255.0 {
        }
}
```

This declaration defines two IP subnets, 204.152.188.0 and 10.0.0.0, which share a single network segment.

13.3.2 Option Scoping with Shared Networks

Although the process of selecting the subnet on a shared network on which a client will be assigned an address is somewhat arbitrary, after that subnet is selected, the client can be assigned parameters specific to the subnet. In many cases, this will be required. For example, each subnet must have its own default route and may have a different broadcast address. Options that are not globally defined for all subnets but that are common to all clients on a shared network can be declared within the shared-network statement, before the subnet statements, as Example 13.15 illustrates.

EXAMPLE 13.15

```
shared-network FLOOR1 {
        option domain-name-servers 204.152.188.10;

        subnet 204.152.188.0 netmask 255.255.255.240 {
            option routers 204.152.188.14;
        }
        subnet 10.0.0.0 netmask 255.255.255.0 {
            option routers 10.0.0.254;
        }
}
```

13.3.3 Avoiding Routing on a Shared-Network Segment

When a machine on one IP subnet wants to send a packet to a machine it has determined is on the same subnet, it acquires the link-layer address of the second machine and then sends the packet directly to that machine. This is done with the *Address Resolution Protocol(ARP)*.

Say a machine with address 10.0.0.1 wants to communicate with a machine with address 10.0.0.2. It broadcasts an ARP packet asking the question "Who has IP address 10.0.0.2?" The machine with that IP address replies: "I have 10.0.0.2, and my link-layer address is 08:00:2b:4c:29:3d." The machine at 10.0.0.1 then sends the packet directly to the machine at 10.0.0.2.

When a machine on one IP subnet wants to send packets to a machine on a different IP subnet, it chooses a router from its routing table. It then ARPs for the link-layer address of that router (routers in a computer's routing tables must always be on a subnet to which that computer is directly connected), and then sends the packet to the router. That router then sends the packet on toward its final destination. On a shared network, this means the packet is sent on the local network segment to the router, which then sends it back on the same network segment to the destination machine.

Proxy ARPing with Microsoft Windows 95

The IP implementation has a special mode, not specified by the IP protocol standard, which enables machines on one subnet on a shared-network segment to send packets directly to machines on a different subnet of that same segment. It does this by sending the client's own new IP address in the routers option. When Windows 95 sees that its default route points at its own IP address, it treats *all* IP addresses as if they are local—it never tries to send IP packets through a router. Example 13.16 shows how to make the ISC DHCP server send the client's IP address for its default route.

EXAMPLE 13.16

```
use-lease-addr-for-default-route on;
```

In Example 13.16, imagine that you have a Windows 95 computer whose IP address is 204.152.188.10 and whose default route points to its own IP address. If it wants to send a packet to a computer at 10.0.0.19, it broadcasts an ARP packet asking for the link-layer address corresponding to the IP address 10.0.0.19. Because 10.0.0.19 is on the same network segment, it receives a response from that machine, and then sends its packet directly to that machine without going through a router.

However, what if that same machine wants to send a packet to another machine at 204.152.186.112? That machine is *not* on the same network segment. When the first machine sends out an ARP request asking for the link-layer address of 204.152.186.112, it will receive no reply because ARP broadcasts are never routed off of a network segment.

This can be solved using a feature of many dedicated routers called *proxy ARP*. If a computer on the network to which the router is connected sends an ARP request asking for the link-layer address of a machine whose IP address is not on the same network segment, the router replies with its own link-layer address. This fools the ARPing machine into sending the off-network packet to the router, which then correctly forwards it to its final destination.

Note

This is not a good solution, of course. No standard exists for describing how to accomplish it; it is just a collection of ad-hoc solutions that various vendors have provided. In a very constricted, homogeneous environment, it might work well, but it will fail if machines from vendors that do not support it are installed.

In particular, if the DHCP server behavior is enabled, as in Example 13.16, then clients that do not support proxy ARP will receive an incorrect default route, and therefore cannot route packets off of their local network segment.

Proxy ARP also generates extra ARP traffic. Every time a machine must communicate with a new machine that is not on the local network segment, it must send another ARP packet. Normally, packets sent off the network segment are forwarded to the same router, whose link-layer address is cached, so it requires only one ARP request to get the link-layer address for all such machines.

13.3.4 Shared-Network Pitfalls

DHCP administrators commonly make the mistake of omitting necessary information when they first set up a shared-network configuration. For example, you may have a network segment with two IP subnets, and you intend to supply IP addresses for one subnet with one DHCP server and IP addresses for the other subnet with a second DHCP server. You may be tempted to just write a subnet declaration in each server's configuration file for the subnet that server is intended to serve and not mention the other subnet. The problem with this is that DHCP servers are responsible for telling DHCP clients whether their IP address is correct for a given network.

DHCPNAK **Wars**

Imagine that a DHCP client on this shared network broadcasts a DHCPDISCOVER packet. Both DHCP servers may respond with a DHCPOFFER packet, each offering an IP address on a different subnet. The client chooses one, and sends out a DHCPREQUEST for that IP address. The DHCP server whose address was not chosen sees that the requested address is not on the subnet that it knows is connected to the network segment on which the DHCPREQUEST was sent. So, it sends the client a DHCPNAK. If that DHCPNAK arrives before the other server's DHCPACK, the client will not get its address, and must start over. This DHCPNAK war can go on indefinitely.

If both servers know about both subnets, however, neither server will send DHCPNAK messages in response to DHCPREQUEST messages for IP addresses on the subnet being served by the other server. Clients can, therefore, be configured successfully.

If both DHCP servers are being used, it is possible to see what is happening by examining the server logs; if one or both of the servers are sending DHCPNAK messages in response to client requests that are correct, their configurations must be fixed. If one network administrator controls one of the DHCP servers and a second administrator controls the other, a network analyzer may be used to solve this problem. Chapter 23, "Debugging Problems with DHCP," discusses this in more detail.

Cable Modem Networks

Cable modem networks are broadcast networks, just like Ethernets. Most ISPs providing cable modem service use DHCP to perform address assignment on their networks. Some cable modem networks have extensive filtering so that you only see packets meant for your home. However, many cable modem networks are just big LANs, where you can see every packet sent to anybody on your network segment. This information also includes DHCP packets. If you set up a DHCP server but do not configure it carefully, it is likely that the server will see a DHCPREQUEST sent by your neighbor's machine down the street, deduce that the machine is asking for an IP address on the wrong network, and thus send it a DHCPNAK. Your neighbor will then be unable to use the Internet.

Private DHCP Server at the Office

You may also be tempted to set up a DHCP server at your office to serve your own set of clients on a subnet setup that just happens to run on the same network segment as your own workstation. Say, for example, that the network drop in your office connects to a network segment with a network number of 10.0.128.0 and a netmask of 255.255.255.0. Now, say you decide to set up a subnet for your own use on the same network segment with a network number you know is not in use—for instance, 10.192.0.0 with a netmask of 255.255.255.240. You configure your DHCP server as Example 13.17 illustrates.

EXAMPLE 13.17

```
subnet 10.192.0.0 netmask 255.255.255.240 {
        option domain-name-server 10.192.0.1;
        option routers 10.192.0.1;
        range 10.192.0.2 10.192.0.14;
}
```

The minute you turn on your network, your DHCP server starts listening for DHCP messages. The DHCP protocol doesn't generate much traffic on a typical network. After a DHCP client has its initial configuration, all further exchanges with the DHCP server are unicast, which means your DHCP server does not see requests from clients unless they are just starting out on the network. If you set up a server in this way, chances are the first DHCP request it sees from a computer other than your own will be the next morning, when computers that were powered down for the night are powered on again.

Configuration Hazards

Recently, a new ISC DHCP server user (call him Persona N. Grata) set up a server configured just this way, went home, and came back the next day to find that nobody could get onto the network, and the system administration staff could not figure out why.

The system administration staff didn't know about the other DHCP server. When they looked at their own server logs, they saw a perfectly normal sequence of events. A DHCP client turned on when its user arrived in the morning, broadcast a DHCPPRE-QUEST message, and the DHCP server sent back a DHCPACK. Unfortunately, what the system administrators did not see in their server's log was the DHCPNAK message Mr. Grata's DHCP server sent whenever it saw these clearly erroneous requests for IP addresses on the 10.0.128.0 subnet.

Mr. Grata had no idea he was causing the problem; indeed, Ted Lemon only figured it out because Mr. Grata sent a message to the ISC DHCP mailing list, reporting some unrelated trouble that he was having with his client. The message happened to mention the circumstances under which the server was installed and the fact that his work network was down. Ted was able to guess why Mr. Grata's network was "down" and suggest a fix.

The lesson here is that when setting up a server such as this, the configuration in Example 13.18 is preferable, even though it mentions a network for which your DHCP server should never be providing IP addresses.

EXAMPLE 13.18

```
shared-network MY-OFFICE {

not authoritative;

    subnet 10.192.0.0 netmask 255.255.255.240 {
      option domain-name-server 10.192.0.1;
      option routers 10.192.0.1;
      range 10.192.0.2 10.192.0.14;
    }
}
```

continues

Mr. Grata configured his DHCP server so that it believed it knew the configuration of the network to which it was attached, when in fact it knew only about the private sub-net Mr. Grata wanted to set up. Unfortunately, other DHCP clients were connected to the same network segment as Mr. Grata's workstation and used the officially sup-ported DHCP server to obtain their IP addresses. Whenever these clients sent DHCPREQUEST packets asking for IP addresses on the official subnet, Mr. Grata's server decided that these DHCPREQUEST packets were invalid, and responded with DHCPNAK packets. Because the server Mr. Grata set up was faster than the primary DHCP server for the network, clients could not get IP addresses—they were always stopped halfway through the process.

By adding the not authoritative directive to the shared-network declaration, the DHCP server is told that the shared-network declaration is not complete. This prevents the DHCP server from aggressively sending DHCPNAK packets when it sees DHCPREQUEST packets for IP addresses on networks it does not know about.

In version 3.0 of the ISC DHCP server, the server assumes it is not authoritative for any network—it must be explicitly told to send DHCPNAKS whenever it sees an address that doesn't belong. Without this behavior, DHCP clients moving from network to net-work will not detect that they have moved until their leases expire. When setting up an official DHCP server without knowing the layout of the network, always specify the authoritative directive.

One last problem exists with the configuration shown in Example 13.18. It declares a range of addresses for dynamic allocation. Any client attached to the MY-OFFICE shared network will be offered an address on the 10.192.0.0 subnet, even if it doesn't belong to Mr. Grata. The solution to this is for Mr. Grata to explicitly specify to which clients IP addresses may be assigned. Chapter 14 demonstrates this in more detail.

If you are not the network administrator for a given network segment, the pre-ceding example demonstrates why it is not a good idea to set up a DHCP server for yourself on that segment. Even if you set up your server as shown in Example 13.18, you still run the risk that the official DHCP server will NAK *your* DHCP clients when they get addresses from your DHCP server. Also, it is not guaranteed that you will be able to choose an address range that is really avail-able and will remain so, unless you acquire it from your network administrator or from the IANA.

Finding Unauthorized DHCP Servers

But what if you are the network administrator for a network segment, and users start complaining that they are being denied access to the network? What if you look in your server log for a particular user's machine, and you see a completely normal start sequence? It may be time to break out a network analyzer and look for unauthorized or otherwise misbehaving DHCP servers. Chapter 24 discusses this in greater detail.

Summary

To configure a DHCP server, the network administrator must describe to the server all the network segments for which it is to provide DHCP service. The server must also be configured with a set of options to send to clients so that the clients can operate on the network, and it must be provided with IP addresses on each network segment so that it can allocate IP addresses for clients.

If the DHCP server is managing more than one network segment, the network infrastructure must be configured to deliver requests from every network segment to the server. You can configure your network either by attaching the DHCP server to every network segment it supports, or by setting up DHCP relay agents on all the network segments to which the DHCP server isn't directly attached.

You can configure more than one IP subnet on each network segment, and you can configure the DHCP server to provide addresses on each of those subnets as well as to provide different parameters for different subnets. If a DHCP server is set up on a network segment but does not have authoritative information about the network configuration, the DHCP server must be configured not to send inappropriate DHCPNAKs.

The next few chapters talk about how to refine and customize this configuration to meet site-specific needs.

## CHAPTER 14

Client Identification and Fixed Address
Allocation

Chapter 13, "Configuring a DHCP Server," describes how to set up a simple
DHCP server configuration in which all addresses are allocated dynamically.
This chapter describes how the DHCP server associates a lease with a particu-
lar client, and how to

- Assign a client a static IP address, either manually or automatically

- Mix both static and dynamic IP address allocation on the same network

- Control access to the DHCP server's resources based on each client's
  identification

14.1 Identifying Clients

For the DHCP server to track the association of a lease to a particular DHCP
client, it must be able to uniquely identify that client. This is true even for
dynamic allocation, described in Chapter 13. If you want to control the server's
behavior with respect to particular clients, you must know how clients are
identified.

A DHCP client can identify itself to a server in two ways.

1. First, the client may use the `dhcp-client-identifier` option to send an arbitrary name for itself to the server.

2. Second, if the client does not use the `dhcp-client-identifier` option, then the server uses the client's link-layer address from the hardware address field of the DHCP packet to identify the client.

The remainder of this section discusses these two ways of identifying a client.

14.1.1 The `client identifier` Option

DHCP specifies an option, the `dhcp-client-identifier`, which is used to uniquely identify clients. DHCP clients are expected to send this identifier whenever they communicate with the server. The protocol enables a client to send this option when it first contacts a server and requires that if it uses the option once, it must continue to use it thereafter. If a client chooses to send this option, the server can use it to differentiate between clients.

Client Identifier Problems

Some problems with client identifiers do exist. First, although the protocol requires that they be unique on any given network segment, no mechanism is defined for ensuring that this is the case. RFC2132 recommends that the DHCP client identifier consist of a network hardware type and the client's link-layer address but permits it to have any value. With some DHCP clients (for example, Apple's OpenTransport client and the ISC client), users can configure the client identifier themselves. If a user assigns the same identifier to two clients, a collision can occur—the DHCP server treats both clients as if they are the same. The protocol provides no mechanism for preventing this. It is simply up to the user to ensure that *collisions* (the use of the same identification for two or more different clients) do not occur.

Problems with Using the Link-Layer Address as a Unique Identifier

Most DHCP clients follow RFC2132's recommendation with respect to choosing client identifiers. This can have some negative consequences, however. Several sites at which the ISC DHCP server is deployed have invested in laptop computers for users (for example, for salespeople or faculty). These users connect to the network through dial-up links part of the time, and plug their laptop computers into docking stations with built-in Ethernet adapters when they are onsite.

Because the Ethernet adapter is built into the docking station, the client identifier is unique to the docking station, not to the laptop inserted into it. As docking stations are expensive, and these users are not usually all onsite at once, docking stations are considered to be interchangeable—a user plugs a laptop computer into whatever docking station happens not to be in use. Unfortunately, this means the client identifier for that laptop computer changes each time the user inserts it into a docking station.

Sites can avoid this problem by configuring their DHCP clients to send a client identifier that is not based on the link-layer address. To do this, the user must manually configure a client identifier. Unfortunately, the Microsoft Windows 95 and Windows 98 DHCP clients do not provide this capability. So, some sites made nonstandard modifications to their DHCP servers to use the host name option as a client identifier. These modifications are discussed in detail later in this chapter.

Example 14.1 shows how to specify to the DHCP server the client identifier for a particular client when that client uses its network hardware type and link-layer address to construct the dhcp-client-identifier option it sends. The Microsoft Windows 95 and Windows 98 DHCP clients generate their client identifiers from their link-layer addresses. In the example, the hardware type is 1, for Ethernet, and the remaining six hexadecimal digits following the 1 are the Ethernet address.

EXAMPLE 14.1

```
option dhcp-client-identifier 1:8:0:2b:4c:72:17;
```

Example 14.2 shows how to configure a DHCP server with a client identifier when the client identifier is an ASCII text string.

EXAMPLE 14.2

```
option dhcp-client-identifier "joe's computer";
```

14.1.2 Using the Link-Layer Address as an Identifier

RFC2131 does not require that the client send a dhcp-client-identifier option. Some DHCP clients, such as version 2 of the ISC client, choose not to send the dhcp-client-identifier option. When the server does not find a dhcp-client-identifier option in a request from a client, it uses the client's network hardware type and link-layer address instead.

Example 14.3 shows how you can configure a DHCP server with a client's link-layer address and network hardware type when the client is identified through its link-layer address. For comparison, Example 14.3 illustrates the identification of the same client as in Example 14.1.

EXAMPLE 14.3

```
hardware ethernet 8:0:2b:4c:72:17;
```

Notice that in Example 14.1, the network hardware type is specified as the number 1, but in Example 14.3, it is specified as the name of the type of network hardware (ethernet).

14.1.3 How the DHCP Server Identifies Clients

Because all clients send their link-layer address and network hardware type but not their dhcp-client-identifier option, the server must choose one of the forms of identification.

When a client is initially allocated an address, the server creates an entry in its database for the client. The entry includes the link-layer address identification and the dhcp-client-identifier option, if supplied. If a lease is recorded that has a link-layer address and a client identifier, the ISC server ignores the link-layer address. This enables a client with the same link-layer address to acquire more than one IP address.

This could happen in a number of ways. The most common way occurs when a user's computer is configured to start up two or more different operating systems, both of which obtain their IP address using a DHCP client. If both DHCP clients send the same identification information, the computer has the same IP address regardless of the operating system it is running. This may be advantageous in some cases and disadvantageous in others.

For example, if the system is configured so that it can start up either Linux or Windows 98, when it is running Linux it might actually be configured to provide some network services. Those services are unavailable when it runs Windows. To avoid the appearance that the machine is connected to the network and running Linux, you may want to arrange for the Linux DHCP client to get a different IP address than the Windows 98 DHCP client.

To prevent both DHCP clients from getting the same IP address, simply configure either the Linux or Windows 95 client to send a different client identifier. For example, if the computer uses the ISC DHCP client to get its IP address when it runs Linux, the statement in Example 14.4 configures the Linux client with a different client identifier.

EXAMPLE 14.4

```
send dhcp-client-identifier "my-linux-box";
```

14.1.4 Choices in Specifying Client Identification

The preceding section describes how to configure the DHCP client so that the server will allocate addresses dynamically and assign a different IP address depending on which operating system is running on the computer. However, if static address allocation is performed, the network administrator must also configure the DHCP server to work with the identification information the user configured into the DHCP clients.

The Microsoft DHCP client chooses a client identifier consisting of the network hardware type followed by the link-layer address. If the link-layer address is 0:a0:4c:2b:e9:ac, and the network hardware type is ethernet (1), and if the Linux client is configured to send the text string my-linux-box as its client identifier, the two host declarations given in Example 14.5 match the Windows and Linux clients, respectively.

EXAMPLE 14.5

```
host ardmore-win95 {
  option dhcp-client-identifier 1:a0:4c:2b:e9:ac;
}
host ardmore-linux {
  option dhcp-client-identifier "my-linux-box";
}
```

Problems occurring when DHCP users choose their own client identifiers are discussed later in this chapter.

Nonstandard Means of Identifying Clients

At the time of this writing, administrators at a number of sites decided that neither the link-layer address nor the client identifier option is a viable way of identifying clients. Instead, they chose to implement nonstandard solutions based on the known behavior of the Microsoft DHCP clients.

Users cannot easily configure Microsoft DHCP clients to send a client identifier other than one formed from the link-layer address. They do send a host name option (12) in every request, however. Users can configure this easily using the Identification section of the Network Setup dialog box.

continues

continued

To avoid collisions, the host name the user supplies must be unique on networks on which the client is used. As with the client identifier, no protocol exists to ensure that the name chosen is unique—it is necessary to trust the user to arrange for this.

Some sites using nonstandard client identification use the host name the client supplies in preference to the client identifier. This involves customizing the DHCP server. Several sites have customized the ISC DHCP server in this

way. One major ISP specializing in cable modem and DSL service is using a customized DHCP server from another vendor in the same way.

This nonstandard use does (to some extent) solve the docking station problem described earlier. However, it works only with Microsoft DHCP clients; clients that do not send a host name option are identified by their client identifier, or possibly not at all. In addition, the potential for client name collisions can be a major problem.

14.1.5 Client Identification Name Collisions

As previously discussed, two clients can have the same identification. If the identification is a user-supplied text string (for example, a host name), a collision occurs when two users choose the same name. For example, if *The Lord of the Rings* (a popular fantasy trilogy) has a lot of fans at any given site, several users may choose the name *Gandalf* for their computer.

Using the client's link-layer address as an identifier mitigates this name collision problem; link-layer addresses are usually guaranteed unique, at least to a particular machine, if not to a particular network interface. Even if the link-layer address is used, however, it is possible to run into trouble because you can change the link-layer address on many network adapters and workstations with per-workstation link-layer addresses. For instance, an Ethernet adapter that was widely used at a particular site had a device driver bug that caused its Ethernet Mac address to reset to all zeros. Whenever two cards entered this state at the same time, it caused serious confusion.

When a collision occurs between the identification of two clients, the DHCP server thinks both clients are in fact the same. If one client is connected to the network and sends a DHCPDISCOVER message with its identification: *gandalf*, the DHCP server allocates an address (for example 10.240.17.7) and sends a DHCPOFFER, to which the client responds with a DHCPREQUEST. The server then sends a DHCPACK, and the client begins using its new address.

However, if a different client with the same identification tries to obtain an address—by sending a DHCPDISCOVER with its identification *gandalf*—the DHCP server looks up *gandalf*, finds an entry for the first client that started up with that identifier, and, not knowing any better, sends a DHCPOFFER with the same address, 10.240.17.7. The client accepts the address, binds to it, and begins using it, at which point both clients receive packets intended for each other, and the users of the two computers begin experiencing seemingly random unreliability in their network service.

Collision Detection

Chapter 8, "DHCP Message Exchanges," explains how a DHCP server probes an address with an *ICMP echo request* to detect if it is about to assign an address that is already in use. Chapter 8 also discusses how a DHCP client checks for collisions with its newly assigned address using the *Address Resolution Protocol (ARP)*. These two collision detection mechanisms are intended to detect situations in which a computer that does not have a valid lease from the DHCP server is nonetheless using an IP address the DHCP server believes belongs to it. In this situation, no collision occurs between the identification of two clients. The DHCP server notifies the administrator of the conflict and then stops using the IP address in question.

When a client identification collision occurs, these strategies do not help because the assumption upon which they are based is not valid.

When a DHCP server notices that an IP address it thinks is not in use is, in fact, in use, it generally marks that address as abandoned—that is, it is no longer available for assignment—and tries to allocate it a different address. If a client later specifically requests the abandoned address in a DHCPPREQUEST message, the ISC DHC server assumes the address was abandoned because the client incorrectly responded to an ICMP echo request when it should not

have, so it gives the client that address. At that time, it notices the other address the client supposedly holds, and because one client cannot hold two leases on the same subnet at the same time, it frees the "unused" address for allocation to a different client.

When the second client tries to renew its lease, the ISC server renews it if the address is still available. It may try to allocate the address to a different client, notice the second client is using it, and abandon it. In either case, both clients may appear to function normally, but the network administrator may see a lot of warning messages from the server. If either client is powered down or nonresponsive at any time, users may experience inexplicable interruptions in network service, or clients may cause the server to abandon all the free addresses in its allocation pool for the network segment.

The IETF DHC working group discussed devising a "universally unique client identifier," but for now, you can avoid this situation in three ways:

- Do not use user-defined client identifiers.

- Offer a strong education program for new users that teaches them how to avoid this situation.

- Handle collisions when they occur, assuming they will not occur very often.

14.2 Static Allocation

Now that you know how the DHCP server identifies clients and how you can identify clients to it, it is time to discuss static IP address allocation (the Microsoft DHCP server uses the term *reservation* instead of *static IP address allocation*).

In static allocation with DHCP, the server administrator maintains a list of known DHCP client identification information, and assigns an IP address (or possibly more than one IP address, if the client can roam from network to network) for each client thus identified. Static IP address assignments are not permanent—the server still leases the IP address to the client for a limited time, which the network administrator can specify. Chapter 16, "Tuning Your DHCP Service," discusses this in greater detail.

Completely static address allocation is surprisingly prevalent, considering how much extra work it involves. The most common reason people give when asked why they use static IP address allocation is that the network administrator (or, often, management) at a site wants to control which clients have access to the network. This can seem natural at sites performing static IP address allocation without the help of a DHCP server, and switching to the DHCP server can save quite a bit of work, even though the protocol's full labor-saving capabilities are not exploited.

When a client tries obtaining a lease, the DHCP server looks it up in the list of clients the administrator provides. If the server finds an entry for the client, it sees whether any of the IP addresses provided are appropriate for the network to which the client is connected. If it finds an appropriate address, it assigns it to the client.

If you have configured the DHCP server to perform only static address assignment and the server does not find an appropriate address for the client, it simply does not respond to the client's requests. Exceptions do exist, however; if the client sends a DHCPREQUEST for an address that the server knows is invalid for the network segment to which the client is connected, the server always responds with a DHCPNAK. The server also sends a DHCPNAK if the requested address is known to the DHCP server and is not available for the client. If the server finds an appropriate address for the client, it offers that address to the client.

Consider an example of how static allocation works. Dave Weiner is the vice president of network operations for WebMasters, Inc., a small company producing customized web pages and providing Internet hosting services. On some days, he works in his home office, where he has a small 10BASE-T Ethernet network to which five computers running Linux and Windows are connected. The network is connected to the Internet through an ISDN link.

Dave runs the ISC DHCP server on a RedHat Linux 5.1 system. Example 14.6 shows his configuration file.

EXAMPLE 14.6

```
option domain-name "webmast.com";

option domain-name-servers 10.140.171.8, 10.136.226.8,
                            10.152.193.2, 10.152.193.2;
subnet 10.152.204.64 netmask 255.255.255.240 {
  option routers 10.152.204.65;
  option broadcast-address 10.152.204.79;
  option netbios-name-servers 10.152.204.65;
}
host DW1.webmast.com {
    fixed-address 10.152.204.66;
    hardware ethernet 00:20:78:11:F9:14;
}
host DW2.webmast.com {
    fixed-address 10.152.204.67;
    hardware ethernet 00:C0:6D:16:68:A2;
}
host DW3.webmast.com {
    fixed-address 10.152.204.68;
    hardware ethernet 00:60:67:2D:20:81;
}
host DW4.webmast.com {
    fixed-address 10.152.204.69;
    hardware ethernet 00:40:05:37:6b:c8;
}
```

As you can see in this example, Dave defined a few global options to send to clients, wrote a subnet definition for his home office subnet, and wrote a host declaration for each client that he uses on his network. Dave used the link-layer address as a client identifier rather than the DHCP client identifier.

14.3 Mixing Static and Dynamic Allocation

It is common for a site to define fixed IP addresses for its DHCP clients that are not mobile, or are otherwise known to the network administrator, and still enable dynamic addressing for clients that are mobile, or are not known to the network administrator. To do this, simply supply a range of IP addresses in each subnet declaration for subnets on which IP addresses will be allocated.

The configuration file in the previous example does not support dynamic IP address assignment. In fact, when visitors to Dave's home office want to use their laptop computers, or when he must test new equipment, he configures his DHCP server to provide automatic address assignments. Example 14.7 shows the actual subnet statement from Dave's configuration.

EXAMPLE 14.7

```
subnet 10.152.204.64 netmask 255.255.255.240 {
  range 10.152.204.70 10.152.204.74;
  option routers 10.152.204.65;
  option broadcast-address 10.152.204.79;
  option netbios-name-servers 10.152.204.65;
}
```

When a client broadcasts a DHCPDISCOVER packet on Dave's home office network, the DHCP server there first tries to match the client identification information to one of the host entries he defined in his DHCP configuration. If the client's identification matches one of these entries, the DHCP server uses that entry to determine what address to send the client.

If the client's identification does not match one of these entries, the DHCP server allocates an IP address from the list of available leases on the network, and offers that IP address to the client.

14.3.1 Moving a Client from Dynamic to Static Address Allocation

Some sites may want to register clients by enabling them to obtain dynamic leases, extracting the client identification information from the lease database and creating a static address allocation for each client. Chapter 18, "Automatic Client Registration," demonstrates how to automate this process. This chapter uses a simple case to describe how to convert a client from dynamic to static allocation by simply hand-editing the configuration file.

The ISC DHCP server stores leases in an unstructured text file providing a history of all lease assignments during server operation.

Each lease is stored as a `lease` statement, and the last lease statement in the file for any given IP address is the most current lease for that IP address. Imagine that Dave just bought a new computer and plugged it into his network for the first time. When it receives an address, the lease is logged in the `dhcpd.leases` file (Chapter 13 explains how to find out where the ISC DHCP server stores the `dhcpd.leases` file). Example 14.8 shows what the client's lease entry may look like.

EXAMPLE 14.8

```
lease 10.152.204.70 {
  starts 3 1999/03/10 00:34:38;
  ends 3 1999/03/10 00:40:38;
  hardware ethernet 08:00:2b:81:65:56;
  uid 63:73:30:3a:6d:61:69:6e;
}
```

In a `lease` statement, the `dhcp-client-identifier` option is stored using the `uid` keyword. In Example 14.8, the DHCP client sends a client identifier option that is not derived from the client's link-layer address. Translated into ASCII, the hexadecimal shown in the example spells out `cs0-main`. If Dave wants to turn this lease entry into a fixed allocation, he writes a host declaration such as the one in Example 14.9.

EXAMPLE 14.9

```
host cs0-main {
  option dhcp-client-identifier 63:73:30:3a:6d:61:69:6e;
  fixed-address 10.152.204.75;
}
```

Notice that Dave does not include a `hardware` statement because the `dhcp-client-identifier` option statement supersedes it. He also does not enter the ASCII client identifier as a text string. Instead, he copies the hexadecimal from the `lease` statement. Either choice is perfectly valid.

Dave could have followed his usual policy of using the link-layer address as a client identifier. In this case, because the client identifier option always supersedes the `hardware` statement, he would also delete the client's lease from the lease database file. Example 14.10 shows what the host declaration looks like using the `hardware` statement.

EXAMPLE 14.10

```
host cs0-main {
  hardware ethernet 08:00:2b:81:65:56;
  fixed-address 10.152.204.75;
}
```

After the static entry for a host is set up, the DHCP server must be told about the new information. Normally, you do this by terminating the DHCP server process and restarting it. When the server restarts, it rereads the dhcpd.conf file and the dhcpd.leases file and picks up the new host declaration. If the dhcpd.leases file must be modified, you should stop the server *before* it is modified and not restart it until the modification is complete.

After the DHCP server reads the host declaration for the client, the DHCP client attempts to renew its lease. Remember that although the server was told about the client's fixed address, the client is still unaware that anything changed. So it sends a DHCPREQUEST to the server asking for the renewal of its old dynamically assigned address.

When the ISC DHCP server finds the host declaration for the client, it assumes the declared IP address is the one the network administrator wants the client to have. So, it does not renew the client's lease. Indeed, if it can, it sends a DHCPNAK, forcing the DHCP client to immediately try to obtain a new IP address. If it cannot, the client runs to the end of its lease without getting a renewal. After the lease expires, the client automatically obtains the new IP address.

However the client gets to the INIT (reinitializing) state, it broadcasts a DHCPDISCOVER packet. The server looks for a matching host entry, finds it, and sends the fixed IP address in that entry to the client, at which point the client has its permanent address.

14.3.2 Converting a DHCP Server from Static to Dynamic Allocation

The ISC DHCP server assumes that statically allocated IP addresses are allocated permanently so that it doesn't actually record lease entries for such addresses. Instead, it assumes that the static entry will be available the next time the client contacts the server—when it must renew the lease. This can cause problems for sites that decide they want to convert from static to dynamic address allocation.

When requests are received for help from people who were performing such a conversion, two main problems exist

- Moving formerly fixed addresses into a dynamic pool

- Getting clients to take dynamic address allocations after their static allocations are deleted

Problems with Moving Static Addresses to a Dynamic Pool

When you move statically assigned IP addresses into a dynamic pool, the server does not know when statically assigned leases expire. When you delete the static assignment from the server's configuration file, it forgets that assignment existed. The client, on the other hand, is probably still using the address. Therefore, there is always a period between the time when the client thinks it is entitled to use its static IP address, but the server is not aware of it.

If the client extends the lease on its address before the server tries to assign it to another client, this is not a problem. However, if the server tries to allocate the lease to another client before the old client renews its lease, the server will most likely abandon the lease. At a minimum, this generates an unexpected warning message to the server administrator. In a worst-case scenario, one or both clients may have trouble using the network until the conflict is resolved.

The easiest way to avoid this conflict is to remove the static IP address assignment but not put that address back into the pool for allocation, until you are certain that any lease the client is holding has expired. After you are certain the client lease has expired, you can add the address to the pool of available addresses. The network administrator can configure a default maximum lease length into the DHCP server—if the network administrator does not do this, the default is 1 day on the ISC DHCP server and 3 days on the Microsoft server. After removing the entry, simply wait for that amount of time before reusing that IP address. Of course, you can also contact the owner of the machine and ask him or her to release the lease.

Problems Getting a Client to Accept a New Address

Some older DHCP clients do not accept a different address than the one they are bound to unless the DHCP server tells them the address they have is no longer valid by sending them a DHCPNAK. If the static IP address allocation is deleted for a client, the server simply ignores renewal requests from the client until the client goes back into the INIT state, at which point the server offers the client a new IP address. The client does not take this new address because it wants the old address and did not receive a DHCPNAK. Thus, it continues to send DHCPDISCOVER messages indefinitely.

The ISC DHCP server sends a DHCPNAK to a client trying to get an address belonging to a different client. To create a situation in which DHCPNAKs are generated, you may want to modify the client identification information on static assignments you are converting so that the identification does not match a real client. When a client whose static assignment is doctored in this way tries to renew its lease, the server sends it a DHCPNAK message, at which point it always gives up that IP address and returns to the INIT state.

14.4 Automatic Allocation

In some cases, you may want the benefits of static address allocation without the costs; that is, you may want clients to have permanent, fixed IP addresses, but you do not want to configure them into the DHCP server. DHCP defines an address allocation strategy that enables automatic allocation of static addresses. RFC2131 refers to this mode as *automatic allocation*.

When a client first sends a DHCPDISCOVER on a network segment, the server allocates it a lease from an address range, just as in dynamic allocation. However, instead of offering a limited lease, the server offers an unlimited lease. DHCP specifies that a lease interval of 4294967295 (FFFFFFFF$_{16}$) must be treated as having an infinite duration—the lease never expires.

Until the 3.0 release, the ISC DHCP server did not explicitly support this mode. However, in version 3.0, the "unlimited" keyword was added, enabling leases to be specified as unlimited. The DHCP server does not expire an unlimited lease, which means that an unlimited lease has the same effect as a static IP address allocation does. Chapter 16 explains how to declare unlimited leases.

14.5 Access Control

In addition to identifying DHCP clients and assigning fixed addresses to them, you may want to identify clients for other reasons. For instance, some sites want to control access to leases the DHCP server supplies. Even though these sites may support dynamic IP address allocation, they do not want to allocate IP addresses to clients the network administrators do not know. Some sites may want to group clients in some way—for example, allocating IP addresses for known clients on a particular network segment on one subnet, and allocating IP addresses for unknown clients on the same network segment from a different subnet. Chapter 17, "Conditional Behavior," explains this second scenario in more detail.

If you want to set up a DHCP server that provides IP addresses only to clients it knows, write host declarations for all known hosts, but do not specify fixed addresses for those hosts. Then configure the DHCP server not to provide IP addresses to unknown clients. Example 14.11 shows a simple server configuration file that limits access to the DHCP server to those clients for which host entries exist, and allocates addresses dynamically. This works whether the client stays in the same location or moves from network segment to network segment.

EXAMPLE 14.11

```
deny unknown-clients;
option domain-name "acl.example.com";
subnet 10.227.94.0 netmask 255.255.255.0 {
  range 10.227.94.2 10.227.94.253;
  option routers 10.227.94.254;
  option domain-name-servers 10.227.94.1;
  option broadcast-address 10.227.94.255;
}
host blaznorf {
  hardware ethernet 00:2b:5c:e9:ad:11;
}
host gzarond {
  hardware ethernet 00:e9:ac:22:08:ee;
}
```

In Example 14.11, the `deny unknown-clients` statement causes the DHCP server to ignore requests from clients it does not recognize. The `subnet` declaration provides a set of addresses to allocate and some options to send, and the two `host` declarations define the two DHCP clients with which the server is willing to communicate. Most DHCP server configurations of this type define more than two hosts, of course.

The ISC DHCP server also enables you to deny access to specific clients. You may want to provide general access to clients without a registration process, but you may not want to assign addresses to some DHCP clients. Revisiting Dave Weiner's home network again (shown in Examples 14.6 and 14.7), suppose Dave has a networked printer he wants to use, but he does not want it to have an IP address; he wants it to be accessible only through AppleTalk (EtherTalk). He can set up a host declaration for that printer (as shown in Example 14.12), and it will never get an IP address.

EXAMPLE 14.12

```
host laserwriter {
  option dhcp-client-identifier "treekiller";
  deny booting;
}
```

Unfortunately, using DHCP, you cannot get the printer to stop requesting an address. However, you can prevent the server from giving it one.

> **Note**
>
> *Access control is not synonymous with authentication. As mentioned previously, some DHCP clients can be reconfigured with different client identifiers. It is also possible with almost any network adapter to supply a link-layer address other than the one assigned to that adapter. This means you can set up access controls based on the DHCP client identifier or the client's link-layer address, but you still must trust that the client is telling the truth—a malicious client can easily fool the DHCP server.*
>
> *The DHCP authentication protocol, described in Chapter 21, "DHCP Authentication," provides a way in which you can actually authenticate the client's identification. Using this protocol, you can ensure that malicious clients do not masquerade as legitimate clients. However, even with authentication and access control, you still cannot prevent unauthorized users from simply picking an address they know is not in use at the moment and using it.*
>
> *Chapter 21 discusses how to enforce real network access control using the DHCP server.*

Summary

The DHCP server must uniquely identify DHCP clients, and it does so using the `dhcp-client-identifier` option, the client's link-layer address, or a nonstandard mechanism. If the mechanism does not guarantee the uniqueness of the identifier, conflicts can occur. DHCP does not provide a way to deal with these conflicts; it simply mandates that clients' identifications must be unique.

In a process called static address allocation, you can configure DHCP servers with user-supplied mappings between IP addresses and client identification. You also can configure servers to automatically make permanent assignments between IP addresses and client identification in a process called automatic address allocation. Plus, you can configure servers to perform a combination of static and dynamic address allocation.

In addition to using the client's identification as a key to its IP address, you may also configure DHCP servers to enable or deny access to leases using the client's identification, although without an authentication mechanism, this capability is not considered reliable.

## CHAPTER 15

Setting Up a Reliable DHCP Service

As discussed in Chapter 1, "An Introduction to DHCP," loss of DHCP service can be a major problem if you depend on such service for automated management of IP addresses and computer configurations. If a client can't access DHCP service, it can't obtain a new address or extend the lease on an address it already has. Thus, when DHCP service is unavailable, new computers and computers that move to new network segments may be unable to use network services, although computers with existing leases on IP addresses will be unable to use the network when those leases expire. Applications running on computers that depend on network service will also be disrupted.

This chapter discusses specific ways in which the DHCP service might fail and presents solutions for those failure modes. It also describes some more general DHCP service implementations that provide additional reliability through redundant DHCP servers.

15.1 Determining Your Level of DHCP Service Reliability

Before deciding on an implementation strategy for providing reliable DHCP service, it is appropriate to review how a loss of DHCP service will affect you and to determine the appropriate level of reliability for your organization and network infrastructure. The loss of DHCP service has two major effects. DHCP clients are unable to obtain new addresses, and they are unable to extend leases on addresses previously assigned through DHCP.

15.1.1 Effects of Loss of Service

In many circumstances, the loss of DHCP service does not immediately affect most DHCP clients and network users and, in fact, may be less disruptive in the short run than the loss of DNS or network file services. DNS service is used with every new connection that requires resolution of a DNS name, so loss of DNS service is immediately obvious to users. On the other hand, a DHCP client that was assigned an address will continue to function normally, and won't attempt to contact the DHCP server until half the duration of its lease expires. Even after it begins to request an extension on its lease, the DHCP client will continue to use its address. Only if the DHCP service is still unavailable when the lease actually expires must the DHCP client stop using its address and terminate network connections.

DHCP clients that restart while DHCP service is unavailable simply continue to use their previously assigned addresses until their leases expire. As long as a client's IP address is still appropriate for the network segment to which it is connected—that is, the client hasn't moved to a new network segment, or the network segment hasn't been assigned a new network number—the client can use its old address. The client notices the loss of DHCP service only when its lease actually expires.

Of course, clients that require DHCP service cannot access the network until such service is restored. If you administer a network to which laptop computers are frequently connected and disconnected, or if clients that you support request a short lease duration, many of your clients may be quickly affected by the loss of DHCP service. And, unfortunately, this loss of service may cause DHCP clients to fail in ways that your end users may not understand (and may not be patient about!). Different DHCP clients react in different ways when they cannot contact a DHCP server. In many cases, the user experiences long startup times while the DHCP client attempts to contact the DHCP server, along with unexplained loss of network access.

Note

Recent DHCP clients from Microsoft and Apple have an additional feature that may cause confusion when DHCP service is unavailable. If these clients cannot contact a DHCP server, they pick an address from a range of addresses that are reserved for auto-configuration. Unfortunately, a computer that performs this auto-configuration appears to be operating normally, but in effect it is using a IP address that cannot be used to reach destination computers not connected to its local network segment. The user has no indication of network initialization failure, but cannot access network services. A DHCP client that performs auto-configuration assigns itself an IP address on the 169.254.0.0/16 network. This mechanism for auto-configuration is currently documented as an Internet Draft, "Automatically Choosing an IP Address in an Ad-Hoc IPv4 Network," and is available at `draft-ietf-dhc-ipv4-autoconfig-04.txt`.

Because of the potential problems this auto-configuration mechanism may cause, the DHC working group developed a DHCP option that controls the use of auto-configuration in DHCP clients. This option, described in RFC2563, "DHCP Option to Disable Stateless Auto-Configuration in IPv4 Clients," enables a network administrator to turn off the use of auto-configuration in DHCP clients through DHCPOFFER *messages.*

You must determine your own requirements for the reliability of your DHCP service based on the ways in which your clients access your network, the length of the leases you choose, and your tolerance for calls to your help desk. Although no single solution exists that fits the needs of every network, the next section covers some specific failure modes and suggests some solutions for those scenarios.

15.2 Specific Failures in DHCP Service

DHCP service can fail for quite a few reasons. The most obvious is that the computer on which the DHCP server is running fails. Another obvious reason is that network connectivity may be lost between the DHCP client and DHCP server. Less obvious are failures of network infrastructure, such as relay agents, and IP address starvation caused by buggy clients, misconfigured servers, and denial of service attacks. Chapter 21, "Authentication of DHCP Clients and Servers," and Chapter 23, "Debugging Problems with DHCP," cover debugging of incorrectly configured servers and denial of service attacks.

15.2.1 Server Failures

The most common server failure is simply a power outage. This can result from a power loss on the electrical circuit to which the server computer is connected, or an accident that causes the computer to power off or causes a site-wide power loss. A different set of problems accompanies each of these scenarios. In addition, server hardware failures can cause an interruption (or, in some cases, a complete loss) of service.

Limited Power Failure

In the event of a power failure that is limited to the server machine and a small number of other machines, few of which are DHCP clients, there shouldn't be much of a problem. The DHCP protocol requires that the server record leases on some kind of stable storage (for example, a hard-disk drive) before confirming them. As long as the DHCP server vendor takes this requirement seriously, the server can simply be restarted.

The easiest way to mitigate this problem is to make sure that the duration of the power failure is short, and to fix the problem quickly. The longer the server is powered off, the more likely it is that a DHCP client without a valid lease will attempt to acquire one. Such clients must wait until DHCP service is restored before they can use the network. Because of the way lease renewal works, clients with existing leases usually have at lease one-half of the lease duration left at any given time, so you can safely take a little less than one-half of the lease duration you assign to restore service.

Major Power Outages

When power goes off throughout your site, the recovery process is a bit different than it is for failures in which only the DHCP server is affected. The problem in this scenario is that all the DHCP clients powered off at the same time and will likely power back on at the same time. If the DHCP server is not available when the clients' power is restored, the clients may not get addresses and will continue to retry. This creates the following three problems:

- Until the clients are assigned addresses, they can't use the network.

- While the clients try to obtain addresses, they may create a significant amount of broadcast traffic on the network.

- All that traffic will be directed at the DHCP server. So, when it comes back online, it may experience an even higher load than if it was available when the first clients started requesting addresses. In general, the more up-to-date your DHCP client software is, the less likely this is to be a problem.

For these reasons, it is recommended that you arrange for your DHCP server to be available before the clients start requesting service. The easiest way to do this is to power the computer which hosts your DHCP server by an *uninterruptable power supply (UPS)*. This is a lovely misnomer for a battery-backed-up power supply that, although not actually uninterruptable, can be purchased in configurations that enable your server computer to run for a reasonable period of time during a power outage. If you can afford it, you may choose to provide backup power for your network equipment using a generator. If you have more limited funds, however, you may find it useful to run the DHCP server on a computer with very low power consumption, so as to reduce the cost of the UPS you will need to keep it running for whatever duration you plan.

Note

Laptops or notebook computers come with their own built-in UPS. Although notebook computers are usually thought to be inappropriate for network services because they are often limited in processing and storage capacity, they may be suitable for supplying DHCP service. In many installations, the number of DHCP requests and the computing power required to process them are low enough that an inexpensive, obsolete notebook computer is sufficient. If you leave the notebook plugged in all the time, you'll get a few hours of continuous service in the event of a power failure. If you power the computer through UPS, it will take a very long time before the UPS's battery dies.

Another solution is to put your DHCP server on a computer that starts up more quickly than your DHCP clients. If you run DHCP on a machine running UNIX, BSD, or Linux, you may be able to arrange to start the DHCP server very early in the start-up process. If you do this, you must arrange for the disk partition on which the server stores its files to be cleaned early in the start-up process.

A very cheap solution to the problem of extremely high server load after a power outage is to simply ask users to shut down their computers if power fails. Obviously, not everybody will comply, but if you get even 50 percent compliance, you will cut your power-on DHCP server load in half.

Hardware Failures

Hardware failures are usually less common than power failures, but they have much the same effect: A DHCP server stops running and doesn't come back again until some problem is corrected. In the worst case, a hardware failure may actually cause the loss of the DHCP database, and it may be necessary to recover the database from backups. This is discussed in Chapter 24, "The DHCP Database."

15.2.2 Planned Outages

You may choose to shut down the DHCP server to perform maintenance on it. Unless the maintenance takes a long time, the potential problems that occur in such cases are much the same as in a power outage. DHCP clients without leases will be unable to obtain them while the server is down. As long as the server is working again before half of the lease duration is assigned to clients, however, clients with valid leases when the server is down will continue to operate normally.

At some point you may also choose to move your network's DHCP service to a different computer with a different IP address. The easiest way to make this infrastructure change is to shut down the DHCP server on the old computer, copy all the configuration files to the new computer, and restart the DHCP server on the new computer. The new server will acquire all assigned addresses and lease information.

This move affects only those computers still running with a valid lease assigned by the old server. A computer in that situation gets no response when it attempts to extend its lease through the old server, and eventually, the computer broadcasts a message to locate an available server. The new server receives the message and then extends the client's lease. Other computers requesting a new address or broadcasting a message when restarting to confirm their address immediately locate the new server and begin using it.

15.2.3 Resource Starvation

Network servers are also susceptible to resource starvation problems. For most sites, DHCP is a fairly low-demand service that is unlikely to place a heavy load on a DHCP server machine. However, if the DHCP server machine also provides other services, some of which are high-demand, resource starvation caused by those services can impact the DHCP server. Also, if a DHCP server is configured to support enough clients, it is possible to create a load so large that the server is unable to keep up (although this has not been observed in practice). Finally, if a great deal of broadcast or multicast traffic is on the network to which the DHCP server machine is connected, this creates a load as well.

To avoid resource starvation caused by competing network services on the same host computer, make sure not to overcommit the machine on which DHCP service is running. If you envision providing high-demand NFS service, consider running the DHCP server on a different computer. If you run a very large DNS service, run it on a separate computer (this should be a problem for only very large sites).

To avoid resource starvation caused by a very high DHCP client load, you may want to install DHCP service on multiple computers rather than on a single DHCP server. Load-sharing for a single network segment isn't practical with the DHCP protocol alone, although if you can use the DHCP Failover Protocol (described in Chapter 25, "Communication between DHCP Servers"), you can share the DHCP client load between the primary and secondary servers for any given network segment.

Broadcast and Multicast-Induced Loads

Broadcast and multicast traffic on a network can require computers connected to the network to process every broadcast or multicast packet, even if the packet is of no interest. In general, IP networks have relatively little broadcast traffic, but networks running other protocols in addition to IP may see more broadcast traffic.

Multicast traffic is intended to reach only computers with clients that are interested in such traffic. Unfortunately, the way multicast is implemented on some network cards requires that the computer examine all multicast traffic, even if it is not of interest. If you run heavy multicast traffic on the network to which your DHCP server is connected, make sure that the DHCP server does not subscribe to this traffic. Also, be sure that the network adapter and the driver for that adapter have efficient multicast filters and do not require the computer to perform multicast filtering. Even if the network interface card correctly supports multicast, the presence of high-bandwidth multicast traffic on a broadcast network can consume enough bandwidth that all other services experience a loss of reliability.

For example, the thrice-yearly Internet Engineering Task Force meeting always provides a terminal room where people can log in and check their email or surf the Web using their own laptop computers or computers the IETF host company provides for the meeting. Many IETF sessions are recorded with digital video cameras and are multicast over the Internet Multicast Backbone (MBONE) so that people can watch these sessions from anywhere on the Internet, including in the terminal room. This traffic consumes about 1.5 megabits per second of bandwidth—about 15 percent of the bandwidth of the Ethernet segment, and 100 percent of the bandwidth of the wireless Ethernet segment.

The terminal room also usually has a DHCP server so that people with laptops can get IP addresses easily. However, people commonly complain about the DHCP server, which generally acts as though it's suffering from resource starvation. Although the reason for this is unclear, one likely explanation is that the DHCP server does not have good multicast filtration, and is, therefore, starved for resources by the large amount of multicast traffic on the terminal room network. Another explanation is that the multicast traffic is simply swamping other traffic and preventing DHCP clients from getting packets through to the DHCP server, or vice versa.

15.2.4 Network Infrastructure Failures

DHCP service requires a working network connection between the DHCP client and the DHCP server. If the client and server are not connected to the same network segment, a working DHCP relay agent must exist.

Failure of Network Hardware

If you experience a network outage that prevents computers holding valid IP addresses from using the network, it probably doesn't matter if DHCP service is interrupted—nobody can use the network anyway. However, if you have local services on a network that a DHCP user might access, you probably want the DHCP service to be at least as reliable as the network to which that user is connected. DHCP service should always be at least as reliable for any given DHCP user as the network connection between that user and the services he or she uses.

The easiest way to meet this goal is to simply have a reliable DHCP server close to the other services any given DHCP user needs. For example, if you have several LANs, each with its own servers and clients, a DHCP server should run on each LAN. If you have several LANs with client machines and a single LAN in a machine room with all the servers, you really need only a DHCP server in the machine room.

Note

As mentioned earlier, however, one of the primary reasons for installing DHCP is to reduce the administrative load of IP address assignment. If a DHCP server is installed in every possible place it is needed, the administrative load increases. Also, deploying more servers can cost more money. So, a definite tradeoff can be made between reliability and cost.

Another way to avoid losing DHCP service when other services are still available is to increase the network's reliability. Within a single site, you may want to set up a redundant power source—provide battery backup or generator power for network routers, switches, and bridges. If you run a central DHCP server to manage addresses across a large corporate network, serving sites connected only by wide area links, you must establish redundant paths. This means that any given site must be connected to the central DHCP site by more than one wide area link. This is harder to accomplish than it sounds; it is quite common to buy WAN links from two different telephone companies, only to learn that both links run through the same conduit between your site and some central distribution point. One company may also be buying bandwidth from the other, in which case both links could be running on the same optical fiber from one site to the other.

Even if each site is connected to two or more different sites, this does not prevent a single point of failure. Your links may still run through the same conduit to a single switching office before they are routed to two different sites. A catastrophic failure at the switching site can take down your network *and* your DHCP service, which means that your site can't talk to the outside world or operate independently while steps are taken to restore connectivity.

Misconfigured or Failed Relay Agents

DHCP service can also fail if relay agents that are not embedded in routers fail. Such agents can fail for most of the same reasons a DHCP server can fail, and the cures are the same as those mentioned in Section 15.2. A relay agent embedded in a dedicated router most likely will not fail unless the router itself fails.

Relay agents can also be misconfigured; for example, if the DHCP server receives a new IP address, relay agents that aren't reconfigured with the server's new address will fail. When changing the DHCP server's IP address, you must update all relay agents as well.

15.3 Improving Reliability Through Long Leases

As mentioned earlier, one way to maintain DHCP service across an outage is to define leases so that they don't expire during a normal outage. This solution has the virtue of simplicity, but it has some disadvantages as well.

The first and most obvious disadvantage is that you may have to define leases that are shorter than the length of time during which you expect a server might be down. Although a client that is expected to move from network to network frequently may work better with a very short lease duration, it will be more susceptible to outages.

You can give a client a very long lease but still force it to renew frequently. You can do this by defining very short renewal and rebinding times; for example, the lease duration might be two days, but the renewal time might be 2 minutes and the rebind time 4 minutes. In this case, the client renews frequently but does not lose connectivity until the server is unavailable for two days. Unfortunately, such a client begins broadcasting renewal requests 4 minutes after the last successful lease renewal. Therefore, configuring the renewal and rebinding times requires that the DHCP client be cooperative—if the client doesn't ask the server for renewal and rebinding times, the server doesn't send any, and the client just computes them on its own. Configuring lease durations is discussed in more detail in Chapter 16, "Tuning Your DHCP Service."

The second disadvantage is that a DHCP client that is powered on or connected to the network for the first time while a DHCP server is unavailable cannot contact the server to get an address. If the client still has a valid lease from the last time it started up, it can continue using that lease after it stops trying to contact the DHCP server. However, if it is on a different network, or if its old lease expired, it must wait for the DHCP server to become available again before it can begin using the network.

This is a problem for mobile clients that roam from network to network. A mobile client may work perfectly well on one network but then fail completely when it moves to a different network during a DHCP server outage.

15.4 Setting Up a Secondary DHCP Server

Another way to maintain DHCP service in the presence of a partial power loss or partial network outage is to set up two DHCP servers and enable them to both serve the same network. It may be worthwhile to set up each server on a different network. Therefore, if you lose connectivity to or power for one network but not the other network, DHCP service continues.

In order for two DHCP servers to provide DHCP service for the same network segment (or segments), the servers must coordinate their behavior. Each server must either know what the other is doing, or be configured so that it can operate without knowing what the other is doing. In order for each server to know what the other is doing, you must use the DHCP failover protocol or a protocol that provides similar functionality. Chapter 25 describes the use of the DHCP failover protocol.

Note

In this chapter, it is assumed that the servers are unable to coordinate, and thus must be configured to operate without knowledge of one another's actions. Although the failover protocol solves many of the problems described in this chapter much more elegantly than the solutions presented here, it is still under development. At the time of this writing, two vendors are known to have deployed implementations of a previous version of the failover protocol, and the protocol draft was undergoing a major revision. By the time this book is published, some preliminary implementations of the new failover protocol may be available.

15.4.1 Dynamic Address Allocation

In order for two servers to perform dynamic (or automatic) address allocation on the same network, they must allocate addresses from separate address pools. If both servers are configured with the same address pools, over time they will independently give the same addresses to different clients. DHCP is a fairly robust protocol in the face of this—you may not notice that anything is wrong, although you will see an abundance of abandoned leases. Unfortunately, over time this means both servers will perform less and less well, and may eventually stop working entirely.

The solution is to give each server a disjoint address pool on each network segment. Examples 15.1 and 15.2 show a likely configuration.

EXAMPLE 15.1

```
subnet 10.127.42.0 netmask 255.255.255.255 {
 range 10.127.42.5 10.127.42.130;
}
```

EXAMPLE 15.2

```
subnet 10.127.42.0 netmask 255.255.255.255 {
 range 10.127.42.131 10.127.42.253;
}
```

In this case, when a client tries to start up for the first time, both servers try to offer addresses. Server 1 may offer 10.127.42.5, and Server 2 may offer 10.127.42.131. The client chooses one of these addresses, requests it from the appropriate server, and starts using the lease. As long as the client needs the lease, and the server from which it got the lease is working, it operates normally.

If the server fails, the client continues using the address it was assigned until its lease expires. During that period, it tries from time to time to renew its lease. As long as the server comes back before the lease expires, the client continues to operate normally. If the server isn't reachable by the time the lease expires, the client must acquire a new lease from the other server, assuming that server is running.

A client might also obtain a lease from Server 1, for example, and then either release the lease or be powered down until the lease expires. If Server 1 is no longer available when it tries to obtain a new lease, Server 2 assigns it a different lease.

15.4.2 Static Address Allocation

When assigning clients addresses statically, as described in Chapter 14, "Client Identification and Fixed-Address Allocation," setting up redundant DHCP service for such clients is much easier. Both servers should be configured with the same list of static addresses for the same clients.

When a client with a static address tries to start up, if both servers are running, both offer it the same address. The client selects one server or the other, requests the address from it, receives the address, and continues to renew its lease.

Remember that when the client first gets a confirmed lease, it goes into the BOUND state. After the lease renewal interval (usually half the lease duration) expires, it goes into the RENEWING state and starts unicasting DHCPREQUEST messages to the server from which it received its address. If that server goes down while the client is in the RENEWING state, the client continues to try to renew its lease until the lease rebind interval expires (usually seven-eighths of the lease interval).

After the rebind interval expires, the client goes into the REBIND state and broadcasts DHCPREQUEST messages. At this point, either server can respond to the DHCPREQUEST message, so if the server from which the client previously obtained its address is still not responding, it binds to the other server and continues operating normally, with no interruption of service.

> **Note**
>
> *In a sense, when you set up two DHCP servers to provide static address assignment for the same network, you set up communicating DHCP servers. The servers communicate through whatever mechanism you choose to use to provide them with identical static address configurations. The effectiveness of this strategy depends on the degree to which the server configurations remain synchronized.*

15.4.3 Hybrid Allocation Models

As mentioned in Chapter 13, "Configuring a DHCP Server," and in Chapter 14, you can set up a DHCP server that performs static address allocation for some clients on some networks, and dynamic allocation for other clients on other networks. If this is the case, you can still set up redundant DHCP service.

For static address assignments, simply maintain duplicate DHCP configurations on both servers. For dynamic assignments, maintain separate address allocation pools for each server. Clients with statically assigned addresses see no apparent interruption in service when a server goes down for longer than their lease duration. Clients with dynamically assigned addresses see an interruption if the server from which they got their address goes down for longer than their lease duration.

Note

When you run a redundant DHCP server configuration that mixes static and dynamic addressing, it is vitally important that the static address assignments for each server are consistent. If both servers are running and one server has a static address assignment for a particular client, while the other has no such assignment, when that client tries to start up, each server will offer it a different address. This could mean the server that knows it has a valid static address would send a DHCPNAK message whenever the client sends a DHCPREQUEST message for the nonstatic address offered by the other server.

Also, if the client gets the dynamically assigned address from Server 1, and then Server 1's static address mapping is updated to include a mapping for that client, the client will be forced to reinitialize with a new IP address, resulting in an interruption of network service for the user.

To avoid this, shut down both servers when installing a new server configuration, install the new configuration on both servers, and then start up both servers. As long as you follow this sequence, both servers can run at the same time with inconsistent states. Of course, this also means both servers will be down at the same time, but as long as the startup time on both servers is reasonably short, this shouldn't be a problem.

15.5 Problems with Setting Up Redundant Servers

Setting up redundant servers that don't speak an inter-server protocol is not a good solution to the problem of providing redundant service. If you can find a server that provides a reliable inter-server protocol, such as the IETF DHCP failover protocol, it is better to use that protocol because it solves all the problems described in this section.

15.5.1 Address Consistency Rule Violations

When two servers are set up in a redundant configuration with dynamic address allocation, clients may not be assigned the same IP address every time they start up. This can happen even in situations in which no outage exists; if a client relinquishes its address on shutdown or simply doesn't remember its previous address across restarts, each time it comes up, both DHCP servers will compete to give it an IP address. This means the client will not have a consistent address across restarts. Because the DHCP protocol tries to ensure that the client always gets the same IP address, this means that a redundant DHCP server setup with dynamic allocation will behave differently than a single server with dynamic allocation, which may be a problem for some users.

15.5.2 Loss of Address While in Use

If a client gets a lease from one server and is unable to renew the lease with that server before it expires, the other server assigns it a new lease with a different IP address. Any network connections in use when the lease expired will be broken, probably without warning. For this reason, it is a good idea to use longer leases—even with a redundant server configuration—as an additional strategy for improving reliability.

15.5.3 Dynamic Allocation Pool Starvation

If you set up two DHCP servers to perform dynamic address allocation on a particular network segment, you must assign each server a part of the address pool. In the event of an outage, it may be necessary to support the entire network segment with only the addresses assigned to the server that has not failed. This means you may have to allocate twice as many addresses as are actually needed. If addresses are in short supply, you may not have enough IP addresses to adequately serve that network segment.

15.5.4 Duplicate Responses from Redundant Servers

Whenever a client transmits a DHCPDISCOVER message on a network with redundant DHCP servers—whether the servers use static or dynamic address allocation—both servers respond. This means the client generally must choose between two offers, one from each server. This creates extra network traffic and causes both servers to do work rather than just one server. Also, this means that you really cannot have a primary and a secondary server; the two servers compete as equals.

When a DHCP client sends a request, the secs field in the DHCP packet is initialized to the number of seconds that elapsed since the client first started sending the request. One possible way to set up a primary and secondary server is to have the secondary server respond only if the secs field is larger than some predetermined amount. Because the secs field is zero for the first request a client sends, the secondary server will not respond to it, but it will respond if the client sends a second request. You can configure version 3.0 or later of the ISC DHCP server to do this, as shown in Example 15.3.

EXAMPLE 15.3

```
min-secs 15;
```

In Example 15.3, the server is configured not to respond unless the secs field in the client's request has a value of at least 15. Whether all clients use the secs field correctly is unknown. This is something to be aware of; if redundant DHCP service is set up in this way, clients that don't correctly set the secs field are simply ignored by the secondary server.

Summary

The major causes of DHCP server failure are power failures, hardware failures, and network problems. To improve reliability, you can use long lease times and set up secondary DHCP servers. These tactics work best when you combine them, although you can also use them separately. Long lease times by themselves are a very easy solution, but they don't solve all the reliability problems that can come up; in particular, they work poorly for mobile clients and for clients that are powered on during a DHCP service outage.

You can improve reliability by having more than one DHCP server serve a given network segment. This is advantageous because it means that even clients that lose their addresses while one DHCP server is unavailable can still use the network. Redundant DHCP service is not an ideal solution—the DHCP failover protocol is a future solution that better handles the problem of setting up redundant service.

CHAPTER **16**

Tom Hickman, Cisco Systems
Ralph Droms, Ph.D
Ted Lemon

Tuning Your DHCP Service

If you already read the preceding six chapters, you should have a very good idea of the mechanics of installing and configuring a DHCP server. This chapter describes how to tune your DHCP service to provide the best assistance for your DHCP clients, and it explains some of the tradeoffs you may have to make to get the smoothest possible service, given the needs at your site. It also describes some ways to monitor your DHCP server's activities so that you know when it is in trouble and whether you tuned it correctly.

16.1 Network Device Configuration and Address Assignment Strategies

Although you no doubt prefer to use DHCP to configure your network devices automatically wherever possible, you will need to (or choose to) configure some computers in some other way. In practice, you can manually configure some legacy devices with an IP address (and a static Domain Name System [DNS] hostname). Your network also includes well-known servers (such as the DHCP server, the DNS servers, Web servers, mail servers, and so on) that you *should* (or must) configure manually to avoid dependence on other services (such as DHCP) and to improve reliability. Additionally, network infrastructure, such as router interfaces, must be configured manually. Other legacy devices that use BOOTP for configuration, such as printers and some network hubs, may require manual configuration or provision of BOOTP service.

As you deploy and refine your DHCP service, keep in mind how to handle devices that aren't configured using DHCP and how to ensure that those devices don't interfere with your DHCP service.

16.1.1 Manual Configuration

You may have legacy devices in your network that you must manually configure with a IP address and other information, such as a default router and a DNS server. UNIX systems include these configuration parameters in an initialization script. Windows systems are configured through the Network control panel. In the long run, you should try to identify these manually configured devices and transition them to use DHCP service.

However, you may want to use manual configuration for well-known server and network infrastructure devices, and, of course, you must use manual configuration for any devices that don't have an implementation of DHCP available. To summarize, consider manual configuration for:

- Mission-critical protocol servers (for example, DNS, DHCP, Simple Mail Transfer Protocol [SMTP], the Web, and so on)

- Mainframe and multi-user computers (for example, IBM 3090s, VAX/Alpha clusters, and high-end UNIX workstations)

- Any server hosting an application that is accessed via the computer's IP address (for example, some database applications)

- Router and switch interfaces

- Any computer that cannot operate as a DHCP (or BOOTP) client

Problems with Manual Configuration

Clearly, manual IP address configuration has some problems; otherwise, the BOOTP and DHCP protocols wouldn't have been developed. Any manually configured host ceases to function correctly if:

- The user changes the IP address or TCP/IP configuration parameters.

- The computer is moved to a different subnet.

- The computer remains stationary, but the subnet is renumbered.

- The TCP/IP parameters (such as DNS server addresses or router addresses) are changed, without a corresponding change to the computer's TCP/IP configuration.

> **Note**
>
> You can also handle one of the major drawbacks of static allocation through the DHCPINFORM message, which enables a host with a manually configured IP address to request other configuration parameters, such as router addresses, DNS servers, and printer servers.

16.1.2 Reclamation of Manually Assigned IP Addresses

In many networks, thousands of legacy manual IP address allocations are scattered through the address range. Because most networks employ manual methods of tracking these static allocations, you cannot ensure that a computer is still using its manually assigned IP address. Some manually configured computers may still be in use, some may have been converted to use DHCP, and some may no longer be in use.

One frequently used method of reclaiming manually assigned IP addresses is to write a script that periodically pings IP addresses that are suspected of being in use by manually configured hosts. You can run this script until you are confident that the devices using any of the addresses you are trying to check are turned on. If your program receives a reply to its ping messages, that IP address is still in use. However, this method is not totally reliable, and it can possibly lead to address conflicts.

When it is determined that a manually assigned IP address is no longer in use, it can be reclaimed. You can add the IP address to the DHCP pool of addresses, and you can delete the DNS resource records.

16.1.3 Strategies for Supporting BOOTP Devices

As mentioned previously, BOOTP is the predecessor of the DHCP protocol. Your intranet will likely include computers and devices that can use BOOTP and not DHCP to acquire their network configuration. For example, ... older printers support BOOTP but not DHCP, such as Macintosh computers using MacTCP instead of OpenTransport, and many older diskless workstations may be capable of using BOOTP but not DHCP. This doesn't represent a significant problem because BOOTP and DHCP can inter-operate on the same network.

Prior to any discussion of how to deal with legacy BOOTP devices, it's worth noting that you can configure DHCP servers to respond to BOOTP messages so that your DHCP server provides both DHCP and BOOTP service. That said, you can handle legacy BOOTP devices in one of several ways:

- Eliminate all BOOTP devices and only use DHCP.

- Provide static IP address assignments for BOOTP clients.

- Automatically allocate permanent IP addresses for BOOTP clients.

- Keep BOOTP and DHCP services separate.

Elimination of All BOOTP Devices

One method of dealing with legacy BOOTP devices is to turn them all into DHCP devices. Where possible, this is an attractive method of dealing with the issue because it leaves the administrator with only *one* method of allocating addresses automatically/dynamically. Many computers and network devices that use BOOTP can also use DHCP. In some cases (as with many network printers), converting devices from BOOTP to DHCP is as simple as selecting DHCP from a network configuration screen. Firmware upgrades for BOOTP-only devices may be available that support DHCP. A large number of different kinds of BOOTP devices exist, so it is difficult to provide details on the method of converting any specific device from BOOTP to DHCP.

A certain amount of work is involved in identifying all BOOTP clients on your network and upgrading them to use the DHCP protocol instead. Likewise, if you decide to continue supporting BOOTP, you must do some extra work because the BOOTP protocol does not provide for any way of automating the maintenance of BOOTP address assignments. Even if you choose to have the DHCP server automatically allocate these addresses, you cannot have it reclaim them when they are no longer in use. Whether you choose to convert from BOOTP to DHCP depends on which of these two options is likely to require the least amount of work.

If you can convert all your BOOTP devices to DHCP, you still must consider whether those devices require the same IP address every time they start up. If this is not a requirement, you can enable the DHCP server to serve the next available address to the devices, and your dynamic allocation takes care of all your legacy BOOTP devices (because they are not DHCP devices).

If all your legacy BOOTP devices must continue using the same IP address they always had, it probably isn't worth the work required to convert the clients from BOOTP to DHCP. This is discussed in the next section.

Static Address Assignments for BOOTP Clients

If your legacy BOOTP devices require the same IP address they got from a BOOTP server, you can choose to use static allocation or automatic allocation. If you choose static allocation, you must add an entry for each BOOTP device. To continue providing BOOTP clients with their old IP addresses, you must take the following steps:

- Configure your DHCP server to respond to BOOTP requests.

- Examine your `BOOTP server configuration` file, and for each entry in the file, create a static address assignment on your DHCP server that includes the hardware address and the IP address to be assigned to that client.

- Make sure that all the appropriate DHCP options are configured in the DHCP server to correspond with all the options specified in the `bootptab` file.

- Turn off your old BOOTP server.

- Restart your BOOTP devices.

Note

Often, entries in your `bootptab` file are very regular. You may find it easiest to simply write a PERL or shell script to convert your `bootptab` file into the format your DHCP server expects. Unfortunately, you cannot do this for the Microsoft DHCP server, but it does work with the ISC DHCP server and with DHCP servers provided by quite a few other vendors.

You might also want to ask whether your vendor already has scripts that you can use. The `bootptab` file format varies between different versions of the BOOTP daemon, and from site to site. One site's script probably doesn't work for another site without changes, but it can still be useful to start from somebody else's conversion script instead of writing a completely new one.

Many BOOTP devices perform a second-stage startup process, in which they download a file from a Trivial File Transfer Protocol (TFTP) or network file system (NFS) server—for example, a startup image or a configuration file. The BOOTP protocol requires that the IP address of the server from which to load this file is included in the `siaddr` and `sname` fields of the BOOTP packet. However, some newer BOOTP clients actually use the DHCP `tftp-server-name` and `bootfile-name` options. You must make sure that you configure the DHCP server to send the second-stage start-up information to the BOOTP client in the same way that the BOOTP server does.

You can tell very quickly whether you have this issue. Scan (or *grep*) through your `bootptab` file, looking for the tag symbol `sa=value`. This is the tag for the TFTP server address. If this tag is present, you should configure the DHCP server with the `tftp-server-name` option instead of telling it to use the `sname` field in the BOOTP header.

Note

Static IP address assignments do not enable BOOTP clients to roam across multiple subnets, unless you create multiple reservations for a given hardware address. Also, if a network is renumbered, the address assigned to a particular BOOTP client might be incorrect for the network segment to which that client is connected. So, this method is effective for enabling BOOTP clients to continue receiving their old IP addresses, but it provides little of the benefit of DHCP.

Automatic IP Address Assignment for BOOTP Clients

Rather than completely eliminating BOOTP, or providing and maintaining static address allocations for all BOOTP clients, you can also have some DHCP servers automatically allocate IP addresses to BOOTP clients. This form of BOOTP service is sometimes called *dynamic BOOTP*.

This method is attractive because it enables you to serve BOOTP clients from the same pool of addresses as dynamic clients. It doesn't require you to create DHCP reservations; yet it isn't adversely affected if you do. This configuration has the added advantage of enabling BOOTP clients to function correctly even if they roam across multiple subnets, or if the network is renumbered. The disadvantage is that the DHCP server must permanently reserve any IP addresses it assigns to BOOTP clients because BOOTP does not include any mechanism for automatically recovering IP addresses that are no longer in use.

Note

The ISC DHCP server provides some ways of working around the BOOTP protocol's inability to provide for automatic IP address reclamation. The first of these is the dynamic-bootp-lease-length *parameter, which you can set to some length shorter than infinity. To use this parameter safely, you must be able to assume that any BOOTP client on your network is always powered off and back on again at least once during the specified interval. For example, if your site is an office that operates Monday through Friday, and all network devices in the office are always powered off on weekends, you can set this interval to one week and be sure that no BOOTP device retains its address for that long.*

The ISC server also provides the dynamic-bootp-lease-cutoff *parameter. This parameter specifies a specific date when all BOOTP leases end. You can use this, for example, in a college dormitory environment, where it is known that all students leave the dorm on a certain day. If the cutoff is set to the next day, all IP addresses assigned to students in the dorm using BOOTP are reclaimed at once. Of course, it's important to reset this cutoff when it expires!*

Separate DHCP and BOOTP Servers

Another alternative is to leave your BOOTP server unchanged, and provide service for all BOOTP devices through the BOOTP server. BOOTP and DHCP servers can inter-operate on the same network or subnet, however you must run the two servers on separate computers. Therefore, if you choose this option, you must manage two servers. In such a scenario, making changes to network topology is complicated because you must update both servers. If the number of legacy BOOTP devices is extremely large, or if for other reasons you do not want to move your BOOTP service to your DHCP server, you can leave the BOOTP server intact and configure the DHCP server not to respond to BOOTP requests.

Whichever approach you select, be very careful not to allocate leases to a DHCP dynamic pool if they are either in use by a BOOTP server, or reserved for a BOOTP device in some other scope. This can result in a duplicate IP address assignment.

16.2 Configuring Lease Lengths

The question of DHCP lease length is a topic of heated debate among network administrators. Some networks run DHCP lease times of one year; some use 30 seconds. Generally speaking, the *right* lease time depends on your network's characteristics and performance requirements. However, you should consider a few relevant issues which, when weighed accordingly, can inform your decision about your optimal DHCP lease time.

The pros and cons of long and short lease times are best illustrated by considering two hypothetical networks that use extremely long and short DHCP leases: one with a lease duration of one year, and another with a lease duration of 1 minute.

16.2.1 A Network with One-Year Leases

On Day 1, several DHCP computers and devices start up in this network. The first, a DHCP-configured laser printer, sends two DHCP messages to the server to obtain its IP address. This printer never moves and is never powered off, so it keeps its address, and people use it via its IP address. After half of the lease expires, six months after Day 1, the printer renews its lease by sending a message to the DHCP server. Six months later, it renews its lease again. The DHCP server processes a total of four messages from the printer in the course of one year.

The second device, a DHCP-configured workstation, also starts up on Day 1. It receives its DHCP lease and is fully functional on the network. Each night, this device is turned off. Every morning, it is turned back on and sends one DHCP message to the server to confirm its IP address and to extend its lease on the address. The DHCP server sees one DHCP message per day from this device.

The third device, a mobile laptop, starts up in one subnet on Day 1 and sends two messages to the DHCP server to obtain an address with a one-year lease. The next day, it starts up in a different subnet and gets another address with a one-year lease. The third day, it starts up in a third subnet and gets yet another address with a one-year lease. The laptop, therefore, has an address with a one-year lease on each subnet to which it is connected.

When the administrator changes a parameter for DHCP clients, the server returns that new value to DHCP clients in the next message it sends to each client. However, because the protocol relies on the *client* to initiate communication, any change to a DHCP option is not sent to a DHCP client until the client sends a message to the server. So, on this network, the printer doesn't see a change to a DHCP option for six months. The workstation and desktop system receive the new parameter value more quickly because they contact the server each time they are powered on, but even 24 hours might be too long to wait for changes to DHCP options to propagate to DHCP clients.

Long leases may also lead to exhaustion of the pool of addresses available for dynamic assignment by the DHCP server. Because the server must wait until the lease expires before reassigning an address to a new client, every device that connects to the network—even a laptop that is connected for only a few hours—is assigned an address that can't be reused for a year. Over time, many addresses may no longer be in use and may not be reused because the leases for those addresses did not expire.

When subnets are assigned new IP addresses, or are *renumbered*, another problem may appear. The laptop and workstation are renumbered according to the new subnet address as soon as they restart. The printer, which is left powered on all the time, is not assigned an IP address on the new network until it extends the lease on its address, which could be as long as six months after the network is renumbered.

Long Lease Times: Benefits

- Stable.
- No renumbering.
- Low DHCP packet traffic.
- Limits impact of DHCP server outages (see Chapter 13, "Configuring a DHCP Server").

Long Lease Times: Caveats

- Leases don't expire, and address allocation pools may be depleted.
- Changes to DHCP option values aren't propagated quickly.
- Networks can't be renumbered automatically.

16.2.2 A Network with One-Minute Leases

On Day 1, several DHCP computers and devices start up in this network. The first, a laser printer that uses DHCP, sends two messages to the DHCP server to obtain an IP address. As in the previous example, this printer never moves and is never powered off. After 30 seconds (half of the lease interval) pass, the client sends the DHCP server a request to renew the lease. This happens every 30 seconds, meaning that in any given day, the DHCP server processes 2,880 lease renewals for this printer. Over the course of one year, the server processes more than 1 million requests from this printer.

The second device, a DHCP-configured workstation, also starts up on Day 1. It receives its address by sending two messages to the server, and it is fully functional on the network. The workstation also renews its lease every 30 seconds while it is powered up and on the network. Each night, this workstation is turned off. The workstation's lease on the address expires 1 minute after it is turned off. Every morning, when the workstation is turned back on, it obtains a new address from the server because the lease on its previous address expired. Because the lease expired, the server may give to another client the IP address previously assigned to the workstation. The workstation may or may not get the same IP address each day.

The third device, a mobile laptop, starts up in one subnet on Day 1 and gets a 1-minute lease. While on this subnet, it renews its lease every 30 seconds. The lease expires 1 minute after the laptop is turned off. The next day, it starts up on a different subnet and gets another 1-minute lease. The third day, it starts up on a third subnet and gets yet another 1-minute lease. Because the leases are short, they always expire before the laptop connects to a new subnet, and the client has only one lease at any given point. While the client is connected to the network, it renews its lease every 30 seconds with a message to the DHCP server.

Suppose the administrator of this network changes a network parameter. The server passes that new value to DHCP clients in the next packet it sends to each client. Because each client sends a message to the DHCP server to extend the lease on its assigned address every 30 seconds, any change to a network parameter is delivered to the DHCP clients almost immediately.

Also, because the DHCP client's lease expires soon after the client is turned off, leases for unused addresses on each subnet do not become stale. Thus, as more and more devices are added to subnets in Network B, the likelihood of running out of IP addresses in a dynamic pool is reduced.

When subnets are renumbered in this network, the computers are renumbered within 30 seconds if they are connected to the network, or the next time they are turned on.

Short Lease Times: Benefits	Short Lease Times: Caveats
• They are very flexible and self-correcting. • Changes propagate to the DHCP clients quickly. • DHCP dynamic pool depletion is unlikely. • When the network is renumbered, clients get addresses on their new subnets very quickly.	• Clients' IP addresses may change frequently. • Leases expire overnight. • They can cause a high load on the DHCP server. • DHCP service must be highly available because even a short outage terminates network service for all clients.

16.2.3 One Lease Per Client

As seen in networks described in Section 16.2.1, scope depletion is possible when you use long lease times. This happens because the DHCP server grants multiple leases to a single client as it moves across subnets.

You can configure the ISC server to enable only one assigned address for each DHCP client. When this feature is enabled, the server terminates any existing leases when it assigns a new address to a DHCP client. As a laptop roams across subnets, it has only one lease at a time, preventing the DHCP server from depleting its dynamic pools unnecessarily.

16.2.4 Tradeoffs Between Number of Clients and Lease Length

Generally speaking, it is a bad idea to attach more computers to a network segment than you assign available IP addresses to that network. You can do this with DHCP, as long as only as many computers are turned on at once as you have available addresses. If you do have nearly as many computers on a network segment as available addresses, you must keep your lease times relatively short to avoid running out of available addresses due to unexpired leases on unused addresses.

One Benefit of Short-Term Leases

At a recent technical convention, the terminal room had a large table with network connections for attendees to use for their laptop computers. Attendees wandered in and out of the terminal room, connecting and disconnecting their laptop computers. Unfortunately, a limited number of IP addresses were available to assign. The terminal room staff initially chose a lease interval of 1 hour. The turnover rate of users of the terminal room was quite a bit shorter than this, so the pool of available IP addresses was quickly depleted. When this occurred, new arrivals in the terminal room were unable to get IP addresses when they first connected to the network, but they mysteriously received IP address assignments if they waited long enough. After adjusting the lease interval to 15 minutes, this problem was virtually eliminated.

16.2.5 The Effect of Lease Length on DHCP Server Load

One consideration when deploying DHCP, and when tuning the parameters of the DHCP server, is how a given parameter impacts the load on the DHCP server. In the previous example, where the DHCP lease time is 1 minute, you can see how even one DHCP client can generate more than 2,000 DHCP packets per day. Imagine that this network handles 10,000 DHCP clients. This leads to a DHCP packet rate of more than 20 million transactions per day. The load generated by a single DHCP packet may seem trivial, but magnify it by 20 million and it becomes substantial. This represents more than 200 packets per second that the DHCP server must process. Considering that the "last transaction time" for each packet is written to disk, this becomes an insurmountable load. When tuned incorrectly, even a relatively small network of 10,000 DHCP clients can totally swamp a server. The same network, with a DHCP lease time of 1 hour, sees only about 5 packets per second. This is a much more sustainable load.

16.2.6 The Effect of Lease Length on Reliability

This topic is discussed in detail in Chapter 13, so it's described briefly here. If you are providing DHCP service on a given network segment using only a single DHCP server, whenever that server is not operating, clients cannot renew leases. If the DHCP server might stop operating for an extended period of time (for example, a long weekend while no network support staff are available), it might be wise to choose a lease interval that enables DHCP clients to continue operating if the server fails. Even if the server is very reliable, you may need to shut it down for maintenance from time to time, so the lease interval you choose should be long enough that network users are not inconvenienced by a server outage.

16.2.7 DHCP Leases with DDNS Updates

With the advent of RFC2136 *Dynamic DNS Updates (DDNS)*, DNS data is more closely tied to DHCP lease data. Because of this, DNS data is now itself dynamic and time-based. When a new DHCP lease is granted, a DDNS update is performed to change the DNS information for the DHCP client. The details of this process are described in more detail in Chapter 23, "Debugging Problems with DHCP."

If the DHCP client leaves the network and the lease expires, the DHCP server must delete the DNS information for the client. However, if the DHCP client stays on the network, periodically renewing its lease, the information in the DNS servers can remain unchanged. This fact, coupled with the way that changes to DNS are propagated through a network, leads to an obvious recommendation for DHCP lease time in DDNS implementations. The DHCP lease time should be at least twice as long as the longest "down time" that a DHCP client normally experiences. In most networks, this is some event such as a three- or four-day weekend. A DHCP lease time of eight days ensures that even if the DHCP client shuts down just before it renews its lease (leaving four days and one second on the lease), the lease doesn't expire when it returns. This prevents unnecessary changes to the DNS name space.

It may be better, however, to simply provide static IP address allocations for DHCP clients that require a consistent and reliable presence on the network, and to configure the DNS records for those clients statically.

16.2.8 DHCP Renew Time

As noted in Section 16.2.1, a long lease time on a network leads to a long delay between changes to network parameters and to delivery of the new parameter values to DHCP clients. By default, the DHCP client attempts to renew its DHCP lease after one-half of the duration of the lease expires. However, you can set a *renew time* parameter on the server, which overrides the default time the client uses for DHCP lease renewal. Setting this parameter to a low value causes DHCP clients to communicate with the DHCP server more frequently, without running the risk of expiring the DHCP lease.

For instance, suppose you set the DHCP lease time to eight days. Using the default renewal time, a DHCP client renews its lease every four days. If you set the renewal time to 12 hours, all the DHCP clients on the network renew their leases and get any new parameter values within 12 hours. Of course, this solution doesn't solve the problem of unexpired leases on unused addresses, but it does enable you to reduce the number of unwanted lease expirations by using longer leases while delivering new parameter values to clients quickly.

16.2.9 Customizing Lease Durations

Some DHCP servers enable you to choose different lease intervals for different DHCP clients. If your DHCP server provides this capability, you may want to configure your DHCP server to provide shorter lease lengths to laptop computers than to desktop workstations, and still longer lease lengths to devices that are always present and whose IP addresses are unlikely to change. Chapter 15, "Setting Up a Reliable DHCP Service," describes ways of classifying clients into groups to which you can give different lease lengths based on their particular needs.

Making Adjustments to Lease Durations

As noted previously, if you choose to renumber your network, having a long lease interval can be very inconvenient. One way to resolve this problem without using short leases all the time is to change your DHCP server configuration in anticipation of a network renumbering. If you choose to provide seven-day leases by default, you might shorten the maximum lease duration to six hours, seven days before the day on which you renumber your network. When the network renumbering is complete, you can once again lengthen the lease interval to seven days.

Reaching a Compromise Lease Length

Using a few simple rules, you can choose a DHCP lease time and DHCP renew time that best fit your needs:

- Keep the DHCP packet rate as low as possible. Although DHCP service doesn't require large amounts of processing and system resources, minimizing DHCP traffic is a good idea.

- If DDNS is deployed, or if you are not providing redundant DHCP service, set the DHCP lease time to a value sufficiently large to prevent DHCP leases from expiring over long weekends.

- If you require rapid propagation of changes to DHCP options, use a low DHCP renew time.

16.2.10 Configuring the Lease Length on the DHCP Server

When you choose a lease duration, you must configure the DHCP server to provide leases of that duration to clients. Different DHCP servers handle this task differently.

The Microsoft DHCP server enables you to configure a maximum lease length for each scope (that is, each subnet). If a DHCP client doesn't request any particular lease length, it is assigned the maximum. If the DHCP client requests a lease length that is less than the maximum, it is assigned a lease with that duration. If it requests a lease longer than the maximum length, it is assigned a lease of the maximum length.

You can configure the ISC DHCP server in any given scope with a minimum, maximum, and default lease length. The minimum is provided because many DHCP clients specifically request a particular lease length, and if the administrator uses long lease intervals to increase reliability, this benefit cannot be obtained without requiring such clients to take longer leases. For example, the Microsoft DHCP client always requests a 24-hour lease.

Example 16.1 shows an ISC DHCP server configuration that sets an appropriate minimum, default, and maximum lease duration for a network with a single DHCP server that you expect is reliable, but that you may need to restart from time to time.

EXAMPLE 16.1

```
default-lease-time 7200;
max-lease-time 86400;
min-lease-time 7200;
```

Remember that these parameters can be different in every scope. This means that, for example, it is possible to globally declare the maximum lease length to be one day, but then provide servers that have static IP address allocations with a maximum lease of a month.

16.3 Monitoring the Server

The *Simple Network Management Protocol (SNMP)* is a mechanism through which you can monitor the operation of network devices via protocol messages. Any device managed by SNMP has an associated *Management Information Base (MIB)* that defines the information on the device that is to be monitored via SNMP.

The DHC Working Group of the IETF has produced a draft DHCP server MIB, authored by R.B. Hibbs and G. Waters. This document and the use of SNMP to access the DHCP server database is described more thoroughly in Chapter 24, "The DHCP Database." This section focuses on the use of SNMP and the DHCP MIB for gathering operational statistics and server configuration information.

To use the information defined by the DHCP server MIB, you use an SNMP management station to contact the DHCP server and fetch the information about the server operation that is of interest to you. This SNMP management station is configured to poll the DHCP server, gather and correlate information, and, when necessary, generate alarms, email messages, pages, and so on, to inform network administrators of problems with the DHCP server.

16.3.1 Gathering and Using Traffic Statistics

Traffic and usage statistics are always useful parameters to monitor. Significant increases or decreases in traffic on a given server generally indicate a change or event that the system administrator should investigate. The draft DHCP server MIB defines several objects that you can use to determine traffic statistics. Most notably, you can compute the total number of DHCP and BOOTP packets the server receives and sends by adding the total count numbers for each message type. The MIB also includes information about message response time, so you can understand how any load on the server is affecting system performance.

On your own network, you might configure your management stations to alert you if the total number of packets you receive is more than 30 percent higher than the total number of packets sent. You might also choose to be alerted if the total number of packets you receive in a 1-hour period exceeds a threshold level. If you know that your DHCP server can handle a packet arrival rate of only 50 packets per second without excessive latency, seeing a packet arrival rate of 180,000 packets per hour is "interesting." If the message response time exceeds 3.5 seconds, you might also generate an alarm because the server is nearing the maximum response latency the protocol enables.

Note

The ISC server generates an entry in its log file for every DHCP message it processes. You can easily extract information about the activity levels in your server by parsing the log file with a program such as a PERL script.

16.3.2 Verifying Server Configuration

It should be obvious that server configuration is *critical* to reliable DHCP service. In a dynamic network, this becomes even more critical. Changes to subnets and to the DHCP server must occur simultaneously. Any inconsistency between the physical network and the DHCP server's view of the subnets and netmasks on the network results in a failure of DHCP service.

The draft DHCP server MIB provides a number of server configuration objects that describe in detail the configuration state of the server. This includes information about subnets and subnet masks, secondary (equivalent) subnets, dynamic pool ranges, dynamic pool usage, static addresses, dynamic addresses, and reserved addresses. This is very useful, as it enables the SNMP management station to view the entire server configuration.

In a real-world network, the SNMP management station should either *know* or *discover* information about the subnets on a network. You can then configure the management station to compare what *it* thinks about the network with the DHCP server's list of subnets and masks and to generate an alarm of some sort if they are mismatched. This is much better than the old method of waiting for someone to complain that he or she can't get a lease!

16.3.3 DHCP Address Pool Depletion

The most common error a properly configured DHCP server encounters is DHCP dynamic pool depletion. Imagine the following scenario: Your company is having a training seminar in a large room, with a network hub on Subnet A. One of the organizers of the seminar brings in a couple of Ethernet hubs and daisy-chains two 12-port hubs off of one Ethernet port. Then, 20 people bring their laptops into the room, plug them in, and try to get DHCP leases in Subnet A (they all normally work in a different building, hence a different subnet). Suddenly, 20 more devices than expected are in Subnet A. Unfortunately, only 19 leases are available on that subnet. Someone doesn't get an address, and calls the help desk.

The draft DHCP MIB enables a method to automatically catch occurrences such as this. As mentioned previously, some MIB objects define the DHCP dynamic pool ranges, as well as the usage of a dynamic pool. You can configure the network management station to generate an alarm if a dynamic pool falls below 15 percent availability, so problems such as the one described here are discovered before they escalate.

Monitoring Address Pool Usage

You can check the status of any scope the Microsoft DHCP server manages through the DHCP Manager application, as described in Chapter 11. To determine the number of available addresses in a pool managed by the ISC server, you must have a program that determines the active leases in the pool from the leases file and the number of addresses in the pool from the configuration file. Subtract the number of active leases from the total available addresses and you have the number of available addresses. Several PERL scripts are available that perform this task.

Summary

Effective deployment of DHCP service requires careful consideration of your current network architecture and device configurations. You can choose from several alternatives when you move to DHCP. Probably the best choice is to use DHCP for all your networked devices. If that strategy isn't feasible, you can accommodate manually configured devices with careful configuration of your DHCP service. You may also benefit from some of the advantages of DHCP in configuring legacy BOOTP devices by integrating your DHCP and BOOTP service.

The choice of address lease lengths and the mobility patterns of your networked devices have a significant effect on the behavior of DHCP clients and on the computing resources your DHCP server consumes. The essential tradeoff is between flexibility and processor load: Shorter leases decrease the delay in reclaiming addresses and getting new configuration parameters to clients, at the expense of increased load on the computer providing the DHCP service. You cannot address the question "How long should my DHCP leases be?" with only one answer; in fact, you may choose different lease lengths for different parts of your network.

## CHAPTER 17

Conditional Behavior

A few of the previous chapters discuss how to set up the DHCP server so that it configures all clients with essentially the same parameters. They also show some simple ways to specify whether the server provides addresses to specific clients, or to clients the server doesn't know about.

These chapters do not discuss how to manually customize the configuration of computers, which is what network administrators must do when they don't have DHCP servers. As a network administrator, if you must configure each machine manually, you can do so based on its user's needs, rather than configuring each system identically.

This chapter describes how to program the ISC DHCP server so that it can perform many of the same customizations you might perform when configuring clients manually, as well as some automatic customizations that are difficult to perform manually. It also shows how to classify clients more accurately, and it describes the capabilities of the ISC DHCP server *class* construct. You will also learn how to set up different address allocation pools so that you can use different address allocation strategies for different clients. In addition, you will learn how to send different parameters or use different settings for specific clients, different classes of clients, and clients whose addresses come from different pools.

For the most part, this level of customization is specific to the ISC DHCP server version 3.0 and higher. Customizations that are also possible for the Microsoft Windows NT DHCP server, or for older ISC DHCP servers, are noted when appropriate.

17.1 Differentiating Between Clients

The DHCP server differentiates between clients based on what each client
sends in its messages to the server. Chapter 14, "Client Identification and Fixed-
Address Allocation," discusses how the DHCP server identifies a specific client
using either the DHCP `client identifier` option or the client's link-layer
address.

The DHCP server can also make decisions about the client based on other
options the client sends, or on the other contents of the client's packet. Unlike
the `client identifier` option and link-layer address, the other contents of a
DHCP packet generally aren't guaranteed to be unique. Configuring the server
to use them to differentiate between clients enables you to control the server's
behavior with respect to *classes* of clients, rather than just to specific individual
clients.

17.1.1 Conditional Statements

The simplest way to differentiate between clients is to use *conditional statements*.
Conditional statements work by testing some logical expression that you write;
if the result of evaluating that expression is true, some special configuration
parameters or options are defined—otherwise, they are not defined.

> **Note**
>
> *You can use many different kinds of expressions to determine what sort of client sent a request.
> Appendix B, "ISC DHCP Server Configuration File Reference," gives a complete list of the different
> kinds of expressions that the DHCP server recognizes.*

If you provide an `else` clause, the parameters or options within the `else` clause
are defined. You can chain a series of `if` statements together using the `elsif`
statement as well. Example 17.1 shows such a sequence:

Example 17.1

```
if known {
    max-lease-time 18000;
    default-lease-time 18000;
} elsif option vendor-class-identifier = "acme-printers"
    max-lease-time 90000;
    default-lease-time 90000;
} else {
    max-lease-time 300;
    default-lease-time 300;
}
```

In Example 17.1, the known expression is used to differentiate between clients. For clients that have host declarations, the default lease time is 18,000 seconds; the maximum lease time is also 18,000 seconds. Clients that don't have host declarations but send a vendor class identifier option of acme-printers get longer lease times. (Presumably printers don't need to renew their addresses as often.) Clients that don't have host declarations and don't send that option (for example, mobile clients) receive much shorter lease times.

You can also nest conditional statements, as shown in Example 17.2.

EXAMPLE 17.2

```
if substring (option dhcp-client-identifier, 0, 3) = "RAS" {
    if not known {
        deny booting;
    } else {
        max-lease-time 300;
        default-lease-time 300;
    }
} elsif known {
    max-lease-time 18000;
    default-lease-time 18000;
} else {
    max-lease-time 300;
    default-lease-time 300;
}
```

Example 17.2 checks to see whether the DHCP client identifier option begins with the string RAS. If so—and if no host declaration for that particular client exists—it is not given an IP address. If the client is known, it gets a very short lease. If the client identifier option wasn't sent, or doesn't begin with RAS, it gets a long lease time if the client is known (that is, it has a host declaration). However, if the client is not known, it gets a very short lease time, again because it's presumed to be mobile or transient.

Note

You can use conditional statements only to conditionalize option and parameter definitions. You cannot conditionally define a new option because new option definition happens when the configuration file is processed. Likewise, it's not possible to conditionally define hosts, subnets, shared networks, groups, pools, address ranges, leases, or permits because all these declarations are processed when the configuration file is parsed, not when a client request comes in.

17.1.2 Client Classing

The ISC DHCP server provides a construct called a *class* that you can use to group clients in a more general manner than you can with a host declaration. Like host declarations and subnet declarations, classes have *scope*. (See Chapter 12, "The ISC DHCP Server.") You can also use a client's membership in a class to control how addresses are allocated to it.

Clients become members of classes either because they match a class's matching rule, or because they are inserted into the class by a conditional statement. Class-matching rules are evaluated before any conditional statements that may exist in any scope. Currently, a client can be a member of up to five classes. This limit is arbitrary and may be eliminated in the future.

If a client appears in more than one class, the rules in each class's scope are evaluated in the opposite order in which the classes are matched. Class-matching rules are evaluated in the order that the classes are originally declared. If a client matches two classes based on those classes' matching rules, the scope of the class declared first in the configuration file is considered more specific than the scope of the class declared second.

Class-Matching Rules

Two kinds of class-matching rules exist: *explicit rules* and *subclass-matching rules*. In Example 17.3, if a client sends a vendor class identifier option of acme-printers or united-printers, it is considered to be in the class printers. If it sends a DHCP client identifier option that starts with the string RAS, it is a member of the ras-clients class. As an example of class-based scoping, members of the printers class receive long lease times, while members of the ras-clients class receive very short lease times. Of course, if a more specific scope overrides the class scope's definition of the domain-name option, the particular client receives the option from the more specific scope. The only scope that is more specific than a class scope is a subsequent class scope or a host declaration.

EXAMPLE 17.3

```
class "printers" {
    match if option vendor-class-identifier = "acme-printers" ||
            option vendor-class-identifier = "united-printers";
    default-lease-time 18000;
    max-lease-time 18000;
}
```

```
class "ras-clients" {
    match if substring (option dhcp-client-identifier, 0, 3) = "RAS";
    default-lease-time 300;
    max-lease-time 300;
}
```

Subclass Matching

As discussed earlier, you can use host declarations to group clients as either known or unknown. You can also use this feature to differentiate between clients that are registered with the network administrator and clients that are not. However, you may want to differentiate between clients more acutely than just whether they are registered. At registration time, it might be useful to ask whether the owner of a particular client is in the engineering department or in the sales department, for example.

Master classes and subclasses provide an efficient method of matching many different possible values that might result from evaluating some expression. Instead of specifying a match if statement, as in an explicit class declaration, a master class has a match statement with an expression that extracts some data from the client's DHCP packet. Each subclass declaration refers to its master class by name and includes in its declaration a value for the master class's match expression. If the value extracted from the client's DHCP packet matches the value specified in the subclass declaration, the client matches the master class and the subclass.

Version 3.0 of the ISC DHCP server does not support more than one match expression, although later versions of the server may. The complete syntax of expressions returning data is described in Appendix B.

Note

You can simply write a very long match if *expression for each class that extracts data from the DHCP packet and compares it to a series of different values. Unfortunately, this is very inefficient because the server must evaluate the entire* match if *expression and compare each possible value in that expression to the value extracted from the client packet.*

The lookup operation performed when matching a client to a subclass based on the master class is very efficient because the data is looked up using a hash table. This means the server doesn't have to check every possible matching value individually to see that the client is in a subclass. If you are comparing more than a few possible values, it is far more efficient to use master classes and subclasses.

When determining membership, if a client is a member of a particular subclass, it's also a member of the master class. Indeed, you cannot check that it is a member of the subclass because the subclass has the same name as the master class. Subclass scopes are considered more specific than master-class scopes. Subclasses are not, however, required to have scopes, and it saves memory if no scope is specified.

Example 17.4 shows an example of a master-class declaration and several sub-class declarations, using the DHCP client identifier option to differentiate between clients. One subclass has its own scope; the other two do not.

EXAMPLE 17.4

```
class "engineering" {
    match option dhcp-client-identifier;
}
subclass "engineering" "amee-pc";
subclass "engineering" 1:00:00:ac:42:a9:a6 {
    option root-path "server1.example.com:/var/clients/root-netbsd";
}
subclass "engineering" "nilo1";
```

As you can see from this example, it is possible that some matching data will be in the form of an ASCII string and some will be in the form of a sequence of hexadecimal bytes separated by colons. You may have noticed that subclass declarations look very much like host declarations. Indeed, in many cases you can use them in exactly the same way. However, you can't specify a fixed address in a subclass declaration, and, as Chapter 14 describes, the method a DHCP server uses to determine a client's identity is more complicated than a simple pattern match.

Explicitly Inserting Clients into Classes

Sometimes subclasses aren't sufficiently general. In such cases, you can explicitly add clients to classes, either because they execute a certain scope (for example, the host declaration scope), or because a conditional statement bases its result on some parameters or values the client sent in its request. Example 17.5 shows two host declarations and a conditional statement.

EXAMPLE 17.5

```
host brenda-pc {
    option dhcp-client-identifier "brenda";
    add "engineering";
}
host brad-pc {
    option dhcp-client-identifier 1:0:0:ac:29:ad:ea;
    add "sales";
}
```

```
if suffix (option host-name, 1) = 0 {
    add "sales";
}
```

If a client matches one of the host declarations, it is added to the class specified in that declaration. The conditional statement tests to see if the client is a Windows 95 client by seeing if the host name option it sends is null-terminated. If it is, the client is added to the sales class. This can be an option if, for example, nobody in engineering uses Windows 95.

Note

In Example 17.5, if the client matching the brenda-pc host declaration sends a null-terminated host name option for some reason, it is added to both the sales and the engineering classes. If the configuration file assumes clients can never be in both classes at once, this might be a problem, and it is a good idea to be careful about how class membership information is used.

Note

You can use classing either to assign different options and parameters based on class, or to control address allocation. However, you cannot use class membership based on the add statement to control address allocation because scopes are evaluated after address allocation occurs. So, although classification based on conditional statements can be useful for grouping clients, it is not useful for address allocation. Furthermore, class scopes are evaluated in order of specificity, with more specific scopes evaluated after less specific scopes. Host scopes are evaluated after class scopes. Therefore, a statement in a host scope adding a client to a class has no effect. A statement in a class scope adding a client to a class also has no effect because of the order in which class scopes are evaluated.

17.2 Controlling Address Allocation

You can control address allocation in two ways:

- Group one or more ranges of addresses into a pool declaration, and then control access to those pools by using permit lists.

- Specify a limit to the number of leases that members of a particular class can hold at any one time.

You can also combine these two mechanisms.

17.2.1 Pool-Based Address Allocation

An address allocation pool is a group of addresses that can be allocated on a particular network segment. Pools can contain addresses from more than one subnet, as long as all the subnets are configured on the same network segment.

Allocation Based on Class Membership

Example 17.6 shows clients from different classes grouped onto different subnets configured on the same network segment. The first pool has a permit list enabling only clients in the engineering class to be assigned addresses. The second pool's permit list enables only clients in the sales class, and the third prohibits members of the engineering and sales classes from being assigned addresses, which means all other clients will be assigned addresses from that pool. A pool's permit list is the set of all allow and deny statements within the pool declaration.

EXAMPLE 17.6

```
shared-network BUILDING-1-LAN {
    subnet 10.227.109.0 netmask 255.255.255.0 {
        option routers 10.227.109.1;
        option domain-name-servers 10.227.109.2;
        pool {
            range 10.227.109.10 10.227.109.254;
            allow members of "engineering";
        }
    }
    subnet 10.227.110.0 netmask 255.255.255.0 {
        option routers 10.227.110.1;
        option domain-name-servers 10.227.110.2;
        pool {
            range 10.227.110.10 10.227.110.254;
            allow members of "sales";
        }
    }
    subnet 10.228.0.0 netmask 255.255.255.0 {
        option routers 10.228.0.1;
        option domain-name-servers 10.228.0.2;
        pool {
            range 10.228.0.10 10.228.0.254;
            deny members of "engineering";
            deny members of "sales";
        }
    }
}
```

Example 17.6 shows pools used to contain address ranges on different subnets. However, it is also possible to have more than one allocation pool on the same subnet. For example, you may want to reserve a small pool on each subnet on your network for unregistered clients and reserve the rest of the IP addresses for registered clients. Chapter 18, "Automatic DHCP Client Registration," discusses ways that you can accomplish this.

Other Allocation Controls

In addition to permitting or denying access to a particular pool based on the class to which a client belongs, pool access can be permitted or denied in several other ways. Allocation can be permitted based on whether a client has a host declaration, using the `allow known clients` or `allow unknown clients` directives. You can also permit or deny allocation of addresses to BOOTP clients using the `allow dynamic bootp clients` directive. Finally, it is possible to explicitly permit or deny all access to a pool using the `allow all clients` or `deny all clients` directives.

17.2.2 Class-Based Address Allocation

Sometimes it is useful to restrict the number of addresses assigned to a class of clients without reserving a specific pool of addresses for the members of that class. Reserving a pool requires either that the maximum number of addresses permitted to each class is reserved at all times, or that the pool of available addresses for all permitted classes is shared in an uncontrolled manner.

For example, imagine a cable modem access provider with one large network segment serving all clients in their homes. (In practice, the network might be segmented, but this example discusses a single network segment for simplicity.) Each cable modem accesses the network by exchanging packets with a head-end system at the access provider's site. Whenever a DHCP client at home broadcasts a DHCP request, the cable modem relays that request to the central DHCP server after attaching a `relay agent information` option containing the `circuit ID` and `remote ID` agent options. The remote ID is always unique to the customer site.

This cable modem provider may want to enable customers to obtain more than one IP address, but it does not want to enable customers to obtain an unlimited number of IP addresses. You can do this by declaring a subclass for each client site, based on the contents of the `relay agent information` option, and by specifying a limit on the number of leases members of that class may obtain. Because the `relay agent information` option is appended to every client packet relayed from a particular customer site and is the same for every host at that site, this restricts the number of leases that DHCP clients at that site may obtain. Example 17.7 shows how this can be done:

EXAMPLE 17.7

```
class "customer-sites" {
    match option agent.remote-id;
    lease limit 4;
}
subclass "customer-sites" 0:42:77:a9:c6;
```

```
subclass "customer-sites" 17:a8:ee:0:0;
subclass "customer-sites" f7:aa:90:1c:2b;
subclass "customer-sites" 27:c9:45:12:a0;
subclass "customer-sites" 99:91:a0:1c:22;
```

In Example 17.7, the lease limit is specified as four in the master class. This means a maximum of four members in each subclass may hold a lease at any one time. You can also specify the lease limit on a per-subclass basis, or specify a lease limit in the master class and specify exceptions in those subclass declarations where different limits apply. Example 17.8 shows a subclass declaration with the lease limit specified.

EXAMPLE 17.8

```
subclass "customer-sites" 99:91:a0:1c:22 {
    lease limit 8;
}
```

> **Note**
>
> *If a client is a member of a class that limits the number of leases allocated to it but is also a member of a class that doesn't, it can get an IP address only through the class that limits lease allocation. If a client is a member of two classes that limit lease allocation and one is full but the other is not, its lease is allocated from the class that is not full.*

Automatic Generation of Subclasses

To further automate this process, it is possible for the ISC DHCP server to create subclasses automatically, based on the matching expression in the master class. These classes are then recorded in the lease database so that they persist across restarts of the DHCP server. This is a handy way to get the address allocation limiting described earlier without requiring anybody to, for example, register specific cable modem remote IDs with the DHCP server. Example 17.9 shows an example of a master class that automatically spawns subclasses.

EXAMPLE 17.9

```
class "customer-sites" {
    spawn with option agent.remote-id;
    lease limit 4;
}
```

In this example, whenever a request is received from a client that contains the `relay agent information` option and a `remote ID` suboption, that suboption is first looked up in the class's hash table. If it is present, the existing subclass is used. Otherwise, a new subclass is allocated and recorded in the lease database, and that new class is used to account for leases in use at that site.

17.3 `class identifier` Options

Two options are defined in the DHCP protocol specifically for the purpose of grouping DHCP clients into classes: the `user class identifier` option and the `vendor class identifier` option. The ISC DHCP server doesn't actually treat these options specially, but they have special meanings that relate to client classification. Another class-related option is the `vendor-specific information` option, which is treated specially by the DHCP server.

17.3.1 `user class` Option

The `user class` option is currently a proposed option, but it has not been standardized. It is included here because it may be standardized at some point. The `user class` option is a very simple way to classify clients consisting of a human-readable ASCII text string. DHCP clients can send this string to the DHCP server to indicate what class of user is using the machine. For example, if you support a sales department, an engineering department, and a support department, you might configure sales machines to report their user class as `sales`, engineering as `eng`, and support as `support`. You can then use this information to classify the client, as shown in Example 17.10:

EXAMPLE 17.10

```
class "sales" {
    match if option user-class = "sales";
}
class "engineering" {
    match if option user-class = "engineering";
}
class "support" {
    match if option user-class = "support";
}
```

For this option to be useful, you must configure it into each DHCP client at your site. The presumption is that every time a new DHCP-enabled workstation is installed, either the network administrator or the user configures that workstation with some kind of class identifier.

Two problems exist with this presumption. The first is that somebody must preconfigure clients with special configuration information, which users try to avoid with the DHCP protocol. The second is that the user class option is very new, and DHCP clients do not officially support it, although some clients (for example, the ISC DHCP client) can easily be configured to use it.

The problem of configuring each client that supports it with a user class option is fairly tractable. Unlike IP addresses, user class identifiers are likely to be human-readable text strings that make sense even to a novice user. Presumably, a DHCP client that supports the user class option provides a dialog box asking for the user class when the client is first installed, or provides some other straightforward mechanism so that an end user can configure it.

The second problem is less tractable. The Windows 95 and OpenTransport DHCP clients currently do not support the user class option. Until the option is standardized, it is unlikely to be widely implemented. Even then, it is unlikely, for example, that it will be possible or practical to upgrade all the old machines on a network to use it. One can hope that the usefulness of this option grows in the future, but for now it's more interesting as a hypothetical illustration of client classification than it is a practical solution to the problem.

17.3.2 vendor class identifier Option

The vendor class identifier option is intended for use by DHCP client vendors to identify the vendor that supplied the DHCP client and, possibly, to provide identification information about the hardware on which the DHCP client is running. The vendor defines the format of the vendor class identifier option. Currently, no process exists whereby vendors can ensure that the identifier they choose is unique to them. However, vendors usually use trademarked company names, so conflicts are unlikely. The Sun implementation of the vendor class identifier is used here as an example of how this option works.

Sun specifies vendor class identifiers as a hierarchical ASCII text string. Nodes in the hierarchy are delimited by the "." character. The leftmost node is least specific, with nodes increasing in specificity to the right. For example, a Sun SPARC Ultra 5/10 workstation sends a vendor class identifier of SUNW.Ultra-5_10. The most general node is SUNW, indicating that the computer is a Sun workstation. Ultra-5_10 encodes the hardware type, which is more specific. A PC running Solaris identifies itself with the vendor class identifier of SUNW.i86pc.

A workstation with a SPARC processor running Solaris may require somewhat different options than a workstation with a processor from the Intel x86 family running Solaris, and you can configure it accordingly. Example 17.11 shows how to send a different root-path option, depending on the processor architecture:

EXAMPLE 17.11

```
if option vendor-class-identifier = "SUNW.Ultra-5_10" {
    option root-path "/export/root/sparc";
} else if option vendor-class-identifier = "SUNW.i86pc" {
    option root-path "/export/root/i86pc";
}
```

Example 17.11 is somewhat simplistic; if you support DHCP clients supplied by other vendors, you may wind up with a long list of if, elsif, and else statements. Also, you may support several different types of Sun SPARC hardware and may want to specify the same behavior for all these types without listing them all explicitly.

Example 17.12 shows a more general case. It first checks to see whether the vendor class identifier option starts with the string SUNW., and then it checks the next five characters in the option to see what kind of Sun workstation sent the request.

EXAMPLE 17.12

```
if substring (option vendor-class-identifier, 0, 5) = "SUNW." {
    if substring (option vendor-class-identifier, 5, 5) = "Ultra" ||
        substring (option vendor-class-identifier, 5, 5) = "Sparc" {
    option root-path "/export/root/sparc";
    } else if substring (option vendor-class-identifier, 5, 5) = "i86pc" {
    option root-path "/export/root/i86pc";
    }
}
```

This is a very straightforward example of using the vendor class identifier option. You can also use the vendor class identifier option as a key with which to address and encapsulate a series of vendor-specific options.

17.3.3 vendor-specific information **Option**

Chapter 6, "The Format of DHCP Messages," describes the format of
DHCP messages and, in particular, the format of the DHCP options field. The
vendor-specific information option is actually a DHCP option whose length is
variable. It contains either uninterpreted vendor-specific data or a sequence of
option tags, lengths, and option data in the same format as the options field
itself.

Example 17.13 shows an example of a vendor-specific information option
that contains vendor-specific option tags. It starts with the code for the vendor-
specific information option, 43, followed by the length, and finally the
payload. The payload is a sequence of two vendor-specific options, options 1
and 2. Option 1 is an IP address (10.0.0.1 in Example 17.13), and option 2 is a
32-bit number (227883991).

EXAMPLE **17.13**

```
+—+—+—+—+—+—+—+—+—+—+—.+—+—.+
|43|12| 1| 4|10| 0| 0| 1| 2| 4|13|149|59|215|
+—+—+—+—+—+—+—+—+—+—+—.+—+—.+
```

The ISC DHCP server enables you to define vendor-specific option spaces, and
then define options within those spaces. You can then direct the DHCP server
to use option spaces you defined to generate the vendor-specific information
option. Option spaces are described in Chapter 12.

A Hypothetical Example of the vendor-specific information **Option**

For example, suppose you set up a DHCP server for use in a bank branch. The bank
purchased a customized turnkey system for operating each branch; each teller gets a
workstation, and a central server runs a couple of proprietary protocols. The vendor
defines a set of DHCP options used to configure the teller workstations. Let's call the
vendor *ExampleSoft*, and use the vendor's name for the option space. The vendor
must send two pieces of information to each workstation: the IP address of the central server, and a token that the client workstation uses to identify its location to the
central server, which may actually support more than one branch. The two options are
called central-server and site-token, respectively.

Example 17.14 shows how these options are introduced to the DHCP server.

EXAMPLE **17.14**

```
option space ExampleSoft;
option ExampleSoft.central-server    code 1 = ip-address;
option ExampleSoft.site-token        code 2 = integer 32;
```

The site also has some networked printers that get their IP addresses using DHCP and do not require the ExampleSoft vendor-specific options. Meanwhile, the branch manager has a workstation running NetBSD in her office that she uses to exchange electronic mail with other branch managers and to prepare presentations. Example 17.15 shows the use of the `vendor-option-space` statement to indicate that the ExampleSoft option space should be used to generate the `vendor-specific information` option, but only if the `vendor class identifier` option the client sent consists of the string ExampleSoft. The example also shows two subnet declarations for different branches served by the DHCP server and by the ExampleSoft branch server. It also shows how vendor-specific options can vary by scope, just like any other option.

EXAMPLE 17.15

```
if option vendor-class-identifier = "ExampleSoft" {
    vendor-option-space ExampleSoft;
}
option ExampleSoft.central-server 10.0.0.1;
option domain-name-servers 10.0.0.11, 10.0.0.12;
subnet 10.0.10.0 netmask 255.255.255.0 {
    range 10.0.10.10 10.0.10.200;
    option routers 10.0.10.1;
    option domain-name "101-main.photon-bank.com";
    option ExampleSoft.site-token 227883991;
}
subnet 10.0.11.0 netmask 255.255.255.0 {
    range 10.0.11.10 10.0.11.200;
    option routers 10.0.11.1;
    option domain-name "250-university.photon-bank.com";
    option ExampleSoft.site-token 198283471;
}
```

When a client sends in a request including a `vendor class identifier` option whose value is ExampleSoft, the DHCP server iterates through the in-scope definitions of all the options in that class to create a vendor-specific option buffer containing all the options. It then encapsulates that option buffer as the payload of the `vendor-specific information` option. The sequence of bytes shown in Example 17.13 is the `vendor-specific information` option that is returned to one of the teller workstations connected to the 10.0.10.0 subnet.

Summary

The ISC DHCP server provides a powerful collection of tools you can use to differentiate between clients. You can instruct the server to return different options to different clients based on what they send.

Options can be grouped into classes. This can be done either by testing for options that many clients may send, by having the client's scope determine its class (for example, with host declarations), or by writing conditional expressions that assign each client's class. You can control address allocation policy based on the classes of which clients are members, as well as whether clients have host declarations and whether they use the BOOTP protocol or the DHCP protocol. You can also limit the number of members of a particular class that can hold a lease at the same time. To automate per-class lease limits, you can configure the server to generate new subclasses as it runs.

Several options are designed specifically for use in classifying clients. Clients can be configured to send the `user class` option to indicate what class of user is using them, although the `user class` option is unfortunately not widely supported. Some vendors' clients may also use the `vendor class identifier` option to identify the vendor that sent the option. The `vendor class identifier` option can also be used to determine the contents of the `vendor-specific information` option.

CHAPTER **18**

Automatic DHCP Client Registration

Chapter 14, "Client Identification and Fixed-Address Allocation," explains how the DHCP server identifies clients, how you can configure it to enable only known clients to be assigned addresses, and how one of the problems with keeping a list of all clients is that someone must maintain it. This chapter describes ways of automating a solution to that problem using the ISC DHCP server and provides references for some solutions that ISC DHCP users have implemented.

Note

You may implement any of the methods suggested in this chapter using a DHCP server other than the ISC DHCP server. You can do this as long as that server differentiates between clients as specifically as the ISC server does, and provides a means whereby its database can be modified by a program. You can modify the databases of most DHCP servers, but not the Microsoft server. We are not aware of any DHCP servers that provide the same level of control over address allocation and option assignment, however.

If you want to implement a method discussed in this chapter using your vendor's DHCP server but your current version won't enable it, you should contact your vendor. Several vendors expressed interest in enhancing their DHCP servers to provide this finer-grained control, so it's quite possible your vendor has a solution for you or may be willing to provide one.

This chapter assumes you have a working knowledge of using the World Wide Web to enable users to enter data. If you find the ideas presented here interesting, but you don't understand some of the suggested solutions, it may help to learn more about web authoring: Hypertext Transfer Protocol (HTTP), Hypertext Markup Language (HTML), and common gateway interface (CGI) scripts in particular.

18.1 Registration Issues

Registering DHCP clients is problematic because each DHCP client's registration information must be entered into the DHCP server's database by some entity that is known and trusted. Chapter 14 makes the assumption that this is the responsibility of the DHCP server administrator. But imagine that you have a site with 3000 potential DHCP clients, and you want to register them all. Even if an administrator takes only 1 minute to register each client, it still takes 50 hours—an entire work week and part of the next—to enter the data. Some ISC DHCP server users suggest that this figure is optimistic—they say it can take closer to 150 hours, or nearly four work weeks, to register 3000 clients. The process also requires somebody who actually understands the registration process to resolve problems with the data supplied on registration forms.

After all the data is in, the database must be maintained. If you expect a 100 percent turnover of DHCP clients during any given year, that means you need an additional eight weeks—four weeks to delete the old records and four weeks to add the new ones. To make matters worse, chances are that at many sites, this work comes in bursts and is not spread evenly throughout the year. Generally, a user does not want to wait four weeks for his or her DHCP client to be registered; everybody wants to be first.

The best way to solve this quandary is to get as many people working on the problem as possible. The obvious group of people to put to work is the users themselves; if you have 3000 DHCP clients, you probably have 3000 users, so the total time to register all these clients is about 1 minute per user, if you can make it easy enough.

18.1.1 Individual Client Registration

To enable individual users to register their own DHCP clients in the DHCP server's database, you must provide the following capabilities:

- a way to enable users to enter their DHCP client information
- a way to ensure the user is authorized to register a DHCP client
- a way to update the DHCP server's database

- a way to update the DHCP client after the server database is updated

- a way to update the Domain Name System (DNS) with the new client's registration

Different sites are administered differently, and no standard protocol is available for registering clients. However, you can implement solutions to this problem and adapt them to the particular environment in which you want to set up DHCP service.

18.2 A Registration Application

A registration application must get enough information from the client to satisfy your needs and those of the DHCP server. The DHCP server must be configured either with a link-layer address and a network hardware type for the DHCP client, or the client identifier the client will send. In order to prove that the user is permitted to enter a DHCP client's information, you probably need at least a username and password from the user, or some other way of identifying the user to your satisfaction. You may also want to have the user request a domain name for the client as part of the registration process, and perhaps fill out a questionnaire.

You can collect the information the DHCP server cares about in one of two ways:

- Tell the user how to get the information and have the user enter it.

- Deduce the information based on the location from which the user is connecting.

If the user is running the registration application from the computer he or she is registering, you can use the IP (Internet Protocol) address of that computer to look up the relevant information in the DHCP server's database. Otherwise, the user must enter the information.

Note

In order to get the client's information from the DHCP server, the DHCP server must already be providing service to the client. If that's the case, you are probably wondering what the point of registering is. This is covered later on in the chapter.

The program you write to enable the user to register can be an application the user installs on his or her computer. It can also be run on a computer (or computers) in a central area to which the user has access. Or it can be a CGI program running on a Web server to which the user connects using some secure transport. The simplest of these three alternatives is probably the CGI program.

Because the user must provide authentication, and because Web browsers use a network protocol to submit information, you must use a secure network transport protocol to get the user login information to the CGI program. You can do this by running the HTTP over an SSL (Secure Sockets Layer) connection. SSL encrypts the network traffic between the Web browser and the web server so that it is impossible to snoop on the network and find out what data is sent.

Most commercial Web servers provide integrated support for SSL, and the open source Apache Web server (http://www.apache.org) can be made to support SSL (see http://www.apache-ssl.org or http://www.ravenssl.com for details). Until the relevant patents expire, it is not legal to use SSL in the United States for commercial purposes unless you have paid a license fee to RSA, Inc. (see http://www.rsa.com). If you are using a free SSL implementation, you should make sure you are using it legally.

18.2.1 Getting the DHCP Server Registration Information

The hardest part about getting the user to enter registration information into the database is explaining to the user how to figure out what to enter. This is covered in a general way in Chapter 14, and in a specific way for some DHCP clients in Chapter 19,"DHCP Clients," but you must be *much* more explicit to enable a less experienced user to enter the correct information. Thus, this choice is not advised. If you have a very knowledgeable user base or feel you can explain the process sufficiently, getting the information is a simple matter of having blank places in the form to enter it.

Instead of having the user enter the registration data, it is better to simply collect the information automatically when the user uses the registration Web page. The registration program learns the IP address of the DHCP client when the user submits the registration. Using the IP address, it can look up the client lease in the DHCP server lease database and extract the client's identification information from the lease.

Example 18.1 shows a lease declaration from the ISC DHCP server lease database. The `hardware` declaration records the client's network hardware type and link-layer address. If the client sends a `dhcp-client-identifier` option, a `uid` declaration records the identifier the client sent. If more than one lease declaration exists for a particular IP address in the lease file, the last declaration is the current one.

EXAMPLE 18.1

```
lease 10.0.0.3 {
    starts 0 1999/04/11 20:22:17;
    ends 1 1999/04/12 08:22:17;
    hardware ethernet 00:a0:24:ab:fb:9c;
    uid 01:00:a0:24:ab:fb:9c;
    client-hostname "SNEECH";
}
```

18.2.2 Incentives to Register

This brings up a bit of a chicken-and-egg problem, though. If you want DHCP clients to register before you give them IP addresses, how can the user of a DHCP client machine that is not yet registered get an IP address to connect to the registration server?

The answer is that the DHCP server must be configured to assign IP addresses to unregistered clients, and users of DHCP clients must be given an incentive to register. Essentially, you either have to restrict access to the network to unregistered clients or provide additional services to registered clients.

For example, you can enable registered clients to be given assigned names in the DNS or to be given permanent IP addresses. You can also limit the number of addresses available to unregistered clients, provide different options, provide addresses on subnets that do not have Internet access, or provide restricted routing for some IP addresses.

Limiting Unregistered Clients

You can configure the DHCP server to assign IP addresses to unregistered clients from the same pool as registered clients, but to limit unregistered clients to a very small number of leases. This means that a user who fails to register tends to have trouble getting access to the network. Unfortunately, users of new computers that aren't registered simply because the user didn't have a chance to register them will have trouble registering, so this is probably not the best solution. However, if none of the other solutions works, this one is easy to implement using only the DHCP server.

Example 18.2 shows a class declaration that limits all unknown clients served by the DHCP server on any network segments to a maximum of two leases:

EXAMPLE 18.2

```
class "unregistered" {
  match if not known;
  lease limit 2;
}
```

With this configuration, when a client that is not registered connects to the network, it requests an IP address from the DHCP server. The DHCP server classifies it in the unregistered class, and checks its records for that class to see how many other clients have leases in the class. If fewer than two clients in the class have leases, the server grants the new client a lease. Otherwise, the server does not provide the client with a lease.

Providing Different Options

Another way of limiting access to the network for unregistered clients is to limit or change the options sent to unregistered clients. For example, by referring unregistered clients to a different DNS server than registered clients, you can prevent those clients from looking up any name other than the name of your registration server. A dishonest user can work around this by simply overriding the DNS server setting from the DHCP client, but if you are more worried about combating laziness than dishonesty, this can be a successful tactic.

This particular tactic requires you to set up a special DNS server that only knows about the name of your registrar server. Example 18.3 shows an excerpt from a dhcpd.conf file, the complete named.conf file, and the three complete zone files used to implement a restricted name server and refer unregistered clients to it. The named.conf file format used is for ISC BIND, version 8.1.2.

EXAMPLE 18.3

— -dhcpd.conf — -
```
option domain-name-servers ns1.example.com, ns2.example.com;
class "unregistered" {
  match if not known;
  option domain-name-servers registrar.example.com;
}
```

- -named.conf - -

```
options {
    directory "/tmp";
};
zone "." {
    type master;
    file "dot.db";
};
zone "example.com" {
    type master;
    file "example.com.db";
};
zone "in-addr.arpa" {
    type master;
    file "inaddr.db";
};
```

dot.db

```
$ORIGIN example.com.
.          IN    SOA   registrar postmaster (1999032501 3600 1800 604800 3600)
           IN    NS registrar.example.com.
registrar IN    A 10.0.0.2
```

example.com.db

```
$ORIGIN example.com.
example.com. IN SOA registrar postmaster (1999032501 3600 1800 604800 3600)
             IN NS registrar.example.com.
registrar       IN    A 10.0.0.2
```

inaddr.db

```
$ORIGIN example.com.
in-addr.arpa. IN  SOA registrar postmaster (1999032501 3600 1800 604800 3600)
              IN  NS  registrar.example.com.
registrar       IN  A    10.0.0.2
$ORIGIN in-addr.arpa.
1.0.0.127       IN  PTR registrar.example.com.
2.0.0.10        IN  PTR registrar.example.com.
```

Note

As Chapter 19 mentions, most versions of the Microsoft DHCP client do not use new configuration information they receive in DHCP transactions after they are initially configured, even after the computer is restarted. If you register a Microsoft DHCP client in this way, it does not use the new domain-name-server option, and does not function properly. In version 3.1 of the ISC DHCP server, the registration application will be able to set a flag on a lease instructing the DHCP server to send a DHCPNAK in response to the next renewal request received from the client for that lease.

Assigning Addresses from Restricted Subnets

Another alternative is to simply allocate a separate subnet on each network segment strictly for unregistered clients. If you don't provide routing from that subnet to the Internet (or, for that matter, to anywhere but your registration server), users of unregistered clients are unable to use the network to do anything but register. This method requires you to configure every router on your network to support a second subnet, so it may be too labor-intensive for some sites. However, addresses reserved for unregistered clients are not taken away from the address pool for registered clients, which an be a significant advantage.

Example 18.4 shows a simple configuration file that provides a separate registration subnet for one network segment:

EXAMPLE 18.4

```
class "unregistered" {
  match if not known;
}
shared-network FOO {
  subnet 204.152.184.0 netmask 255.255.255.0 {
    option routers 204.152.184.1;
  }
  subnet 10.0.0.0 netmask 255.255.255.0 {
    option routers 10.0.0.1;
  }

  pool {
    deny members of "unregistered";
    range 204.152.184.10 204.152.184.254;
  }

  pool {
    allow members of "unregistered";
    range 10.0.0.2 10.0.0.254;
  }
}
```

Assigning Addresses with Restricted Routing

Having a separate subnet for unregistered clients on each network segment is a very effective way to encourage users of unregistered clients to register. Unfortunately, as mentioned earlier, you must configure every router on your network with a secondary subnet for each network segment, probably with its own routing information. A similar method exists that is a bit less effective but that also takes a lot less work to maintain. Simply reserve a small group of addresses on every subnet for unregistered clients, and then block those addresses at your external firewall. You may also want to block access from those IP addresses to key servers at your site so that users of unregistered DHCP clients can't, for example, get their mail from the internal Post Office Protocol (POP) server.

Example 18.5 shows how you can configure the DHCP server to do this:

EXAMPLE 18.5

```
class "unregistered" {
  match if not known;
}
subnet 204.152.184.0 netmask 255.255.255.0 {
  option routers 204.152.184.1;
  pool {
    deny members of "unregistered";
    range 204.152.184.10 204.152.184.244;
  }
  pool {
    allow members of "unregistered";
    range 204.152.184.245 204.152.184.254;
  }
}
```

18.2.3 Registering the Client

After the user submits a registration form, the DHCP server's configuration must be updated—a new host declaration describing the client must be added. Generally, you cannot stop a user from registering the same client twice, so it's probably best that the program that updates the configuration file check for a previous host declaration for the client and remove it before making a new one. After this is done, the registration program should make the appropriate changes to the DHCP server's database to add the newly registered client.

When the server's database is updated, you must restart the server. You can do this automatically every time an update is done. However, if registrations are happening frequently and the configuration file is expected to be large, it may be better to have a *cron* job (see your computer system's documentation for the cron command) that checks the configuration file every few minutes and restarts the server if it's changed. The interval should be no longer than the time you expect it to take for a user to restart his or her machine, however.

18.2.4 Getting Registered Clients to Switch

At this point, it is important to think about what happens *after* a DHCP client is registered. When the DHCP server has the client's registration information, the DHCP client should get its newer, better IP address quickly; otherwise, the DHCP client's user still cannot use the network.

Probably the easiest way to solve this problem is to simply instruct the user to restart his or her computer. When the computer restarts, the client should start up either in the INIT or INIT-REBOOT state. In either case, it immediately contacts the DHCP server. If it is in the INIT-REBOOT state, it sends a DHCPREQUEST for the IP address it got when it wasn't registered. In Examples 18.4 and 18.5, the client gets a DHCPNAK because it cannot use the IP address it had before. In Example 18.2, the lease usage for the unregistered class is updated so that a new unregistered client can have a lease.

Another method that requires more patience but less action from the user is to simply provide very short leases to unregistered clients so that they renew quickly and pick up their new IP address or configuration information. Example 18.6 shows a class declaration that gives unknown clients short leases.

EXAMPLE 18.6

```
class "unregistered" {
  match if not known;
  default-lease-time 60

  max-lease-time 60;
}
```

18.3 Authenticating the User Registration Process

To have users register their own DHCP clients without any intervention on the part of the network administrator, you must have a pre-established trust relationship between the network administrator and the user. Without such a relationship, you cannot tell whether a person is authorized to register a DHCP client. Automatic registration, therefore, depends on one of three things:

- A site-wide system for managing and authenticating this trust relationship must already be in place.

- It must be less expensive to install and operate such a system than it is to have the network administrator do all the work.

- You must get more benefit from the system than just the capability for users to securely register their DHCP clients.

If none of these conditions applies, it is probably not worthwhile to try to set up an automatic DHCP registration system.

18.3.1 Leveraging an Existing Authentication System

Many sites already have some kind of site-wide system for enabling users to prove their identities so that they can access shared resources such as file servers and mail servers in a secure manner. The system may be either a distributed, network-based authentication system such as Kerberos, or it may be host-based. For example, servers from which users get their mail and file service may have a password database for all users. A mainframe running MVS has one of several security systems (for example, RACF), and if all (or even most) users have an account on that mainframe, that password database can be used for authentication.

18.3.2 Using Kerberos, DCE, or Windows NT Authentication

Windows NT and DCE (the Open Software Foundation's Distributed Computing Environment) both use Kerberos for authentication. Kerberos acts as a trusted third party to provide secure authentication across a network, using a central database of users and shared secrets.

Note

Kerberos is only one protocol that Windows NT can use for authentication. The mere fact that you are using distributed authentication with Windows NT does not mean you are using Kerberos. Kerberos is discussed here because it's a solution that can work in a heterogeneous environment, unlike other kinds of authentication performed by Windows NT. Also, although Kerberos is the most widely deployed distributed authentication scheme, it is by no means the only one, and any distributed authentication scheme you have can probably implement automatic registration.

For Kerberos-based DCE or NT authentication to be useful, it must be widely used; it never makes sense for you to install any of these systems just so you can automate the user registration process. However, because all these systems use Kerberos authentication as their basis, you can set up a common authentication database that supports UNIX, Windows, and NT systems, and possibly even the newest Mac OS systems.

18.3.3 Using Host-Based Password Authentication

If you are using host-based password authentication, you must provide a secure channel from the registration server to the host on which the password database is stored so that the user's password isn't exposed when the user registers. If possible, run the registration server on the system with the central password database.

18.3.4 A Credit Card-Based Registration System

One way to validate users is to figure out whether they have information that enables them to pay for access to the network. If you are an Internet service provider providing access using the DHCP protocol, your registration server may be just a Web page where users enter their credit card information, enabling you to establish a billing relationship at the same time the client is registered. Depending on how this is set up, you may also want to set up a program that automatically de-registers users when they stop paying.

18.4 Future Work

Development on the ISC DHCP server is ongoing at the time of this writing, and two of the ongoing projects bear directly on the registration process. One project will make writing registration applications a lot easier by providing the ability to communicate directly with the DHCP server to read and write its database. The second project is an implementation of the DHCP authentication protocol described in Chapter 21, "Authentication of DHCP Clients and Servers." After the DHCP authentication protocol is implemented, it will be necessary to provide a mechanism for managing keys; a registration program will be a great way to accomplish this.

Summary

Many sites want to keep track of the DHCP clients for which they provide service. The DHCP protocol doesn't include a way to do this directly, but the ISC DHCP server provides tools for registering clients, and for differentiating between registered and unregistered clients. Additional features of the ISC DHCP server make it possible to force unregistered clients to use different addresses or parameters than registered clients. You can take advantage of this by writing a user-friendly registration application that enables users to register DHCP clients themselves, removing this workload from the network administrator.

## CHAPTER 19

DHCP Clients

Previous chapters go into great detail about the DHCP protocol and about various aspects of how DHCP servers work and are configured. This chapter describes:

- How a DHCP client works

- Some specific DHCP clients and what is unusual about them

- Some of the problems you may have when using or providing DHCP service for clients

19.1 Theory of Operation

In describing the theory behind how a DHCP client operates, this chapter refers primarily to the ISC DHCP client because readers can examine the source code of this client. However, the issues raised here should be similar for any DHCP client. As such, this chapter also discusses how the behavior of another client differs from the behavior of the ISC client.

The DHCP client runs as a daemon process; that is, it is started when the computer first starts up, and it continues to run until the computer is halted. The DHCP client actually drives the DHCP protocol; it has an internal state machine that makes transitions as the client moves through the protocol. The DHCP client finite state machine is illustrated in Figure 8.1 and described in more detail in Chapter 8, "DHCP Message Exchanges."

19.1.1 Getting an IP Address

When the client is first started, it reads in a database of old leases, examines each lease in the database, and discards the lease if it has expired. If any leases remain when this process is completed, the client chooses the lease acquired most recently and enters the INIT-REBOOT state. In this state, the client broadcasts a DHCPREQUEST message to ensure that the lease it remembers is valid for the network segment to which it is connected. If it gets no response, it resends the DHCPREQUEST message. If it receives no response after a certain period of time elapses, it tries to use the IP address in the lease.

When they fail to confirm their lease during the INIT-REBOOT state, most DHCP clients simply use the IP address they tried to confirm. If the ISC DHCP client fails to confirm its lease using a broadcast DHCPREQUEST message, it tries to confirm that the address is appropriate for the subnet to which it is attached. It does this by configuring its network connection with that address and sending an Internet Control Message Protocol (ICMP) echo request to its default router. If it gets a response, it uses the old address; otherwise, it tries to determine whether any of the other unexpired addresses work on the current subnet. If the client can't contact the default router with any of its unexpired addresses, the client reverts to the TIMEOUT state.

As DHCP is specified in RFC2131, a client is expected to start in the INIT state if it has no unexpired leases. Many clients implement this behavior and immediately broadcast a DHCPDISCOVER message when starting with no unexpired leases. However, you can interpret the text in RFC2131 to enable a client to first try to renew an expired lease and then revert to the INIT state it the renewal fails. Some versions of the ISC DHCP client start in the INIT-REBOOT state if they have a record of an old lease, even though that lease expired. If the ISC client is unable to renew the lease, it reverts to the TIMEOUT state.

If the ISC client receives no response to its broadcast message in the INIT state, it continues retransmitting DHCPDISCOVER messages for some configurable period of time (usually 60 seconds). If it doesn't find a valid lease within that time period, it reverts to the TIMEOUT state.

19.1.2 When the Client Fails to Get an Address

The TIMEOUT state mentioned in the preceding section is not included in the protocol specification, but many DHCP client implementors added it (or something like it) to their state machines. The purpose of the TIMEOUT state is to enable the client to "give up" and notify the user in some way that it failed to acquire an IP address.

When the ISC DHCP client is started, it runs in the foreground until it has either found an IP address or entered the TIMEOUT state. This enables daemons that are started after the client to assume that the network is configured before they are started, but it prevents the client from holding up the system startup indefinitely. After the purpose of the TIMEOUT state is fulfilled, the client waits for a configurable interval and then reverts to the INIT state.

The Microsoft DHCP client included in Windows 95 will time out after a certain period of time elapses and display a pop-up window notifying the user that it failed to acquire an IP address. The user is asked to indicate whether the DHCP client should continue periodically displaying this message. While the client waits for the user to make a choice, and then after the choice is made, the DHCP client continues to try to acquire an IP address. If the dialog box is still being displayed when the IP address is acquired, the client removes it.

> **Note**
>
> *The Microsoft DHCP client that comes with Windows 98 behaves very differently. When it reaches the TIMEOUT state, it temporarily gives up on getting an IP address through DHCP, and instead goes on to the IPv4 auto-configuration protocol. When using this protocol, it simply chooses an IP address out of the 65,534 possible IP addresses in the 169.254.0.0/16 subnet. It then sends an Address Resolution Protocol (ARP) request to see whether the address is in use; if it is, it chooses a different address from the same subnet at random. It continues to do this until it finds an address that isn't in use, and then it configures that address. It then periodically attempts to use DHCP to get an IP address. If it finally contacts a DHCP server, it stops using the auto-configured IP address.*

19.1.3 Using an IP Address After It Is Acquired

After the DHCP client acquires an IP address, it enters the BOUND state. When it initially enters this state, it configures the network interface with the new IP address. If the server provides a default route, it installs that route. The ISC DHCP client also uses the domain-name option (if the server provides one) and the domain-name-servers option to create an /etc/resolv.conf file. This is a standard configuration file on most UNIX and UNIX-like systems that is used to configure domain name service.

In addition to configuring the network interface, when the DHCP client enters the BOUND state, it also makes a persistent record of the lease it acquired in a disk file. This record includes any DHCP options the server sends; you can use that lease information later if the client is restarted.

19.1.4 Maintaining a Lease on an IP Address

After the DHCP client acquires a lease, it must maintain it. When half of the duration of the lease expires, the client enters the RENEWING state, and periodically unicasts a DHCPREQUEST message to the server that assigned it its lease, requesting an extension. If it gets a response to this request that extends its lease, it re-enters the BOUND state until half of the duration of the new lease once again expires. The client need not reconfigure the network interface when it renews its lease, but it does make use of any changes in the options that the server sends—for example, the default route and the domain name service configuration. The new lease is also recorded on disk for later use.

If seven-eighths of the lease time expires and it still receives no response, the client enters the REBINDING state and begins broadcasting DHCPREQUEST messages to locate some other DHCP server that will renew its lease.

19.1.5 When the Lease Expires

If for some reason the client is unable to renew its lease before the entire duration of the lease expires, the client must stop using the IP address it is leased. The client deletes the IP address from its interface configuration and goes back to the INIT state to try to get a new address.

19.1.6 Multiple Network Interfaces

The above discussion assumes the client can operate on only one network interface. This is not far from the truth; if more than one network interface must be configured, the DHCP client program actually sets up a separate state machine for each interface. These state machines operate independently from one another; one interface can be in the BOUND state, while another interface is in the INIT state, for example.

As far as IP address configurations go, this state of affairs works perfectly well; each interface is configured with an IP address as soon as a server provides one. Unfortunately, with respect to DHCP options, if two interfaces get different configurations, no mechanism exists within the ISC DHCP client to decide which set of options to use. Instead, the set of options most recently received prevails. This problem is expected to be a matter for future work on the ISC DHCP client.

Note

Generally, it is not known how the problem is resolved in the Microsoft DHCP client, if it is resolved at all. The Solaris DHCP client provides a mechanism whereby one interface can be declared primary and all others secondary. The DHCP client then installs the options obtained when the primary interface gets an IP address and ignores options obtained for any other interface.

19.1.7 More Than One IP Address Per Interface

Occasionally, users ask for a mechanism for obtaining more than one IP address for a single network interface. The ISC DHCP client included in Version 3.0 of the ISC DHCP distribution actually supports this capability. A pseudo-interface can be declared and associated with a real interface, and the DHCP client allocates a separate state machine for that pseudo-interface.

You must give the pseudo-interface a different DHCP client identifier than is sent for the primary interface, or the DHCP server cannot differentiate between the two requests and assigns the same IP address to both interfaces. The standard DHCP client does not provide any way to actually use the second IP address.

19.2 The Microsoft DHCP Client

Microsoft has included a DHCP client with Windows since it released Windows for Workgroups. DHCP clients are included with Windows 95, Windows 98, and Windows NT 4.0. Windows 2000 is also expected to include a DHCP client. These DHCP clients are in some ways quite similar to each other and in other ways quite different from each other. This section tries to capture the essential similarities and differences.

The coverage concentrates on Windows 95, Windows 98, and Windows NT 4.0 because Windows for Workgroups is nearly obsolete at the time of this writing. NT 4.0 Service Pack 4 (SP4) is described here, but the differences between NT 4.0 SP4 and other service packs should be minimal.

19.2.1 Installing and Enabling the Microsoft DHCP Client

To use the DHCP client in Windows 95 and Windows 98, you must install Internet Protocol (IP) networking. You can do this by right-clicking the Network Neighborhood icon on the Windows Desktop and selecting Properties.

Windows 95

In Windows 95, when you right-click the Network Neighborhood box and select Properties, Windows displays the Network dialog box. If you select the Configuration tab, you see a window within the dialog box that lists a series of protocols and the network interfaces to which these protocols are bound. If the TCP/IP protocol is already bound to the interface you intend to use, you don't need to install it again. If it is not, click Add.

Windows 95 displays the Select Network Component Type dialog box. Click the line that reads Protocol, and then click the Add button. This opens the Select Network Protocol dialog box, which contains two windows: The one on the left displays a list of manufacturers, and the one on the right displays a list of protocols. The manufacturer for the TCP/IP protocol is Microsoft; if you click Microsoft in the left window, you should see TCP/IP as one of the choices in the right window. You can click TCP/IP, and then click OK to install it. Windows may prompt you to insert a floppy disk or CD-ROM from which it can install the TCP/IP software.

Figure 19.1 shows the Network dialog box, the Select Network Component Type dialog box, and the Select Network Protocol dialog box, as they look if you follow the above instructions to the point just before you click OK.

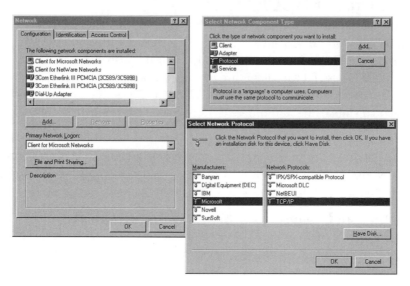

FIGURE 19.1   *Dialog boxes used when installing TCP/IP on Windows 95.*

After you install TCP/IP protocol support, you can configure it by selecting a TCP/IP binding from the Network dialog box; you should select the binding for the network card on which you want to enable DHCP. Then click Properties, and Windows displays the TCP/IP Properties dialog box. Select the IP Address tab as shown in Figure 19.2, and click the radio button labeled "Obtain an IP address automatically" to enable DHCP.

You can configure the Windows 95 DHCP client to obtain its IP address from DHCP, but still use a statically configured Domain Name System (DNS) configuration. If you do not want it to do this, you should go back to the TCP/IP Properties dialog box and select the DNS Configuration tab. Then click the Disable DNS radio button. If DNS is enabled, even if you didn't provide configuration information, Windows 95 does not use the DNS configuration the DHCP server provides.

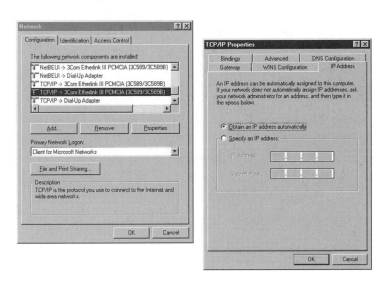

FIGURE 19.2 *The TCP/IP Properties dialog box.*

Windows 98

The Windows 98 DHCP installation and configuration process is essentially the same as the Windows 95 process. The only difference you might notice is that in the Select Network Protocol dialog box, when you select Microsoft as the manufacturer, many more protocol types show up. The TCP/IP protocol is at the very end of the list, so you must scroll down to see it.

Windows NT 4.0

In Windows NT 4.0, after you right-click Network Neighborhood and select Properties, you see the Network dialog box. Within this dialog box is a window labeled Network Protocols. If you see a line of text in this window that reads TCP/IP Protocol, the protocol is already installed. Otherwise, click the Add button, and the Select Network Protocol dialog box is displayed. You must then select the line that reads TCP/IP Protocol from the Network Protocol: window. Figure 19.3 shows the Network dialog box and the Select Network Protocol dialog box.

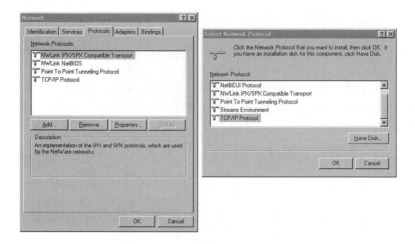

FIGURE 19.3   *Dialog boxes used when installing TCP/IP on Windows NT 4.0.*

After you install the TCP/IP protocol, it is displayed in the Network Protocols:
window. You can then highlight it by clicking it. Click Properties to open the
Microsoft TCP/IP Properties dialog box, which has a series of menu tabs at the
top. Select IP Address, as shown in Figure 19.4. To enable the DHCP client,
simply click the radio button labeled Obtain an IP Address from a DHCP
Server. The dialog box does not allow you to enable the DHCP client if you
configure NT to act as a DHCP server.

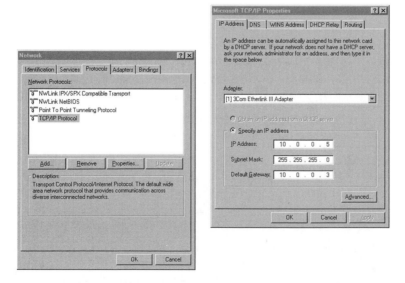

FIGURE 19.4   *The Microsoft TCP/IP Properties dialog box.*

19.2.2 User Interface

The Microsoft Windows DHCP client for Windows 95 and Windows 98 has a user interface program called winipcfg. This is not available as a selection on the start menu; to use it, you must choose the Run selection from the Start menu, and then type winipcfg into the Open dialog box and click OK.

winipcfg then pops up its own dialog box displaying the status of the DHCP client. To see the complete status, click the More Info button. Figure 19.5 shows winipcfg after More Info is selected.

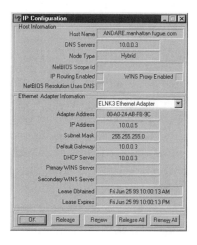

FIGURE 19.5 *The winipcfg dialog box.*

You can use the winipcfg dialog box to see what options the DHCP server sends, to see what IP address the server provides, and to display various other details of the DHCP client's state. If the client is configuring more than one network adapter, you can change the adapter whose state is being displayed or affected by selecting the network adapter from the text widget below the Ethernet Adapter Information label.

You can also use winipcfg to release and renew the DHCP client's lease; to release the lease, click the Release or Release All button. To renew the lease, click the Renew or Renew All button. Release and Renew affect only the configuration for the network interface whose state is currently displayed, whereas Release All and Renew All affect the state of all network adapters.

19.2.3 Behavior Specific to the Microsoft DHCP Client

This section describes some of the unique behavior of the Microsoft DHCP client. Although this behavior is, by and large, unique to the Microsoft DHCP client, these differences are due to interpretation of the protocol specification. Nothing that the Microsoft DHCP client does that is documented here is specifically forbidden by the protocol specification.

Hostname

The DHCP protocol standard, and indeed the documentation for many DHCP servers, leads you to believe that if you define a host-name option for a particular DHCP client, that client uses the defined host-name option. Unfortunately, the Microsoft DHCP client does not use the host-name option in this way. Indeed, it ignores the host-name option in any DHCP packets it receives.

Instead, it uses the host-name option to tell the DHCP server what it thinks its name is. It does this by sending its NetBIOS Name Service (NBNS) name in the host-name option whenever it sends a DHCPDISCOVER or DHCPREQUEST message. Some DHCP servers take advantage of this by using the NBNS name to do a DNS update. Also, as mentioned in Chapter 14, "Client Identification and Fixed-Address Allocation," you can configure some DHCP servers to use the NBNS name as a client identifier. Some problems occur with this, but to understand them, you must know a bit about NBNS.

Microsoft historically has used NBNS, also known as Windows Internet Name Service (WINS), to name Windows network clients. NBNS is a distributed naming protocol, which can function over IPX or IP, and can operate whether or not a centralized NBNS server is present. If no centralized NBNS server is present, the protocol operates by broadcasting NBNS queries to the network and waiting for responses. NBNS is in the same class of protocol as Sun's Network Information Services protocol; it is easy to manage, and therefore advantageous, on a small network, but it does not scale to use throughout the Internet.

When Microsoft Windows is first installed, one of the questions it asks the person installing it is the name of the system. This question is mandatory; you can't finish the install without answering it. People tend to answer the question in a variety of ways; if an individual is installing a single Windows workstation, he or she might give it a name such as "TEDSPC" or "SNEECH." A systems administrator who is installing large numbers of Windows machines might have a standard way of choosing the name of the PC—either the name of the person to whom it is delivered, or some counting scheme, such as "PC001," "PC002," and so on. You can determine the NBNS name of a Windows machine by right-clicking the Network Neighborhood icon, selecting Properties from the menu, and then selecting the Identification tab, as shown in Figure 19.6.

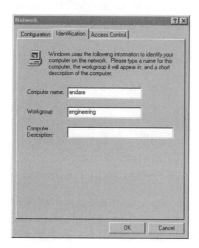

FIGURE 19.6 *Finding the NBNS name of a Windows computer.*

When the Windows machine first becomes active on the network, it uses the NBNS protocol to ensure that its name is unique within its workgroup. If an NBNS server is serving the administrative domain in which the workstation is installed, this process succeeds; if the user chooses a name in use by some other user in the same workgroup, Windows chooses a different name. If no NBNS server exists, you cannot ensure that the name is unique. Note also that NBNS only ensures that a name is unique within a workgroup, so if you have more than one active workgroup on your network, the NBNS name alone is not guaranteed to be unique.

Note

You can determine whether a client broadcasts WINS requests by the response it gets from the DHCP server. You can do this because the DHCP server can send a netbios-node-type *option to indicate whether Windows should broadcast or contact a WINS server, and it can also send the* netbios-name-servers *option to indicate which name servers should be contacted. Because a response from the DHCP server can affect the conflict resolution process, the DHCP server cannot assume that WINS has checked the hostname for uniqueness before the DHCP client starts.*

As a consequence, although it would be handy to be able to count on the uniqueness of the name that the Microsoft DHCP client sends in the host-name option, it is not possible to do so. If a DHCP server is going to use this name as a unique identifier, this may result in an identifier conflict, as described in Chapter 14. If a DHCP server wants to update the DNS using the host-name option sent by the Microsoft client, it must perform its own conflict resolution process prior to doing so, and it must ensure that the name is not already claimed by some other client.

Client Identifier

The Microsoft DHCP client does not provide a user interface by which the user can choose the client identifier that it sends. Instead, it uses the format suggested in RFC2132; the client identifier is a series of bytes beginning with a single byte containing the network hardware type, followed by the link-layer address of the network interface that the DHCP client is configuring.

Option Updates

When the Microsoft DHCP client renews its lease, it does not use any new values for options that it may receive. For example, consider the case in which a Windows 95 machine starts up, acquires an IP address, and learns that its domain name is radish.org and its domain name server is 10.0.0.7. If the DHCP server administrator later updates the DHCP server configuration so that the correct name server IP address is 10.0.0.9, Windows continues to use 10.0.0.7 as the domain name server IP address. The only way to stop Windows from doing this is to run the winipcfg application, and release and renew the lease.

Note

Both Windows 95 and Windows 98 have been observed to behave this way, but tests were not done to verify that this problem persists in Windows NT, nor are we certain that the problem exists in all service pack levels of Windows 95 or Windows 98.

DHCPINFORM

Some Windows applications may need information from the DHCP server that is not requested or sent when the DHCP client acquires its lease. In that case, the application can send a DHCPINFORM message requesting further information. For this reason, recent versions of Windows frequently generate DHCPINFORM requests, and it's helpful to have a DHCP server that supports DHCPINFORM.

19.3 The ISC DHCP Client

The ISC DHCP client is a general-purpose client intended for use on computers running UNIX and UNIX-like operating systems. The DHCP client protocol engine is implemented using the same underlying network code that's used to implement the DHCP server. On top of that is a protocol engine written in C. When an address is acquired, the portion of the DHCP client that is written in C does not perform the system-specific operations required to install the new IP address. Instead, it invokes a shell script that is programmed with system-specific commands to handle configuration of interfaces and routes, and to install the domain name service configuration.

19.3.1 Installation

The ISC DHCP client is included in the ISC DHCP distribution. The instructions for installing the DHCP server, included in Chapter 12, "The ISC DHCP Server," and in Appendix H, "DHCP Server and Operating System Versions," also apply to the client. The client program is called dhclient, and it is installed automatically when you type make install after building the distribution, as shown in Chapter 12.

Because the underlying network interface code is the same for the ISC DHCP client and server, the system-specific caveats mentioned in Appendix H all apply to the client as well as the server. Like the server, the client should be installed in the system startup script so that it automatically configures network interfaces on system startup.

19.3.2 Operation

As mentioned in Section 19.1, the ISC DHCP client normally starts up and runs in the foreground until it acquires an IP address. After it does so, the foreground process exits, and the client continues running in the background as a daemon.

You can take advantage of this behavior by starting the DHCP client in the system startup script before any daemons that depend on the network being configured. Because the client does not exit until the network is configured (or until it can no longer successfully be configured), daemons that are started after the DHCP client's foreground process exits can reasonably depend on having network connectivity when they are started.

If, for some reason, it is not considered desirable to have the DHCP client go into the background on startup, you can specify the -d switch. You can specify the -q switch to make the client startup process completely silent. You can obtain a complete listing of DHCP client switches in the dhclient manual page by typing man dhclient at the shell prompt.

You can control which broadcast interfaces the DHCP client should configure by providing a list of those interfaces on the command line. The names of the interfaces should be the same names shown when you type `netstat -i`.

19.3.3 Configuration

The ISC DHCP client does not require any special configuration. However, it is possible to provide a configuration to change the default behavior of the DHCP client. You can widely adjust the DHCP client's protocol timing through the configuration file. You can also configure the client to send different values to the DHCP server.

Requesting Additional Options

For example, if you are adding a custom DHCP client script that takes advantage of DHCP options that the default DHCP client script does not use, you may want to configure the DHCP client to specifically request those options. You can do this using the `request` statement, as shown in Example 19.1 (note that if you set up a parameter request list, you must explicitly request the `subnet mask`, `routers`, `domain-name`, and `domain-name-servers` options, or the client does not receive those options):

EXAMPLE 19.1

```
request subnet-mask, routers, domain-name, domain-name-servers,
      ntp-servers;
```

Rejecting Unacceptable Offers

You can instruct the DHCP client to reject DHCP offers that do not provide options the client needs. For example, you might say that at a minimum, the client needs a `subnet-mask` and `routers` option, as shown in Example 19.2:

EXAMPLE 19.2

```
require subnet-mask, routers;
```

Overriding Options Sent by the DHCP Server

You can also configure the DHCP client to override or augment some values that the DHCP server returns to it. For instance, the DHCP server may return a domain name of "fugue.com," but you may want to have the `/etc/resolv.conf` specify a domain search path of `manhattan.fugue.com fugue.com`. You can do this with the `prepend` statement. If the computer on which you are running the DHCP server has a local name server, you may want to use only your own name server. You can accomplish this using the `supersede` statement.

Example 19.3 shows a sample configuration that performs these two customizations.

EXAMPLE 19.3

```
prepend domain-name "manhattan.fugue.com";
supersede domain-name-servers 127.0.0.1;
```

Interface-Specific Customizations

You can also specify different customizations for different network interfaces. One useful customization is simply to specify a list of network interfaces to configure in the configuration file, rather than having to specify them on the command line. Only those interfaces that are mentioned in the configuration file (or on the command line) are configured.

Example 19.4 shows an example of the interface statement being used to send different client identifier options for two different network interfaces. If the send statement is specified outside of an interface declaration, it causes the same value to be sent for all interfaces.

EXAMPLE 19.4

```
interface "ln0" {
  send dhcp-client-identifier 1:8:0:2b:4c:a9:ad;
}

interface "fpa0" {
  send dhcp-client-identifier "snorg-fddi";
}
```

19.3.4 Emulating the Microsoft DHCP Client

To emulate the behavior of a Windows 95 or Windows 98 DHCP client, it is sometimes useful to send a host-name option and a standard client identifier. Example 19.5 shows how to do this.

EXAMPLE 19.5

```
send dhcp-client-identifier 1:0:0:ad:a9:22:10;
send host-name 41:42:41:43:55:53:0;
```

Notice that the hostname is specified as a sequence of hexadecimal octets, rather than as an ASCII text string, so as to emulate the Windows 95 behavior of NUL-terminating the host-name option. You can use this feature to convince a DHCP server that is programmed to serve only Windows DHCP clients to serve an ISC DHCP client as well. The example assumes that the client's network interface is an Ethernet card with a link-layer address of 0:0:ad:a9:22:10. The ASCII value of the host-name option is ABACUS.

19.3.5 Network Setup Script Customization

Because the ISC DHCP client does its network setup through a shell script, it's possible to customize the network setup process quite extensively. You are not supposed to modify the shell script directly; instead, the standard client script invokes two scripts: one before it takes any action, and one when it exits. The first script is called /etc/dhclient-enter-hooks, and the second is called /etc/dhclient-exit-hooks. The manual page for the DHCP client script, dhclient-script, describes how you can program these customization scripts.

19.3.6 Debugging

If the DHCP client is having trouble getting an IP address, it can be useful to observe its startup messages to see what is happening. The progress of the client through the phases described in Section 19.1, at the beginning of this chapter, displays up to the time at which the client gets an IP address. After the client has an IP address, you can track its progress by looking in the system log; like the ISC DHCP server, the client logs all its activity using the LOG_DAEMON facility.

A normal client startup should look something like this:

```
grosse# dhclient
Internet Software Consortium DHCP Client V3.0alpha 19990507
Copyright 1995, 1996, 1997, 1998, 1999 The Internet Software Consortium.
All rights reserved.
Please contribute if you find this software useful.
For info, please visit http://www.isc.org/dhcp-contrib.html
Listening on BPF/ep0/00:10:4b:ec:93:61
Sending on BPF/ep0/00:10:4b:ec:93:61
Sending on Socket/fallback/fallback-net
DHCPDISCOVER on ep0 to 255.255.255.255 port 67 interval 1
DHCPOFFER from 10.0.0.3
DHCPREQUEST on ep0 to 255.255.255.255 port 67
DHCPACK from 10.0.0.3
New Network Number: 10.0.0.0
New Broadcast Address: 10.0.0.255
bound to 10.0.0.2 — renewal in 1800 seconds.
grosse#
```

If no DHCP server is on the network segment to which the client is connected, you simply see a series of DHCPDISCOVER messages, and finally, after about 1 minute, the client announces that it's giving up and goes into the background. This can also happen if the network is very busy and the DHCP server or the network is dropping packets, or if the DHCP server has no IP addresses available to offer to the client.

If two DHCP servers are competing, and one is incorrectly configured, you see a slightly different sequence:

```
[...]
DHCPDISCOVER on ep0 to 255.255.255.255 port 67 interval 1
DHCPOFFER from 10.0.0.3
DHCPOFFER from 10.0.0.7
DHCPREQUEST on ep0 to 255.255.255.255 port 67
DHCPNAK from 10.0.0.7
DHCPDISCOVER on ep0 to 255.255.255.255 port 67 interval 2
[...]
```

In this case, the client fails to get an IP address because when it selects an address from the DHCP server at 10.0.0.3, the DHCP server at 10.0.0.7 sends a DHCPNAK, indicating that the address is incorrect and causing the client to start over. If you are not the administrator for this site, and you have no immediate way to fix the DHCP server at 10.0.0.7, you can instruct the DHCP client to ignore responses from that server, as shown in Example 19.6:

EXAMPLE 19.6

```
reject 10.0.0.7;
```

If the DHCP client already has an IP address, it starts up in the INIT-REBOOT state and initially broadcasts a DHCPREQUEST, rather than a DHCPDISCOVER. When the network configuration it's requesting is correct and the DHCP server is available, this looks exactly like what's shown in Example 19.6, minus the DHCPDISCOVER and DHCPOFFER messages. If the address is incorrect, the transaction (if it goes well) looks like the one shown in Example 19.7:

EXAMPLE 19.7

```
grosse# dhclient
[...]
DHCPREQUEST on ep0 to 255.255.255.255 port 67
DHCPNAK from 10.0.0.3
DHCPDISCOVER on ep0 to 255.255.255.255 port 67 interval 1
DHCPOFFER from 10.0.0.3
DHCPREQUEST on ep0 to 255.255.255.255 port 67
DHCPACK from 10.0.0.3
New Network Number: 10.0.0.0
New Broadcast Address: 10.0.0.255
bound to 10.0.0.2 — renewal in 1800 seconds.

grosse#
```

If the DHCP server can't provide an IP address to a DHCP client that starts in the INIT-REBOOT state, the log shows the DHCPREQUEST/DHCPNAK exchange, and then the client sends DHCPDISCOVER messages until it gives up because the server isn't responding.

Summary

This chapter describes the theory of operation of a DHCP client, and then describes two popular DHCP clients, how to install them, how to configure them, and some problems that you may see with the clients in the event of a server misconfiguration.

The DHCP client drives the DHCP protocol; it contains a state machine, handles message timeouts, configures the network interface according to the responses it gets from the DHCP server, and unconfigures the interface if it loses contact with the DHCP server for such a long time that its lease expires.

All DHCP clients follow pretty much the same process in acquiring IP addresses, but each DHCP client behaves slightly differently in some cases, depending on the design goals of the implementor.

## CHAPTER 20

Setting Up DHCP in a Small Office or Home

Most of this book is targeted at professional network administrators who are setting up DHCP service for a large site, and who have a great deal of control over how their network is configured. This chapter describes how to set up DHCP service for a smaller network, which may be connected to the Internet using an analog, Integrated Services Digital Network (ISDN), Digital Subscriber Line (DSL), or cable modem. Seamless integration of DHCP service from an Internet service provider (ISP) and DHCP service on a local network can pose some specific problems. This chapter addresses these problems, and includes some discussion about firewalls that may also be of interest to network administrators at large sites.

The networks discussed in this chapter are in a small office of some kind—perhaps an ophthalmologist's office, a home office, or (as is the case for both of the authors) a network that enables them to share their Internet connection transparently with their families. Setting up a DHCP server for such an application isn't much different from setting one up for a large site; just about everything you learned in previous chapters applies equally well to a small office environment. However, some of the things you might do to work around the limitations of a small networking environment could interact badly with DHCP service. This chapter informs you of some of these problems and provides ways of working around them.

You may need the information in this chapter if any of the following is true:

- You are connected to your ISP through a bridge, not a router (for example, with DSL or cable modem service).

- You are running your DHCP server on the same computer that you are using to do Internet Protocol (IP) IP address translation between your office network and the Internet.

- You are running your DHCP server on the same computer that you are using as a router or firewall between your network and the Internet.

20.1 Small Office Network Architectures

A very common configuration in small office environments is a computer running Linux or NetBSD that is connected to the Internet on one interface and to the local office LAN on a second interface, acting as a router *and* as a DHCP server. Often, the Internet connection provides only one IP address, so the router must be configured to do *IP IP address Translation* (*IPNAT* or *NAT*, also known as *IP Masquerading*). Even when the ISP provides more than one IP address, the router is often configured to act as a firewall. In some cases, the router may need to act as a DHCP client on the interface connected to the Internet, but as a DHCP server on the other interface.

In this situation, you may use one of the three topologies shown in Figure 20.1.

In Topology A, the router/server is connected directly to the ISP through some kind of point-to-point link: an analog or ISDN modem, a leased line, or something similar.

In Topology B, the ISP provides a device that is connected to the ISP's network on one side and to the local network on the other. This device is a bridge, forwarding packets from one network to the other. It probably also filters what it sends so that it doesn't forward packets on one side of the bridge that aren't intended for computers on the other side of the bridge.

Topology C has the same sort of device, but instead of connecting your side of the device to your local network, you connect it to a separate network that only your router/server is connected to.

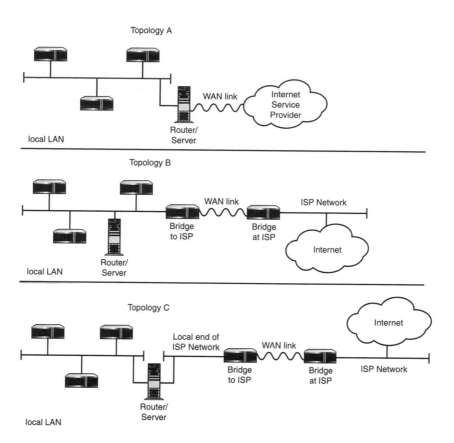

FIGURE 20.1 *Three topologies for a small office network.*

Bridging Devices

If your ISP provides you with a bridging device to connect your local office network to the ISP's network, you should use Topology C if possible. Topology B may inappropriately allow packets from your ISP's customers or your ISP onto your network, and it may inappropriately allow your packets onto their network. Because your ISP is providing the interface, you must trust your ISP to configure the bridge— so as not to for-ward packets containing private information from your network to the ISP's network. Even if the ISP doesn't intend to do this, you may not want to assume that your ISP knows how to configure the bridge so that this won't happen. In addition to the obvious potential security problems, your DHCP service may interfere with the ISP's DHCP service, and vice versa.

continues

continued

Ralph Droms tried to use Topology B to set up a home network when he could not locate a router/server computer to use that had two network interfaces. He found that his DSL link failed whenever he tried to connect a second computer to the hub in his home. After a few calls to the ISP, Ralph learned that the DSL link functioned with only one device; as soon as the DSL equipment in the ISP's office detected a second computer on the hub, it shut down. Ralph tracked down a second network interface for his router/server and set up his home network using Topology C, which worked fine.

20.2 IP address Translation (IP Masquerading)

If you are connecting through an Internet connection that provides you with only one IP address, but you have more than one computer in your office that needs to use the Internet, you must provide *IP address translation*. A IP address translation router operates by rewriting packet headers so that packets sent from your office network to the Internet appear to be coming from the router (which has a valid IP address on the Internet). Packets sent from the Internet to your router are rewritten and forwarded to the correct machine on your local network.

You can visit two Web pages that explain IP address translation in detail. Table 20.1 shows URLs that describe how to set up (or purchase, in the case of Windows NT) IPNAT for various operating systems.

TABLE 20.1 SETTING UP IPNAT FOR VARIOUS OPERATING SYSTEMS

Operating System	URL
NetBSD	http://radon.moof.ai.mit.edu/~armenb/ipnat.html
Linux	http://metalab.unc.edu/LDP/HOWTO/mini/IP-Masquerade.html
Windows NT	http://www.checkpoint.com
Other	http://coombs.anu.edu.au/~avalon/ip-filter.html

If you are using private IP addresses and NAT on your small office network, you can use DHCP to manage the private IP addresses. Configuring the ISC server for a small network using private IP addresses is discussed in more detail later in this chapter.

You may configure your IP address translation router using any of the topologies shown in Figure 20.1. If your router also acts as a firewall, Topology B provides less security than Topology A or C because packets from outside the firewall actually run on the same network segment as packets running inside the firewall.

20.3 Running a DHCP Server and Client on the Same Computer

If you are connecting to the Internet using DSL or a cable modem, your ISP most likely expects you to use DHCP to get an IP address to communicate on the Internet. In that case, you must set up both a DHCP client and a DHCP server on your router/server machine.

20.3.1 Running the DHCP Server and Client on Different Interfaces

If you set up your network using Topology B, you must make sure that the DHCP server running on your server/router doesn't try to provide the DHCP client running on your server/router with an IP address. You can easily exclude the DHCP client from receiving DHCP service with a host declaration in the server's configuration file, such as the one shown in Example 20.1.

EXAMPLE 20.1

```
host router-server {
  hardware ethernet 08:00:2b:5a:19:22;
  deny booting;
}
```

To run the client and server on different interfaces, you *must* use an operating system on which the DHCP distribution supports multiple that network interfaces. You can find a list of these operating systems in Appendix H, "DHCP Server and Operating System Versions."

You also must make sure that your DHCP client and server use the correct interfaces; that is, the DHCP client configures the interface connected to your ISP, and the DHCP server listens for DHCP messages on the interface connected to your small office network. For both the client and server, you can specifically identify the interfaces on the command line for each, as shown in Example 20.2.

EXAMPLE 20.2

```
dhclient if0
dhcpd if1
```

Configuring the Client

The DHCP client normally configures all broadcast interfaces that it finds. To prevent this, either specify the name of the interface that it should configure on the command line when you invoke it, or write an interface declaration for that interface in the /etc/dhclient.conf file. The declaration can be as simple as the one shown in Example 20.3, or as complex as you need to make it.

EXAMPLE 20.3

```
interface "ep0" {
}
```

Configuring the Server

You can either invoke the DHCP server with the name of the interface connected to your local office net, or write a shared-network declaration for the network connected to the subnet on which your Internet connection is terminated. Example 20.4 shows how you can do this.

EXAMPLE 20.4

```
not authoritative;


shared-network ISP {
  subnet 192.168.0.0 netmask 255.255.255.0 {
  }
}


subnet 10.0.0.0 netmask 255.255.255.0 {
  authoritative;
}
```

In this example, the configuration file includes the not authoritative; statement mentioned previously. The ISP subnet declaration identifies the ISP subnet to ensure that the server does not send DHCPNAKs to DHCP messages received from the ISP subnet. The subnet declaration for the local office network then states that the server *is* authoritative for the local office network, meaning that it sends DHCPNAKs in response to DHCP messages received from the local office subnet. In addition, the subnet declaration for the local office network also needs some configuration parameters and some IP addresses to assign.

20.3.2 Running the DHCP Client and Server on the Same Interface

If you are using Topology B, it's more difficult to guarantee that the DHCP server and client don't interfere with each other because they are both using the same interface. The DHCP client normally initializes the interface on startup into a state where it has no IP addresses, which means that it discards any addresses from the small office network previously configured for that interface. If the DHCP client on the operating system you are using uses the BSD socket Application Programming Interface (API), you cannot prevent this from happening; the BSD socket API doesn't provide a mechanism for working around it.

You can tell which API the client is using by starting it up with `dhclient -d`. The startup message looks something like the one shown in Example 20.5.

EXAMPLE 20.5

```
Internet Software Consortium DHCP Client V3.0alpha 19990507
Copyright 1995, 1996, 1997, 1998, 1999 The Internet Software Consortium.
All rights reserved.
Listening on Socket/ep0
Sending on Socket/ep0
```

At the end of the client's output are two lines that start with `Listening on` and `Sending on`. After that is the name of the API being used; in this case, `Socket`, meaning the BSD socket API.

Avoiding the `PREINIT` Problem

If the DHCP client is not using the BSD socket API, you can install a `/etc/dhclient-enter-hooks` script as shown in Example 20.6.

EXAMPLE 20.6

```
if [ x$reason = xMEDIUM ] || [ x$reason = xPREINIT ]; then
  exit 0
fi
```

The `PREINIT` phase of the client script normally starts the network interface, but the script in Example 20.6 disables the `PREINIT` phase. This means the network must already be started before the client runs. To complete this workaround, you must arrange to configure the interface with the IP address on your office network *before* you start the DHCP client.

Configuring an Alias in the DHCP Client

When the DHCP client acquires a new IP address for a given interface, it normally gets rid of the old network configuration for that interface and installs the new one. To have the DHCP client reinstall the IP alias as it configures the network interface, you must write an `alias` declaration in the `/etc/dhclient.conf` file. The alias declaration tells the DHCP client that a second IP address needs to be configured on the interface in addition to the one it got from the DHCP server. Example 20.7 shows an alias declaration for the DHCP client whose startup output is shown in Example 20.6.

EXAMPLE 20.7

```
alias {
  interface "ep0";
  fixed-address 10.0.0.1;
  option subnet-mask 255.255.255.0;
}
```

This example assumes that your local network has a network number of 10.0.0.0 and a subnet mask of 255.255.255.0, and that your NAT router's IP address on that subnet is 10.0.0.1. You need the interface declaration within the alias declaration to tell the client that the IP alias should be configured on interface `ep0`, along with whatever address is received from the ISP's DHCP server.

Limiting the DHCP Server's Authority

As mentioned previously, if you're using Topology B, your local DHCP service and other DHCP services can be connected to the ISP to interfere with each other. In particular, your DHCP server may receive DHCP messages from clients on other networks, and it can interpret those messages as coming from a client that has an invalid IP address. Therefore, it is very important that you configure your DHCP server so that it does not send DHCPNAK messages in response to packets it receives from other networks. If you skip this step, you risk causing your ISP a great deal of trouble.

Fortunately, it is easy to configure the ISC server so that it does not send DHCPNAK messages. Just include `not authoritative`; at the top of the `/etc/dhcpd.conf` file.

20.4 Running the DHCP Server on your Firewall

A firewall is a computer that sits between one network and another, and forwards some packets while not forwarding others. You generally place a firewall between your "trusted" internal network—in this case, your office network—and the Internet, which you probably don't trust. The firewall is configured to prevent packets from being sent from the Internet that might compromise the security of machines on your internal network. This book does not describe the detailed workings of firewalls. If you don't know how they work and are curious, you may want to read *Firewalls & Internet Security: Repelling the Wily Hacker* by Steven M. Bellovin and William R. Cheswick.

Ideally, no network services should run on your firewall. Your firewall should just be filtering packets between your network and the outside world, and preventing bad packets from getting in. If you install a DHCP server on a firewall, you risk the possibility that a bug in the DHCP server might enable an attacker outside your firewall to subvert the firewall and penetrate your network.

However, people who are setting up small office environments with only a few machines generally can't afford a separate machine to use as their firewall. They also tend not to be as concerned about active attacks from the Internet as they might be if they are involved in E-commerce or have a serious Web presence at their site. If you are involved in either of these applications, you're probably already paying more every month for your Internet connectivity than a dedicated firewall machine costs.

You are likely to run into two problems when running the DHCP server on your firewall: filtering rules that prevent DHCP from working, and the use of a server identifier that all clients may not be able to reach.

20.4.1 Filtering Rules

The DHCP protocol requires that clients be able to send packets from a source address of 0.0.0.0 to a destination address of 255.255.255.255.

A firewall is normally configured to allow only packets from or to your local subnet, and it may reject packets from 0.0.0.0 or to 255.255.255.255. Some firewall implementations examine packets when they receive them, rather than when the routing decision is made. If you have such a firewall, you must configure it to accept packets from 0.0.0.0 to 255.255.255.255. It must also be able to send replies from its own IP address to 255.255.255.255. If you omit the first rule, the DHCP server never sees any DHCP packets. If you omit the second rule, it sees them and tries to respond, but the client never sees its response.

20.4.2 Server Identifier

The DHCP protocol requires clients that are in the RENEWING state to unicast their renewal request (a DHCPREQUEST packet) to the IP address that the DHCP server provides in the dhcp-server-identifier option. The ISC DHCP server normally sends the primary IP address of the interface on which it receives the client's request in the dhcp-server-identifier option.

Firewall rules may prevent clients on the local network from sending packets to that address. This most likely occurs with Topology B, in which your firewall has one interface configured with two IP addresses: one on your office subnet and one on the ISP's subnet. In that case, the DHCP server may choose to use the IP address on the ISP's subnet for the server identifier. If your router is not configured to pass DHCP packets, your DHCP clients may not be able to unicast renewals to that IP address. To solve this problem, simply write a server-identifier statement that uses the server's IP address on the office subnet.

20.5 Problems with DSL Routers

Some DSL routers are known to have problems. The routers in question are marketed as complete solutions; they have built-in firewall support, built-in IP address translation support, and built-in DHCP service. Although you should use the firewall support and IP address translation support in these routers, the DHCP support can be a problem if you aren't aware of its existence.

For instance, consider this scenario. A DSL router comes preconfigured with DHCP service enabled, but the DHCP server setup is completely incorrect. The router is connected to the same subnet on which a legitimate DHCP server is operating. Whenever a DHCP client tries to get an IP address, it sends a DHCPDISCOVER, gets a DHCPOFFER, sends a DHCPREQUEST, and gets a DHCPACK from the legitimate server. Unfortunately, before the DHCPACK from the legitimate server arrives, a DHCPNAK from the DSL router arrives, causing the client to report that it is not permitted to obtain an IP address.

The solution to this problem is to reconfigure the router to disable DHCP service. After this is done, the DHCP clients on the network can be configured with no trouble at all.

Summary

DHCP service can be useful in a small office environment. Although for the most part setting up DHCP service in such an environment is the same as setting it up in any other environment, you may encounter some special difficulties. For instance, you should be aware of the possible interference that a firewall can cause to a DHCP server running on it. You should also know about the problems DHCP clients and servers can encounter when running on the same computer, and the problems that a misconfigured DHCP server can cause when connected to a network segment that is bridged to an ISP's network. You can solve these problems in a number of ways, as this chapter outlines.

CHAPTER 21

Authentication of DHCP Clients and Servers

In some circumstances, DHCP clients and servers need to reliably authenticate each other's identities as part of the DHCP message exchange. Unfortunately, the current DHCP protocol does not provide a way to do this. The IETF DHC Working Group is currently working on a protocol draft to solve this problem. Because the draft is sufficiently mature at the time of this writing, it's worth describing in this chapter.

21.1 Reasons for Authenticating the DHCP Protocol

The DHCP authentication protocol seeks to accomplish two goals. The first goal is to protect both the client and the server in the DHCP protocol from attack. The second goal is to establish a trust relationship, enabling the server to ration access only to authorized DHCP clients and to trust the information that the client presents.

In considering potential DHCP security issues, the network administrator must operate under the assumption that some people may harm the network either intentionally, or otherwise. Some forms of intentional harm include simply causing trouble, intercepting information, planting false information, or intercepting requests for information and substituting incorrect information. Some forms of unintentional harm include a naïve person incorrectly configuring a DHCP client or server in such a way that it causes a disruption.

Which of these problems occurs likely depends on the context; in a school environment, disruptive pranks by students are common, and configuration errors by students and guests are even more common. In an environment where monetary transactions are conducted, or where valuable information is passed, criminals may use the computer to try to steal money or information (for example, account balances) that they can resell.

21.1.1 Protecting the Client from Attack

Consider a DHCP client attached to a network. It wants to get an IP address and needs to know the IP address of its router, name server, and possibly some other services. Now, imagine that somebody with bad intentions (the "attacker") wants to prevent the client from using the network.

Such an attacker can simply set up a DHCP server that provides incorrect addressing information. As long as this server is faster than the official DHCP server and is configured to serve only the client being attacked, the client almost certainly selects the invalid IP address. When the client tries to use this address, it doesn't work, and the client cannot use the network. A clever attacker might use a legitimate IP address but supply an incorrect value for the name server; such an attack is less obvious to somebody looking at the server log or at the client's network configuration.

What if the attacker wants to steal information from the client? The easiest way to do this is to simply eavesdrop on the network. However, most large network installations today use Ethernet switches that prevent devices connected to the network from eavesdropping on one another. These devices do not, however, prevent devices connected to the network from hearing broadcasts. An attacker on such a network can set up a DHCP server, provide the client with a legitimate IP address, but provide the client with its own IP address in the routers option, causing the client to send all off-network traffic to the attacker. The attacker can transparently forward this information off the network so that the client is unaware of the attack.

Finally, what if the attacker wants to provide incorrect information to the client? For example, imagine an attacker with a pathological dislike for radishes. This attacker wants to prevent anybody from reading the world-famous radish.org Web site. To do so, he sets up a DHCP service that mimics the address allocation process of the legitimate DHCP server, but he provides a different domain name server address. This domain name server provides incorrect information for the radish.org domain, leading the attacked client to a site promoting turnips.

21.1.2 Protecting Clients from Errors

DHCP servers can also unintentionally interfere with the operation of DHCP clients because DHCP clients may not have a way to differentiate between DHCP servers in an organization. Also, an end user can easily install a DHCP server without understanding that this "personal" DHCP server may affect DHCP service for all users of the network.

Unintentional Interference Between DHCP Servers

DHCP servers may unintentionally interfere with each other because RFC2131 does not provide a mechanism through which servers and clients can identify themselves in a reliable way. Ralph Droms once worked with an organization whose data center used a large, bridged network configured as a single IP subnet. Development and production groups shared this network, and each of them ran their own DHCP servers. But because both the production and development DHCP servers received DHCP client broadcasts, production DHCP clients risked receiving an address assigned by the development server.

In this network, a DHCP client from the development group could accept an address from the production DHCP server, and the DHCP server in the development group processed requests from clients in both the production and development groups. Although most DHCP clients could function with an address from either server, some production clients received incorrect parameters such as a default Domain Name System (DNS) server from the development server.

At the same time, the development server processed the incoming requests from clients in the production organization, and the development server responded to both development and production group servers. These interactions with the production clients interfered with DHCP client-server design and implementation experiments between development clients and servers conducted by the development organization.

Another common source of disruption to your DHCP service can result from the inclusion of the DHCP server with Windows NT 4.0. An NT user can easily start up the Microsoft DHCP server, perhaps to provide DHCP service to a few local computers, or just to explore DHCP. These DHCP servers may be incorrectly configured so that the server hands out invalid addresses or duplicate addresses, or sends inappropriate *DHCPNAK* messages in response to client requests. Any of these situations results in disruption of service to DHCP clients.

The authentication mechanism for DHCP enables a client to be configured with a list of legitimate servers and with a key enabling each server to prove its identity. The client can then be configured either to simply discard offers from unknown servers, or to respond only to offers from unknown servers if it does not hear any offers from known servers within a specific period of time. By using the authentication mechanism, clients configured with a list of legitimate servers never accept IP addresses from an unauthorized server because the owner of that server does not know the secret key that the client and the legitimate server share.

21.1.3 Protecting Servers from Attacks by Clients

Without authentication, an attacker can easily exhaust a DHCP server's pool of available addresses by repeatedly requesting and confirming leases, each time with new identification information, until the server runs out of IP addresses to allocate. When this happens, the server cannot provide addresses to legitimate clients. If you can program the server to allocate addresses only to legitimate clients that can prove their identities, or at least to reserve most addresses for such clients, such an attack can't succeed.

21.1.4 Reliably Restricting Address Allocation

Chapters 14, "Client Identification and Fixed-Address Allocation," 17, "Conditional Behavior," and 18, "Automatic DHCP Client Registration" describe ways of restricting the address allocation process to only authorized clients. Unfortunately, although the DHCP protocol provides an identifier through which you can specify client authorization rules, without authentication, nothing prevents a user from configuring a client to present a false identity; the DHCP protocol doesn't require proof of the client's identity. The DHCP authentication protocol provides a means for imposing and enforcing such a requirement.

21.1.5 Authenticating Client Assertions

Some uses of the DHCP protocol require the DHCP client to provide information to the DHCP server that the DHCP server can't validate on its own. For example, a client may claim that its hostname is "alice," and the DHCP server may be unable to decide whether this is true. With authentication, you can program the DHCP server to accept the name "alice" if a certain identity is proven and to reject it otherwise. You can also program it to create an association between a name it has never seen before and a particular identity. This means that when one client claims to be named "alice," that client is always believed if it subsequently claims to be named "alice." Other clients that subsequently claim to be "alice" are not believed. You can use this, for example, to implement a first-come, first-served dynamic DNS naming system.

21.1.6 Securing Other Services

The DHCP protocol includes a mechanism for making the client aware of other network services. As discussed previously, an attacker can arrange to eavesdrop on network services and steal information, or provide incorrect information. Securing the DHCP protocol makes doing this somewhat harder for an attacker, but it is still possible. To prevent eavesdropping and falsification of information, you must secure all the network protocols that a DHCP client uses. You can do this using Internet layer security (IPsec), transport layer security (TLS or SSL), or protocols that are secure themselves.

21.2 Objectives the DHCP Authentication Protocol Cannot Accomplish

The DHCP authentication protocol does not accomplish, and probably can't accomplish, a number of desirable security goals. These include:

- preventing denial-of-service attacks against the server

- preventing clients from using the network without authorization

- securing other services

21.2.1 Denial-of-Service Attacks

The DHCP authentication protocol can't prevent effort-related denial-of-service attacks. An effort-related denial-of-service attack is one in which an attacker sends packets to the server that the server is forced to process. These attacks come so rapidly that the requests of legitimate clients are lost in the flood. The authentication protocol can't prevent this from happening because it actually takes extra work to authenticate a packet; authentication uses an algorithm that consumes a significant amount of CPU time for every authentication that it conducts.

21.2.2 Preventing Access to the Network

DHCP service is not, in itself, an access-control mechanism. If the DHCP server is configured not to grant IP addresses to clients that can't prove their identities, or to clients that aren't permitted access to the network, those clients cannot get IP addresses legitimately. However, a user can quite easily *guess* an

IP address that works on the network, either through prior knowledge or by capturing packets from the network. For example, an attacker might write a program to pick a IP address based on network traffic. A sophisticated program might watch DHCP traffic to monitor addresses assigned by the DHCP server and watch for an address with an expired lease. The attacking computer can then use that address and pretend to be an authorized computer on the network.

You can use other devices in your network infrastructure to provide network access control, enabling only authorized devices to access the network. For example, you can program filtering switches or hubs so that they exchange frames only from authorized network devices, and you might configure your routers to forward datagrams for network devices with legitimately assigned IP addresses.

Ideally, your DHCP server dynamically updates the rest of your network infrastructure so that hubs, switches, and routers can enforce access control based on the addresses managed by your DHCP server. Unfortunately, no protocol or standard mechanism currently exists through which a DHCP server can forward address assignment information to other network devices. You can use the DHCP authentication protocol to good effect as part of a network access control system, but network access control is not closely related to DHCP authentication. Therefore, the DHCP authentication protocol specification does not attempt to provide network access control.

21.3 Protocol Design

The `authentication` option for DHCP is currently described in an Internet Draft, `draft-ietf-dhc-authentication-11.txt`. The design goals for the authentication mechanism in DHCP are as follows:

- Provide a mechanism through which clients and servers can reliably identify each other and confirm that the contents of DHCP messages were altered while in transit

- Avoid changing the current protocol and maintain backward compatibility with existing clients and servers

- Allow for multiple authentication mechanisms and algorithms

- Allow for automated selection of authentication tokens

- Minimize manual configuration of DHCP clients

The authentication mechanism and option are actually a framework for the definition of multiple authentication protocols. The authentication option itself carries an identification of the protocol and the algorithm used within the option.

The current Internet Draft defines two authentication mechanisms: a simple plain-text token used to identify clients and servers, and a keyed-hashing technique based on *Hashed Message Authentication Code (HMAC)* (RFC2104). Both authentication mechanisms use the same format for the authentication option, which is given in Figure 21.1.

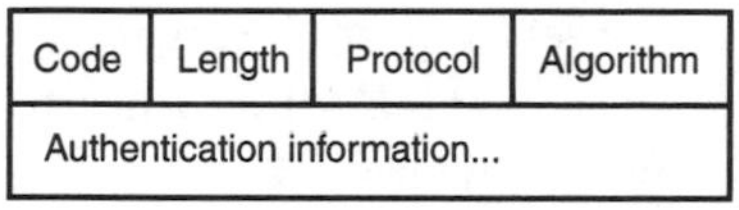

Code	Length	Protocol	Algorithm
Authentication information...			

FIGURE 21.1 *Format of the DHCP* authentication *option.*

The difference between the two mechanisms is in the contents of the authentication information field. The fields in the authentication option are described in Table 21.1.

TABLE 21.1 FIELDS IN THE DHCP authentication OPTION

Field	Definition
code	Undefined (to be assigned when the authentication option is accepted as an Internet Standard)
length	Number of bytes in protocol, algorithm, and authentication information fields
protocol	Protocol in use in this option: 0: authentication token (see Section 21.3.1) 1: delayed authentication (see Section 21.3.2)
algorithm	Specific algorithm used with protocol from protocol field; interpreted according to definition of protocol
authentication	Additional information as required by the information protocol and algorithm; interpreted according to definition of protocol

21.3.1 Authentication Token Protocol

The authentication token protocol provides minimal identification of DHCP clients and servers. The protocol is intended for protection against DHCP servers that are inadvertently started or incorrectly configured and for simple segregation of clients and servers in shared networks. The authentication protocol provides no defense against an active intruder who can simply examine local network traffic to determine the appropriate authentication token to use to gain unauthorized service.

The protocol number for the authentication protocol is 0, and the `algorithm` field must be set to zero. The authentication information is a simple plain-text string. For example, it might be the name of the server or of the organization that manages the server. The format of the `authentication` option when used to carry the authentication token protocol is shown in Figure 21.2.

Code	n+2	0	0
Authentication token (n bytes)			

FIGURE 21.2 *Format of the DHCP* `authentication` *option.*

In the sidebar in Section 21.1.2, the development organization might configure its DHCP clients and servers to use the authentication protocol with a token value of `Development`, whereas production might configure its DHCP clients and servers to use the token value `Production`. Each of the servers uses the authentication token value supplied by DHCP clients to filter and ignore messages from clients that server is not managing.

21.3.2 Delayed Authentication Protocol

The second protocol defined in the `authentication` option specification is called the *delayed authentication protocol*. In this protocol, the authentication is delayed until the server sends a `DHCPOFFER` message in response to a client's `DHCPDISCOVER` message. The delay enables the server to announce to the client what specific algorithm and key the server accepts, without requiring the client to divulge any information.

This protocol assumes that DHCP clients and servers are provided with a shared secret key through some mechanism independent of the authentication protocol. The mechanism enables the use of multiple keys so that a mobile DHCP client that might frequently contact different DHCP servers can use a different key for each DHCP server it knows about.

Authentication Option Formats

A client first sends a DHCPDISCOVER message with an authentication option requesting use of the delayed authentication protocol. Figure 21.3 illustrates the format of the delayed authentication option in a DHCPDISCOVER message.

Code	2	1	Algorithm

FIGURE 21.3 *Format of the delayed* authentication *option in a* DHCPDISCOVER *message.*

The algorithm field defines the specific algorithm to be used to generate the authentication information in subsequent messages.

Subsequent messages between the client and server contain the authentication option in the format shown in Figure 21.4. In this version of the authentication option, the secret ID is an identifier for the secret the sender uses to generate the *message authentication code*, or *MAC*. The secret identifier enables the client and server to agree on the use of one of possibly several shared secrets. The counter field is a 64-bit, monotonically increasing value used to avoid replay attacks. The MAC field is generated from the contents of the DHCP message using the HMAC and MD5 (RFC1321) algorithms, and it ensures the integrity of the DHCP message.

Code	n+14	1	Algorithm
Secret ID			
Counter (8 bytes)	...		
MAC (n bytes)	...		

FIGURE 21.4 *Format of the delayed* authentication *option in subsequent messages.*

Computing the MAC Field

The sender computes the MAC field for the delayed authentication option using the HMAC and MD5 algorithms. The entire DHCP message, with two exceptions, is used as input to the HMAC-MD5 algorithm, including the fixed-format and options sections of the message. Because the giaddr and hops fields may be altered by a relay agent, those fields are not included in the MAC, and their contents are set to zero for computation by the MAC. In addition, if a relay agent information option appears at the end of the DHCP packet, the bytes in this option are not included in the HMAC computation.

The secret ID field of the delayed authentication option is set to the identifier of the shared secret the sender uses to generate the MAC. The counter field is set to a 64-bit, monotonically increasing counter. The current time of day, in Network Time Protocol (NTP) format (RFC1305), is a good value for the counter field.

Validating a Message

To validate an incoming message, the receiver first compares the contents of the counter field to the previous value used by the sender. If the current value is not larger than the previous value, the receiver discards the message. Next, the receiver uses the contents of the secret ID field from the delayed authentication option to identify the key used to generate the MAC in the message. The receiver then computes the MAC for the message using the algorithm described in the previous section. It sets the contents of the MAC field in the authentication option, sets the giaddr and the hops field in the fixed-format section of the message to zero for the computation, and ignores the relay agent information option if one exists. If the MAC value the receiver computes does not match the contents of the MAC field in the authentication option, the receiver discards the message.

Use in INIT State

When using the delayed authentication option in INIT state, the client uses the option format shown in Figure 21.3. At present, only one algorithm is defined, and the only valid value for the algorithm field is 1, selecting the HMAC-MD5 MAC computation algorithm.

After receiving the delayed authentication option in the DHCPDISCOVER message, a server selects a key and composes the delayed authentication option to insert in its DHCPOFFER response. The server must be configured with enough information so that it can select a key and an identifier for the key for clients that it did not communicate with previously. When the server selects a key and an identifier for the client, it records that information along with any other information it keeps about the client. The server computes the MAC for the DHCPOFFER message according to the procedure described previously in this section, and sends the MAC to the client as the MAC field in the authentication option. The server then sends the DHCPOFFER message to the client.

The client validates incoming messages as described previously in this section and discards any messages that do not pass the validation tests. The client then chooses one of the DHCPOFFER messages, and it looks up the secret key identified in the message in its local database of secret keys. The client composes a DHCPREQUEST message with a delayed authentication option containing a value for the MAC field computed by the secret key used for the selected server. Finally, the client sends the DHCPREQUEST as specified in RFC2131.

Any server receiving the DHCPREQUEST message validates the incoming message. The server selected in the DHCPREQUEST message constructs a DHCPACK message that contains all the options as required by RFC2131. The server includes the authentication option in the DHCPACK, composed as described previously. The server sends the DHCPACK to the client, which validates the incoming DHCPACK message, extracts the assigned IP address and other configuration parameters, and uses those configuration parameters to configure its protocol stack.

Note

The sequence of messages exchanged between the client and server for authenticated DHCP is the same as described in RFC2131. This enables backward compatibility with clients and servers that do not include an implementation of the authentication *option, and it minimizes the impact of the* authentication *option on the DHCP specification.*

Use in INIT-REBOOT State

When starting in INIT-REBOOT state, the client uses the secret it recorded when it obtained its configuration information in INIT state to compose an authentication option to include with its DHCPREQUEST message. The client then sends the DHCPREQUEST message.

The client performs the validation test on responses it receives and discards messages that fail. Messages that pass the validation test are processed as specified by RFC2131:

- A DHCPACK message confirms that the client may continue using its address, and the client uses any configuration parameters from the DHCPACK message.

- A DHCPNAK message forces the client into INIT state.

- If the client receives no responses that pass the validation test, it may continue to use its previous address until the lease on that address expires.

Use in RENEWING or REBINDING State

At the time specified to extend the lease on its address, the client composes a DHCPREQUEST message and includes the authentication option with the MAC value computed using the secret it recorded when it initially obtained the address. The client sends the DHCPREQUEST message and performs the validation test on responses it receives. The client discards messages that fail the validation test.

If the client receives a DHCPACK message that passes the validation test, it uses the configuration information from the message to configure its protocol stack. If the client receives no responses, or none of the received responses passes the validation test, the client behaves as though it received no responses to its DHCPREQUEST message.

21.4 Status

At the time of this writing, the DHC Working Group has accepted the protocol specification in principle, and the Internet Draft with the specification is undergoing final revision. Working Group approval is expected on completion of the final revisions, and the authentication protocol should be accepted as an Internet Standard and as part of DHCP by the end of 1999.

Summary

Both DHCP clients and servers can be subject to intruder attacks, and they may also be affected unintentionally by misconfigured or badly implemented DHCP protocol agents. The DHC Working Group developed a mechanism through which DHCP clients and servers can reliably identify each other. This authentication gives network administrators a tool to minimize or eliminate the hazard of malicious or unintentional interference with their DHCP service.

The DHCP authentication option is really a framework for defining authentication mechanisms for DHCP messages. The specific mechanism used in a DHCP message is identified in the message itself, so clients and servers can agree on the authentication mechanism they use.

The current DHCP authentication option specification defines two protocols. The first is based on a simple plain-text password that provides limited protection against unintentionally instantiated DHCP servers. The second protocol uses a shared secret key for reliable identification of DHCP clients and servers, a message digest to prevent modification of DHCP messages, and a counter to prevent replay attacks. The secret key protocol enables selection among multiple keys so that a client that interacts with different DHCP servers can automatically select the correct key for each server.

The DHC Working Group reviewed the authentication option specification and approved the specification in principle. The option should be accepted as an Internet Standard and as part of the DHCP specification by the end of 1999.

CHAPTER 22

Mark Stapp, Cisco Systems
Ralph Droms, Ph.D.
Ted Lemon

DHCP/DNS Interaction

The *Domain Name System,* or *DNS,* enables you to refer to a computer by name rather than by its IP address. Every time you use a ".com" name, your computer queries DNS to find the IP address for that name.

DNS holds information about computer names and IP addresses. It stores the information in *DNS servers,* which are located throughout the Internet. DHCP servers make address assignments which affect two types of name information in DNS. The most commonly accessed entries in DNS are the familiar *domain names,* such as `www.bucknell.edu`, which are translated, or *resolved,* by DNS servers into IP addresses.

DNS servers also manage entries that resolve IP addresses into domain names. As a DHCP server assigns IP addresses to computers, you must add or modify entries in the DNS database to reflect the new address assignments.

This chapter describes the ways in which DHCP servers and clients interact with the DNS service, and it looks at the difficulties and potential pitfalls in these interactions. The chapter focuses on the aspects of DNS that DHCP affects.

For a more detailed description of DNS, we suggest that you read *DNS and Bind* by Cricket Liu and Paul Albitz (1998), or *Internetworking with TCP/IP: Principles, Protocols, and Architecture* by Douglas Comer (1995).

22.1 The Domain Name System

The information in DNS is stored as a distributed database on the DNS servers. The names in the DNS comprise a tree-structured hierarchy of names, or *namespace*, and each DNS server manages a subtree of the namespace. The administrator for each DNS server establishes policies about DNS name allocation and management for the names that server stores.

Resource records (often abbreviated as *RRs*) represent DNS data and are associated with names in the DNS namespace. Many different types of resource records exist, and each is associated with a different type of information. The DNS specification defines several record types and acknowledges that additional types continue to be proposed as the needs of the community evolve.

The *A (address)* and *PTR (pointer)* records contain the data that's most clearly related to IP addresses: the address of a host and the name of the host associated with an address, respectively.

The data in a PTR record is a domain name in a reserved part of the DNS namespace. A special domain, called in-addr.arpa, contains a hierarchy of names that represent IP addresses. To convert an IP address into a name, convert each octet in the address into a label and arrange the labels in most-to least-specific order, from left to right. For example, the IP address 192.168.11.25 is represented in the in-addr.arpa domain as 25.11.168.192.in-addr.arpa. When one host knows the IP address of another, perhaps because it receives an IP datagram from the other host and wants to know its DNS name, it can issue a query for the PTR record on the corresponding in-addr.arpa name.

Some application servers, such as File Transfer Protocol (FTP) servers, look up the names of the hosts that access them and compare the data to the name with the IP address that the client is using. If a prospective client does not have a PTR record, if the name in the PTR record is not within a certain domain, or if the data in the A record named by the PTR record does not match the IP address that the client is using, the server may refuse further communication with the client. This simple crosscheck assumes, of course, that the DNS data is reliably administered and transmitted.

22.2 Dynamic Updates to the DNS Database

IP address assignments made by DHCP servers do, of course, change the name and address information that the DNS database represents. When a DHCP client is assigned a new IP address, the DNS database should have an A record containing the IP address for the client's domain name, and a PTR record for the new IP address containing the client's domain name.

The problem with keeping the DNS database current with domain names and IP addresses assigned through DHCP is that the changes are traditionally made directly by a DNS administrator. An administrator modifies the DNS data stored in a file and tells the DNS server to read the new data. Requiring manual update of the DNS database whenever the DHCP server assigns an IP address to a client, eliminates much of the advantage of dynamic address allocation through DHCP.

One solution is to prepopulate the DNS server with preassigned domain names in A and PTR records for all the addresses DHCP manages. That is, the DNS database is preconfigured with all the IP addresses and domain names assigned to each address. For example, if a DHCP client on the GSI internet is assigned 192.168.11.25, it is also assigned the preregistered domain name `net11-host25.genstart.com`. The DNS database is preconfigured with an A record mapping `net11-host25` to 192.168.11.25 and a PTR record mapping `25.11.168.192.in-addr.arpa` to `net11-host25.genstart.com`. Of course, this solution is not very flexible and doesn't enable the use of mnemonic domain names.

RFC2136, "Dynamic Updates in the Domain Name System," describes a mechanism through which you can change the contents of the DNS database using DNS protocol messages. RFC2136 describes a new type of DNS message; a message that does not ask a server just to retrieve DNS data, but to change DNS data as well. Dynamic update messages can add and remove A and PTR resource records.

The dynamic update mechanism enables clients to supply prerequisites, which are conditions about data in the DNS zone that must be satisfied before the DNS server performs an update. A DNS server performing a dynamic update first checks all the prerequisites in the update request. If all those prerequisites are met—that is, all the conditions specified as prerequisites are true—the server performs all the requested changes to the DNS data. As an example, DHCP clients and servers use prerequisites in DNS update messages to detect duplicate domain names.

22.3 Dynamic Updates and DHCP

DHCP clients and servers can use dynamic DNS updates to keep the DNS database synchronized with the addresses that servers assign. As a server assigns an address, the client and the server use dynamic update messages to add or update the A resource record for the client's domain name and the PTR record for the IP address assigned to the client.

Several knotty problems are associated with dynamic DNS updates from DHCP clients and servers:

- What computers do you trust to do dynamic updates?

- Does the DHCP client or the server select the client's name?

- Does the client or the server perform the dynamic update?

- What is the relationship between a client's lease on an address and the DNS entries for that client?

- What happens if two DHCP clients select the same name?

- What happens if a client moves?

- What happens if a client's name changes?

These issues and some proposed solutions are described in an Internet Draft, "Interaction Between DHCP and DNS" (`draft-ietf-dhc-dhcp-dns-09.txt`), by Yakov Rekhter and Mark Stapp. The mechanisms for DHCP clients and servers to make dynamic updates to DNS in the remainder of this section are taken from this Internet Draft.

Note

The use of dynamic updates to DNS by DHCP servers and clients is still under discussion by the DHC Working Group. The details may change before the draft specification is accepted as an Internet Standard.

22.3.1 DNS Dynamic Update Security Issues

Dynamic updates to the information in DNS represent a significant potential for security problems. Without some restrictions on the acceptance of dynamic updates, anyone can send a dynamic update request to a server to change the IP address for a DNS name. So, if you want to intercept all the traffic aimed at www.genstart.com, you can simply send a dynamic update to dns.genstart.com that changes the IP address for www.genstart.com to your computer's IP address.

At the time of this book's publication, DNS servers that support dynamic updates most commonly offer a way to restrict the IP addresses from which they accept update queries. This is currently the most common form of protection against malicious updates.

Another form of protection against unauthorized updates is to restrict the acceptance of dynamic updates to DNS information entered by a network administrator. For example, if the www.genstart.com server has a manually configured IP address, the network administrator can mark its DNS entry to disallow dynamic updates. This restriction on dynamic updates prevents another computer from using a dynamic update to assign a different IP address. Although no standard mechanism exists to disallow dynamic DNS updates, many DNS servers implement some form of this feature.

Controls based on the address from which an update is received are inadequate when DHCP is in use. Simply acquiring an address from a DHCP server does not provide a sufficient level of trust to enable a DHCP client to make changes to the DNS database. Two methods for adding an authorization mechanism to dynamic DNS updates were proposed within the IETF. Both mechanisms include additional information in dynamic DNS update messages that is based on an authorization key that the updater holds.

For example, if a network administrator chooses to enable DHCP clients to make DNS updates, the administrator distributes a key to the clients authorizing each client to make changes to its own DNS name. Whenever the client is assigned a new IP address through DHCP, it sends a corresponding DNS update message, along with its authorization information, to the DNS server. The DNS server uses the authorization to confirm that the client can make the update.

22.3.2 DHCP Client DNS Name Selection

Two reasonable sources exist for DHCP client DNS names: the DHCP server, and the DHCP client itself. Most modern DHCP clients, including those from Microsoft, enable a host's administrator to configure it with a hostname, and include that hostname in the host-name option in requests to the DHCP server.

A site may prefer this policy if it decides that it wants its network administrators to configure hostnames into each new client as they install it, or that it wants to enable individuals to pick (and change) their machines' names. Other sites may implement a policy in which the DHCP servers are the source for clients' hostnames. There tend to be fewer DHCP servers, which makes it easier to centralize name management, and they tend (as do most network

servers) to be relatively tightly controlled. The administration model on most
Windows desktop clients does not presently prevent the client's user from
changing its hostname, so it is difficult for sites with these clients to enforce
client-side policies that depend on limiting administrative access to DHCP
client configuration.

A number of server-centric possibilities do exist, however. The DHCP server
could:

- Be configured with a name for each client

- Generate a name for each client based on some algorithm or heuristic

- Transform the name presented by the client in its DHCP request

None of these alternatives is mandated; it's up to the site administrator to
choose the source of DNS names.

22.3.3 Responsibility for Performing DNS Updates

Enabling DNS updates to be performed by DHCP clients is a tricky issue.
Because the DHCP server controls IP allocation, it is the natural source for
updates to the PTR records for IP addresses. Whether the DHCP server is the
best source for A record updates, however, is the subject of intense discussion
in the DHC Working Group.

One alternative is to enable individual DHCP clients to manage their own DNS
names. Each client should have the appropriate credentials to add and delete its
own A record as it enters and leaves the network. If you have a laptop computer
and it has permission to update its domain name, it can presumably update that
name from any location that has IP access to your company's primary name-
server. If you travel to my company's site and if your laptop receives a new IP
address there through DHCP, the laptop can update its A record to reflect its
new IP address. This is quite useful: others who know your laptop's domain
name can determine the laptop's address even though the address in the record
isn't inside the IP address space controlled by my company.

For some administrators, however, significant risks are involved in enabling
DNS updates from DHCP clients. Clients may add DNS names and then be
removed from the network, leaving the names in the DNS database long after
the clients' DHCP leases expire. The administrative cost of distributing security
credentials to every DHCP client may be onerous. Sites with these concerns

choose to permit DNS updates only from their DHCP servers. In this configuration, the DHCP server adds both the A record for the client's domain name and the PTR record for the address when it assigns a new address to a client.

22.3.4 DHCP Client Name Collision

If the users of DHCP clients are permitted by local policy to select their own hostnames, one problem that can arise is that two users may choose the same name for their computer. Currently no provision exists in the DHCP protocol to resolve such conflicts, although as discussed in Chapter 19, "DHCP Clients," the Microsoft DHCP client tries to use the Windows Internet Name Service (WINS) protocol to resolve naming conflicts.

The DHCP-DNS interaction draft refers to the situation in which two DHCP clients have the same name as a *name collision*, or a *name conflict*, and provides a method that clients and servers can use to detect this. The draft proposes that you add an additional resource record along with the A record. This additional record is a form of the KEY resource record that is described in RFC2535, "Domain Name System Security Extensions." This form of the KEY record contains data that identifies the client: the client identifier that the client uses in its DHCP requests, or its link-layer address if it does not include the DHCP client-id option.

Whether the A record update is performed by the DHCP client or by the server, the updater can use the prerequisites section of the update query to assert that no other client is currently using the name in question. The DHCP updater first sends an update request including a prerequisite that the name does not exist and uses the update section to add the A record and the KEY record.

If the first prerequisite test fails because the name being added already exists, the updater tries another update request; this time with the prerequisite that the name include a KEY record matching the client-identifier of the DHCP client. If the prerequisite test in this second request succeeds, the DNS server updates the A record for the client to reflect the client's new IP address.

If this prerequisite test fails, however, the updater must conclude that some other client is using the domain name to be updated. The second client's update replaces an existing name only if the local administrator explicitly configures the updaters to replace existing names: This is not the default behavior as the mechanism is currently specified.

Note

Because it can be very useful to clients to be represented in the DNS, some DHCP servers attempt to add some fully qualified domain name (FQDN) even if the preferred FQDN is not available. The updater must know the name of the zone in which it is attempting to perform updates so that it can attempt to generate a hostname that can be added to the zone. Imagining several possible ways to generate names is not difficult: A server can generate a pseudo-random hostname, or a hostname based on the client's client-identity (which must be unique), or a name that appends a counter value to the preferred hostname.

22.3.5 Client Relocation

Many organizations that use dynamic DNS also use multiple DHCP servers; therefore, you should consider several issues concerning the DNS database when DHCP clients interact with more than one DHCP server.

Suppose a site has two buildings and uses a separate DHCP server in each building. What happens when a laptop is shut down at a user's desk in Building A and is restarted on the network in a conference room in Building B?

Presumably, the DHCP server in Building A (Server A) doesn't know that this happened: It knows only that the client has an active lease with it. When the DHCP server in Building B (Server B) leases an IP address to the client, it expects to add a PTR record corresponding to the IP address, and an A record corresponding to the client's domain name. However, Server A already had an A record (one that contains the IP address it leased to the client). The client's A record should represent the most recent active lease, so Server B attempts to add an A record and a KEY record for the client's domain name.

Server B generates an appropriate client-identity, either from the client's client-identifier, or from its link-layer address. Server B sends a DNS update message to the DNS server, including the prerequisite that the client's FQDN does not exist and containing an update section that adds an A record and a KEY record. The data in the A record is the new IP address, and the data in the KEY record is the client-identity.

This message's prerequisites fail because the FQDN is already present. When Server B is notified of this failure, it then forms another update message, which includes the prerequisite that the KEY record for the client's domain name matches the client-identity that B generates. The second message updates the A record to include the new address that B assigns to the client. The KEY record must already match for the prerequisites to be satisfied so that the update in the message does not affect it. If the second message succeeds, the client's current IP address is in its A record.

DHCP Server A sees none of this activity. As far as it is concerned, the client has a valid lease with it, and the client just isn't around. In fact, Server A's lease may expire while the client is in Building B.

As described in the following section, Server A should attempt to remove the DNS records that represent the expired lease. What prevents Server A from removing the data that Server B replaced? Server A requires in the prerequisites for its update message that the data in the A record matches the IP address that Server A assigned to the client. Because Server B changed the IP address in the A record, A's test fails, and A does not change the client's A record.

22.3.6 Lease Expiration

When a lease expires (or is released), the updaters of the A and PTR records must attempt to remove the records from the DNS database. Removing the DNS records that represent a DHCP lease enables the DNS data to accurately represent the current IP addresses and hostnames.

In particular, the A records on names added as part of a DHCP update have associated KEY records; you should remove these records so that the name is available to any other host. A and KEY records left behind after a lease expires prevent any other host (or even the same host which is given a new client-identity—for example, a new network interface card with a new Ethernet address) from associating its IP address with the name.

Above all, DHCP clients and servers must avoid deleting DNS data they do not add. The updaters can use the dynamic update prerequisites to detect cases in which another DHCP transaction or some administrative action creates a situation in which they should not delete records.

Because the DHCP server controls the IP address, the server is responsible for updating and deleting the PTR record that corresponds to the DHCP lease. To delete the PTR record, the DHCP server prepares an update query specifying a prerequisite that the PTR record's data matches the client's FQDN. The update section of this query deletes the in-addr.arpa name.

If the DHCP server performs the DNS A record update, it is also responsible for deleting the A and KEY RRs when the client's lease expires. If the DHCP client performs its own A record update, it is responsible for removing the A record when its DHCP lease expires, or when it releases its lease.

The KEY record associated with the client's A record enables the DHCP client or server to determine whether the host that is associated with the A record is the same as the host whose DHCP lease expired.

The updater of the A RR forms an update query specifying a prerequisite that the data in the KEY RR associated with the name matches the client-identity data generated for the client whose lease expired. The presence of the KEY RR guarantees that the updater's notion of the client associated with the FQDN is still accurate.

An administrator may enable another client to take over the name for some reason, or may decide to associate the name with some host manually. The query contains a second prerequisite: that the IP address contained in the A record matches the lease that expired.

As described previously, this prevents a DHCP server from deleting the A record of a client that moves and receives a new lease from a different server. The second lease causes the second server (or the client itself) to replace the A record with one containing the second IP address. If the prerequisite tests succeed, the update section of the query deletes the FQDN, removing both the A and KEY records.

22.3.7 Client Name Change

As noted previously, the DNS database should reflect the most current information about the DHCP client. The entity responsible for updating the A record attempts to add a new A record and KEY record to the new FQDN, performing the tests described here. You must remove the old A and KEY records because they prevent any other DHCP client from using the name that they are attached to. The DHCP server then updates the PTR record matching the client's IP address to point to the new FQDN.

Summary

The *Domain Name System (DNS)* provides a mapping between mnemonic names for networked devices and the IP addresses assigned to those devices. The mapping information is stored as a database, whose contents are distributed among DNS servers throughout the Internet.

Dynamic address assignments that DHCP makes affect the name and address information that DNS manages. As DHCP servers assign IP addresses to clients, you must either add database entries to the DNS database, or you must modify existing entries to reflect the new address assignments.

The dynamic DNS update mechanism in RFC2136 defines a mechanism through which you can update the DNS database using network messages. The DHC Working Group developed a proposal describing techniques for DHCP servers and clients to use dynamic update messages that keep the DNS synchronized with addresses assigned by DHCP servers.

Several specific problems arise when DHCP clients and servers make dynamic DNS updates. The mechanisms for DHCP-DNS interaction described in the Internet Draft, "Interaction between DHCP and DNS," include proposed solutions to these problems. As this book is written, work on DHCP/DNS mechanisms is still in progress; the Working Group should complete a final version in the second half of 1999.

CHAPTER **23**

Kim Kinnear, Cisco Systems
Ted Lemon
Ralph Droms, Ph.D.

Debugging Problems with DHCP

Previous chapters discuss how the DHCP protocol works and how to configure DHCP servers and clients. This chapter discusses problems that can occur when DHCP servers and clients are configured incorrectly. It also provides an overview of the process of debugging DHCP clients and servers when they aren't working correctly and describes some specific problems that occur rather frequently.

23.1 The Debugging Process

The debugging process includes three basic parts:

- Discovering that you have a problem

- Determining what the problem is

- Solving the problem

This may seem obvious, but each of these parts can be fairly subtle. It's worth describing them in detail before talking about specific problems that you may encounter.

23.1.1 Discovering That You Have a Problem

A computer using DHCP is likely to encounter two fundamental problems:

- The DHCP client may fail to acquire or renew a lease.

- If the DHCP client does acquire a lease, the information the server provides may be incorrect.

Depending on which version of the DHCP client you are using and on the nature of the problem, it may be difficult to tell which of these two problems occurred.

Failure to Acquire or Renew a Lease

Some DHCP clients notify the user if they fail to acquire or renew a lease. The DHCP client included in Windows 95 does this; if it can't get a lease, it displays a dialog box saying that either it is unable to contact a DHCP server, or the DHCP server denied access to the network. Other clients, such as the one included in Windows 98, assume that if they are unable to get an Internet Protocol (IP) address from a DHCP server, they should use an IP address chosen according to the IPv4 auto-configuration procedure described in Chapter 15, "Setting Up a Reliable DHCP Service."

These clients do not display a dialog box if they fail to acquire an IP address. Instead, they choose an IP address on the 169.254.0.0/16 subnet. The only way to tell that the client chose an auto-configuration address is to run the winipcfg command and examine the IP address it displays. If the command displays an IP address that starts with 169.254, the DHCP client is unable to acquire an IP address from the DHCP server.

Note

DHCP clients on multiuser machines, such as UNIX, Linux, NetBSD, and Windows NT, do not display a dialog box indicating that a problem exists in acquiring an IP address. Instead, the DHCP client reports the error through the system error log. To determine that these systems failed to acquire an IP address, you can either look in the error log, or check the status of each network interface that the DHCP client is instructed to configure. If the network interface doesn't have an IP address, the DHCP client failed to acquire one.

On UNIX-like systems, the syslog daemon, which is configured through the /etc/syslog.conf file, writes the system error log. If you don't know where DHCP client errors are logged, consulting this file and the documentation for the DHCP client should help. On Windows NT, you can run the Event Log program to examine the event log for errors.

Incorrect Information from the DHCP Server

If the DHCP server is providing a lease but is providing incorrect information about network services with that lease, the DHCP client generally cannot tell, and it does not display a dialog box or log a message indicating that an error occurred. The only evidence that something is wrong is that the client cannot access some or all network services.

For example, if the DHCP server supplies an incorrect value for the Domain Name System (DNS) server or the default route, the DHCP client cannot resolve DNS names and contact other network computers even though it has a valid IP address. A DHCP client for a diskless workstation (for example, a network computer) that is provided either with incorrect information about the name of its bootfile, or with an incorrect IP address for the server that provides that file, may display an error message such as "File not found" on startup.

If you suspect that something of this nature is occurring, you probably should examine the client's configuration in detail to discover the problem. The Windows 95/98 `winipcfg` command displays the IP address of the domain name servers that it receives, as well as the default route, so it is possible to verify that these configuration parameters are correct. DHCP clients for UNIX systems generally write the IP addresses of the DNS servers into the `/etc/resolv.conf` file, and the `netstat.m` command can be used to display the routing table, including the default route provided by the DHCP server.

23.1.2 Characterizing the Problem

After you discover that you have a problem, you must figure out why you have the problem. The client may fail to acquire or renew a lease for four general reasons:

- The client may be unable to get DHCP packets to the server.

- The server may be receiving DHCP packets, but it may be unable to get its responses to the client.

- The server may have no IP addresses to allocate to the client, or it may be configured not to allocate the IP addresses that it has available to that client.

- More than one DHCP server may exist, and the servers may be configured in such a way that they interfere with each other.

If the information the client receives is incorrect, either the DHCP server is incorrectly configured, or more than one DHCP server exists and the DHCP server from which the client acquired its lease is not the right DHCP server for that client.

To determine what the problem is, you may need one or more tools. You should have documentation for your DHCP server and have a reasonable understanding of it. You must be able to access the server log files for your DHCP server, you must know the identity of the client that is having difficulty, and you may need a network analyzer to monitor the DHCP traffic between the client and the server.

> **Note**
>
> A network analyzer *is a tool that reads and interprets packets on a network segment. A network analyzer may be a separate device such as a* Network General Sniffer, *or a program you run on a general-purpose computer such as* tcpdump *or* snoop. *In either case, you can use the network analyzer to examine the contents of DHCP messages and determine the nature of your problem.*
>
> *Although you can't easily debug some problems without using a network analyzer, you can debug many DHCP problems without such a tool. If you don't have one easily available to you, you may still be able to debug your problem.*

23.1.3 Solving the Problem

After you determine the problem, solving it may be easy. For example, if the problem is network connectivity, you need to fix the connectivity problem. If you are running out of addresses, you need to figure out some way to allocate more. However, if the problem is more complex—for example, two DHCP servers are interacting badly—you may need to learn more about the protocol, or call in your server vendor for help. If you ask for help from the vendor, you should provide your vendor with as much information as possible; don't try to leave out details you think are irrelevant. If you can't figure out the problem, you probably don't know which details are important.

The rest of this chapter discusses actual problems you may run into while operating DHCP and how to solve them.

23.2 Establishing Connectivity

To acquire a lease, a DHCP client must first be able to communicate with a DHCP server. Although this seems obvious, in many cases a DHCP client can't acquire a lease for an IP address simply because it is unable to communicate with the DHCP server.

Most DHCP servers log informational messages when they receive packets from clients. Therefore, the first place to look to see whether the client and server are communicating is the DHCP server log.

The ISC DHCP server logs this information using the syslog daemon. Where the syslog daemon stores the log messages varies on different versions of UNIX and UNIX-like operating systems. You can find out where your syslog daemon stores these messages by looking in the /etc/syslog.conf file for a line that indicates where messages of the class daemon are logged. You can then use the grep command to search this file for entries that include the string "dhcp"; this shows you whatever is logged. The ISC DHCP server logs routine events at the info level, so your syslog.conf file must specify that messages at that level be logged.

The Microsoft DHCP server logs events to one of seven files, one for each day of the week. Each file's name is DhcpSrvLog. followed by the first three letters of the English name for the day of the week, the first letter of which is capitalized. For example, the log for Monday is DhcpSrvLog.Mon. Each log file contains a message at the top explaining the format of the entries in the file.

To find an event associated with a particular client, and thus prove that the DHCP server is receiving messages from that client, you must know the information that the server uses in its log message to identify the client. This is generally the client's link-layer address or client identifier option (see Chapter 14, "Client Identification and Fixed-Address Allocation," for details on client identification).

If you can find a record of the client's request in the server log file, you know that the server is receiving requests from the client. You can then try to figure out why the client isn't receiving a response.

If you do not see some record of the client's request in the server log file, you have found at least one problem. To discover why the server didn't receive the client's request, you must consider the path that a client packet should follow from the client to the server.

23.2.1 Local Connectivity

The first step in the path is the client's network interface card and the wiring between the network interface card and the rest of the network segment to which it is connected. If the network interface card is not working, the client cannot communicate on the network. Likewise, if the network wiring isn't working, the client cannot communicate.

> **Note**
>
> *Remember that if the client is connected to a network segment other than the one to which you think it's connected, this can cause unexpected results. Be sure to correctly identify the network segment the client is connected to.*

The first step in determining whether the network card is working is to manually configure the network interface with an IP address and see whether the client can send packets to the local router.

UNIX systems, UNIX-like operating systems, and Windows systems provide a `ping` command, which you can use for this purpose. Just type `ping xxx.xxx.xxx.xxx`, where `xxx.xxx.xxx.xxx` is the IP address of the router. If you don't get a response, either the network card isn't working or the wiring between the network card and the router isn't working. To determine which of these two is the problem, try connecting the network interface to a network port that's already working for some other computer. If that enables the client to ping the router, you have a wiring problem, a bad port on a network switching device, or some other network hardware configuration problem.

If the client can't ping the router, even with a network port that you know is working, make sure that the cable you're using to connect the network interface card to the network is working by trying a different cable. If none of these tests enables you to ping the local router, you may have a bad network card or a bad driver for the network card. If this is the case, contact your operating system vendor or your network interface card vendor. If the problem is a network card, you may want to try swapping in a different network card of the same type to see whether it works. Again, if this is the problem, you may have to go to your network interface card vendor for help.

If you don't find a problem with the client's connection to its local network segment, the next step is to figure out why. If the DHCP client and server are on the same network segment, and the client can, when manually configured with an IP address, ping its router, a problem exists with the DHCP server machine or the DHCP server itself. If the DHCP client and server are on different network segments, you must have a relay agent to convey the client's request to the server.

23.2.2 Relay Agent Connectivity

When the DHCP client and DHCP server are not connected to the same network segment, the DHCP server does not see a packet broadcast by the DHCP client unless a relay agent is on the network segment to which the client is connected. In this case, the most frequent problem is that the relay agent on the network segment to which the DHCP client is connected either is not configured, or is configured incorrectly. Chapter 13, "Configuring a DHCP Server," describes how you can configure DHCP relay agents.

If other DHCP clients on the same network segment are being configured correctly, you do not have to check the relay agent. However, if no other clients are configured on the network segment, or no clients on the network segment are able to acquire IP addresses, it's worth checking that the relay agent is correctly configured.

23.2.3 Server Connectivity

If you can verify that the client's connection to its local network segment is working, that the client and server are on the same network segment, and that the relay agent between the client and the server is configured correctly, it's time to look to the server. If you have a network analyzer you can run on the network to which the DHCP server is connected, it may be worthwhile to make sure that the packet is actually arriving on that network segment.

Determining Whether the DHCP Server Is Receiving Client Messages

Although it might sound obvious, the first thing you should do is to make sure that the DHCP server is actually running. Check to make sure a DHCP server process exists. If you find that no DHCP clients are getting DHCP service, you might try restarting the DHCP server.

The DHCP server might not see a DHCP packet that is sent to the correct network and is actually arriving on that network because the network stack is dropping the packet. The network stack might drop the packet for two common reasons: it is configured with firewall rules that block receipt of DHCP packets, or there is a bug in the stack.

If you run firewall filtering on your DHCP server machine, you should refer to Chapter 20, "Setting Up DHCP in a Small Office or Home," for details about setting this up correctly. Otherwise, you should probably contact your DHCP server vendor to figure out why it's not receiving packets. Excessive network traffic can also temporarily prevent a client from obtaining an address, but unless your network is badly over-utilized, this is unlikely to result in a persistent outage.

After you establish that the DHCP server is receiving your DHCP client's requests, you should see whether the DHCP server is responding. If you see in the log that the server is sending a positive response to the client, but you know that the client is failing to acquire the lease the server is offering, either the server is unable to get its responses to the client, or some other server is interfering.

Determining Whether the Client Is Receiving Responses

If the server is sending responses to the client, but the client isn't succeeding in acquiring or renewing its lease, it is possible that the responses are not reaching the client. This might be happening for a variety of reasons.

The most common reason is that the server is sending the responses to the wrong IP address. The DHCP protocol requires that the DHCP server or relay agent send responses to one of two IP addresses: either the IP address that is assigned to the client, or to 255.255.255.255. The client may specifically request that responses be sent using the broadcast bit in the flags field of the DHCP message—otherwise, the server unicasts if it can, and broadcasts if it cannot unicast.

Note

When DHCP was first defined, the protocol specification required that any responses be sent to the newly assigned IP address, avoiding the use of the IP broadcast address. Experimentation with existing TCP/IP implementations showed that some implementations do not accept User Datagram Protocol (UDP) datagrams with a unicast address before an IP address is configured. The broadcast bit was invented to enable implementations to request the use of IP broadcast if necessary.

Some DHCP server implementations also broadcast instead of unicast because of limitations in the IP stack of the operating system on which they are running. The ISC DHCP server broadcasts to local clients if it is using the BSD socket Application Programming Interface (API) because this API does not specify a standard way of unicasting to clients that can't respond to Address Resolution Protocol (ARP) messages. Otherwise, the server unicasts unless the client specifies otherwise or unless the DHCP relay agent on the network segment to which the client is attached can't unicast.

Unfortunately, some IP stacks do not work correctly when a destination IP address of 255.255.255.255 is specified for an outgoing datagram. Instead of sending the packet to 255.255.255.255, the IP stack sends the packet to the subnet broadcast address. For example, if the DHCP client is on a subnet numbered 109.117.221.0, with a subnet mask of 255.255.255.0, a server or relay agent with this problem sends the response to 109.117.221.255 instead of to 255.255.255.255. You can see whether this is happening by using a network analyzer connected to the same network segment as the client to examine the response messages. Appendix H, "DHCP Server and Operating System

Versions," lists some of the operating systems on which this can be a problem, and describes some workarounds.

If the server is on a different network segment than the client, the relay agent must relay the packet back to the client. The relay agent stores its IP address in the giaddr field of the DHCP header. More precisely, the relay agent must write the address of the interface on which the DHCP message is received from the client in the giaddr field. If the IP address in the giaddr field is wrong, either the DHCP server is unable to get its response to the relay agent, or the relay agent is unable to deliver the message to the client.

Likewise, if the relay agent fails to honor the broadcast bit, or sends the response to the wrong IP destination address, the client will not receive it. You can use a network analyzer to see exactly what the relay agent is sending to the server, and also what it is sending to the client.

Some clients can accept only broadcast replies from the DHCP server prior to receiving an IP address, but they fail to set the broadcast flag. This behavior does not comply with the DHCP protocol specification.

If a network analyzer indicates that the broadcast bit is not set in a DHCPDISCOVER packet—and the DHCP client doesn't receive an offer, yet it appears as though the DHCP server sent one—you might suspect a unicast issue. If you can configure your DHCP server to always broadcast (and never unicast), despite setting the broadcast flag, you might try configuring it in that way to see whether the DHCP client receives the DHCPOFFER packet.

Conversely, some clients accept only a unicast packet and do not accept broadcast packets. These clients typically signal their intentions by not setting the broadcast bit. However, if your server doesn't support unicast on the platform on which it is operating, it cannot honor the setting of the broadcast bit as set by the DHCP client.

Note

Unicast support is very operating-system specific and is not possible on some operating systems. Again, RFC2131 specifies that a server should unicast when the broadcast flag is not set, and that a client must be able to handle a broadcast, even if the broadcast flag is not set. However, some clients do not fully comply with the DHCP specification in this point.

23.3 When the Server Does Not Respond

If the server is receiving requests from the client but is not responding to them, you should look in the server's log file to see why. Most DHCP servers log some kind of an error message when a client's DHCP request is received but no

IP address is ultimately offered to the client. If you find a useful log message describing the problem, you need only fix it. If you cannot locate the problem from the log entries, you can check for a couple of potential obstacles.

23.3.1 No Available IP Addresses

For the DHCP server to assign an IP address to the client, it must have an address that is available for dynamic assignment, or a static assignment for the client that is valid on the network to which the client is connected. The DHCP specification requires that a server not respond to a client if the server has no addresses left to assign. If the server does not respond when the client requests an IP address, it may be because no address is available to assign to the client.

23.3.2 Server Not Configured for Client's Network Segment

Another potential problem is that the server does not have a configuration entry for the network segment to which the client is attached. The DHCP specification requires that a server simply ignore requests for addresses from network segments for which it is not configured. If you don't include the client's network segment in the server's configuration, the server does not respond to the client's request.

23.3.3 BOOTP Clients and DHCP Servers

Most DHCP servers respond to BOOTP messages, but they must be explicitly configured to offer such support. If a device uses BOOTP and is unable to get an IP address from a DHCP server, first ensure that the DHCP server is configured to offer services to BOOTP devices. Then ensure that either an explicit IP address is configured for the BOOTP device (which is the original approach for BOOTP support), or that the server is configured for *dynamic BOOTP*.

Dynamic BOOTP enables the DHCP server to assign an available address to a device using BOOTP the first time that server sees a request from that device. For compatibility with the BOOTP specification, the server gives that device an infinite lease on the IP address. From then on, whenever the DHCP server sees a BOOTP request from that device, it sends it the same IP address.

23.4 Server DHCPNAK Behavior

The DHCP protocol specifies that if a DHCP server receives a DHCPREQUEST message from a DHCP client for an IP address that it knows to be incorrect, it must send a DHCPNAK to the client. This causes the client to stop using that IP address and go back into the INIT state, after which it should acquire a different one. If a DHCP server sends a DHCPNAK when it shouldn't, or doesn't send one when it should, this can prevent the client from acquiring or renewing a lease.

23.4.1 Server Sends DHCPNAK When Inappropriate

If two DHCP servers are providing DHCP service for a single network segment, both DHCP servers must agree on the subnet configuration and on any static IP address assignments they have for that network segment. If they are performing dynamic IP address allocation, they must not be allocating from the same set of IP addresses unless they have some way to communicate with one another about which addresses they assign.

If two DHCP servers do not agree on the configuration of a given network segment, it is likely that each server is preventing clients from completing the DHCP protocol with the other server. If you have access to the logs of both DHCP servers, you can compare them to see whether this is happening. If a client sends a DHCPDISCOVER message, gets a DHCPOFFER from one server, sends a DHCPREQUEST for that IP address, and gets a DHCPNAK from the other server, the server that sent the DHCPNAK is not configured correctly. The DHCP client is thus unable to acquire an IP address from the other server.

Multiple Servers

Even if you think you have only one DHCP server configured to support a given network segment, you may be wrong; perhaps some user of that network segment configured his or her own DHCP server and got the configuration wrong. You may be able to determine that this happened by running a network analyzer on the network and watching the DHCP packets that are exchanged with a client. If you see DHCP packets coming from some IP address on which you aren't aware that a DHCP server exists, you have a rogue DHCP server on your network.

A common configuration error can occur when two servers are providing service on the same network segment. As the DHCP server begins to run low on addresses for a network segment, a subnet is added on one server to make more addresses available, but the administrator forgets to add it to the other DHCP server. The new subnet is configured on the same network segment as the old subnet. Thus, one server's idea of what IP subnets are configured for the network segment is different from the other.

This configuration error does not show up until some DHCP client is offered an address on the newly allocated subnet. At this time, the DHCP client broadcasts a DHCPREQUEST message for the offered IP address. The server that offered the IP address responds with a DHCPACK. Because the other server does not have the new subnet in its configuration, it decides that the IP address the DHCP client is requesting is invalid for the network segment to which it is attached. The protocol requires DHCP servers to send DHCPNAK messages to clients whose configurations are incorrect for the network to which they are attached, so the second DHCP server sends a DHCPNAK to the client.

This can be very difficult to detect because most DHCP clients accept the first response they receive. Sometimes the client receives the DHCPACK first and sometimes the DHCPNAK. If the client receives the DHCPACK first, it uses the newly assigned address; if the DHCPNAK arrives first, the client starts its initialization process again. If you think you have a problem with conflicting server configurations, you can use a network analyzer to determine which server is sending a DHCPACK and which is sending a DHCPNAK.

The solution to this problem is to configure the second server to be aware of the existence of the newly allocated subnet on the first server. If you do this, the server knows that addresses on the new subnet are valid for the network segment, and remains silent when it sees a DHCPDISCOVER from the DHCP client that received an IP address on the new subnet from the first DHCP server.

23.4.2 Server Fails to Send DHCPNAK Messages When Appropriate

DHCP servers are expected to validate IP addresses requested by clients. If a client requests an IP address that is not valid for the network segment to which it is attached, the DHCP server is expected to send a DHCPNAK in response to the client's request. This DHCPNAK causes the DHCP client to move to the INIT state and broadcasts DHCPDISCOVER messages so that the local DHCP server can offer it a valid IP address.

If a DHCP server fails to send a DHCPNAK when it should, the DHCP client may continue to use the IP address if time remains on the lease. If the IP address is not valid for the network segment to which it is connected, the client cannot use the network.

Note

To protect against misconfiguration by naïve users, Version 3 of the ISC DHCP server does not send DHCPNAK messages in this situation unless it is positively configured to do so, using the authoritative *option. The Microsoft DHCP server should always send a DHCPNAK in this situation, so this isn't a problem for installations where this server is used.*

23.5 Incorrect Option Values

Sometimes a client receives incorrect option values from the server along with the lease for an IP address. Most frequently, this is the result of a configuration error in the server and the association of the various option values with the different subnets and DHCP clients.

If the server doesn't provide some way to report the option values that it sends directly, you can use a network analyzer to display the option values in the DHCP messages and diagnose the problem. The DHCP client may also send a `parameter request list` option, specifying the parameters it is expecting. The treatment of this list varies from server to server, and the server and client may not always agree on what this list means. In such a situation, the server may not send the client all the options that it needs to operate.

If you use a network analyzer and determine that the server is not sending all the options that the client is requesting, you may have to override the `parameter request list` option on the server.

23.6 Uniqueness of Client Identifiers

DHCP client identifiers *must* be unique within an administrative domain for the DHCP protocol to operate correctly. If two clients choose the same client identifier, the server cannot differentiate between the two clients. In many cases, the user does not have control over the identifier the DHCP client chooses to send. In many of those cases, the client identifier is based in some way on the client's link-layer address, which should guarantee uniqueness.

However, for cases in which the user can configure the client identifier, it is important that he or she be very sure that it is unique because it is the identity or key that the DHCP server uses to tell one client from another. This problem is discussed in detail in Chapter 14.

23.7 Dual-Boot Client Systems

A *dual-boot client system* is one in which a user can run two different operating systems on the same hardware. For example, you might have an Intel-based system with a partitioned disk that has Windows loaded in one partition and Linux loaded in another partition. You can choose which operating system to use when the system first starts up. Because the two operating systems are completely independent of one another, they are using two separate DHCP clients, each with its own state.

In some cases, those two different operating systems generate an identical client identifier (typically from the link-layer address); the DHCP server is then unable to distinguish one operating system from the other. Each operating system may, however, have a different expiration time for the lease, though they share the same IP address.

If each DHCP client is configured with the same host name and the DHCP server is configured to enable the client to specify the host name and to enable the DHCP server to perform the dynamic DNS update, the server will simply leave the DNS entry unchanged. If the DHCP clients are configured with different host names, whenever one starts up the other operating system, it appears to the DHCP server as though the client changed its name, and the server responds accordingly.

Sometimes dual-boot systems develop different client identifiers for the same machine. Most commonly, one operating system develops a client identifier from the link-layer address, and the other does not use a client identifier at all. In this case, many DHCP servers see these two operating systems as fundamentally different DHCP clients and give each of them a different IP address.

If, however, the client is supplying a host name to the DHCP server to place into DNS using the dynamic DNS service, and both clients are configured with the same host name (which makes sense because this is the same computer), unexpected behavior can result. Precisely what happens is highly dependent on your server, and possibly even on its version. This is something to watch out for in dual-boot scenarios.

23.8 Duplicate IP Addresses

Whenever two network interfaces are configured with the same IP address, problems result. A DHCP server does not give one client a lease on an IP address while some other client still holds a valid lease on that same address. However, some network user may misappropriate an IP address without using DHCP by knowing the network number and subnet mask and testing each valid IP address on the subnet until he or she finds one that is not in use. If the DHCP server subsequently assigns this IP address to a DHCP client, both the client and the manually configured computer are using the same IP address simultaneously.

Some DHCP servers try to avoid allocating duplicate IP addresses by sending an Internet Control Message Protocol (ICMP) Echo message to the address before allocating it to a client. If the server receives a response, the address is already in use. The server marks the address as unusable and tries another address for the client.

This check works only if the other computer using that IP address is operational at the time the DHCP server checks the address. If the rogue user's machine is active when the server checks, the server notifies the system administrator through a log message that a conflict exists. If the machine is not active, the user of the DHCP client notices the problem when the rogue machine is again powered on.

In addition to the DHCP server's ICMP Echo check, DHCP clients are expected to use ARP to check the newly assigned IP address prior to using it. If they find some other system using it, they should send the DHCP server a DHCPDECLINE, and then go back to INIT state to acquire a different IP address. If a client doesn't support DHCPDECLINE, you may need to manually mark the IP address as unusable through the server configuration, and then restart the client that experienced difficulty.

Duplicate address situations can result from a variety of reasons when using DHCP, and they are, in general, completely preventable. Keep in mind the following things:

- Do not supply for dynamic allocation an address to a DHCP server that is manually assigned to a network client.

- When using redundant DHCP servers (as described in Chapter 15), do not supply the same IP address to two different servers to be dynamically allocated.

- Do not lose your DHCP server's database of active leases.

If you avoid doing these things, you should have problems only with duplicate IP address allocation if you have users whom you cannot convince to use DHCP for address allocation.

23.9 Client Fails to Get Reserved IP Address

Most DHCP servers enable you to reserve a particular IP address for a particular client. The DHCP server does not offer that IP address to any other client, and if the client appears on the network segment where the reservation exists, it should get that IP address.

For cases in which redundant DHCP servers are used, as described in Chapter 15, both DHCP servers must be aware of the static allocation. Otherwise, the DHCP server that is not configured with the static allocation may make a dynamic IP address assignment to the client. This can be a problem if the client depends on having a consistent IP address because the dynamically allocated address is almost certainly different. So, when configuring redundant DHCP servers, the dynamic IP address must be different on the two DHCP servers, while the static IP address allocations must be the same.

Summary

Successful DHCP client configuration requires that several parts of your network work correctly. Specific characteristics of clients and servers, failure or incorrect configuration of network components, and even uncooperative users may all cause DHCP to fail. Any time you suspect a problem with DHCP, first examine your server's log files to see whether you can find some clues about the problem there.

When working on problems with DHCP, you should first ensure that the DHCP client and DHCP server can communicate. If the client and server are on different network segments, you must ensure that a correctly configured DHCP relay agent is supporting the client's network. You can use a network analyzer on the client's network segment to confirm that the client is sending DHCP messages and that the server's responses are reaching the client. You can also check whether the replies from the server are being delivered to the correct IP address.

Configuration problems in DHCP servers can often cause difficulties. The DHCP server must be configured with information about the network segments to which clients may be attached. The server must also have addresses available to assign to clients on those network segments.

Redundant DHCP servers are especially prone to configuration problems. Be very careful to ensure that all servers are configured with the same list of subnets, that the dynamic address pools are separate, and that the reservations for IP addresses are identical. Only one server should support dynamic BOOTP for any subnet.

Although no one can anticipate every problem you might encounter with your DHCP service, this chapter describes several common dilemmas. If you follow the strategies described here, you should be able to diagnose and fix all your DHCP problems.

CHAPTER **24**

The DHCP Database

Every DHCP server manages an internal database of policies and information that guide the server's operation. This database includes statically configured information about management policies and network infrastructure architecture, dynamic information about leased addresses and addresses that are available for assignment, and other runtime information about the server's operation.

A DHCP server obtains its policies and a description of the network architecture from a configuration file that the server reads when it first starts up. Details regarding the configuration files the ISC server and the Microsoft server are included in Chapter 11, "The Microsoft DHCP Server," and Chapter 12, "The ISC DHCP Server." This chapter describes the following:

- The requirements for managing the lease information set out by the DHCP specification

- The ways in which the ISC and Microsoft servers meet these requirements

- The two proposals, one based on a *Simple Network Management Protocol (SNMP)* and the other based on the *Lightweight Directory Access Protocol (LDAP)*, that provide access to the dynamic information managed by the DHCP server while it's running

24.1 The Lease Database

For a DHCP server to manage lease information, the server must be able to recover lease information and reinitialize its internal database whenever the server restarts. That is, the server must be able to get itself back to its previous state, regardless of whether it was shut down gracefully or it suddenly stopped running because of a power failure or a system crash.

24.1.1 Requirements for Lease Databases

The DHCP specification requires that a DHCP server record lease transactions to some local, permanent storage file before it sends a response to a client. In practice, this means the server must write the new lease information to its disk before responding to the client. The way in which the information is recorded is up to the server developer. The ISC server keeps the lease information as a journal or log file, adding a new entry at the end of the file for each transaction. The Microsoft server stores configuration and lease information in several disk files.

A server need not keep a lot of information about each lease in its lease file. Each lease entry needs to include some identification of the client to which the lease is assigned, the address associated with the lease, and the lease expiration time. The server can determine other configuration parameters delivered to the client based on the server's policies and infrastructure information. These parameters need not be saved in the lease database.

24.1.2 The ISC Database

The ISC server records every transaction with a client that modifies the server's database of leases as a new entry at the end of a journal file dedicated to recording lease information. Each time an address is assigned, or the lease on an address is extended or released, the information about that lease is recorded in the lease file. The lease file usually contains more than one entry for a particular address. The last entry in the file for that address has the current information about the address assignment and lease.

ISC Lease File Entries

Each entry in the lease file describes a single IP address, as identified in the lease statement in Example 24.1.

EXAMPLE 24.1

```
lease ip-address {        }
```

The starting time for the lease is specified in the `starts` statement, and the expiration time is specified in the `ends` statement. The dates in these statements are specified in the format described in Example 24.2.

EXAMPLE 24.2

```
day-of-week year/month/day hour:minute:second<
```

The day of the week is included to make it easy to read the lease file and is not used by the ISC server. The day and time are stored in Universal Time Coordinated (UTC) (also known as Greenwich Mean Time, or GMT) for consistency. A DHCP server may manage clients in multiple time zones or even clients that move between time zones, so the information about leases must be stored in a format that is independent of time zone and location. The other required piece of information in a lease file entry is the identification information for the computer to which the address is assigned. As mentioned in Chapter 14, "Client Identification and Fixed-Address Allocation," the identification information for a client can be either its link-layer IP address or the `client identifier` option (option 61) that it sends. The link-layer address is specified in Example 24.3.

EXAMPLE 24.3

```
hardware hardware-type link-layer-address
```

In the case of an Ethernet interface, the hardware-type is specified as `ethernet` and the link-layer-address is specified as six hexadecimal numbers, each representing one byte in the Ethernet address and separated by colons. An example of an entry from the lease file of `dhcpserve` for IP address 192.168.11.25, which is assigned to a computer with Ethernet address 39:8f:ad:7e:17:84, is shown in Example 24.4.

EXAMPLE 24.4

```
lease 192.168.11.25 {
        starts Friday 1998/12/04 00:55:01;
        ends Friday 1998/12/04 00:57:01;
        hardware ethernet 39:8f:ad:7e:17:84;
}
```

A DHCP client may identify itself to the DHCP server with the client-identifier option. The ISC server records the value in the client identifier with the uid statement.

EXAMPLE 24.5

```
uid client-identifier;
```

The client-identifier option is recorded as a sequence of hexadecimal values. Some Windows clients may send their host names using the hostname option (option 12), which the ISC server records as a character string with the hostname statement.

EXAMPLE 24.6

```
hostname "desktop1";
```

> **Note**
>
> The hostname *option is designed for use by servers to supply a DNS name to a client. The Windows DHCP client implementation uses the* hostname *option to pass its locally configured name to the server, instead of using the preferred* client-identifier *option.*

If the ISC server determines that an address in one of the server's pools of assignable addresses is already in use by another computer, the server *abandons* the address. The server may determine that an address should be abandoned because a DHCP client finds the address is already in use and returns a DHCPDECLINE message when the server offers the address. It may also determine that an address should be abandoned because the server itself discovers that the address is in use when it checks the address prior to assigning it to a client. The server records abandoned addresses in its database with the abandoned statement, as shown in Example 24.6.

EXAMPLE 24.6

```
abandoned;
```

24.1.3 Microsoft NT DHCP Server Database

The Microsoft NT DHCP server, described in Chapter 11 and Chapter 12, stores its address lease information in a structured binary file. The formats of the database, the lease file, and the configuration file are proprietary and undocumented. You can access the contents of the files only through the Microsoft server manager. As the server makes changes to the lease database, it records the changes as entries in a lease file. Each time the server restarts, it integrates the lease file with the database file so that the database file reflects the current state of the lease database.

DHCP Manager Interface Program

You can review the current leases and available addresses through the *DHCP Manager* interface program. You can look at the active leases in a scope by first selecting the scope and then clicking on Active Lease in the Scopes menu. The Active Leases window lists both active and expired leases for the scope, sorted either by IP address or client identifier. This window also displays the number of addresses defined for the scope, how many of those addresses are excluded, assigned, or reserved, and how many are still available in the scope. Clicking on the Properties button displays a window with the IP address, client identifier, client name, and expiration date for the lease.

The Microsoft server manager gives you access to the DHCP server configuration information for individual leases, but it does not give you access to all the configuration information for the server in one window. You cannot generate a summary list of active leases and reservations from all the scopes, nor can you obtain a report of statistics, such as percentage of addresses still available for assignment.

Note

The ISC server distribution does not include tools for managing the server configuration or generating reports about available addresses. However, because the configuration and lease information is stored in simple text files, you can access that information through a text editor or with a program such as a PERL script.

24.2 Accessing Information from a Running Process

In addition to the initial configuration information the DHCP server reads from a file when it first starts up, you may want to access information about dynamically allocated addresses and monitor other operational information within your DHCP server. The IETF DHC Working Group is considering two solutions to this problem: a SNMP *Management Information Base (MIB)* for DHCP servers, and a *LDAP* directory schema to identify DHCP services and servers.

24.2.1 DHCP and SNMP

SNMP (RFC1905) is used to retrieve operational statistics and control the operation of network elements such as hubs, switches, and routers. SNMP defines the communication between the network *manager* that monitors the operation of network elements and *agents*, or the network elements themselves.

In the client-server network application paradigm, an SNMP manager is a client and an SNMP agent is a server. The SNMP manager typically runs on a network administrator's computer, and sends requests for information or control messages to the network elements. An SNMP agent that receives and processes the requests and returns requested values to the manager is on each network element. The manager collects and displays the information from the network elements for the network administrator.

You can use SNMP for many different monitoring and management tasks. SNMP itself defines only the control messages exchanged between a manager and agents. A MIB defines the structure of the information referenced by the SNMP messages. A MIB is a hierarchical data structure that contains the management information. The manager can name and access each member of the MIB through the SNMP messages.

24.2.2 An MIB for DHCP Servers

To enable the use of SNMP with DHCP, the DHC Working Group has developed a proposed MIB for the administration of DHCP servers (DHCP-MIB). This MIB describes the information that is exchanged between DHCP servers and SNMP managers. Figure 24.1 illustrates the use of SNMP for monitoring and controlling the operation of a DHCP server. The following sections give an overview of the current DHCP MIB.

The DHCP MIB is mostly a read-only file and is designed for monitoring activity, not active management. Therefore, the DHCP MIB is not appropriate for exchanging information between DHCP servers.

The MIB for DHCP servers has eight major groups, which are described in Figure 24.2. Within the MIB, information about BOOTP services and DHCP services is managed separately; the SNMP manager can combine the information into composite information for the server.

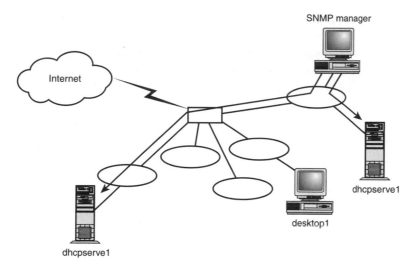

FIGURE 24.1 *Using SNMP to monitor and control a DHCP server.*

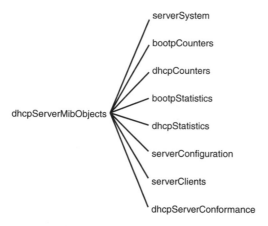

FIGURE 24.2 *The major groups of the DHCP MIB.*

Note

The current DHCP server MIB is published as an Internet Draft and is currently in review by the IETF. The DHC Working Group is likely to approve the DHCP server MIB soon in something close to its current form.

The serverSystem group includes the name and version information for the
server. The bootpCounters and dhcpCounters groups hold running counts of the
different types of messages the server receives. The groups also count the messages the server does not process because the server is not configured for the
client from which the message is received, or for the subnet to which the client
is attached. The bootpStatistics and dhcpStatistics groups hold information
about the intervals between messages and the response time for messages. The
elements of these groups are summarized in Table 24.1.

TABLE 24.1 ELEMENTS OF serverSystem, BOOTP, AND DHCP OBJECTS

Group	Object	Type	Description
serverSystem	serverSystemDescr	string	Textual description of this server, including name and version
	serverSystem ObjectID	object identifier	Vendor's identifier for the system instantiating this server
bootpCounters	bootpCountRequests	32-bit integer	Number of BOOTP requests received
	bootpCountInvalids	32-bit integer	Number of invalid BOOTP/DHCP packets received
	bootpCountReplies	32-bit integer	Number of BOOTP replies sent
	bootpCountDropped UnknownClients	32-bit integer	Number of BOOTP requests ignored because the server was not config-ured to supply BOOTP service to the requesting client
	bootpCountDropped NotServingSubnet	32-bit integer	Number of BOOTP requests ignored because the server was not config-ured to supply BOOTP service to the subnet from which the request was received
dhcpCounters	dhcpCountDiscovers	32-bit integer	Number of DHCPDISCOVER messages received
	dhcpCountRequests	32-bit integer	Number of DHCPREQUEST messages received
	dhcpCountReleases	32-bit integer	Number of DHCPRELEASE messages received

Group	Object	Type	Description
	dhcpCountDeclines	32-bit integer	Number of DHCPDECLINE messages received
	dhcpCountInforms	32-bit integer	Number of DHCPINFORM messages received
	dhcpCountInvalids	32-bit integer	Number of messages received with an unknown DHCP message type
	dhcpCountOffers	32-bit integer	Number of DHCPOFFER messages sent
	dhcpCountAcks	32-bit integer	Number of DHCPACK messages sent
	dhcpCountNacks	32-bit integer	Number of DHCPNAK messages sent
	dhcpCountDropped UnknownClient	32-bit integer	Number of DHCP messages ignored because the server was not configured to supply DHCP service to the requesting client
	dhcpCountDropped NotServingSubnet	32-bit integer	Number of DHCP messages ignored because the server was not configured to supply DHCP service to the subnet from which the request was received
bootpStatistics	bootpStatMin ArrivalInterval	milli-seconds	Minimum time between arrival of two BOOTP messages
	bootpStatMax ArrivalInterval	milli-seconds	Maximum time between arrival of two BOOTP messages
	bootpStatLast ArrivalTime	date and time	Time at which last valid BOOTP message is received
	bootpSumSquares ArrivalTime	64-bit integer	Sum of the squared inter-arrival times between BOOTP messages
	bootpStatMin RepsonseTime	milli-seconds	Minimum time between arrival of BOOTP message and transmission of reply

continues

TABLE 24.1 CONTINUED

Group	Object	Type	Description
	bootpStatMax ResponseTime	milliseconds	Maximum time between arrival of BOOTP message and transmission of reply
	bootpStatSum ResponseTime	milliseconds	Sum of the response time intervals between the receipt of BOOTP messages and the transmission of associated responses
	bootpStatSum SquaresResponse Time	64-bit integer	Sum of the squared response time intervals between the receipt of BOOTP messages and the transmission of associated responses
dhcpStatistics	dhcpStatMin ArrivalInterval	milliseconds	Minimum time between arrival of two DHCP messages
	dhcpStatMax ArrivalInterval	milliseconds	Maximum time between arrival of two DHCP messages
	dhcpStatLast ArrivalTime	date and time	Time at which last valid DHCP message was received
	dhcpSumSquares ArrivalTime	64-bit integer	Sum of the squared inter-arrival times between DHCP messages
	dhcpStatMin ResponseTime	milliseconds	Minimum time between arrival of DHCP message and transmission of reply
	dhcpStatMax ResponseTime	milliseconds	Maximum time between arrival of DHCP message and transmission of reply
	dhcpStatSum ResponseTime	milliseconds	Sum of the response time intervals between the receipt of DHCP messages and the transmission of associated responses
	dhcpStatSumSquares ResponseTime	64-bit integer	Sum of the squared response time intervals between the receipt of DHCP messages and the transmission of associated responses

Server Configuration

The serverConfiguration group contains information obtained from the initial configuration file and information such as leases on addresses assigned while the server is running. The serverSubnetTable lists the current IP subnets known to the server. Each entry in the table includes the IP address and subnet mask of the subnet and lists the other subnets that share the same network segment.

The serverRangeTable lists the addresses that the server may assign to DHCP clients. The addresses are specified in *ranges*, with a beginning address, an end address, and an associated subnet mask.

The assigned addresses known by the server are stored in the serverAddressTable. Each address is accessed through a separate entry in the table, along with the link-layer address, the client identifier (if supplied), the range from which the address is assigned, and the time remaining on the lease for the address. Table 24.2 lists all the information associated with each address.

TABLE 24.2 ELEMENTS OF AN ENTRY IN THE serverAddressTable

Object	Type	Description
serverAddress	IP address	IP address of this entry
serverAddressSubnetMask	IP address	Subnet mask associated with this address
serverAddressRange	IP address	Address range from which this address was assigned; identified by starting address of the range
serverAddressType	integer	Type of address assignment: static, dynamic, reserved through initial configuration, reserved for pending assignment
serverAddressTimeRemaining	32-bit integer	Time remaining until lease on this address expires, measured in seconds
serverAddressAllowedProtocol	integer	Type of protocol allowed to serve this address: BOOTP, DHCP, both, none (reserved)
serverAddressServedProtocol	integer	Type of protocol used when this address was assigned: BOOTP, DHCP, none (address is unassigned)

continues

TABLE 24.2 CONTINUED

Object	Type	Description
serverAddressMacAddress	byte string	Type of hardware and hardware address of interface to which this address was assigned; first byte is hardware type from htype field and remaining bytes are client's hardware address from chaddr field
serverAddressClientId	byte string	Client identifier for interface to which this address was assigned
serverAddressHostName	string	Host name assigned to this client
serverAddressDomainName	string	Domain name assigned to this client

BOOTP and DHCP Clients

The clients known to a server are reported through the serverClientTable. The list includes clients that contact the server to obtain configuration information and clients that are identified to the server through its initial configuration.

The entry for each client includes its link-layer address, the IP address and subnet mask currently assigned to the client, and information about the time and type of the last request received from the client. The elements of an entry in the serverClientTable are shown in Table 24.3

TABLE 24.3 ELEMENTS OF A CLIENT ENTRY IN THE serverClientTable

Object	Type	Description
serverClientTypeAndMacAddress	byte string	Type of hardware and hardware address of interface to which this address was assigned; first byte is hardware type from htype field and remaining bytes are client's hardware address from chaddr field
serverClientSubnetMask	IP address	Subnet mask assigned to this client
serverClientAddress	IP address	IP address of this entry
serverClientLastRequestTime	date and time	Time when last request was received from this client
serverClientLastRequestType	integer	Type of last message received from this client: BOOTP, DHCP message type, unknown
serverClientLastResponseType	integer	Type of last message sent to this client

An Example of the DHCP MIB

Figure 24.3 gives an example of the DHCP MIB containing information about the example network from Chapter 2, "An Example of DHCP in Operation." In this example, the DHCP server (dhcpServer) manages five subnets. The DHCP client (desktop1) is assigned an address, 192.168.11.25, on one of the subnets so that MIB entries exist for both the client and its assigned address.

dhcpServerMibObjects

- serverSystem
  - serverSystemDescr   - "Demo Server; ISC DHCP server 3.0"
  - serverSystemObjectID   -1.3.6.1.4.1.9999.1.3
- bootpCounters
- dhcpCounters
- bootpStatistics
- dhcpStatistics
- serverConfiguration

  - serverSubnetTable

Subnet address	Subnet mask	Shared subnet
192.168.11.0	255.255.255.0	0.0.0.0
192.168.11.0	255.255.255.0	0.0.0.0
192.168.11.0	255.255.255.0	0.0.0.0
192.168.11.0	255.255.255.0	0.0.0.0
192.168.11.0	255.255.255.0	0.0.0.0

  - serverRangeTable

Range start	Range end	Subnet mask	In use	Offers
192.168.11.1	192.168.11.251	255.255.255.0	0	0
192.168.12.1	192.168.12.253	255.255.255.0	1	0
192.168.13.1	192.168.13.253	255.255.255.0	0	0
192.168.14.1	192.168.14.253	255.255.255.0	0	0
192.168.15.1	192.168.15.253	255.255.255.0	0	0

  - ServerAddressTable

IP Address	Subnet mask	Range	Time remaining	Hardware address	Client identifier
192.168.12.25	255.255.255.0	192.168.12.1	86400 seconds	8 : 0 : 20 : 76 : f : 8	"desktop1"

- ServerClient

Hardware address	Assigned address	Subnet mask
1 8 : 0 : 20 : 76 : f : 8	192.168.12.25	255.255.255.0

- dhcpServerConformance

FIGURE 24.3 DHCP MIB example.

24.2.3 DHCP and LDAP

Broadly defined, LDAP (RFC2253) is a networked directory service. Strictly speaking, LDAP defines just the access protocol used between an application and a directory server. LDAP now includes the access protocol, as well as the directory service and the mechanism for defining the contents of the directory.

LDAP was originally defined as a replacement for the *Directory Access Protocol (DAP)* component of the X.500 directory service (ISO 9594). X.500 is a framework through which information is organized into a hierarchical namespace. An X.500 directory can store many different types of data, and X.500 defines search mechanisms for information retrieval.

DAP requires the entire OSI protocol suite, which is not widely available. LDAP implements a subset of the functions of DAP, and it uses the TCP/IP protocols. Initially, LDAP was designed to interact with an LDAP server, which, in turn, passed requests via the OSI protocols to an X.500 server. Today, the directory service may be provided directly by an LDAP server.

The structure of the information stored in an LDAP directory is defined by a *schema*. The LDAP schema for DHCP serves the same purpose as the SNMP MIB for DHCP; the schema provides a framework through which an LDAP client can access the information in the DHCP server.

Overall Structure of the DHCP Schema

The LDAP schema for DHCP is a structure for the representation of information about DHCP on an Intranet. The DHCP schema is logically divided into two major components that describe the DHCP service and DHCP servers separately. In the DHCP schema, a `dhcpService` consists of configuration information about clients, and a `dhcpServer` refers to a specific instance of DHCP server software providing DHCP configuration information defined by a `dhcpService`.

The separation of DHCP service parameters and information about specific DHCP servers is designed to accommodate the implementation of a common DHCP service through multiple DHCP servers. One or more DHCP servers may provide a DHCP service. The network administrator and the DHCP servers access the DHCP service component of the schema to define and retrieve information about DHCP clients. The DHCP server component holds information such as the name of a server and the services that the server provides.

Note

The LDAP schema of DHCP is defined in an untitled document produced by the IETF DHC Working Group and is available through `http://www.dhcp.org`. *The Working Group expects to publish the specification as an Internet Draft for eventual acceptance as an Internet Standard.*

The dhcpServer Object

Each DHCP server is represented in an LDAP directory by a dhcpServer object, which includes the server name, the services this server provides, and the type of server; for example, the server's vendor. The services provided by this vendor are dhcpService objects, as defined in the next section. Table 24.4 gives the components of the dhcpServer object.

TABLE 24.4 COMPONENTS OF A dhcpServer OBJECT

Name	Type	Description
dhcpServerName	string	Name of this DHCP server
dhcpService	list of distinguished names	Services provided by this server
dhcpImplementation	string	Description of this server

The dhcpService Object

Each dhcpService object includes the components listed in Table 24.5. The proposed LDAP schema assumes that DHCP services provided through multiple DHCP servers are structured so that each service has a primary DHCP server and one or more secondary servers. The dhcpPrimaryServer and the dhcpSecondaryServer components identify the DHCP servers responsible for the dhcpService object.

TABLE 24.5 COMPONENTS OF A dhcpService OBJECT

Name	Type	Description
dhcpServiceName	string	Name of this DHCP service
dhcpPrimaryServer	distinguished name	Primary server for this DHCP service
dhcpSecondaryServer	list of distinguished names	List of secondary servers for this DHCP service
dhcpParentService	distinguished name	Parent service from which configuration information is included
dhcpIncludeFromParent	list of objects	Objects to be included from the parent service identified in dhcpParentService
dhcpLocator	list of objects	Objects such as subnets, ranges, and addresses to be included in this service

The dhcpParentService component identifies another dhcpService from which this dhcpService obtains some of its configuration objects. The specific objects from the parent service are listed in the dhcpIncludeFromParent object.

Configuration objects included in the service object specify configuration information for this service. Such configuration objects include dhcpAddress, dhcpClient, and dhcpSubnet objects, which are defined in the next sections. The configuration objects exist elsewhere in the DHCP LDAP directory, and so they can be managed independently. The configuration objects are identified by name in the dhcpLocator component of the dhcpService object.

Configuration Objects

dhcpSubnet objects describe the subnets that a DHCP service manages. Each subnet has an IP address and subnet mask that define the addresses that make up the subnet. A subnet may be identified as belonging to a group of subnets that share the same network segment. Associated with each subnet is a list of IP addresses assigned from that subnet. The assignable addresses within a subnet may be restricted to a subset of the addresses associated with the subnet.

dhcpAddress objects identify individual IP addresses within the DHCP service. Along with the IP address itself, the dhcpAddress stores the lease expiration time for the address, the client to which the address is assigned, and other information.

A dhcpClient object represents a DHCP client known to the DHCP service. The client identifier, the address assigned to the client, and the classes to which the client belong are stored in the dhcpClient object.

An Example of the DHCP LDAP Schema

Figure 24.4 gives an example of the DHCP LDAP schema used to represent the example DHCP service described in Chapter 2. As in the previous example in this chapter, the LDAP directory describes a DHCP service that includes five subnets, the DHCP client desktop1, and a DHCP server dhcpserve. desktop1 is assigned the IP address 192.168.12.25, which is represented in the directory.

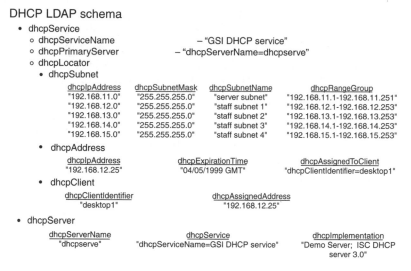

DHCP LDAP schema

- dhcpService
  - dhcpServiceName — "GSI DHCP service"
  - dhcpPrimaryServer — "dhcpServerName=dhcpserve"
  - dhcpLocator
    - dhcpSubnet

dhcpIpAddress	dhcpSubnetMask	dhcpSubnetName	dhcpRangeGroup
"192.168.11.0"	"255.255.255.0"	"server subnet"	"192.168.11.1-192.168.11.251"
"192.168.12.0"	"255.255.255.0"	"staff subnet 1"	"192.168.12.1-192.168.12.253"
"192.168.13.0"	"255.255.255.0"	"staff subnet 2"	"192.168.13.1-192.168.13.253"
"192.168.14.0"	"255.255.255.0"	"staff subnet 3"	"192.168.14.1-192.168.14.253"
"192.168.15.0"	"255.255.255.0"	"staff subnet 4"	"192.168.15.1-192.168.15.253"

- dhcpAddress

dhcpIpAddress	dhcpExpirationTime	dhcpAssignedToClient
"192.168.12.25"	"04/05/1999 GMT"	"dhcpClientIdentifier=desktop1"

- dhcpClient

dhcpClientIdentifier	dhcpAssignedAddress
"desktop1"	"192.168.12.25"

- dhcpServer

dhcpServerName	dhcpService	dhcpImplementation
"dhcpserve"	"dhcpServiceName=GSI DHCP service"	"Demo Server; ISC DHCP server 3.0"

FIGURE 24.4 *An example of an LDAP directory.*

Summary

DHCP servers use statically configured information to set up their DHCP service and generate dynamic information while running. The DHCP service administrator often must access the information to monitor or debug the operation of the DHCP service.

The ISC DHCP server reads its initial configuration from a file, and saves address assignment information to a lease file while running. The ISC server reads the address assignment file when restarting to obtain information about all the currently active leases. The ISC server lease file is written in ASCII text, and you can read it using any text editor.

The Microsoft DHCP server stores its dynamic information in a binary file. The Microsoft server reads this dynamic information when starting to find out about active leases. You can use a graphical management tool for the Microsoft server to examine the server's configuration information and write the lease information to an ASCII text file.

The IETF DHC Working Group is working to establish standard techniques for accessing server information. One project is aimed at defining an SNMP MIB for DHCP servers, and the other is working toward an LDAP schema for DHCP services and servers. Both the SNMP MIB and LDAP schema include definitions for common information about a DHCP server, such as clients managed by the server, addresses assigned by the server, and addresses still available for assignment. The DHCP MIB includes many operational statistics. The LDAP schema uses a more flexible model, in which DHCP services and servers are defined separately. This model accommodates multiple DHCP servers managing a common pool of available and assigned addresses.

Both the DHCP MIB and the DHCP LDAP schema are in early stages of development. Information about the status of both projects is available through the DHC Working Group website, `http://www.ietf.org/html.charters/dhc-charter.html`, or through `http://www.dhcp.org`.

CHAPTER 25

Ralph Droms, Ph.D.
Kim Kinnear, Cisco Systems

Communication between DHCP Servers

DHCP reliability is an important issue because DHCP is part of a network infrastructure without which DHCP clients cannot operate. As discussed in Chapter 10, "Theory of Operation of a DHCP Server," you may choose to use multiple servers for load sharing and to ensure reliability.

However, you may encounter a serious problem when using multiple DHCP servers. To be effective, servers must coordinate their activities by exchanging information so that all servers are aware of which addresses are available for assignment, and when the leases on assigned addresses are set to expire. In the abstract, the servers must maintain a distributed database in which the contents of the dynamic database are replicated among the DHCP servers. Keeping the data consistent across all locations is difficult to do in a timely fashion.

This chapter looks at the reasons servers must communicate and why this communication is a complicated problem. It also reviews the protocol for inter-server communication currently under development by the DHC Working Group.

25.1 Why Should DHCP Servers Communicate?

In a network with multiple DHCP servers, a client may contact any of several servers for each DHCP transaction. That is, a client may obtain its initial address assignment from server A, extend its lease through server B, and release its address to server C. The details of DHCP message transmission and relay agent operation enable clients to locate and use different servers over time. In this way, you can make DHCP service more reliable through the use of redundant DHCP servers.

The information about available addresses, client configuration rules, assigned addresses, and leases really represents a distributed database shared among the DHCP servers. Some of this information is relatively static and is config-ured by the network administrator. But the information about assigned addresses, leases, and available addresses changes frequently as clients obtain addresses and extend leases, and as leases expire.

25.1.1 Why Is This a Problem?

A strategy for improving reliability using multiple DHCP servers is not easy to implement. Fully redundant service requires that the servers notify each other about transactions with DHCP clients so that the servers have consistent infor-mation about the clients. Sharing network configuration among multiple DHCP servers is difficult to do reliably and quickly.

Reliability is an issue because the servers communicate over a network that may fail. As soon as the servers lose contact with each other, their configura-tion information becomes inconsistent. For example, if one server fails to notify other servers that it assigned a particular address to a DHCP client, some other server may try to assign that same address to a different client.

Reliable communication is further complicated by the fact that a server cannot differentiate between another server being down and a network failure between the servers. Thus, a server must not assume that another server is not running just because contact between the servers is lost.

Speed of communication among servers is an issue because inter-server com-munication may increase a server's response time. The expedient solution of forwarding notification of lease assignments to other servers imposes an unac-ceptable performance penalty on DHCP servers, especially in cases in which a network or server failure necessitates retransmission of notification messages. Long server response times slow down the operation of a DHCP client. In addition, the client may time out and retransmit its original request if the delay is too long, adding to the load on the DHCP servers.

25.1.2 Solving the Difficult Problems

Although in the abstract the solution to DHCP redundancy appears to be a generic distributed-database issue, the particular requirements for server availability and performance create difficult problems. You can solve these problems by exploiting the DHCP server's control over the difference between the information exposed to the DHCP client and the other DHCP server.

In particular, the primary DHCP server strictly limits the duration of the lease that it offers to a DHCP client to be less than a well-known constant beyond the lease time known by the secondary server. In this way, the secondary server can know that, after that interval, it will hear from any DHCP client that is allocated one of the leases belonging to the primary server, or that DHCP client's lease will expire.

25.2 Inter-Server Protocol

The DHC Working Group has developed a proposal for a new protocol that servers can use to provide high-reliability DHCP service. The goal of this inter-server protocol, usually referred to as the *failover protocol,* is to enable pairs of servers to coordinate their activities so that one server is always available. The next few sections look at the components of the failover protocol and describe its operation.

25.2.1 Introduction to the Failover Protocol

The two servers in the failover protocol have different roles: The *primary* server handles DHCP client transactions under normal circumstances, and the *secondary* server takes over if the primary server is unavailable. The protocol enables the secondary server to act as a hot backup for the primary and for DHCP service to be transferred to the secondary if the primary fails ("failover"). This organization can provide a reliable service that is transparent to DHCP clients and that handles several common types of server and network failures. Figure 25.1 illustrates the normal operation of the primary and secondary servers, and Figure 25.2 shows the secondary server taking over for the failed primary.

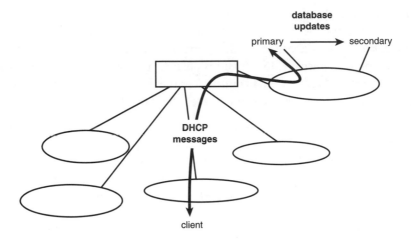

FIGURE 25.1   *Normal operation of primary and secondary servers.*

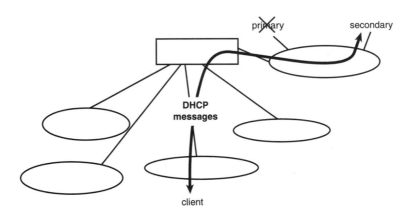

FIGURE 25.2   *Failover operation of primary and secondary servers.*

In normal operation, although the primary server handles all client transactions, the client messages are delivered to both servers. Conceptually, the network is configured to operate with the DHCP servers in either normal or failover mode. Any relay agent is configured to forward copies of client messages to both the primary and secondary servers. So, while the primary is managing client transactions, the secondary receives copies of the DHCP messages forwarded by relay agents, but simply discards them. This design simplifies the operation of the network infrastructure and DHCP clients; the servers can go into failover mode without changing the rest of the network infrastructure.

25.2.2 Configuring Relay Agents for the Failover Protocol

In addition to configuring the primary and secondary servers to use the failover protocol, you must arrange for DHCP client messages to be delivered to both servers. Of course, if both servers are on the network segment that all your clients are on, the clients' broadcast messages are received by both servers. If you use relay agents in your network, you must configure them to forward client messages to both servers.

For example, you can simply configure the relay agents with the IP addresses of both servers. If both servers are on the same network segment, you can configure the relay agents with the broadcast address of the network. This technique has the advantage of enabling you to change the IP addresses of the DHCP servers without reconfiguring all the relay agents. In fact, you can configure the relay agents to broadcast the forwarded messages even if the servers are on different network segments; use the broadcast addresses of the two network segments instead of the servers' IP addresses. In any case, you must ensure that the client broadcast messages are forwarded to both servers for transparent failover operation.

25.2.3 Normal Operation

In normal operation, the primary server does all the work, receiving all DHCP client messages and handling all client transactions. In general, the primary server performs all the functions of a single DHCP server. In addition to these normal DHCP functions, the primary server sends information about changes to its client information to the secondary server, such as newly assigned addresses and extended leases. The secondary server performs no DHCP functions; it simply tracks the changes the primary server sends and keeps its local client information synchronized with the primary's information. So, the secondary is always ready to take over from the primary, but it doesn't take part in any load sharing while the primary is functioning.

25.2.4 Operation When Primary Fails

While the primary server is managing client transactions, the secondary server monitors the primary's operation by tracking the messages from the primary and by sending status requests to it. The secondary can detect when the primary server is no longer functioning because it stops receiving transaction updates, and the primary fails to respond to status requests.

When the primary server fails, the secondary begins to answer DHCP client requests that it receives. In this mode, the secondary handles all client transactions: assigning addresses, extending leases, and returning released addresses to the pool of available addresses. After the secondary takes over the DHCP service, clients continue to operate normally.

A DHCP client sees a difference after the primary server fails when it attempts to extend a lease on an assigned address. Because the client unicasts its initial requests to the primary server to extend the lease on its assigned address, it cannot contact the primary server for the extension. At time T2, the client broadcasts its extension request, which the secondary server receives and answers.

As the primary server comes back up, it contacts the secondary server to reacquire control of the DHCP service. At that point, the secondary server stops responding to client requests, and the primary again handles most DHCP client transactions. Upon re-establishing contact, each server updates the other with the results of any DHCP client activity that occurred while they were out of contact.

At this point, the two servers are back in normal operation, with the primary handling client messages and the secondary available as a hot backup, as shown in Figure 25.3.

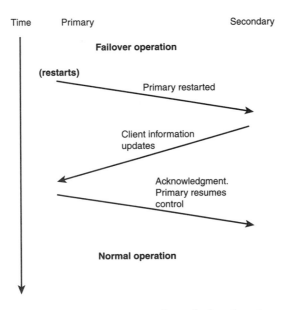

FIGURE 25.3 *Messages exchanged when the primary server returns to normal operation.*

25.2.5 Simultaneous Operation of Both Servers

The failover and recovery cycle described in the previous section assumes that the secondary server can always tell when the primary fails. Unfortunately, in real networks the secondary server cannot differentiate a failure of the primary server from a failure of the network between the two servers. This means the secondary might conclude that the primary failed when, in fact, the primary is still functioning. But if both servers are handling client requests simultaneously, they may assign the same IP address to two different clients.

Another potential problem results from the time it takes the primary to send an update to the secondary. If the primary assigns an address to a client but then fails before passing that new assignment along to the secondary, it might assign the same address to another client in the future. Similarly, if the primary extends a lease and then fails immediately, the secondary may mark the lease as expired and make the address available for reassignment while the client continues to use the address under the extended lease. Once again, the servers can potentially assign the same address to two different clients.

The failover protocol addresses the problem of potential parallel operation by ensuring that the primary and secondary servers never assign addresses out of the same pool of addresses, even if they are running in parallel. In normal operation, the secondary maintains a small pool of addresses that are not available for assignment by the primary. If the secondary detects that the primary may have failed, the secondary begins to assign addresses out of its reserve pool. Even if the primary is still functioning, the two servers are assigning addresses from different pools, so each server will not assign the same address to different clients.

Sometimes, the secondary server may have no recorded information from the primary about a client attempting to extend a lease. Although this scenario is unusual, it may occur because the primary crashed just after allocating the IP address to the client. If this occurs, and if the secondary has no conflicting information, it extends the client's lease, and all clients with existing leases can continue to use them.

When both servers are running but not communicating with each other, the primary server might extend a client's lease on its assigned address without the secondary server learning of the extension. In that situation, the secondary might determine that the lease expired and make the address available for reassignment while the client is still using it. To avoid duplicate assignment of addresses in this case, the secondary does not reassign an address even after the lease on the address expires. Only after the secondary is in contact with the primary and can confirm that the lease definitely expired does the secondary make an address available for reassignment.

In these cases of primary outages, as long as the secondary does not exhaust its reserve pool of addresses, the two servers can resynchronize their client information by passing updates to each other when they re-establish communications. If the primary and secondary can't communicate for a long enough period of time, the secondary may exhaust its reserve pool of addresses.

At any time prior to that point, the network administrator need only inform the secondary that the primary is, in fact, out of operation. Then, the secondary server automatically takes over the primary's address pool in complete safety because it received confirmation that the primary is not operating in parallel. The secondary can do this safely because the primary can extend a lease for a certain period of time beyond that known by the secondary, and the secondary will wait that time before using any of the primary's available leases or reallocating an expired lease. When the primary re-establishes contact with the secondary because the primary was actually out of service, the two servers can recover automatically.

Alternatively, under rules established by the network administrator, the secondary may optionally begin to function as the primary without any intervention, assigning addresses and extending leases, without any guarantee that the primary is truly out of service.

When the primary re-establishes contact with the secondary, if the primary is actually out of service, the two servers can recover automatically. If the secondary started functioning as the primary and the primary wasn't actually out of service, in some circumstances you may have to intervene manually to resolve address assignment and lease extension conflicts.

25.2.6 Details of the Failover Protocol Architecture

One important detail of the architecture is the granularity of the groups of clients managed by primary and secondary servers. Primary and secondary servers can be defined for subsets of clients so that one group of clients might use server A as a primary and B as a secondary, while another group of clients might use C as a primary and D as a secondary. You can think of the primary and secondary servers as "virtual" servers, implemented within a DHCP server process.

In fact, this organization enables a DHCP server to act as the primary server for some clients and the secondary server for other clients, while ignoring requests from other clients altogether. The smallest grouping of clients that you can define are the clients on a single network segment. As a server receives an incoming DHCP message, it processes that request as a primary or a secondary server or simply discards the message based on the network segment to which the client is connected.

The failover protocol, then, doesn't require that the primary server do all the work while the secondary sits idle. By splitting your network among the two physical servers so that each server acts as primary for one-half of your clients and secondary for the other half, you can share the processing load while providing reliable DHCP service.

Another potential organization for primary and secondary servers is to deploy several primary servers, each of which manages some of your DHCP clients, and then use a single DHCP server as the secondary for all the primaries. Figure 25.4 illustrates this strategy. Depending on your DHCP client load, you might choose to implement the secondary server on a relatively inexpensive hardware platform, as you are likely to use the secondary only occasionally and for short periods of time. If your network is physically distributed among several sites, you might consider deploying a primary server at each site and a single, centralized server acting as the secondary for all your sites.

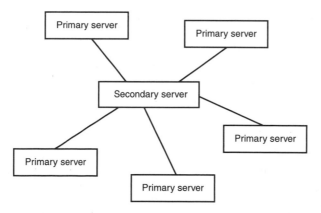

FIGURE 25.4 Using a single server as the secondary for multiple primary servers.

Summary

One strategy for improving the reliability of DHCP service is to add additional servers for redundancy. DHCP clients can accommodate networks with more than one DHCP server and will search for any available server when requesting a new address, checking that a previously assigned address is still appropriate for its network segment and extending a lease on an assigned address.

Although multiple, independent DHCP servers can add reliability, servers must communicate with each other for maximum effectiveness. As one server assigns new addresses or extends leases, it must pass the new information along to other servers if those servers are to provide redundancy. The unreliability and timing delays of network message delivery make reliable exchange of DHCP client information among servers a hard but solvable problem by exploiting characteristics of the DHCP protocol itself.

The DHC Working Group developed a proposal for the *failover protocol* to provide redundant DHCP service. This proposed protocol defines the operation of *primary* and *secondary* servers for groups of DHCP clients. By taking over if the primary server fails, the secondary server can improve the reliability of the DHCP service. The failover protocol is currently under development, and the specification is available in an Internet Draft. Check `http://www.dhcp.org` for the current status and specification of the failover protocol.

## CHAPTER 26

Guiding the Evolution of DHCP

The options DHCP uses were defined over time, and the procedure for accepting new options into the protocol evolved with the protocol specification itself. Some of the new options added to the protocol simply carry addresses for different types of servers, while other options change DHCP's fundamental operation. Many factors, in addition to correctness and effectiveness, should be considered when defining and accepting a new option. This chapter looks at:

- Causes for concern about defining new DHCP options in the future

- The current process for reviewing new options

- The recommendations from a panel of IETF DHC Working Group members who reviewed the current DHCP options and processes for defining new options

Several important new DHCP functions and options, including DHCP authentication, an inter-server protocol for DHCP, DHCP-DNS interaction, and DHCP for IPv6, are covered separately in other chapters.

26.1 Motivation for Review of DHCP Options

In 1996, the DHC Working Group identified two potential problems with the DHCP options: exhaustion of the option codes, and the inability to carry domain names and IP addresses in options.

One of the authors of this book, Ralph Droms, defined two new DHCP options that would expand the range of available option codes and allow the use of domain names in existing options:

Option Code	Purpose	Name
127	Extended option code	Encode 16-bit option codes
126	Extended option code request option	Request extended option code

The Working Group reviewed and rejected these new options. Rather than adopt a quick-and-dirty engineering solution, the group decided to thoroughly review the DHCP options and the procedures for defining new options.

Having initially suggested that a more thorough review was in order, Mike Carney of Sun Microsystems graciously agreed to bring together a panel of DHC Working Group members (dubbed the Futures Panel) to review the current options and procedures and to develop recommendations for the issues that are described in the following sections of this chapter.

26.1.1 Exhaustion of Options Space

What appear as *options* in the current DHCP specification were defined in RFC1048 as *vendor information*. RFC1048 defined the basic format of options, including the 1-byte option code field and the 1-byte length field. RFC1048 also defined 12 information options (codes 1 through 12 in RFC2132) as well as the END and PAD options, and reserved option codes 128-254 for local (site-defined) use. Later RFCs (RFC1084, RFC1395, and RFC1497) specified the original definitions for option codes 1 through 18. These option codes were also defined in RFC2132 for backward compatibility with BOOTP clients.

Option formats, as originally defined in RFC1048, are significantly limited. Most importantly, the 1-byte option code field, combined with the reservation of codes 128-254 for local use, allows only 127 different DHCP options to be defined. Furthermore, the 1-byte length field restricts the data area to a maximum of 255 bytes. These limitations did not seem restrictive when they were adopted; only 18 of the 127 option codes were used in RFC1497, which was published in 1993.

However, as DHCP became widely deployed and used to manage more complex configuration environments, more options were defined. RFC2132 defines 76 options (including the original 18 from RFC1497), and three subsequent RFCs (RFC2241, RFC2242, and RFC2485) define six additional options. Other codes are allocated for options that are not yet defined. One cause of the exhaustion of option codes is the process through which option codes are assigned, which is discussed in the next section. Fewer than 20 codes are currently available for assignment to new options.

26.1.2 Recovery of Assigned Option Codes

One of the reasons the DHCP option codes are nearly exhausted is because codes are assigned to *proposed* options instead of *accepted* options.

RFC2132 describes the process for defining new options. In this process, each new option is assigned a code when it is proposed. Unfortunately, quite a few proposed options have not completed the process for acceptance, and their assigned option codes are in limbo. The DHC Working Group is reviewing the status of option codes assigned to proposed options and has recovered several codes for reassignment to new options.

To address this problem in the future, RFC2489 modifies the process described in RFC2132. The new process assigns an option code to a new option when it is accepted as part of the DHCP specification. Under this new process, option codes are assigned only as required. This reserves as many codes as possible for new options.

26.1.3 The Effect of New Options on the Protocol

Also significantly affecting the definition of new DHCP options are changes to the semantics of the protocol itself. It is difficult to accommodate extensions or re-definitions of the ways in which DHCP works. Existing client software must be replaced with new software that implements the new protocol. Servers must retain backward compatibility with clients using the original protocol, and servers must be able to differentiate between old and new clients. Many new options simply carry different configuration parameters, such as a list of domains to search when resolving domain names, and do not affect the semantics of DHCP. Other options affect the way clients and servers interact, but do not fundamentally change the protocol itself. One such proposed option is the user class option, which allows a client to inform a server of the client's characteristics or organizational membership. The user class option does not change the sequence of DHCP messages, but it requires that server implementations are extended to interpret the option and to modify address allocation and configuration rules based on the data provided by the client.

Some options may fundamentally change the way in which DHCP works. For example, the authentication mechanism discussed in Chapter 21, "Authentication of DHCP Clients and Servers," may change the sequence and semantics of DHCP messages that clients use when they first obtain an address. The `relay agent information` option requires that relay agents examine the contents of DHCP messages and add new option information that servers then process.

26.1.4 Data Types in DHCP

Currently, DHCP options use a variety of data types, including IP addresses, lists of IP addresses, integers of various lengths, and Boolean values. Some options contain a single value or a simple list of values, while others have a more complex internal structure. Each option defines its own data types and structure within the option, and the protocol specification provides no guidance on how to share types or structures with other options.

This diversity in data types and structures complicates the implementation of clients and servers and allows for potential confusion about the definition of options. Options with new data types require implementers to add code to generate and interpret the option data values; network administrators must then deploy the new code.

Note

The Internet Software Consortium (ISC) DHCP server and client are implemented in such a way that it is relatively easy to extend them to support new options. As you read in Chapter 12, "The ISC DHCP Server," new DHCP options can be specified in server and client configuration files by indicating the data type and structure of the option. This syntax for specifying options means the ISC DHCP server installations can be extended without installing new server software.

26.2 DHC Panel Recommendations

At the time of this writing, the panel had drafted its recommendations and the DHC Working Group was reviewing them. The panel's report includes:

- The primary findings upon reviewing the current options and processes for defining new options

- A proposed set of guidelines for analyzing and accepting future options

- A set of format rules for new options

26.2.1 Review of Current Options and Processes

After reviewing the DHCP specification and options, the panel reported four primary findings:

- The available option codes might be consumed before a replacement, such as IPv6 or DHCPv6, becomes available. Although recovering assigned option codes might mitigate this problem, exhaustion of option codes is still a possibility.

- No guidelines exist for assessing the impact of new options on DHCP and on existing implementations.

- No mechanism exists through which clients and servers can identify which version of DHCP they are using.

- Parts of the DHCP specification in RFC2131 and RFC2132 are not precise, and differing interpretations by vendors have led to interoperability problems.

Note

As an example of interoperability problems resulting from vagueness in the DHCP specification, a recent release of Apple's OpenTransport TCP/IP stack sent a DHCPRELEASE message relinquishing the lease on the client's address every time the stack was shut down. RFC2131 does not explicitly state the client's action after issuing a DHCPRELEASE, and the stack was implemented so that when it restarted, it went to INIT-REBOOT state and sent a DHCPREQUEST for the old address, for which the client no longer had a valid lease. After the DHCPRELEASE, the client should have gone to INIT state and sent a DHCPDISCOVER message to initiate the four-message exchange for obtaining a new address.

To address these issues, the panel's report makes several recommendations, described in the following sections.

26.2.2 New Guidelines for Reviewing and Assigning Options

The panel's report includes guidelines and extensions to the process described in RFC2489. The new guidelines define three option categories.

Category 1: Defines new configuration parameters that existing clients and servers can accommodate without modifying or re-deploying implementations.

Category 2: Defines new configuration parameters that do not change the underlying protocol but may require modifying or re-deploying implementations.

Category 3: Changes the semantics or the operation of the protocol itself.

Category 4: Changes the semantics or the operation of the protocol in a way that is incompatible with previous clients and servers.

The extensions to RFC2489 in the panel's report add detail to the process of deciding whether a new option should be accepted as part of the DHCP specification. These extensions are summarized as follows:

- If this option handles data used by an application layer protocol, then it should be considered for inclusion in the Service Location Protocol (SLP) (RFC2165).

- If this option handles data specific to a particular vendor's implementation, it should be encoded as a vendor-specific option.

- Category 1 options require DHC Working Group or IETF review and assignment of an option code number from IANA.

- Category 2 options require DHC Working Group or IETF review, assignment of an option code number from IANA, and interoperability testing.

- Category 3 options require DHC Working Group or IETF review, assignment of an option code number from IANA, interoperability testing, and a change of the DHCP version number.

- Category 4 options are not acceptable for inclusion in DHCP.

26.2.3 New Format for Options

The panel's recommendation defines a new format for DHCP options. This format accomplishes three goals:

- An expansion of the number of available option codes

- An increase in the maximum length of an option data item

- Better handling of data typing

Data typing and the option format the panel proposed are discussed in the following sections.

Data Types

Three issues are related to data types in DHCP options:

- The proliferation of dissimilar data types used in options

- The structure of data types (single item, simple list of items, or structured item)

- The use of alternate data types within an option; for example, IP address or FQDN

The panel's recommendation addresses these issues by defining a set of known data types and encoding the type of the data item within the option itself. The report defines the following listed data types.

- Single variable-length NVT-ASCII string (not null-terminated).

- Single variable-length string of bytes.

- List of integers, each of length 1, 2, 4 or 8 bytes; length of data item must be a multiple of the size of the integer.

- List of IPv4 addresses; length of data item must be a multiple of four.

- Single variable-length UNICODE string (not null-terminated).

- List of IPv6 addresses; length of data item must be a multiple of 16.

- Boolean; a single byte value that represents value true if non-zero and false if zero.

- Structured data values, composed of a list of simple data types (as defined above).

In each case, the data type may hold a list of items whose length is defined by the option header. For example, if the length of an option containing IPv4 addresses 12, the option holds three addresses.

Option Format

The report defines a new format for options as listed in Figure 26.1.

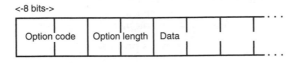

FIGURE 26.1   *Proposed format for new options.*

The option code and length are unsigned 16-bit integers, and the data is structured according to the data types described earlier in this section. This format expands the available option codes and allows for longer data items, addressing the issues of option code exhaustion and interoperability of data types in RFC2312 format options.

26.2.4 Interoperability with Clients and Servers

The panel's recommendation defines several specific interoperability mechanisms to accommodate the proposed extensions to DHCP.

Option Syntax

The first of these mechanisms is to encapsulate options carried in the format described in the previous section in an `options` field prefixed with a new 4-byte `cookie` value. The use of a new cookie allows clients and servers to differentiate between old (RFC2132) and new option syntaxes. For backward compatibility, the first 256 option codes in the new option format are reserved to mirror the 256 options available in the RFC2132 option format.

The function of the RFC2132 options is preserved by the first 256 options in the new option specification. Those options are encoded in the new option format.

`option block request` Option

Next, the recommendation defines an RFC2132 format option, DHCP `option block request`, through which a client requests new format options from a server. That is, the client includes this new option in an RFC2132 format message to inform the server that the client can process new format options. In fact, the DHCP `option block request` option carries the magic cookie value of the requested format, so it can be used for any option formats defined in the future. This option's format is listed in Figure 26.2.

FIGURE 26.2 *Format of an* option block request *option.*

IANA will assign the option code when the panel's proposal is accepted.

version number **Option**

The recommendation also defines a second RFC2132 format option giving the DHCP version number for a message. As new Category 3 options are defined, the DHCP version number is incremented to accommodate the new semantics included with the new option. The version number option has the following format, shown in Figure 26.3.

FIGURE 26.3 *Proposed* version number *option.*

The version number is a 16-bit integer, and IANA will assign the option code.

Coordinating Operation

The recommendation specifies how clients and servers use these options to coordinate their operation. Clients should select responses from servers that match the DHCP version the client is implementing, in preference to earlier, lower-numbered, versions. Servers identify their DHCP version using the DHCP version number option. Clients accepting new option formats should announce that capability by including a DHCP option block request option with the magic cookie from the desired option format in the option.

Servers use the protocol version number in incoming messages to determine which protocol version to use with a client. If the server uses a version number lower than that which the client has requested, the server either ignores the message or uses its (lower) protocol number, as configured by the network administrator. Otherwise, the server uses the protocol version requested by the client. Servers use RFC2132 format options unless the client has requested another format in a DHCP option block request option.

Summary

DHCP is available from many vendors and is widely used. As new services were defined and added to network infrastructures, new options for configuring these services were added to DHCP. Experience with DHCP in different operational environments, such as organizations with multiple sites, universities, and Internet service providers, and with new types of network hardware such as wireless LANs and cable modems, prompted the definition of new functions within DHCP.

Recognizing the issues raised by the rapid expansion of the use and required functions in DHCP, the DHC Working Group formed a panel to review the state of DHCP and guide its evolution. The committee produced a draft report defining guidelines for review of future options and a new format for options that allows for growth.

As this chapter was being written, the IETF had not yet adopted the panel's recommendations as a standard part of the DHCP specification. The panel's report, currently an Internet Draft, is under review by the DHC Working Group and should be considered for acceptance some time in 1999. Until the recommendations are accepted and published as an RFC, the documents are available through http://www.dhcp.org.

CHAPTER 27

DHCP for IPv6

The IETF developed a new version of IP intended to replace the current version of IP, version 4, with as few changes as possible to the rest of the TCP/IP protocol suite. This new version, called *IPv6*, is the result of several investigations into limitations in IP version 4. More than twenty vendors and research organizations developed the preliminary implementations of IPv6. These implementations were demonstrated and tested for interoperability, and an IPv6 experimental testbed, the *6bone*, has been established on the Internet.

IPv6 is named after the version number stored in the version field of the IP header. Version 4 of IP, which is the current version defined in RFC791, is sometimes referred to as *IPv4* to differentiate it from IPv6. Early versions of IPv6 were called *IP next generation (IPng)* after the popular television show, *Star Trek: The Next Generation*.

> **Note**
>
> *IP version numbers 0, 1, 2, and 3 are unassigned. IP version number 5 was assigned to Internet Stream Protocol Version 2 (ST II) (RFC 1819) before IPng was developed. Thus, when the IETF settled on the preliminary design of its new version of IP, IANA assigned it version number 6.*

Several motivations exist for the development of IPv6. One of these motivations, improving several aspects of IP addressing, is directly related to DHCP. The changes to IPv6 are significant enough to warrant the development of a new version of DHCP for IPv6, called *DHCPv6*.

> **Note**
>
> *For clarity, this chapter explicitly refers to IP version 4 as IPv4 and to DHCP for IPv4 as DHCPv4. Elsewhere in the book, these protocols are referred to as IP and DHCP.*

This chapter discusses the differences between IPv4 and IPv6 that affect DHCP, and the details of DHCPv6.

> **Note**
>
> *As this book was being written, DHCPv6 was defined in two Internet Drafts. The details of the protocol may change before they are accepted as an Internet Standard. Check* http://www.dhcp.org *for the latest details about DHCPv6.*

27.1 An Introduction to IPv6

This section presents a brief introduction to IPv6, including those features directly connected to DHCP functions. The IPv6 documents define several terms describing components of an IPv6 internet. Some of those definitions are included here because they are used in some of the IPv6 mechanisms discussed in this chapter.

- Node: Any device that implements IPv6

- Router: A node that forwards IPv6 datagrams

- Host: A node that is not a router

- Link: A mechanism through which nodes can exchange datagrams at the link layer (for example, Ethernet)

- Interface: A node's connection to a link

- Address: An IPv6 identifier for an interface

- Prefix: The initial bits of an IPv6 address identifying a link; equivalent to a network number in IPv4

27.1.1 IPv6 Addressing

IPv6 IP addresses contain 128 bits and, unlike the Class A, B, and C addresses in IPv4, have no inherent structure. Instead, addresses are organized into types by prefix. A prefix in IPv6 is always some number of contiguous bits, starting with the most significant bit of the address. It is identified, when necessary, by a 1-byte *prefix length*, giving the number of bits in the prefix.

At present, most of the IPv6 address space is reserved for future use. Prefixes are allocated for unicast addresses, addresses with limited scope (described in more detail in Section 27.1.2), and multicast addresses. Also, a compatibility mode exists in which IPv4 addresses can be represented in the IPv6 address space.

Because of their length, IPv6 addresses use a different format than IPv4 for textual representation. IPv6 addresses are written by converting them into hexadecimal notation in 16-bit groups separated by colons. This notation is known as *colon hexadecimal*, or *colon hex*. The colon hex format includes two additional notational shortcuts: Any leading zeros from the hexadecimal representation of each 16-bit group can be dropped, and a pair of colons can indicate a string of groups containing zeros (::).

An IPv6 address is represented in colon hex as

    3356:0:4C2D:1F:C34:3F:54CA:B

Several addressing mechanisms in IPv4 are formalized in IPv6. In IPv4, the address 0.0.0.0 may be used as a source address during initialization when the computer is not assigned an address and the address 127.0.0.1 is used as the loopback address. IPv6 also defines the address of all zeros, 0:0:0:0:0:0:0:0, for use during initialization, and the loopback address is 0:0:0:0:0:0:0:1. In IPv6, an interface can have multiple addresses. Finally, the private addressing scheme introduced in RFC1918 is extended to scoped addresses restricted to a node's local link or site.

Note

RFC1918 reserves several IP IP addresses for use in private internets. Organizations can use these addresses for any internal networks, and computers attached to these networks can use IP addresses from the IP addresses without coordinating with any number assignment authority, such as IANA. The addresses reserved in RFC1918 include one Class A IP address, 10.0.0.0; 16 Class B addresses, 172.16.0.0-172.31.0.0; and 256 Class C addresses, 192.168.0.0-192.168.255.0.

Use of these private addresses postpones the imminent shortage of unique IP addresses by allowing organizations to reuse parts of the IP address space on their internal networks. The primary drawback is that a computer using a private address cannot exchange packets with a computer outside its own internal network.

Address Types and Scoping

IPv6 addressing formalizes the notion of *scope*, introduced for IPv4 in RFC1918. In IPv6, an address can be

- Global: Unique among all addresses on the Internet and deliverable ("routed") to any Internet destination

- Site-local: Unique among all addresses within a site and deliverable to any destination within the site

- Link-local: Unique among all addresses on the link (local network) and deliverable only to destinations on the same link

IPv6 also introduces the *interface identifier* (RFC2373), a 64-bit value that can be generated from an interface link-layer address. For example, to construct an interface identifier for Ethernet hardware, insert $ffff_{16}$ (16 one bits) between the first three bytes and the last three bytes of a 48-bit Ethernet address. Interface identifiers are then used with a specific prefix to generate a 128-bit link-local address. For example, the Ethernet address 0:80:3e:6d:31:ea

00000000 10000000 00111100 01101101 00110001 11001010

This is translated to the interface identifier 0:80:3e:ff:fe:6d:31:ea

00000000 10000000 00111100 11111111 11111111 01101101 00110001 11001010

Note

The technique for creating the interface identifier for an interface is defined in the document specifying the techniques for transmission of IPv6 datagrams over the particular interface hardware; for example, RFC2464, "Transmission of IPv6 Packets over Ethernet Networks," in the case of Ethernet hardware.

RFC2644 describes the use of the EUI-64 identifier in creating an interface identifier for an Ethernet interface, and the way in which an EUI-64 identifier is constructed from a 48-bit IEEE 802 address.

Multicast

Scoping also applies to multicast addresses. A 4-bit scope field defines several classes of increasing scope, including link-local and site-local. Thus, it is possible to define a multicast address that can be used at different sites without conflict. For specific services or technologies using multicast, a single multicast address can be defined for use at all sites.

27.1.2 IPv6 Auto-Configuration

One of IPv6's design goals is to enable the automated configuration of IPv6 devices. Several specific mechanisms—some of which are formalizations of IPv4 practices and others new to IPv6—enable computers using IPv6 to determine or obtain a IP address without manual configuration or intervention by a network server.

Link-Local Address

In simple network configurations with no routers, an IPv6 node can use a link-local address with no knowledge of a local IP address. The node selects an address that is not in use by other nodes on its network.

Note

This scenario of a single network with no connections to other networks is often called the "dentist's office" network. This describes an ad-hoc network, created by nonexpert users plugging some computers into a hub. Why dentists were chosen as the canonical nonexpert users is unclear, but the name stuck.

The standard technique for a computer to generate an IPv6 link-local address is to combine the link-local address prefix with the interface identifier. A dentist's office network need not be configured with a network number, and computers on that network can use a link-local address to contact other computers on the network.

Of course, this automatic process does not configure DNS servers, DNS names, or other services. It does guarantee, however, that computers on an isolated network can communicate with each other and support other manually or automatically configured services.

Although the link-local address generated according to these rules is quite likely to be unique, a small chance exists that some other device on the same network is already using the same address. To check the use of its generated link-local address, a device using IPv6 transmits a request on its local network, asking whether other devices are already using that address. If that query receives no responses, the device can safely begin to use the new address.

Prefix Advertisement

Link-local addresses are useful only in communicating with other computers on the same link. To exchange data with computers on other networks, a computer must have a site-local or global address. A computer using IPv6 can pick a site-local or global address for itself by combining the network number or prefix assigned to the local network with the computer's own interface identifier. However, without other information, a computer will not know the prefix for its local network. IPv6 *router advertisement* messages, transmitted by routers to announce their availability on a link, carry prefix numbers for a link.

Computers receiving these messages can find out the prefix for a link and then generate an appropriate address.

27.1.3 Fragmentation and Path MTU

One last difference in IPv6 is that its routers do not perform fragmentation. Only the source of an IPv6 datagram can fragment that datagram. Thus, a computer must know the minimum MTU of all the links along the path to the destination, which it can determine using path MTU discovery. Conceptually similar to path MTU in IPv4, an IPv6 node must use the mechanism for all destinations, including UDP and TCP, to avoid losing packets on links with small MTUs.

27.2 Motivation for DHCPv6

Some difference of opinion exists in the IPv6 community about the need for DHCPv6. A rich set of auto-configuration mechanisms, along with the capability to control network prefixes through router advertisements, means it is possible to have auto-configured operation of IPv6 devices without a centralized address administration service.

Another feature of DHCPv6 is the *Service Location Protocol (SLP)*, which supplies the addresses of application servers and other resources. Most application server options in DHCPv4 are provided through SLP in IPv6, so DHCPv6 has far fewer configuration options than DHCPv4.

Note

Although a specification for SLP for IPv4 exists, it was accepted as a standard in 1997 and is not widely deployed. Because there was a need for server address configuration prior to the availability of SLP for IPv4, DHCPv4 has many options for application server addresses.

Even though formal auto-configuration mechanisms exist in IPv6, some installations still require centralized management and control of IPv6 address allocation and protocol parameter configuration. This function can be provided only through a client-server protocol such as DHCP. Thus, the DHC Working Group began developing a new version of DHCP.

27.3 Design of DHCPv6

DHCPv6 retains the client-server architecture of DHCPv4, and many of the server functions are similar to those in DHCPv4. At the same time, some key differences exist.

27.3.1 Differences between DHCPv6 and DHCPv4

The authors of DHCPv6, Jim Bound and, later, Charlie Perkins, took advantage of the opportunity to start with a clean design slate for DHCPv6 by adding new features to the DHCP service, using the new IPv6 addressing features, and dropping backward compatibility with BOOTP.

Multiple Addresses for an Interface

One key difference between the two versions of DHCP is that DHCPv6 manages multiple addresses for each interface. When DHCPv4 was designed, few (if any) TCP/IP stacks could be configured with more than one IP address. As a simplifying assumption, DHCPv4 was designed with the constraint that each managed interface could be assigned only one IP address.

Note

More precisely, the DHCPv4 specification allows only a single address for each separately identified interface. Because clients can use distinct values in the `client-id` *option, it is theoretically possible to allocate more than one IP address to a single physical interface using DHCPv4. In practice, the DHCP specification does not define how to assign multiple IP addresses to a physical interface, and most DHCPv4 clients cannot support more than a single DHCP address on an interface.*

IPv6 allows for multiple addresses on each interface. This feature enables the use of link-local, site-local, and global addresses through the same interface as well as *virtual hosting*, which provides for multiple copies of a service—for example, multiple WWW servers—through a single physical interface.

DHCPv6 enables a client to request multiple addresses for an interface. The address requests may come as separate DHCPv6 messages, asking for the addresses as required by individual application servers on the DHCPv6 client. The DHCPv6 server implementation manages all the addresses as a set, associated with the interface for which the requests were made.

Use of Link-Local Address

In DHCPv4, using UDP and IP before the client is assigned an address is accomplished using the all-zeros source address and link-level broadcast. The IPv6 link-local address auto-configuration mechanism provides a valid IPv6 address to the client, which the client and server or relay agent use to exchange messages on the local network segment.

Address Lifetime Management

Another difference between DHCPv4 and DHCPv6 is the mechanism through which the assignment duration of addresses is managed. In IPv6, addresses have an associated *valid lifetime*, which defines the time through which an address is used. This lifetime is related to the DHCPv4 lease, and the network administrator uses it to control the length of time over which a client uses an address.

Fewer Protocol Configuration Parameters

At present, the DHCPv6 specification defines far fewer options (called *extensions* in DHCPv6) than DHCPv4. IPv6 has fewer configurable parameters than IPv4, and SLP for IPv6 provides many of the application service addresses defined as options in DHCPv4.

Reconfiguring DHCPv6 Clients

DHCPv6 includes a mechanism through which a DHCP server initiates a message exchange with clients. Using this mechanism, a server informs clients of new configuration parameters, such as new IP addresses in the case of network renumbering.

Note

A similar mechanism was considered for DHCPv4 but was not made part of the protocol specification. When it was evaluated, the proposed reconfiguration function was deemed difficult to implement, both in servers and existing IPv4 protocols stacks. This outweighed the potential advantages. So, it was not included in the DHCPv4 specification.

Use of Multicast in DHCPv6

DHCPv6 defines three multicast addresses reserved for the use of clients, servers, and relay agents:

Name	Scope Use
All-DHCP-Agents	Link-local clients to send messages to servers and relay agents
All-DHCP-Servers Site-local	Relay agents to forward messages to servers
All-DHCP-Relays	Site-local (reserved for future use)

27.4 Client-Server Transactions in DHCPv6

This section describes the specific message exchanges taking place between DHCPv6 clients and servers. These transactions are similar but not identical to the transactions in DHCPv4.

27.4.1 Initial Assignment of Addresses

A DHCPv6 client obtains an initial address by exchanging messages similar to the initial messages in DHCPv4. The client uses multicast to send a message that locates available DHCP servers. This message corresponds to the DHCPDISCOVER message broadcast by a DHCPv4 client to the local broadcast address. A DHCPv6 client locates only servers with the initial message. Any address assignment is performed in the second transaction between the client and server.

The client begins by sending a message to DHCPv6 servers or relay agents on its local link, looking for an available server. This message is sent to the All-DHCP-Agents multicast address. Any servers choosing to respond to the initial discovery message reply to the client, through a relay agent if necessary. The client then selects a server and sends a message requesting an address and other configuration information. Finally, the chosen server responds with the requested parameters.

When it does not have a valid site-local or global address, the DHCPv6 client uses its link-local address as the source address. The DHCPv6 server or relay agent on the same link as the client uses that link-local address to unicast reply messages to the client.

Obtaining Additional Addresses

After obtaining a site-local or global scope address, a client may contact a server directly with subsequent requests for additional IPv6 addresses to be assigned to a particular interface. The server keeps a list of all the addresses assigned to a particular interface, identified by the interface's link-local address. Each of these addresses has an independent valid lifetime. The communication between applications requesting specific addresses and the DHCPv6 client is up to the implementation.

Note

Allowing multiple addresses on a single interface complicates the design and implementation of the protocol. To coordinate the dynamic allocation of multiple addresses, a DHCPv6 client may request that the DHCPv6 server discard all previously allocated addresses, returning them to the pool of available addresses. In response, the server releases the previous addresses and allocates new addresses according to the current request. By clearing the server's record of all allocated addresses, the DHCPv6 client can request initial addresses when the host restarts, and individual applications can request addresses as needed.

Lease Extension

Before the valid lifetime of an address expires, a DHCPv6 client may send a request to the server to extend the lifetime of that address. This action is the equivalent of extending the lease from a DHCPv4 server. In DHCPv6, the expiration of an address is tied to its valid lifetime, and there is no explicit time (equivalent to T1 or T2 in DHCPv4) at which the client is required to extend the valid lifetime on addresses.

Address Release

A DHCPv6 client may return to a server addresses that it no longer needs. The client may choose to return all addresses at once, or it may return some addresses and retain others. In DHCPv6, the server acknowledges returned addresses to the client, using either a IP address specified by the client or through the relay agent on the client's link.

Reconfiguration

The DHCPv6 reconfiguration mechanism allows a server to push new configuration parameters out to clients. The mechanism assumes that every client listens for server messages on the DHCPv6 UDP port, and will process incoming messages as they arrive.

Note

A server can send two types of reconfiguration requests. The first, used when the same parameters are to be passed on to many clients, carries the new parameter values in the message itself. The clients take those parameters out of the message from the server and reply with an acknowledgment message.

The second type of reconfiguration transaction, used when different clients receive different parameters, causes the client to send a request message back to the server. The server can then reply to each client with a message containing the parameters for that client.

Reconfiguration messages may be sent in one of three ways:

- To all DHCPv6 clients at a site through the multicast address reserved for DHCPv6 clients

- To a subset of DHCPv6 clients through a locally configured multicast address

- To individual clients through their unicast addresses

In all these cases, the server is responsible for reliably delivering the reconfiguration messages to all DHCPv6 clients. The server must match replies from the servers and retransmit to any clients that do not respond to the initial message. At the discretion of the server administrator, the server may report to the administrator a list of clients from whom no reply is received.

27.4.2 Interaction with IPv6 Auto-Configuration

DHCPv6 address configuration complements IPv6 auto-configuration, and IPv6 nodes must choose one form of configuration or the other. The IPv6 router advertisement mechanism provides administrative control over that choice through flag bits that indicate whether IPv6 nodes should use auto-configuration or DHCPv6.

Summary

The IETF is developing a new version of IP, called *IPv6*. IPv6 includes several features for address management that are either not included in IPv4 or represent formalization of current practice in IPv4. IPv6 includes *scoped addresses* forwarded only across a single network (link) or only within a single site. With IPv6, computers can obtain information about network numbering and an auto-configuration mechanism through which they can generate addresses based on the network numbering information.

As this book is being written, the DHC Working Group is bringing forward a specification of DHCP for IPv6, called *DHCPv6*. DHCPv6 explicitly allows for multiple addresses on each interface and allows clients to request addresses in more than one transaction. DHCPv6 allows servers to initiate interactions with clients so that servers can push new configuration information to clients on demand. Network administrators can control whether IPv6 devices use auto-configuration or DHCPv6 through the router advertisement protocol.

DHCPv6 is published as an Internet Draft, and the details may change before the specification is accepted as an Internet Draft. To obtain information about the latest version of the DHCPv6 specification, refer to the DHC Working Group charter page, `http://www.ietf.org/html.charters/dhc-charter.html`.

PART IV

Appendixes

A Microsoft DHCP Server Examples

B ISC DHCP Server Configuration File Reference

C The DHCP Message Format

D DHCP Options Summary

E Other DHCP Resources

F Bibliography

G List of Related RFCs

H DHCP Server and Operating System Versions

I Glossary

APPENDIX A

Microsoft DHCP Server Examples

The main text of this book provides examples using the configuration file language of the ISC DHCP server. This appendix shows you how to use the Microsoft DHCP server for every example in the main text that the Microsoft server supports.

This appendix is intended for use as a reference and should not be read sequentially. As a result, some examples are redundant, and in many cases the text illustrating one example refers to another example.

To use these examples, you must have the Microsoft DHCP server installed, as described in Chapter 13, "Configuring a DHCP Server." Before using the examples in this appendix, you should read Chapter 13, which explains how to make the Microsoft DHCP server work.

After you install the Microsoft DHCP server, you must start the DHCP Manager and connect it to the DHCP server you want to modify. Figure A.1 shows the DHCP Manager window.

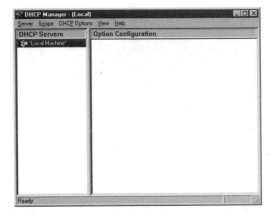

FIGURE A.1   The DHCP Manager window.

A.1 Examples 3.1, 3.2, 3.3, and 3.4

Subnets are called scopes in the Microsoft DHCP server. To add a subnet, go to the DHCP Servers list in the DHCP Manager window and click the name of the server you want to update (generally Local Machine). The server's name should be highlighted and should appear in parentheses in the window's title bar, as shown in Figure A.1.

To add a new scope, pull down the Scope menu and select Create.

Example 3.2, in Chapter 3, "Configuring the DHCP Server," shows examples of five new subnets. Because Microsoft treats scopes as a concept independent of subnets, it is impossible to show an example of an empty scope declaration, as in Example 3.2. Instead, Examples 3.1, 3.2, 3.3, and 3.4 are combined. Figure A.2 shows the full definition of the first of the GSI subnets.

A.2 Examples 3.5 and 3.6

Example 3.5 shows the format of an option declaration, and Example 3.6 shows a simple subnet-specific option declaration. The Microsoft DHCP server enables you to declare options that are specific to the scope, very much like the routers option shown in Example 3.6. To define an option that is local to a scope, highlight the scope in the DHCP Manager Servers subwindow, and select the Scope item from the DHCP Options menu. Then choose an option from the Unused Options list, click the Add-> button, select the new option from the Active Options list, and click the Value>>> button. This adds a dialog box to the

DHCP Options window, enabling you to set the value of the option. Because the routers option includes an array of values, you must click the Edit Array button to open the Array Editor dialog box. This finally enables you to enter the IP address of the router into the New IP Address box and click Add. Figure A.3 shows the routers option being defined.

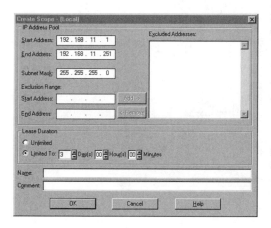

FIGURE A.2   Create Scope *window for subnet 192.168.11.0.*

You may notice that the names of the options are slightly different in the Microsoft DHCP server—for example, the ISC routers option is equivalent to the Microsoft Router option. The subnet-mask option is set up in the Create Scope dialog box, and it can't be configured in the Scope Options dialog box. The ISC domain-name-servers option corresponds to the Microsoft DNS Servers option, and it is defined in the same way as the Router option. Be careful not to mistake the Microsoft Name Servers option for the DNS Servers option—the two are completely different. The Name Servers option refers to IEN116 name service, which is now obsolete. If you define IEN116 name servers and don't define domain name servers, your DHCP clients can't do DNS name resolution.

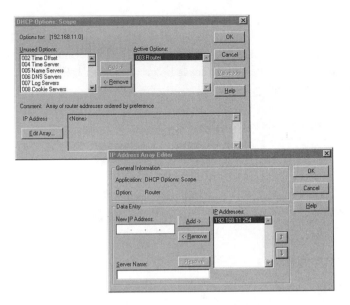

FIGURE A.3   *Entering a router's IP address in the* Array Editor *dialog box.*

A.3 Example 3.7

Example 3.7 configures all five subnets, which involves going through the scope configuration process, described in the preceding eight examples, once for each subnet. This appendix doesn't walk you through that entire process—you should just repeat the instructions given in the preceding examples once for each subnet to fully implement the configuration shown in Example 3.6.

A.4 Examples 3.8 and 3.9

The Microsoft DHCP server enables you to set a per-scope maximum lease time, but it does not enable you to set a different default lease time. If a client does not specify a lease time, it receives the maximum lease time.

The maximum lease time is set in the Create Scope or Scope Properties dialog box. The Create Scope dialog box in Figure A.2 shows a lease duration of three days. The Microsoft DHCP server requires you to set the maximum lease duration for a scope by specifying the number of days, hours, and minutes, rather than just adding it all up and specifying a number of seconds. The 86,400-second max-lease-time value in Example 3.9 represents a one-day lease.

To change the maximum lease duration after you create a scope, highlight in the DHCP Manager window the scope whose value you want to change in the DHCP Servers list, and then pull down the Scope menu and select Properties. Figure A.4 shows the Scope Properties window with the maximum lease duration set to one day.

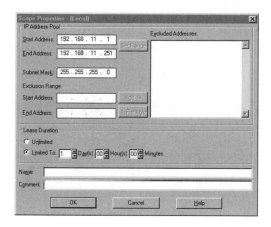

FIGURE A.4 *Setting the maximum lease duration in the* Scope Properties *window.*

Example 3.9 extends Example 3.7 to include lease duration information, as shown in Example 3.8.

A.5 Example 3.10

Example 3.10 is essentially the same as Example 3.5.

A.6 Example 3.11

Example 3.11 shows Example 3.9 with the addition of some *global options,* as well as global values for the default and maximum lease times. You cannot set a global value for the default and maximum lease times in the Microsoft DHCP server.

To define global options, in the DHCP Manager window pull down the DHCP Options menu and select Global Options. This opens the DHCP Options: Global dialog box. Select Domain Name from the Unused Options list and click the Add-> button. Then highlight Domain Name in the Active Options list and click Value>>>. A dialog box is displayed, enabling you to enter a value for the option, as shown in Figure A.5.

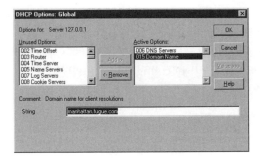

FIGURE A.5 *Entering a domain name in the* DHCP Options: Global *dialog box.*

As mentioned in Section A.2, the domain-name-servers option corresponds to the Microsoft DNS Servers option. To set a global value for this option, use the DHCP Options: Global dialog box described previously. This option takes an array of IP addresses, so you must use the Edit Array dialog box to enter the actual option value, as in the Router option shown in Section A.2.

A.7 Examples 10.1 and 10.2

The Microsoft DHCP server doesn't support multiple address allocation pools or access control on pools. So, no Microsoft equivalent exists for these examples.

A.8 Example 11.1

Chapter 13 provides examples in both Microsoft and ISC forms. Therefore, an example is not provided in the Microsoft form here.

A.9 Examples 12.1 through 12.6

These examples show output of the ISC DHCP server; no equivalent exists for the Microsoft server.

A.10 Example 12.7

The Microsoft DHCP server does not provide equivalents for the default-lease-time, min-lease-time, allow-bootp, and authoritative parameters. The text in this appendix for Example 3.9 explains how to set a maximum lease time.

A.11 Example 12.8

Example 3.11 shows how to accomplish this.

A.12 Example 12.9

It appears that no equivalent to this example exists in the Microsoft DHCP server. A dialog box does exist into which you can enter the BOOTP filename, but you most likely cannot use this to actually configure a client. (You may be able to do so in Windows NT 4.0 SP5 or Windows 2000.) To open the aforementioned dialog box, highlight the server name in the DHCP Servers list of the DHCP Manager window, pull down the Servers menu, and select Properties. Then click the BOOTP Table tab.

FIGURE A.6   *The* BOOTP Table *dialog box.*

A.13 Examples 12.10 and 12.11

Chapter 13, Section 13.3.6, describes how to define new options in the Microsoft DHCP server.

A.14 Example 12.12

No known equivalent exists for the Microsoft DHCP server.

A.15 Example 12.13

Section A.1 provides an example of how to define a subnet for the Microsoft DHCP server.

A.16 Example 12.14

Although the ISC server has a general notion of scopes, the Microsoft DHCP server does not. Instead, it defines three specific scopes—the global scope, the subnet scope, and the reservation scope. Of course, Microsoft does not refer to these as scopes—Microsoft uses the term *scope* to refer to an IP subnet. The explanation in Section A.2 shows how to define an option in the subnet scope. Section A.6 shows how to define an option in the global scope.

To define an option that's specific to a reservation, select the scope in which the reservation appears from the DHCP Servers list in the DHCP Manager window, and then pull down the Scope menu and select Active Leases. This opens the Active Leases window. Select the reservation you want to modify from the Client list, and then click Properties. This opens the Client Properties dialog box. Click the Options button to open the DHCP Options: Reservation dialog box. Then enter any options as you do in the DHCP Options: Scope or DHCP Options: Global dialog boxes. Sections A.2 and A.6 describe how to do this. Figure A.7 shows all three of the dialog box windows described here.

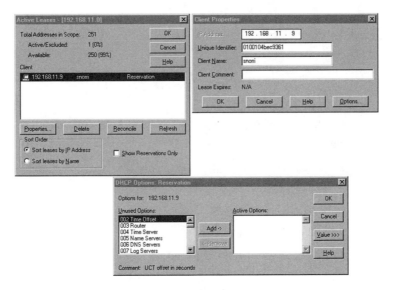

FIGURE A.7   *The dialog boxes that are navigated when setting reservation-specific options.*

A.17 Examples 12.15 and 12.16

These examples show UNIX-specific Bourne Shell scripts used to start the ISC DHCP server, so no equivalent exists for the Microsoft server.

A.18 Examples 13.1 and 13.2

See Section A.1 for the Microsoft DHCP equivalents.

A.19 Examples 13.3, 13.4, 13.5, and 13.6

See Sections A.2 and A.3 for the Microsoft DHCP equivalents.

A.20 Example 13.7

The Microsoft DHCP relay agent is configured using the `Microsoft TCP/IP Properties` dialog box. To get to this dialog box, click the `Network Neighborhood` icon on your desktop using the right mouse button, and select `Properties` from the menu. This opens the `Network` dialog box, as shown in Figure A.8. Click the `Protocols` tab, highlight `TCP/IP Protocol` in the `Network Protocols:` list, and click `Properties`.

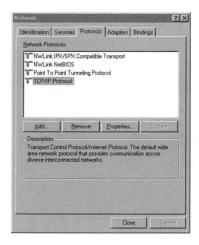

FIGURE A.8   *The Windows NT* Network *dialog box.*

After you open the `TCP/IP Properties` dialog box, click the `DHCP Relay` tab to configure the relay agent. To configure a list of DHCP servers, click the `Add` button. This opens the `DHCP Relay Agent` dialog box, at which point you can add a DHCP server by typing in its IP address and clicking the `Add` button. Figure A.9 shows these two dialog boxes.

You can also configure the Microsoft DHCP relay agent not to relay DHCP packets until a certain number of seconds have passed since the client started trying to acquire an IP address. To do this, set the number of seconds in the `TCP/IP Properties` dialog box as shown in Figure A.9. You can also limit the number of hops a DHCP packet can make before the relay agent discards it. Every time a client request is relayed through a relay agent, the hop count is incremented by one. When this number reaches the number you choose in the `TCP/IP Properties` dialog box, the relay agent does not relay the packet. In practice, it is rarely useful to relay DHCP packets more than once, so you should set this number to 1.

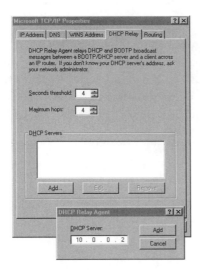

FIGURE A.9 *The* TCP/IP Properties *and* DHCP Relay Agent *dialog boxes.*

A.21 Example 13.8

This example is Cisco-specific. No Microsoft equivalent exists.

A.22 Example 13.9

See Section A.6, as it refers to setting up global options. The ntp-servers option is equivalent to the Microsoft DHCP server's NTP Servers option.

A.23 Examples 13.10 and 13.11

See Section A.2 for an explanation.

A.24 Example 13.12

This example is specific to a Cisco router, so no Microsoft equivalent exists.

A.25 Example 13.13

See Section A.6 for an explanation.

A.26 Example 13.14

Section 13.3.2 of Chapter 13, discusses *superscopes* and explains how to implement the equivalent of what is shown in Example 13.14.

A.27 Example 13.15

The Microsoft DHCP server does not provide a way to define options that apply to a superscope.

A.28 Example 13.16

No known equivalent method exists for doing this with the Microsoft DHCP server.

A.29 Example 13.17

See Section A.2 for an explanation.

A.30 Example 13.18

No known equivalent exists for the Microsoft DHCP server.

A.31 Example 14.1 and 14.2

DHCP client identifiers are entered in the `Add Reserved Clients` or `Client Properties` dialog, in the `Unique Identifier` box. You must enter client identifiers in hexadecimal, so it's not easy to enter an ASCII identifier, as in Example 14.2. Figure A.10 shows a new reservation added with the same client identifier shown in Example 14.1. Note the difference in the way identifiers are entered—the ISC DHCP server expects the numbers to be entered as a sequence of byte values separated by colons, whereas the Microsoft server expects a sequence of two-digit hexadecimal values with no separator.

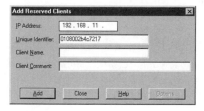

FIGURE A.10 *Entering a unique identifier in the* `Add Reserved Clients` *dialog box.*

A.32 Example 14.3

You cannot enter a client's link-layer address as a separate entity from the client identifier in the Microsoft DHCP server. If you enter a client identifier by specifying the link type as the first byte and the link-layer address in subsequent bytes, the Microsoft server may recognize this and use it to identify clients that do not send a `dhcp-client-identifier` option (for example, BOOTP clients). (However, we were unable to verify this at the time of this writing.) Figure A.10 shows an example of this, using the same link-layer address and network hardware type as are specified in Example 14.3.

A.33 Example 14.4

No known equivalent exists for doing this using the Microsoft DHCP client.

A.34 Example 14.5

As mentioned previously, you cannot enter a text client identifier. Figure A.11 shows a reservation being added for host `ardmore-win95`.

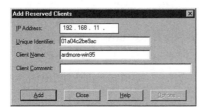

FIGURE A.11 *A reservation being entered for host* `ardmore-win95`.

Note

Examples 14.1 through 14.5 assume that it's possible to talk about client identification separately from static IP address assignment, but this is not possible with the Microsoft DHCP server. This is why the Add Reserved Client *dialog box shown in Figures A.10 and A.11 has a space to enter an IP address.*

A.35 Example 14.6

This example provides a complete static configuration, including global options, a subnet declaration with subnet options, and four static IP address assignments. See Section A.2 for information on how to define global options.

The explanation in Section A.1 shows how to create a new scope, which is equivalent to a subnet declaration. The Microsoft DHCP server requires that reservations are allocated from the set of addresses that are available within the scope. If you do not want to do any dynamic allocation, you must exclude all addresses in the scope for which no reservations are made. To define a subnet as shown in Example 14.6, then, you must access the Create Scope dialog box as shown in Section A.1. Enter into the scope all the IP addresses in the subnet that you can allocate, and then exclude all the IP addresses for which you don't already have static allocations by entering exclusion ranges. Figure A.12 shows the subnet in Example 14.6 being added, with all the addresses except for those that are reserved for the four hosts in the example.

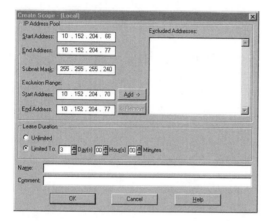

FIGURE A.12 *Adding a scope with no dynamically allocatable addresses.*

To add the reservations for the four hosts, select the new scope from the DHCP Servers list in the DHCP Manager window, pull down the Scope menu, and select Add Reservations. Figure A.13 shows the host DW1 being added using the Add Reserved Clients dialog box. This dialog box enables you to enter more than one client—after you click Add, the dialog box is cleared so that you can enter a new static IP address assignment.

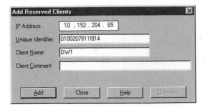

FIGURE A.13   *Adding a reservation for the DW1 client.*

A.36 Example 14.7

Example 14.7 is equivalent to Example 14.6, but without the address range exclusion.

A.37 Examples 14.8 and 14.9

To find a client's lease information in the Microsoft DHCP server's lease database, you must know in which scope the DHCP client got its IP address. The easiest thing to do is to examine the client's configuration information to find out what IP address it was assigned. Select the scope containing that IP address from the DHCP Servers list in the DHCP Manager window, pull down the Scope menu, and select Active Leases. This opens the Active Leases dialog box, as shown in Figure A.14.

FIGURE A.14   *Finding a DHCP client's lease in the* Active Leases *dialog box.*

Highlight the client's IP address in the Clients list, and then click Properties. This opens the Client Properties dialog box. The box labeled Unique Identifier contains the client's identifier. Figure A.15 shows the Client Properties dialog box, with the client identifier one of the author's DHCP clients is using (it was too difficult to exactly reproduce the lease shown in Example 14.8).

FIGURE A.15 *Finding a client identifier in the* Client Properties *dialog box.*

The client identifier is the hexadecimal string that appears in the Unique Identifier box. After you have this identifier, you can use it to create a reservation, as shown in Example 14.9. Figure A.16 shows how to create a reservation using the information in Figure A.15.

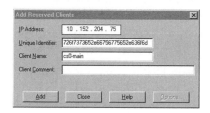

FIGURE A.16 *Creating a reservation using the client identifier from a lease.*

A.38 Examples 14.10, 14.11, and 14.12

No known equivalent exists for the Microsoft DHCP server.

A.39 Examples 15.1 and 15.2

You can duplicate these examples by configuring two Microsoft DHCP servers on two separate NT servers. On each server, create a scope containing one of the address ranges shown in the examples. Refer to Section A.1 to see how to create a scope.

A.40 Examples 17.1 through 17.10

No known equivalent exists for the Microsoft DHCP server.

A.41 Examples 17.11 through 17.14

No known equivalent exists for the Microsoft DHCP server. However, Windows 2000 uses the vendor-specific information option, so you may be able to do this using the Windows 2000 DHCP server. If more information on this exists, it will be posted on the http://www.dhcp-handbook.com Web site.

A.42 Examples 18.1 through 18.6

No known equivalent exists for the Microsoft DHCP server. Example 18.3 also includes configuration information for the BIND DNS server. An equivalent way to do this with the Microsoft DNS server probably exists, but it is beyond the scope of this book to cover that.

A.43 Example 20.1

No known equivalent exists for the Microsoft DHCP server.

A.44 Example 20.2

You can enable the Microsoft DHCP client on some interfaces and not enable it on others. See Chapter 17, "Conditional Behavior," for more information. (However, we know of no way to configure the Microsoft DHCP server not to provide service on some interfaces.)

A.45 Example 20.3

See the section in Chapter 17 on the Microsoft DHCP client for more information.

A.46 Example 20.4

No known equivalent exists for the Microsoft DHCP server.

A.47 Examples 20.5 and 20.6

No known equivalent exists for the Microsoft DHCP client.

A.48 Examples 24.1 through 24.7

Except for Examples 24.3 and 24.7, these examples are covered in Section A.37. No known equivalent exists for Examples 24.3 and 24.7 for the Microsoft DHCP server.

A.49 Examples in Appendixes

These system-specific examples are not applicable to Windows NT.

ISC DHCP Server Configuration File Reference

This appendix provides a complete reference for the ISC DHCP server's configuration file. Every possible statement or syntax that can appear in the **dhcpd.conf** file is described here. This appendix begins with a description of the organization of the file and, then, documents all types of declarations and statements. It ends with a complete list of predefined DHCP options and their formats.

Material adapted from material found at `ftp://ftp.isc.org/isc/dhcp/3doc/dhcp-eval.5` and `ftp://ftp.isc.org/isc/dhcp/3doc/dhcpd.conf.5`. Copyright © 1996 – 1999 Internet Software Consortium.

B.1 How to Use this Appendix

This appendix is organized into groups of statements and declarations of similar types. It is not organized alphabetically. To look something up alphabetically, refer to the index. Furthermore, this appendix does not attempt to explain *how* to use the syntax it describes. For this information, refer to the relevant chapters in this book, particularly Chapter 12, "The ISC DHCP Server," Chapter 13, "Configuring a DHCP Server," Chapter 14, "Client Identification and Fixed Address Allocation," Chapter 15, "Setting Up a Reliable DHCP Service," and Chapter 17 "Conditional Behavior."

Each subsection of this appendix that describes a specific element of syntax from the configuration file also provides a syntax diagram for that element. In a syntax diagram, text appearing in **boldface** is actual syntax that you enter into the file, exactly as it is shown. Text appearing in *italics* is intended to represent some information that you must provide. Such information is explained in the text following the syntax diagram.

Some text in the syntax diagram is specified using neither **boldface** nor *italics*. In such cases, you have a choice as to what syntax to write. If a portion of a syntax diagram is enclosed in square brackets, you can either include or omit that portion, as shown in Example B.1.

EXAMPLE B.1

`range [ `**`dynamic-bootp`**` ] `*`low-address`*` [ `*`high-address`*` ];`

In this example, the **dynamic-bootp** keyword is optional, and you can enter or omit it depending on the desired meaning, which is described in the subsequent text. Likewise, you can omit *high-address*. *low-address* and *high-address* are not meant to be typed in literally, but represent some general syntax described in the text that follows.

When a selection of possible keywords can be entered in a particular part of the syntax diagram, these keywords are enclosed in square brackets and separated by vertical bars, as shown in Example B.2. The text following the syntax diagram explains whether you must enter one of these keywords.

EXAMPLE B.2

`[ `**`allow`**` | `**`deny`**` ] `**`known clients;`**

In this example, you must enter either the **allow** or **deny** keyword, but not both.

Finally, in some cases you can specify one or more values in a particular portion of the syntax. This is shown using square brackets and ellipses, as in Example B.3.

EXAMPLE B.3

`**option** *name* **code** *code* = { *type-1* [ … , *type-n* ] };`

In this example, you can enter one or more types within the braces, separated by commas.

B.2 File Organization

The **dhcpd.conf** file is a sequence of statements and declarations. *Declarations* are evaluated once when the server reads the file, and they tend to persist as structures in the DHCP server's in-memory database. *Statements* are generally evaluated each time a request is received for a client. The scope in which a statement appears determines whether it is evaluated for a given client.

Many declarations have *scopes* within which other declarations and statements can be written. Most scopes are simply collections of statements and declarations enclosed in braces. One exception is the *global scope*, which is the text of the **dhcpd.conf** file that appears outside all pairs of braces. Chapter 12 describes how the DHCP server evaluates scopes.

Statements come in two major categories:

- conditional statements

- statements that define options or parameters

The server handles options and parameters in much the same way. The only difference is that parameters control what the server does, and options tell the server what to send to the DHCP client. Chapter 17 describes how conditional statements can be used.

Declarations can't appear within conditional statements because conditional statements are evaluated every time a packet is received, and declarations are evaluated when the configuration is read and persist thereafter.

B.3 The *shared-network* Declaration

```
shared-network name {
    [ statements ]
    [ declarations ]
}
```

You use the *shared-network* declaration to inform the DHCP server that the subnets declared within it are connected to the same network segment. Parameters specified in the scope of the *shared-network* declaration are considered to be more specific than (and thus override) parameters specified in the global scope.

Name should be the name of the network segment that the ***shared-network*** decla-ration represents. The server uses this name when printing debugging mes-sages, so it should be a name that meaningfully describes the network segment. The name may have the syntax of a valid domain name (although it is never used as such), or it may be any arbitrary name that you choose.

B.4 The *subnet* Declaration

```
subnet subnet-number netmask netmask {
   [ statements ]
   [ declarations ]
}
```

You use the ***subnet*** declaration to provide the DHCP server with enough infor-mation to determine whether a particular IP address is on the subnet. A ***subnet*** declaration should exist for every subnet from which the DHCP server might receive a DHCP request. If the DHCP server allocates an IP address for a client from a particular subnet, statements in that subnet's scope are executed, and are considered more specific than statements in the global scope or in the shared-network scope.

The *subnet-number* should be an IP address or domain name that resolves to the subnet number of the subnet being described. The *netmask* should be an IP address or domain name that resolves to the subnet mask of the subnet being described. You can use the subnet number, together with the subnet mask, to determine whether a particular IP address is on the specified subnet.

If no subnet-mask option is specified in scope for a client receiving an IP address on a particular subnet, the subnet mask from the host declaration is supplied to the client in the subnet-mask option. If a subnet-mask option state-ment in any scope applies to the client, however, it takes precedence over the subnet mask in the ***subnet*** declaration.

B.5 The *range* Declaration

```
range [ dynamic-bootp ] low-address [ high-address ] ;
```

For any subnet on which addresses are assigned dynamically, there must be at least one ***range*** declaration. The ***range*** declaration specifies that the server may allocate to DHCP clients every address, from *low-address* to *high-address*. You can specify a single IP address by omitting *high-address*.

All IP addresses in the range should be on the same subnet. If the *range* decla-ration appears within a *subnet* declaration, all addresses should be on the declared subnet. If the *range* declaration appears within a *shared-network* declaration, all addresses should be on subnets already declared within the *shared-network* declaration.

You may specify the *dynamic-bootp* flag if addresses in the specified range can be dynamically assigned to both BOOTP and DHCP clients.

> **Note**
>
> The **dynamic-bootp** flag was deprecated in version 3.0 of the DHCP server in favor of declaring the address within a pool and specifying in the permit list that dynamic allocation for BOOTP clients is permitted.

B.6 The *host* Declaration

```
host name {
    [ statements ]
    [ declarations ]
}
```

The *host* declaration provides information about a particular DHCP client. *Name* should be a name for the *host* declaration, but a specific meaning is not required. If the *use-host-decl-names* flag is enabled, *name* is sent in the *host-name* option if no *host-name* option is specified.

Host declarations match DHCP or BOOTP clients based on either the clients' link-layer IP address or the dhcp-client-identifier option that the client sends. Chapter 14 discusses how this works in detail. BOOTP clients do not normally send a dhcp-client-identifier option. So, you must use the link-layer IP address for all clients that might send BOOTP protocol requests.

The *host* declaration has three purposes:

- to assign a static IP address to a client

- to declare a client as "known"

- to specify a scope in which statements can be executed for a specific client

You can make the DHCP server treat some DHCP clients differently from others if *host* declarations exist for those clients. Any request coming from a client that matches a *host* declaration is considered to be from a "known" client. Requests that do not match any *host* declaration are considered to be from "unknown" clients. You can use this knowledge to control how addresses are allocated, as described in Chapters 14 and 17.

It is possible to write more than one *host* declaration for a client. This can be useful if the client has a different scope on different subnets—for each IP address that requires a different scope, one *host* declaration should exist. A client can be in the scope of only one *host* declaration at a time. *host* declarations with static address assignments are in scope for a client only if one of the address assignments is valid for the network segment to which the client is connected. The host scope is the most specific scope.

B.6.1 The *hardware* Declaration
```
hardware type address;
```

A *host* declaration that is matched to a DHCP or BOOTP client using the client's link-layer address should include a *hardware* declaration. `type` should be the type of network hardware—currently, `ethernet`, `token-ring`, or `fddi`. `Address` should be the link-layer address—a list of octets specified as hexadecimal numbers, separated by colons.

B.6.2 The *dhcp-client-identifier option* Statement
```
option dhcp-client-identifier identifier;
```

Within a *host* declaration, you can use a `dhcp-client-identifier` option statement to match a *host* declaration to a DHCP client. If it is being used to identify the client, the `dhcp-client-identifier` option must not be specified within any kind of conditional statement. It also must not have a value that is dependent on what the DHCP client sent because it is executed when the configuration file is parsed, not when a packet is received. If the DHCP client sends a `dhcp-client-identifier` option with the value specified in `identifier`, the *host* declaration will match.

B.6.3 The *fixed-address* Declaration
```
fixed-address address-1 [ , …, address-n ];
```

To make a static IP address assignment for a client, the client must match a *host* declaration, as described earlier. In addition, the *host* declaration must contain a *fixed-address* declaration. A *fixed-address* declaration specifies one or more IP addresses or domain names that resolve to IP addresses. If a client matches a *host* declaration, and one of the IP addresses specified in the *host* declaration is valid for the network segment to which the client is connected, the client is assigned that IP address.

A static IP address assignment overrides a dynamically assigned IP address that is valid on that network segment. That is, if a new static mapping for a client is added after the client has a dynamic mapping, the client cannot use the dynamic mapping the next time it tries to renew its lease. The DHCP server will not assign an IP address that is not correct for the network segment to which the client is attached and will not override a valid dynamic mapping for one network segment based on a static mapping that is valid on a different network segment.

You can specify a domain name instead of an IP address in a *fixed-address* declaration. However, you should do this only for long-lived domain name records—the DHCP server only looks up the record on startup. So, if the record changes while the server is running, the server continues to use the record's former value.

B.7 The *pool* Declaration

```
pool {
    [ permit list ]
    [ range declarations ]
    [ statements ]
}
```

You can use the *pool* declaration to declare an address pool from which IP addresses can be allocated, with its own permit list to control client access and its own scope in which you can declare pool-specific parameters. *Pool* declarations can appear within subnet declarations or shared-network declarations. The addresses in a particular pool are declared with range declarations. Specified addresses must be correct for the *subnet* declaration within which the *pool* declaration is made. If it is made within a *shared-network* declaration, the addresses must be on subnets that were previously declared within the same *shared-network* declaration.

B.7.1 Pool Permit Lists

You can control address allocation in pools using the pool permit list. *Permit statements* begin with either the *allow* or *deny* keyword, followed by a statement of what is permitted or not permitted. If a pool has a list of things that are permitted, any client that doesn't match one of the permits cannot be allocated an address from the pool. If a pool has a list of things that are not permitted, any client that doesn't match one of those permits can be allocated an address from the pool.

The *known clients* Permit

```
[ permit ¦ deny ] known clients;
```

This permit either allows or prevents allocation from a pool to any client that
has a host declaration (that is, is known).

The *unknown clients* Permit

```
[ permit ¦ deny ] unknown clients;
```

This permit either allows or prevents allocation from a pool to any client that
has no host declaration (that is, is not known).

The *members of* Permit

```
[ allow ¦ deny ] members of "class";
```

This permit either allows or prevents allocation from the pool to any client that
is a member of the named class.

The *dynamic bootp clients* Permit

```
[ allow ¦ deny  ] dynamic bootp client;
```

This permit either allows or prevents allocation from the pool to any BOOTP
client.

The *all clients* Permit

```
[ allow ¦ deny ] all clients;
```

This permit either allows or prevents allocation from the pool to all clients.
This can be useful when you want to write a pool declaration, but you do not
yet want addresses to be allocated from it. You can also use it to force all clients
that were allocated addresses from a pool to obtain new addresses immediately
the next time they renew.

B.8 The *class* Declaration

```
class "class-name" {
    [ statements ]
    [ declarations ]
}
```

You use *class* declarations to group clients together based on information they
send. A client can become a member of a class through an add statement, based
on the class's matching rules, or because the client matches a subclass of that
class.

Class-name should be the name of the class and is used in add statements and
members of permit statements, as well as in *subclass* declarations for subclasses
of the named class.

When a packet is received from a client, every *class* declaration is examined for a *match, match if,* or *spawn* statement, and that statement is checked to see if the client is a member of the class.

class scopes are considered to be more specific than *pool* or *subnet* declaration scopes, but they are less specific than *host* declaration scopes.

B.8.1 The *match if* Statement
`match if boolean-expression;`

A client is considered a member of a class if, when the server receives a packet from the client, `boolean-expression` evaluates to be true. `Boolean-expression` may depend on the contents of the packet the client sends.

B.8.2 The *match* Statement
`match data-expression;`

If `data-expression`, when evaluated using the contents of a client's request, returns a value that matches a subclass of the class in which the *match* statement appears, the client is considered a member of both the subclass and the class.

B.8.3 The *spawn with* Statement
`spawn with data-expression;`

If `data-expression` evaluates to a non-null value, the server looks for a subclass of the class that matches the result of the evaluation. If such a subclass exists, the client is considered a member of both the subclass and the class. If no such subclass exists, one is created and recorded in the lease database, and the client is considered a member of the new subclass as well as the class. The matching data for the subclass is the result of evaluating `data-expression`.

B.8.4 The *lease limit* Statement
`lease limit limit;`

The *lease limit* statement causes the DHCP server to limit the number of members of a class that can hold a lease at any one time to `limit`. This limit applies to all addresses the DHCP server allocates, not just addresses on a particular network segment. If a client is a member of more than one class with lease limits, the server will assign the client an address based on either class. If a client is a member of one or more classes with limits and one or more classes without limits, the classes without limits are not considered.

B.9 The *subclass* Declaration

```
subclass "class-name" class-data;
subclass "class-name" class-data {
    [ statements ]
}
```

The *subclass* declaration declares a subclass of the class named by *class-name*. *Class-data* should be either a text string enclosed in quotes, or a list of bytes expressed in hexadecimal, separated by colons. Clients match subclasses based on the results of evaluating the *match* or *spawn with* statements in the *class* declaration for *class-name*—if the result of the evaluation matches *class-data*, the client is a member of the subclass and the class. Subclasses can have scopes, in which case their scope is considered to be more specific than the scope of *class-name*; if a subclass has no scope, it inherits the scope of *class-name*.

B.10 The *group* Declaration

```
group {
    [ parameters ]
    [ declarations ]
}
```

You can use the *group* declaration to provide a common scope for whatever is declared within it. For example, if several host declarations require the same set of parameters, you can group them within a *group* declaration, and you can specify the statements defining those parameters once in the group scope instead of once in each host statement's scope.

B.11 The *option space* Declaration

```
option space space-name;
```

The *option space* declaration declares a new option space. This declaration must precede all definitions for options in the space being declared. *Space-name* should be the name of the option space. Currently three option space names are predefined:

- the **dhcp** option space

- the **agent** option space

- the **server** option space

The **dhcp** option space is the default option space—if an option name is specified without an option space, it is assumed that the name refers to an option in the **dhcp** option space. For example, the option names dhcp.routers and routers are equivalent.

B.12 Conditional Statements

The ISC DHCP server provides the ability to conditionally evaluate statements based on the values the client sends. Chapter 17 describes how this can be used.

B.12.1 The *if* Statement

```
if boolean-expression {
    [ statements ]
}
```

The most basic conditional statement is the *if* statement. If, `boolean-expression` evaluates to be true, the statements enclosed in braces following `boolean-expression` are executed. If `boolean-expression` evaluates to be false, those statements are skipped.

B.12.2 The *else* Clause

```
if boolean-expression {
    [ statements ]
} else {
    [ statements ]
}
```

An *if* statement can have an **else** clause. If `boolean-expression` turns out to be false, the statements following it are skipped, but the statements within braces following the *else* clause are executed.

B.12.3 The *elsif* Clause

```
if boolean-expression-1 {
    [ statements-1 ]
} elsif boolean-expression-2 {
    [ statements-2 ]
} else {
    [ statements-3 ]
}
```

It is possible to chain a series of conditionals, so that only one group of statements out of a set is executed. In the preceding example, if `boolean-expression-1` evaluates to true, the collection of statements labeled `statements-1` is executed and `statements-2` and `statements-3` are skipped, regardless of what the result of evaluating `boolean-expression-2` might have been. `Boolean-expression-2` is evaluated only if `boolean-expression-1` evaluates to false. If it evaluates to true, the collection of statements labeled `statements-2` is executed. Otherwise, the statements labeled `statements-3` are executed. An *elsif* clause doesn't have to be followed by an *else* clause, but if there is an *else* clause, it must be the last clause in the chain. It is possible to chain together an arbitrary number of *elsif* clauses.

B.13 Expressions

The DHCP server can evaluate expressions while executing statements. The DHCP server's expression evaluator currently supports expressions returning the following types:

- A *boolean* is simply a true or false, on or off value.

- An *integer* is a 32-bit quantity that may be treated as signed or unsigned, depending on the context.

- A *string of data* is simply a collection of zero or more bytes. Any byte value is valid in a data string—the DHCP server maintains a length rather than depending on a NUL termination.

Expression evaluation is performed when a request is received from a DHCP client. Values in the packet the client sends can be extracted and used to determine what to send back to the client. If you can refer to a value in the client packet for which there is no value, the result is the null value. Null values are treated specially in expression evaluation, as described later. A Boolean expression that returns a null value is considered false. A data expression that returns a null value generally results in the statement using the value not having any effect.

B.13.1 Boolean Operators

This section defines all the operators the ISC DHCP server currently supports that return boolean values.

The *check* Operator
`check "class-name"`

The *check* operator evaluates to true if the packet being considered comes from a client that falls into the specified class. `class-name` must be a string that corresponds to the name of a defined class.

The = Operator
`data-expression-1 = data-expression-2`

The = operator compares the result of evaluating `data-expression-1` and `data-expression-2`. If they are the same, the result is true; otherwise, it is false. If either `data-expression-1` or `data-expression-2` evaluates to null, the result is also null.

The *and* Operator
`boolean-expression-1` **and** `boolean-expression-2`

The *and* operator evaluates to true if `boolean-expression-1` and `boolean-expression-2` both evaluate to true. If either expression evaluates to null, the result is null. If either expression evaluates to false, the result is false.

The *or* Operator
`boolean-expression-1` **or** `boolean-expression-2`

The *or* operator evaluates to true if either `boolean-expression-1` or `boolean-expression-2` evaluates to true. If either expression evaluates to null, the result is null. If both expressions evaluate to false, the result is false.

The *not* Operator
not `boolean-expression`

The *not* operator evaluates to true if `boolean-expression` evaluates to false, and it evaluates to false if `boolean-expression` evaluates to true. If `boolean-expression` evaluates to null, the result is also null.

The *exists* Operator
exists `option-name`

The *exists* operator returns true if the specified option exists in the DHCP packet being examined. Otherwise, it evaluates to false.

The *known* Operator
known

The *known* operator evaluates to true if the client whose request is currently being processed is known—that is, if there is a host declaration for it. Otherwise, it evaluates to false.

B.13.2 Data Operators

This section describes those operators the ISC DHCP server currently supports that return strings of data.

The *substring* Operator
substring (`data-expr`, `offset`, `length`)

The *substring* operator evaluates the data expression and returns the substring of the result of that evaluation that starts `offset` bytes from the beginning, continuing for `length` bytes. `offset` and `length` are both numeric expressions. If `data-expr`, `offset`, or `length` evaluates to null, the result is also null. If `offset` is greater than or equal to the length of the evaluated data, a zero-length data string is returned. If `length` is greater than the remaining length of the evaluated data after `offset`, a data string containing all data from `offset` to the end of the data is returned.

The *suffix* Operator
`suffix (data-expr, length)`

The *suffix* operator evaluates *data-expr* and returns the last *length* bytes of the result of that evaluation. *length* is a numeric expression. If *data-expr* or *length* evaluates to null, the result is also null. If *length* evaluates to a number greater than the length of the data, all the data is returned.

The *option* Operator
`option option-name`

The *option* operator returns the contents of the specified option in the packet being considered. If no such option appears in the packet, or if the expression is evaluated in a situation where no packet exists, the result of the evaluation is the null value.

The *hardware* Operator
`hardware`

The *hardware* operator returns a data string whose first element is the **htype** field of the packet being considered, and whose subsequent elements are first **hlen** bytes of the **chaddr** field of the packet, as described in Appendix C, "The DHCP Message Format." If no packet exists, or if the **hlen** field in the packet is invalid, the result is null.

The *packet* Operator
`packet (offset, length)`

The *packet* operator returns the specified portion of the packet being examined, or null in contexts where no packet exists. *offset* and *length* are applied to the contents of the packet, as in the *substring* operator. The beginning of the packet is actually the first byte of payload in the UDP packet, so it is not possible to examine the link-layer, IP, or UDP headers.

The *text* Operator
`"text"`

A text string, enclosed in quotes, may be specified as a data expression. It evaluates to an ASCII-encoded data string containing the text between the quotes.

The *string* Operator
`byte-1 [ … : byte-n ]`

A list of hexadecimal byte values, separated by colons, may be specified as a data expression. A single hexadecimal number, appearing in a context where a data string is expected, is interpreted as a data string containing a single byte.

The *concat* Operator
concat (*data-expr1, data-expr2*)

The two expressions are evaluated, and the result of concatenating the results of the two evaluations is returned. If either data expression evaluates to null, the result is null.

The *encode-int* Operator
encode-int (*numeric-expr, width*)

numeric-expr is evaluated and encoded as a data string of the specified *width*, in network byte order (with the most significant byte first). If *numeric-expr* evaluates to null, the result is also the null value.

B.13.3 Numeric Operators

Numeric operators are expressions that evaluate to an integer. In general, the precision of numeric expressions is at least 32 bits, but the precision of numeric expressions may be more than 32 bits on some architectures.

The *extract-int* Operator
extract-int (*data-expr, width*)

The ***extract-int*** operator extracts an integer value in network byte order from the result of evaluating *data-expr*. *width* is the width in bits of the integer to extract. Currently, the only supported widths are 8, 16, and 32. If the evaluation of data-expr doesn't provide sufficient bits to extract an integer of the specified size, the null value is returned.

The *number* Operator
number

Any number that can be represented within the maximum precision of numeric expressions—at least 32 bits—may be specified as a numeric expression.

B.14 Parameter Statements

Parameter statements control how the DHCP server behaves—how long leases should be, whether to respond to a client's request, and so on. These statements can appear in any scope, as well as within conditional statements within a scope, and they affect the response to any client for which that scope is valid.

B.14.1 *allow* and *deny* Statements

The *allow* and *deny* statements are one kind of parameter that you can use to control the server's behavior. *allow* and *deny* statements should not be confused with *allow* and *deny* pool permits—although both begin with *allow* or *deny*, they actually have distinct meanings and different syntax. Although permits are evaluated during address allocation, *allow* and *deny* statements are evaluated after the address is allocated, so they cannot affect the address allocation process.

The *unknown-clients* Flag

```
[ allow ¦ deny ] unknown-clients;
```

The *unknown-clients* flag tells the server whether an unknown client may receive a dynamically assigned address. Dynamic address assignment to unknown clients is allowed by default.

The *bootp* Flag

```
[ allow ¦ deny ] bootp;
```

The *bootp* flag tells the server whether to respond to BOOTP requests. Responses to BOOTP requests are allowed by default. In pools that permit dynamic BOOTP address assignment, BOOTP clients must have static IP address assignments.

The *booting* Flag

```
[ allow ¦ deny ] booting;
```

The *booting* flag tells the server whether to respond to queries from a particular client. By default, booting is allowed, but if it is disabled for a particular client, the server will never respond to that client.

B.14.2 The *default-lease-time* Statement

```
default-lease-time time;
```

Time should be the length in seconds that is assigned to a lease if the client requesting the lease does not ask for a specific expiration time.

B.14.3 The *max-lease-time* Statement

```
max-lease-time time;
```

Time should be the maximum length in seconds that is assigned to a lease. Dynamic BOOTP lease lengths are not limited by this parameter.

B.14.4 The *min-lease-time* Statement

```
min-lease-time time;
```

Time should be the minimum length in seconds that is assigned to a lease.

B.14.5 The *min-secs* Statement

`min-secs` *seconds*;

Seconds should be the minimum number of seconds since a client began trying to acquire a new lease before the DHCP server responds to its request.

The number of seconds is based on what the client reports. The maximum value that the client can report is 255 seconds. Generally, if you set this to 1, the DHCP server does not respond to the client's first request, but it always responds to its second request.

You can use this parameter to set up a secondary DHCP server which doesn't offer an address to a client until the primary server is given a chance to do so. If the primary server is down, the client binds to the secondary server; otherwise, clients should always bind to the primary server. Note that this does not, by itself, permit a primary server and a secondary server to share a pool of dynamically allocatable addresses.

B.14.6 The *dynamic-bootp-lease-cutoff* Statement

`dynamic-bootp-lease-cutoff` *date*;

The *dynamic-bootp-lease-cutoff* statement sets the ending time for all leases assigned dynamically to BOOTP clients. Because BOOTP clients do not have a way of renewing leases and do not know their leases could expire, the DHCP server normally assigns unlimited leases to all BOOTP clients. However, it may make sense in some situations to set a cutoff date for all BOOTP leases—for example, the end of a school term, or the time at night when a facility is closed and all machines are required to be powered off.

Date should be the date on which all assigned BOOTP leases end. The date is specified in the form:

`W YYYY/MM/DD HH:MM:SS`

W is the day of the week expressed as a number from 0 (Sunday) to 6 (Saturday). YYYY is the year, including the century. MM is the month expressed as a number from 1 to 12. DD is the day of the month, counting from 1. HH is the hour, from 0 to 23. MM is the minute and SS is the second. The time is always in Greenwich Mean Time (GMT), not local time.

B.14.7 The *dynamic-bootp-lease-length* Statement
`dynamic-bootp-lease-length` *length*;

You use the *dynamic-bootp-lease-length* statement to set the length of leases dynamically assigned to BOOTP clients. At some sites, it may be possible to assume that a lease is no longer in use if its holder has not used BOOTP or DHCP to get its address within a certain time period. The period is specified in length as a number of seconds. If a client restarts using BOOTP during the timeout period, the lease duration is reset to *length*, so a BOOTP client that boots frequently enough never loses its lease.

Needless to say, you should adjust this parameter with extreme caution.

B.14.8 The *get-lease-hostnames* Statement
`get-lease-hostnames` *flag*;

When the *get-lease-hostnames* parameter is enabled in scope and no valid `host-name` option in scope exists, the DHCP server does a reverse lookup on the IP address assigned to the client and supplies the result to the client in the `host-name` option. This parameter is disabled by default.

B.14.9 The *use-host-decl-names* Statement
`use-host-decl-names` *flag*;

When the *get-lease-hostnames* parameter is enabled in scope, scope has no valid `host-name` option, and the client has a valid `host` declaration, the DHCP server sends the name from the `host` declaration in the `host-name` option. This is disabled by default.

B.14.10 The *authoritative* Statement
`[ not ] authoritative`;

When the DHCP server receives a DHCPREQUEST message from a DHCP client requesting a specific IP address, the DHCP protocol requires that the server determine whether the IP address is valid for the network to which the client is attached. If the address is not valid, the DHCP server should respond with a DHCPNAK message, forcing the client to acquire a new IP address.

To make this determination for IP addresses on a particular network segment, the DHCP server must have complete configuration information for that network segment. Unfortunately, experience shows that it is not safe to assume that DHCP servers are configured with complete information. Therefore, the DHCP server normally assumes that it does not have complete information, and thus is not sufficiently authoritative to safely send DHCPNAK messages as required by the protocol.

This default assumption should not be true for any network segment that is in the same administrative domain as the DHCP server. For such network segments, the *authoritative* statement should be specified, so that the server sends DHCPNAK messages as required by the protocol. If the DHCP server receives requests only from network segments in the same administrative domain, you can specify the *authoritative* statement at the top of the configuration file (in the global scope).

Note

Version 2.0 and earlier of the DHCP server makes the opposite assumption: that the DHCP server is configured with all configuration information for all network segments of which it is aware. If this assumption is not valid for your configuration, you must write not authoritative statements for all network segments where this assumption is not true (or at the top of the configuration file). Version 1.0 does not support the authoritative statement.

B.14.11 The *always-reply-rfc1048* Statement
always-reply-rfc1048 *flag*;

Some BOOTP clients expect RFC1048-style responses but do not follow RFC1048 when sending their requests. You can tell a client has this problem if it does not get the options you have configured for it, and if you see in the server log the message (non-rfc1048) printed with each BOOTREQUEST that is logged.

If you want to send rfc1048 options to such a client, you can set the *always-reply-rfc1048* parameter in that client's host declaration to true, and the DHCP server responds with an RFC-1048-style vendor options field. You can set this flag in any scope, and it affects all clients covered by that scope.

B.14.12 The *use-lease-addr-for-default-route* Statement
use-lease-addr-for-default-route *flag*;

If the *use-lease-addr-for-default-route* parameter is true in a particular scope, instead of sending the value specified in the routers option (or sending no value at all), the IP address of the lease being assigned is sent to the client. This supports a Windows 95 feature: If a Windows 95 computer sees its own IP address as its default route, it sends ARP requests for all IP addresses, regardless of whether they are local to the network segment. You can use this if your router is configured for proxy ARP. This is known to work only with Windows 95 and later versions, and it may cause serious problems for other DHCP clients.

B.14.13 The *server-identifier* Statement

```
server-identifier hostname;
```

You can use the ***server-identifier*** statement to define the value that is sent in the dhcp-server-identifier option for a given scope. The value specified must be an IP address for the DHCP server, and it must be reachable by all clients served by a particular scope.

Use of the ***server-identifier*** statement is not recommended. You should use it only to force a value to be sent when it is incorrect to send the default value. The default value is the first IP address associated with the physical network interface on which the request arrives.

Usually, the ***server-identifier*** statement is needed when a physical interface has more than one IP address, and the one being sent by default isn't appropriate for some or all clients served by that interface.

Another common case in which ***server-identifier*** is needed is when you define an IP alias for the purpose of having a consistent IP address for the DHCP server, and you want the clients to use this IP address when contacting the server. If the DHCP server crashes, you can start a hot spare with the same IP alias but with a different primary address, and the spare server will receive DHCPREQUESTs from clients in the RENEWING state.

Supplying a value for the dhcp-server-identifier option is equivalent to using the ***server-identifier*** statement.

B.14.14 The *add* Statement

```
add "class-name";
```

Executing the ***add*** statement causes the client to be added to the class whose name is specified in *class-name*. The ***add*** statement is executed after IP address allocation is completed. Therefore, class membership caused by an ***add*** statement cannot be used in the address allocation process.

B.14.15 The *vendor-option-space* Statement

```
vendor-option-space option-space;
```

The ***vendor-option-space*** statement instructs the server to construct a vendor-encapsulated-options option using all the defined options in the option space. If no vendor-encapsulated-options option is defined, the server sends this option to the client, if appropriate.

B.14.16 The *site-option-space* Statement

`site-option-space` *option-space*;

The **site-option-space** statement determines the option space from which site-local options are taken. Site-local options have codes ranging from 128 to 254. If no **site-option-space** is specified, site-specific options are taken from the default option space.

B.15 Statements Defining Values to Send to Clients

Four statements define specific values to send to DHCP clients:

- the `filename` statement
- the `server-name` statement
- the `next-server` statement
- the `option` statement

The first three define the values to send in the `filename`, `server-name`, and `siaddr` fields of the BOOTP or DHCP packet. The `option` statement is used to define the options sent back to the client in the `option` portion of the DHCP packet.

B.15.1 The *filename* Statement

`filename` "*filename* ";

You can use the **filename** statement to specify the name of the initial bootfile to be loaded by a client. *filename* should be a name of a file that is recognizable to whatever file transfer protocol the client is expected to use to load the file. Some clients may prefer to receive this information in the `bootfile-name` option.

B.15.2 The *server-name* Statement

`server-name` "*name*";

You can use the **server-name** statement to inform the client of the name of the server from which it should load its bootfile. *name* should be the name that is provided to the client.

B.15.3 The *next-server* Statement

`next-server` *server-name*;

You use the **next-server** statement to specify the host address of the server from which the initial bootfile (specified in the `filename` statement) is to be loaded. `server-name` should be a numeric IP address or a domain name. If no `next-server` parameter applies to a given client, the DHCP server's IP address is used.

B.15.4 The *option* Statement

```
option option-name option-values;
option option-name = data-expression;
```

The **option** statement defines the value that is sent to a client for a particular option, if the server finds it is appropriate to send a value for that option. *Option-name* is the name of the option whose value is specified—either an option space name, followed by a '.', followed by the name of that option, or the name of an option in the default option space.

The **option** statement can be in one of two forms. In the first, recommended form, the value or values for an option are specified in the format specified by the option's declaration. The second form allows the entire contents of the option to be specified as the result of a data expression. The second form is not recommended because the configuration file parser can't verify the values are correct, but it is useful for returning an option to the client whose value is derived from what the client sent.

Option-values should include values conforming to the declaration of the option. If the option declaration specifies a record value—that is, a series of types enclosed in braces—those values should be separated by spaces. If the option declaration specifies an array of values, each element in the array should be separated by commas. An option whose values are an array of records should be specified with the individual values in the record separated by spaces, and the records themselves separated by commas. Example B-4 shows option statements that illustrate each of these three possibilities:

EXAMPLE B-4

```
option policy-filter 10.0.0.0 10.0.255.255;
option routers 10.0.0.1, 10.0.0.2;
option static-routes 10.0.0.0 10.0.0.1, 10.0.1.0 10.0.0.2;
```

B.16 The *option* Definition

```
option option-name code code = definition;
```

Option-name should be the name of the option being declared. If the option is in the default option space, option-name should be the name of the option space it is in, followed by a '.', followed by the actual name of the option. *Code* should be the option code—for current DHCP options, a number between 0 and 255.

Definition should be the definition of the structure of the option—what data type or types it is made up of, and whether it is an array. The ISC DHCP server currently supports a few simple types, such as integers, Booleans, strings, and IP addresses, and it supports the ability to define arrays of single types or arrays of fixed sequences of types (records).

The following simple option type definitions are supported.

B.16.1 The *boolean* Type

```
option name code code = boolean;
```

An option of type *boolean* is a flag with a value of either on or off (true or false). Here is an example use of the boolean type:

```
option use-zephyr code 180 = boolean;
option use-zephyr on;
```

B.16.2 The *integer* Type

```
option name code code = [ signed | unsigned ] integer width;
```

Integers can be either signed or unsigned. If neither is specified, signed is assumed. The width can be 8, 16, or 32, and refers to the number of bits in the integer. The following two lines show a definition of the sql-connection-max option and its use:

```
option sql-connection-max code 192 = unsigned integer 16;
option sql-connection-max 1536;
```

B.16.3 The *ip-address* Type

```
option name code code = ip-address;
```

You can express an option whose structure is an IP address either as a domain name or as a dotted quad. The following is an example use of the ip-address type:

```
option sql-server-address code 193 = ip-address;
option sql-server-address sql.example.com;
```

B.16.4 The *text* Type

```
option name code code = text;
```

An option whose type is *text* encodes an ASCII text string. For example:

```
option sql-default-connection-name code 194 = text;
option sql-default-connection-name "PRODZA";
```

B.16.5 The *string* Type

```
option name code code = string;
```

An option whose type is a data string is essentially just a collection of bytes, and can be specified either as quoted text, such as the text type, or as a list of hexadecimal byte values separated by colons. For example:

```
option sql-identification-token code 195 = string;
option sql-identification-token 17:23:19:a6:42:ea:99:7c:22;
```

B.16.6 Arrays

```
option name code code = array of type;
```

Options can contain arrays of any of the above types, except for the text and data string types, which aren't currently supported in arrays. An example of an array definition is as follows:

```
option kerberos-servers code 200 = array of ip-address;
option kerberos-servers 10.20.10.1, 10.20.11.1;
```

B.16.7 Records

```
option name code code = { type-1 [ , ... type-n ] };
```

Options can also contain data structures consisting of a sequence of data types, which is called a *record type*. For example:

```
option contrived-001 code 201 = { boolean, integer 32, text };
option contrived-001 on 1772 "contrivance";
```

It's also possible to have options that are arrays of records. For example:

```
option new-static-routes code 201 = array of {
    ip-address, ip-address, ip-address, integer 8 };
option static-routes
    10.0.0.0 255.255.255.0 net-0-rtr.example.com 1,
    10.0.1.0 255.255.255.0 net-1-rtr.example.com 1,
    10.2.0.0 255.255.224.0 net-2-0-rtr.example.com 3;
```

B.17 The Standard DHCP Options

Option definitions for all the standard DHCP options are shown below:

```
option subnet-mask code 1 = ip-address;
option time-offset code 2 = signed integer 32;
option routers code 3 = array of ip-address;
option time-servers code 4 = array of ip-address;
option ien116-name-servers code 5 = array of ip-address;
option domain-name-servers code 6 = array of ip-address;
option log-servers code 7 = array of ip-address;
option cookie-servers code 8 = array of ip-address;
option lpr-servers code 9 = array of ip-address;
option impress-servers code 10 = array of ip-address;
```

```
option resource-location-servers code 11 = array of ip-address;
option host-name code 12 = string;
option boot-size code 13 = unsigned integer 16;
option merit-dump code 14 = text;
option domain-name code 15 = text;
option swap-server code 16 = ip-address;
option root-path code 17 = text;
option extensions-path code 18 = text;
option ip-forwarding code 19 = boolean;
option non-local-source-routing code 20 = boolean;
option policy-filter code 21 = array of { ip-address, ip-address };
option max-dgram-reassembly code 22 = unsigned integer 16;
option default-ip-ttl code 23 = unsigned integer 8;
option path-mtu-aging-timeout code 24 = unsigned integer 32;
option path-mtu-plateau-table code 25 = array of unsigned integer 16;
option interface-mtu code 26 = unsigned integer 16;
option all-subnets-local code 27 = boolean;
option broadcast-address code 28 = ip-address;
option perform-mask-discovery code 29 = boolean;
option mask-supplier code 30 = boolean;
option router-discovery code 31 = boolean;
option router-solicitation-address code 32 = ip-address;
option static-routes code 33 = array of { ip-address, ip-address };
option trailer-encapsulation code 34 = boolean;
option arp-cache-timeout code 35 = unsigned integer 32;
option ieee802-3-encapsulation code 36 = boolean;
option default-tcp-ttl code 37 = unsigned integer 8;
option tcp-keepalive-interval code 38 = unsigned integer 32;
option tcp-keepalive-garbage code 39 = boolean;
option nis-domain code 40 = text;
option nis-servers code 41 = array of ip-address;
option ntp-servers code 42 = array of ip-address;
option vendor-encapsulated-options code 43 = string;
option netbios-name-servers code 44 = array of ip-address;
option netbios-dd-server code 45 = array of ip-address;
option netbios-node-type code 46 = unsigned integer 8;
option netbios-scope code 47 = text;
option font-servers code 48 = array of ip-address;
option x-display-manager code 49 = array of ip-address;
option dhcp-requested-address code 50 = ip-address;
option dhcp-lease-time code 51 = unsigned integer 32;
option dhcp-option-overload code 52 = unsigned integer 8;
option dhcp-message-type code 53 = unsigned integer 8;
option dhcp-server-identifier code 54 = ip-address;
option dhcp-parameter-request-list code 55 = array of unsigned integer 8;
option dhcp-message code 56 = text;
option dhcp-max-message-size code 57 = unsigned integer 16;
option dhcp-renewal-time code 58 = unsigned integer 32;
option dhcp-rebinding-time code 59 = unsigned integer 32;
option vendor-class-identifier code 60 = string;
option dhcp-client-identifier code 61 = string;
option nisplus-domain code 64 = text;
```

```
option nisplus-servers code 65 = array of ip-address;
option tftp-server-name code 66 = text;
option bootfile-name code 67 = text;
option mobile-ip-home-agent code 68 = array of ip-address;
option smtp-server code 69 = array of ip-address;
option pop-server code 70 = array of ip-address;
option nntp-server code 71 = array of ip-address;
option www-server code 72 = array of ip-address;
option finger-server code 73 = array of ip-address;
option irc-server code 74 = array of ip-address;
option streettalk-server code 75 = array of ip-address;
option streettalk-directory-assistance-server code 76 = array of ip-address;
option nds-servers code 85 = array of ip-address;
option nds-tree-name code 86 = string;
option nds-context code 87 = string;
option agent.circuit-id code 1 = string;
option agent.remote-id code 2 = string;
```

APPENDIX C

The DHCP Message Format

Every DHCP message includes a fixed-format section and a variable-format section. The fixed-format section is divided into several fields that carry the client's hardware and IP addresses, the server's IP address, and other control information. The variable-format section holds options that carry additional control information about the message and configuration parameters.

C.1 Fixed-Format Section

Figure C.1 illustrates the format of the fixed-format section of a DHCP message, and Table C.1 explains the use of each of the fields identified in the figure.

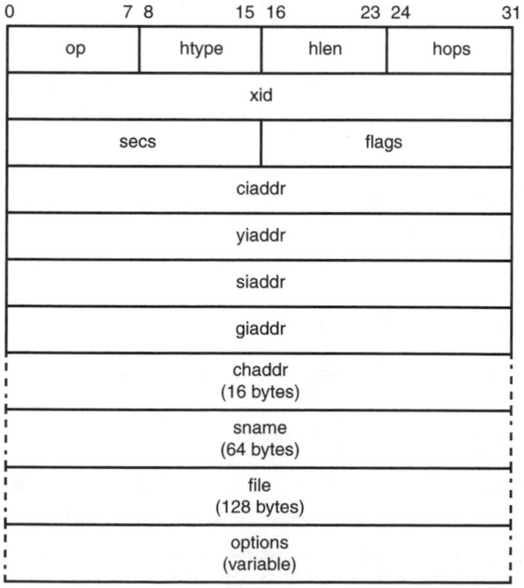

FIGURE C.1 *Fields in the* fixed-format *section of a DHCP message.*

TABLE C.1 SUMMARY OF DHCP Fixed-Format SECTION FIELDS

Field	Description
op	Message operation code; set to 1 in messages sent by a client, and set to 2 in messages sent by a server. The two possible values for op are carried forward from BOOTP for backward compatibility and are sometimes called BOOTREQUEST and BOOTREPLY, respectively.
htype	Hardware address type; definitions are taken from the IANA list of ARP hardware types. For example, Ethernet type is specified by htype to be set to 1.
hlen	Hardware address length (in bytes); defines length of the hardware address in the chaddr field.
hops	Number of relay agents that forwarded this message.
xid	Transaction identifier; used by clients to match responses from servers with previously transmitted requests.
secs	Elapsed time (in seconds) since the client began the DHCP process.
flags	flags field; the leftmost bit, called the broadcast bit, may be set to 1 to indicate that messages to the client must be broadcast (see Section 7.1 for details).
ciaddr	Client's IP address; set by the client when the client confirms its IP address is valid.
yiaddr	Client's IP address; set by the server to inform the client of client's IP address, that is, "your" IP address.
siaddr	IP address of the next server for the client to use in the configuration process; for example, the server to contact for TFTP download of an operating system kernel.
giaddr	Relay agent ("gateway") IP address; filled in by the relay agent with address of interface through which the DHCP message was received.
chaddr	Client's hardware address.
sname	DNS name of the next server for the client to use in the configuration process.
file	Name of file for the client to request from the next server; for example, the name of the file containing the operating system for this client.

C.2 Variable-Format Section

Figure C.2 shows the format each option carries in the variable-format section. Appendix D, "DHCP Options Summary," includes a summary of all the options that can be included in the variable-format section.

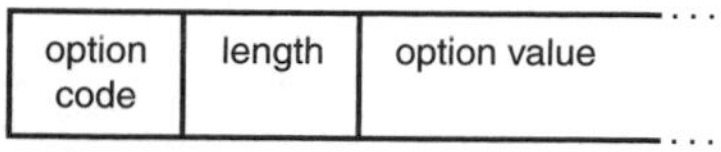

option code	length	option value

FIGURE C.2 *Format of options carried in the* variable-format *section.*

TABLE C.2 FIELDS IN AN OPTION

Field	Length	Description
option code	1 byte	Identifies the specific option; see Appendix D for a list of DHCP options.
length	1 byte	Number of bytes the in option value.
option value	length bytes	Data value for this option.

APPENDIX D

DHCP Options Summary

This appendix includes two tables of DHCP options. Table D.1 lists the options in alphabetical order, while Table D.2 lists the options in numerical order.

Table D.1 includes the names the ISC and Microsoft DHCP servers use to identify DHCP options, along with a short description of each option. The Microsoft DHCP server does not give names to all options; the entries for those options are blank. Unless otherwise indicated, all the DHCP options are defined in RFC2132.

TABLE D.1 DHCP OPTIONS, LISTED ALPHABETICALLY

Option name	Option code	ISC server name	Microsoft server name	Description
All subnets local	27	all-subnets-local	All subnets are local	0 specifies client should assume some IP subnets have smaller MTUs; 1 specifies all subnets have same MTU as subnet to which client is connected
ARP cache timeout	35	arp-cache-timeout	ARP Cache Timeout	Timeout (in seconds) for ARP cache entries

continues

TABLE D.1 CONTINUED

Option name	Option code	ISC server name	Microsoft server name	Description
Autoconfig-uration	116	option-116		0 specifies client should not per-form IP address autoconfiguration; 1 specifies client should perform autoconfiguration[1]
Boot file size	13	boot-size	Boot File Size	Size of client boot-file in 512-byte blocks
Boot file name	67	bootfile-name	Boot File Name	Name of bootfile to use when `file` field is used to carry options
Broadcast address	28	broadcast-address	Broadcast Address	Broadcast address for subnet to which client is attached
Client identifier	61	dhcp-client-identifier		Client's unique identifier
Cookie server	8	cookie-servers	Cookie Servers	Cookie servers[2]
Default IP TTL	23		default-ip-ttl	Default Time-to-live Default TTL client should use for out-going datagrams
DHCP message type	53	dhcp-message-type		Identifies type of DHCP message; see section 9.1.2 for details
Domain Name Server	6	domain-name-servers	DNS Servers	List of DNS servers
Domain name	15	domain-name	Domain Name	Default name for DNS name resolu-tion
End	255	option-end		Indicates end of options in field
Ethernet encapsulation	36	ieee802-3-encapsulation	Ethernet Encapsulation	0 specifies Ethernet Version 2[3] encapsu-lation; 1 specifies IEEE 802.3[4]

Option name	Option code	ISC server name	Microsoft server name	Description
Extensions path	18	extensions-path	Extensions Path	Name of file containing additional options to be interpreted according to RFC2132 format
Finger server	73	finger-server		List of finger servers
Host name	12	host-name	Host Name	Client host name
Impress server	10	impress-servers	Impress Servers	Imagen Impress printer servers
Interface MTU	26	interface-mtu	MTU Option	Value of MTU client should use for this interface
IP address lease time	51	dhcp-lease-time		Lease duration (in seconds) for assigned IP address
IP forwarding	19	ip-forwarding	IP Layer Forwarding	0 specifies datagram forwarding between interfaces is to be disabled; 1 specifies forwarding is to be enabled
IRC server	74	irc-server		List of *Internet* (IRC) servers *Relay Chat*
Log server	7	log-servers	Log Servers	MIT-LCS log servers
LPR server	9	lpr-servers	LPR Servers	LPDP (UNIX lpr)[5] servers
Mask supplier	30	mask-supplier	Mask Supplier Option	0 specifies client should not respond to ICMP subnet mask request messages; 1 specifies client should respond
Maximum datagram reassembly size	22	max-dgram-reassembly	Max DG Reassembly Size	Maximum size of packet client should expect to reassemble

continues

TABLE D.1 CONTINUED

Option name	Option code	ISC server name	Microsoft server name	Description
Maximum DHCP message size	57	dhcp-max-message-size		Maximum DHCP message size accepted by client
Merit dump file	14	merit-dump	Merit Dump File	Name of file for memory dump
Message	56	dhcp-message		Message from server to be dis-played to user by client
Mobile IP home-agent	68	mobile-ip-home-agents	Mobile IP Home Agents	List of mobile IP home agent
Name server	5	ien116-name-servers	Name Servers	IEN 116 name servers
NDS context	87	nds-context		Initial *Netware Directory Service* (NDS) for client[6]
NDS server servers	85	nds-servers		List of *Netware Directory Service* (NDS) servers[7]
NDS tree name	86	nds-tree-name		*Netware Directory Service* (NDS) tree name for client to use[8]
NetBIOS over TCP/IP datagram distribution	45	netbios-dd-server	NetBIOS over TCP/IP NBDD Servers	List of *NetBIOS Datagram Distribution (NBDD)* servers[9] server
NetBIOS over TCP/IP name server	44	netbios-name-servers	WINS/NBNS Servers	List of *NetBIOS Name Server* (NBNS) servers[10]
NetBIOS over TCP/IP node type	46	netbios-node-type	WINS/NBT Node Type	Client's NetBIOS over TCP/IP node type[11]; see section 9.4.11 for details
NetBIOS over TCP/IP	47	netbios-scope	NetBIOS Scope ID	Client's NetBIOS over TCP/IP scope[12]
NetWare/IP domain name	62	option-62		Name of *NetWare/IP* domain for client[13]

Option name	Option code	ISC server name	Microsoft server name	Description
NetWare/IP information	63	option-63		Additional *NetWare/IP* parameters; see section 9.4.14 for details[14]
NIS domain	40	nis-domain	NIS Domain Name	Client's *Network Information Service* (NIS) domain
NIS servers	41	nis-servers	NIS Servers	List of *Network Information Service* (NIS) servers
NIS+ domain	64	nisplus-domain	NIS+ Domain Name	Client's *Network Information Service+* (NIS+) domain
NIS+ servers	65	nisplus-servers	NIS+ Servers	List of *Network Information Service+* (NIS+) servers
NNTP server	71	nntp-server		List of *Network News Transport Protocol* (NNTP) servers
Non-local source routing enable/ disable	20	non-local-source routing	Non-local Source Routing	0 specifies forwarding of datagrams with non-local source routes is to be disallowed; 1 specifies forwarding of such datagrams is to be allowed
NTP servers	42	ntp-servers	NTP Servers	List of *Network Time Protocol* (NTP)[15] servers
Option overload	52	dhcp-option-overload		Specifies whether `file` and `sname` fields are used to carry options
Pad	0	pad		Carries no data; can be used to force option alignment

continues

TABLE D.1 CONTINUED

Option name	Option code	ISC server name	Microsoft server name	Description
Parameter request list	55	dhcp-parameter-request-list		List of options requested by client
Path MTU aging	24	path-mtu-aging-timeout	Path MTU Aging TO	Timeout (in seconds) for aging PMTU values[16]
Path MTU plateau table	25	path-mtu-plateau-table	Path MTU Plateau Table	List of MTU sizes for PMTU discovery[17]
Perform mask discovery	29	perform-mask-discovery	Perform Mask Discovery	0 specifies client should not perform ICMP subnet mask discovery; 1 specifies client should perform subnet mask discovery
Perform router discovery	31	router-discovery	Perform Router Discovery	0 specifies client should not perform router discovery[18]; 1 specifies client should perform router discovery
Policy filter	21	policy-filter	Policy Filter Masks	List of policy filters for non-local source routing
POP3 server	70	pop-server		List of *Post Office Protocol 3* (POP3) servers
Requested IP address	50	dhcp-requested-address		IP address requested by client
Resource location server	11	resource-location-servers	Resource Location Servers	Resource location protocol[19] servers
Root path	17	root-path	Root Path	Name of client's root disk
Router solicitation address	32	router-solicitation-address	Router Solicitation Address	Address client should use for router discovery[20]

Option name	Option code	ISC server name	Microsoft server name	Description
Routers	3	routers	Router	Routers available on client's network segment
Server identifier	54	dhcp-server-identifier		IP address of DHCP server
SMTP server	69	smtp-server		List of *Simple Mail Transport Protocol* (SMTP) servers
Static route	33	static-routes	Static Route Option	List of static routes; each static route includes a destination address and a router (next hop) address for that destination address
StreetTalk directory assistance server	76	streettalk-directory-assistance-server		List of *StreetTalk Directory Assistance* (STDA) servers
StreetTalk server	75	streettalk-server		List of *StreetTalk* servers
Subnet mask	1	subnet-mask		Subnet mask for network segment to which client is connected
Swap server	16	swap-server	Swap Server	Swap server for client
T1	58	dhcp-renewal-time		Time in seconds until client should renew lease on assigned address
T2	59	dhcp-rebinding-time		Time in seconds until client should rebind lease on assigned address
TCP default TTL	37	default-tcp-ttl	Default TTL Option	Default TTL for TCP segments

continues

TABLE D.1 CONTINUED

Option name	Option code	ISC server name	Microsoft server name	Description
TCP keep alive garbage	39	tcp-keepalive-garbage	Keepalive Garbage	0 specifies client should not send garbage byte with TCP "keep alive" messages; 1 specifies client should send garbage byte
TCP keepalive interval	38	tcp-keepalive-interval	Keepalive Interval	Time (in seconds) to wait before sending keepalive message on TCP connection
TFTP server name	66	tftp-server-name	Boot Server Host Name	Name of TFTP server to use when sname field is used to carry options
Time offset	2	time-offset	Time Offset	Time offset in seconds from Coordinated Universal Time (UTC) for client's network segment
Time server	4	time-servers	Time Server	Time servers[21]
Trailer encapsulation	34	trailer-encapsulation	Trailer encapsulation	0 specifies client should not negotiate use of trailers through ARP[22]; 1 specifies client should negotiate trailers
UAP servers	98	option-98		List of URLs specifying *User Authentication Protocol* servers (defined in RFC 2485)
Vendor class identifier	60	vendor-class-identifier		Identifies vendor and client configuration

Option name	Option code	ISC server name	Microsoft server name	Description
Vendor specific information	43	vendor-encapsulated-options	Vendor Specific Info	Vendor specific information; see 9.1.10 for description of contents
WWW server	72	www-server		List of World Wide Web (WWW) servers
X Window System display manager	49	x-display-managers	X Window System Display Mgr. Servers	List of X Window System display managers[23]
X Window System font server	48	font-servers	X Window System Font Servers	List of X Window System font servers[24]

[1] RFC2563
[2] RFC865
[3] RFC894
[4] RFC1042
[5] RFC1179
[6] RFC2241
[7] RFC2241
[8] RFC2241
[9] RFC 1001, RFC1002
[10] RFC 1001, RFC1002
[11] RFC 1001, RFC1002
[12] RFC 1001, RFC1002
[13] RFC2242
[14] RFC2242
[15] RFC1305
[16] RFC1191
[17] RFC1191
[18] RFC1256
[19] RFC887
[20] RFC1256
[21] RFC868
[22] RFC893
[23] RFC1198
[24] RFC1198

Table D.2 lists the options in numerical order.

TABLE D.2 DHCP OPTIONS, LISTED IN NUMERICAL ORDER BY OPTION CODE

Option code	Option name	ISC server name	Microsoft server name
0	Pad	pad	
1	Subnet mask	subnet-mask	
2	Time offset	time-offset	Time Offset
3	Routers	routers	Router
4	Time server	time-servers	Time Server
5	Name server	ien116-name-servers	Name Servers
6	DNS server	domain-name-servers	DNS Servers
7	Log server	log-servers	Log Servers
8	Cookie server	cookie-servers	Cookie Servers
9	LPR server	lpr-servers	LPR Servers
10	Impress server	impress-servers	Impress Servers
11	Resource location server	resource-location-server	Resource Location Servers
12	Host name	host-name	Host Name
13	Boot file size	boot-size	Boot File Size
14	Merit dump file	merit-dump	Merit Dump File
15	Domain name	domain-name	Domain Name
16	Swap server	swap-server	Swap Server
17	Root path	root-path	Root Path
18	Extensions path	extensions-path	Extensions Path
19	IP forwarding enable/disable	ip-forwarding	IP Layer Forwarding
20	Non-local source routing enable/disable	non-local-source-routing	Non-local Source Routing
21	Policy filter	policy-filter	Policy Filter Masks
22	Maximum datagram reassembly size	max-dgram-reassembly	Max DG Reassembly Size
23	Default IP TTL	default-ip-ttl	Default Time-to-live
24	Path MTU aging timeout	path-mtu-aging-timeout	Path MTU Aging TO
25	Path MTU plateau table	path-mtu-plateau-table	Path MTU Plateau Table
26	Interface MTU	interface-mtu	MTU Option
27	All subnets local	all-subnets-local	All subnets are local

Option code	Option name	ISC server name	Microsoft server name
28	Broadcast address	broadcast-address	Broadcast Address
29	Perform mask discovery	perform-mask-discovery	Perform Mask Discovery
30	Mask supplier	mask-supplier	Mask Supplier Option
31	Perform router discovery	router-discovery	Perform Router Discovery
32	Router solicitation	router-solicitation-	Router Solicitation Address
33	Static route	static-routes	Static route option
34	Trailer encapsulation	trailer-encapsulation	Trailer encapsulation
35	ARP cache timeout	arp-cache-timeout	ARP Cache Timeout
36	Ethernet encapsulation	ieee802-3-encapsulation	Ethernet Encapsulation
37	TCP default TTL	default-tcp-ttl	Default TTL Option
38	TCP keepalive interval	tcp-keepalive-interval	Keepalive Interval
39	TCP keepalive garbage	tcp-keepalive-garbage	Keepalive Garbage
40	NIS domain	nis-domain	NIS Domain Name
41	NIS servers	nis-servers	NIS Servers
42	NTP servers	ntp-servers	NTP Servers
43	Vendor specific information	vendor-encapsulated-options	Vendor Specific Info
44	NetBIOS over TCP/IP name server	netbios-name-servers	WINS/NBNS Servers
45	NetBIOS over TCP/IP datagram distribution server	netbios-dd-server	NetBIOS over TCP/IP NBDD Servers
46	NetBIOS over TCP/IP node type	netbios-node-type	WINS/NBT Node Type
47	NetBIOS over TCP/IP scope	netbios-scope	NetBIOS Scope ID
48	X Window System font server	font-servers	X Window System Font Servers
49	X Window System display manager	x-display-managers	X Window System Display Mgr. Servers

continues

TABLE D.2 CONTINUED

Option code	Option name	ISC server name	Microsoft server name
50	Requested IP address	dhcp-requested-address	
51	IP address lease time	dhcp-lease-time	
52	Option overload	dhcp-option-overload	
53	DHCP message type	dhcp-message-type	
54	Server identifier	dhcp-server-identifier	
55	Parameter request list	dhcp-parameter-request-list	
56	Message	dhcp-message	
57	Maximum DHCP message size	dhcp-max-message-size	
58	T1	dhcp-renewal-time	
59	T2	dhcp-rebinding-time	
60	Vendor class identifier	vendor-class-identifier	
61	Client identifier	dhcp-client-identifier	
62	Netware/IP domain name	option-62	
63	Netware/IP information	option-63	
64	NIS+ domain	nisplus-domain	NIS+ Domain Name
65	NIS+ servers	nisplus-servers	NIS+ Servers
66	TFTP server name	tftp-server-name	Boot Server Host Name
67	Bootfile name	bootfile-name	Bootfile Name
68	Mobile IP home agent	mobile-ip-home-agent	Mobile IP Home Agents
69	SMTP server	smtp-server	
70	POP3 server	pop-server	
71	NNTP server	nntp-server	
72	WWW server	www-server	
73	Finger server	finger-server	
74	IRC server	irc-server	
75	StreetTalk server	streettalk-server	
76	StreetTalk directory assistance server	streettalk-directory-assistance-server	

Option code	Option name	ISC server name	Microsoft server name
85	NDS server	nds-servers	
86	NDS tree name	nds-tree-name	
87	NDS context	nds-context	
98	UAP servers	option-98	
116	Autoconfiguration	option-116	
255	End	option-end	

APPENDIX E

Other DHCP Resources

The following is a list of available resources that you will find useful in keeping up with developments in the areas of host configuration and IP address management. You can also use these resources as a source of references. The first of these resources is a Web site designed to accompany this text:

`http://www.dhcp-handbook.com`

DHCP users and implementors can also find helpful information at:

`http://www.dhcp.org`

On the DHCP site you'll find an archive of minutes and other documents from the IETF DHC Working Group, as well as links to DHCP RFCs, Internet Drafts, and other DHCP resources.

Topic	List address	To join
DHC Working Group	`dhcp-v4@bucknell.edu`	Send mail to `listserv@bucknell.edu` with: `subscribe dhcp-v4 Your Name` in the body of the message
ISC software	(various)	Go to `http://www.fugue.com/dhcp/lists/`

continues

Topic	List address	To join
General discussion of DHCP and related products	`dhcp-interest@isc.org`	Go to `http://www.isc .org/view.ogi?/ services/mailing lists/dhcp.interest .phtml`

The Internet Software Consortium Web site is found at:

`http://www.isc.org`

The following Web site includes information about the ISC DHCP server:

`http://www.isc.org/dhcp.html`

The IETF Web site includes information about the IETF, a list of IETF Working Groups, a schedule of upcoming meetings, and proceedings from past meetings. You can find the IETF Web site at:

`http://www.ietf.org`

The IETF Web site also includes a page for the DHC Working Group:

`http://www.ietf.org/html.charters/dhc-charter.html`

The DHC Working Group page maintains links to all current RFCs and Internet Drafts relating to DHCP.

The RFC Editor's Web site is found at:

`http://www.rfc-editor.org`

This site stores copies of all the RFCs, including the DHCP RFCs:

RFC2131 Dynamic Host Configuration Protocol
`http://www.rfc-editor.org/rfc/rfc2131.txt`

RFC2132 DHCP Options and BOOTP Vendor Extensions
`http://www.rfc-editor.org/rfc/rfc2132.txt`

RFC2241 DHCP Options for Novell Directory Services (NDS)
`http://www.rfc-editor.org/rfc/rfc2241.txt`

RFC2242 NetWare/IP Domain Name and Information
`http://www.rfc-editor.org/rfc/rfc2242.txt`

RFC2485 DHCP Option for the Open Group's User Authentication Protocol
`http://www.rfc-editor.org/rfc/rfc2485.txt`

RFC2489 Procedure for Defining New DHCP Options
`http://www.rfc-editor.org/rfc/rfc2489.txt`

RFC2563 DHCP Option to Disable Stateless Auto-Configuration
`http://www.rfc-editor.org/rfc/rfc2563.txt`

Internet Drafts can be found at the IETF Web site:

`http://www.ietf.org/ID.html`

John Wobus at Syracuse University maintains a DHCP FAQ (Frequently Asked Questions) list:

`http://web.syr.edu/~jmwobus/comfaqs/dhcp.faq.html`

APPENDIX F

Bibliography

Albitz, Paul and Cricket Liu. 1998. *DNS and Bind*. Sebastopol, CA: O'Reilly and Associates.

Comer, Douglas. 1995. *Internetworking With TCP/IP: Principles, Protocols, and Architecture*. Upper Saddle River, New Jersey: Prentice Hall.

ISO9594; ISO 9594-1. International Organization for Standardization and International Electrotechnical Committee. 1998. "Information Processing Systems—Open Systems Interconnection: The Directory—Overview of Concepts, Models and Services." December.

RFC791. Postel, J. 1981. "Internet Protocol." September.

RFC792. Postel, J. 1981. "Internet Control Message Protocol." September.

RFC821. Postel, J. 1982. "Simple Mail Transfer Protocol." August.

RFC826. Plummer, D.C. 1982. "Ethernet Address Resolution Protocol: Or Converting Network Protocol Addresses to 48-bit Ethernet Addresses for Transmission on Ethernet Hardware." November.

RFC854. Postel, J. and J.K. Reynolds. 1983. "Telnet Protocol Specification." May.

RFC894. Hornig, C. 1984. "Standard for the Transmission of IP Datagrams over Ethernet Networks." April.

RFC903. Finlayson, R., T. Mann, J.C. Mogul, and M. Theimer. 1984. "Reverse Address Resolution Protocol." June.

RFC950. Mogul, J.C and J. Postel. 1985. "Internet Standard Subnetting Procedure." August.

RFC951. Croft, W.J. and J. Gilmore. 1985. "Bootstrap Protocol." September.

RFC977. Kantor, B. and P. Lapsley. 1986. "Network News Transfer Protocol." February.

RFC1001. NetBIOS Working Group in the Defense Advanced Research Projects Agency, Internet Activities Board, End-to-End Services Task Force. 1987. "Protocol Standard for a NetBIOS Service on a TCP/UDP Transport: Concepts and Methods." March.

RFC1002. NetBIOS Working Group in the Defense Advanced Research Projects Agency, Internet Activities Board, End-to-End Services Task Force. 1987. "Protocol Standard for a NetBIOS Service on a TCP/UDP Transport: Detailed Specifications." March.

RFC1042. Postel, J. and J.K. Reynolds. 1988. "Standard for the Transmission of IP Datagrams over IEEE 802 Networks." February.

RFC1048. Prindeville, P.A. 1988. "BOOTP Vendor Information Extensions." February.

RFC1122. Braden, R.T. 1989. "Requirements for Internet Hosts— Communication Layers." October.

RFC1123. Braden, R.T. 1989. "Requirements for Internet Hosts—Application and Support." October.

RFC1127. Braden, R.T. 1989. "Perspective on the Host Requirements RFCs." October.

RFC1191. Mogul, J.C. and S.E. Deering. 1990. "Path MTU Discovery." November.

RFC1256. Deering, S.E. 1991. "ICMP Router Discovery Messages." September.

RFC1288. Zimmerman, D. 1991. "The Finger User Information Protocol." December.

RFC1305. Mills, David L. 1992. "Network Time Protocol (Version 3) Specification, Implementation." March.

RFC1321. Rivest, R. 1992. "The MD5 Message-Digest Algorithm." April.

RFC1459. Oikarinen, J. and D. Reed. 1993. "Internet Relay Chat Protocol." May.

RFC1497. Reynolds, J. 1993. "BOOTP Vendor Information Extensions." August.

RFC1519. Fuller, V., T. Li, J. Yu, and K. Varadhan. 1993. "Classless Inter-Domain Routing (CIDR): An Address Assignment and Aggregation Strategy." September.

RFC1661. Simpson, W. ed. 1994. "The Point-to-Point Protocol (PPP)." July.

RFC1819. Delgrossi, L. and L. Berger eds. 1995. "Internet Stream Protocol Version 2 (ST2) Protocol Specification—Version ST2+." August.

RFC1878. Pummill, T. and B. Manning. 1995. "Variable Length Subnet Table for IPv4." December.

RFC1918. Rekhter, Y., B. Moskowitz, D. Karrenberg, G.J. de Groot, and E. Lear. 1996. "Address Allocation for Private Internets." February.

RFC1931. Brownell, D. 1996. "Dynamic RARP Extensions for Automatic Network Address Acquisition." April.

RFC1939. Myers, J. and M. Rose. 1996. "Post Office Protocol—Version 3." May.

RFC1945. Berners-Lee, T., R. Fielding, and H. Frystyk. 1996. "Hypertext Transfer Protocol—HTTP/1.0." May.

RFC2002. Perkins, C. 1996. "IP Mobility Support." October.

RFC2104. Krawczyk, H., M. Bellare, and R. Canetti. 1997. "HMAC: Keyed-Hashing for Message Authentication." February.

RFC2131. Droms, R. 1997. "Dynamic Host Configuration Protocol." March.

RFC2132. Alexander, S. and R. Droms. 1997. "DHCP Options and BOOTP Vendor Extensions." March.

RFC2136. Vixie, P. ed., S. Thomson, Y. Rekhter, and J. Bound. 1997. "Dynamic Updates in the Domain Name System (DNS UPDATE)." April.

RFC2165. Veizades, J., E. Guttman, C. Perkins, and S. Kaplan. 1997. "Service Location Protocol." June.

RFC2241. Provan, D. 1997. "DHCP Options for Novell Directory Services." November.

RFC2242. Droms, R. and K. Fong. 1997. "NetWare/IP Domain Name and Information." November.

RFC2253. Wahl, M., S. Kille, and T. Howes. 1997. "Lightweight Directory Access Protocol (v3): UTF-8 String Representation of Distinguished Names." December.

RFC2373. Hinden, R. and S.E. Deering. 1998. "IP Version 6 Addressing Architecture." July.

RFC2464. Crawford, M. 1998. "Transmission of IPv6 Packets over Ethernet Networks." December.

RFC2489. Droms, R. 1999. "Procedure for Defining New DHCP Options." January.

RFC2535. Eastlake, D. 1999. "Domain Name System Security Extensions." March.

RFC2563. Troll, R. 1999. "DHCP Option to Disable Stateless Auto-Configuration in IPv4 Clients." May.

Stevens, W. Richard. 1994. *TCP/IP Illustrated, Volume I: The Protocols*. Reading, MA: Addison-Wesley.

Appendix G

Lists of Related RFCs

The following list includes all RFCs that pertain to DHCP specification, including primary specification documents, options accepted as Internet Standards since the DHCP specification was published, and a description of the current process for submitting proposals for new DHCP options.

RFC	Name	URL
RFC2131	Dynamic Host Configuration Protocol	http://www.rfc-editor.org/rfc/rfc2131.txt (obsoletes RFC1541)
RFC2132	DHCP Options and BOOTP Vendor Extensions	http://www.rfc-editor.org/rfc/rfc2132.txt (obsoletes RFC1532)
RFC1534	Interoperation Between DHCP and BOOTP	http://www.rfc-editor.org/rfc/rfc1534.txt
RFC2241	DHCP Options for Novell Directory Services	http://www.rfc-editor.org/rfc/rfc2241.txt
RFC2242	NetWare/IP Domain Name and Information	http://www.rfc-editor.org/rfc/rfc2242.txt
RFC2485	DHCP Option for the Open Group's User Authentication Protocol	http://www.rfc-editor.org/rfc/rfc2485.txt

continues

RFC	Name	URL
RFC2489	Procedure for Defining New DHCP Options	`http://www.rfc-editor.org/rfc/rfc2489.txt`
RFC2563	DHCP Option to Disable Stateless Auto-Configuration in IPv4 Clients	`http://www.rfc-editor.org/rfc/rfc2563.txt`
RFC951	Bootstrap Protocol	`http://www.rfc-editor.org/rfc/rfc951.txt`
RFC2610	DHCP Options for Service Location Protocol	`http://www.rfc-editor.org/ifc/rfc2610.txt`

For the most current list of Internet Drafts representing work in progress on DHCP in the IETF Dynamic Host Configuration working group, go to `http://www.ietf.org/html.charters/dhc-charter.html`. The following is a partial list of Internet Drafts on DHCP topics:

Name	URL
Authentication for DHCP Messages	`http://www.ietf.org/internet-drafts/draft-ietf-dhc-authentication-11.txt`
DHCP Relay Agent Information Option	`http://www.ietf.org/internet-drafts/draft-ietf-dhc-agent-options-05.txt`
DHCP Failover Protocol	`http://www.ietf.org/internet-drafts/draft-ietf-dhc-failover-04.txt`
Dynamic Host Configuration Protocol (DHCP) Server MIB	`http://www.ietf.org/internet-drafts/draft-ietf-dhc-server-mib-03.txt`
Interaction Between DHCP and DNS	`http://www.ietf.org/internet-drafts/draft-ietf-dhc-dhcp-dns-09.txt`
Dynamic Host Configuration Protocol for IPv6 (DHCPv6)	`http://www.ietf.org/internet-drafts/draft-ietf-dhc-dhcpv6-14.txt`
Extensions for the Dynamic Host Configuration Protocol for IPv6	`http://www.ietf.org/internet-drafts/draft-ietf-dhc-v6exts-11.txt`

DHCP Server and Operating System Versions

This appendix briefly describes the ISC and Microsoft DHCP servers with the intent of providing readers with an idea of the different features to consider in any DHCP server. It also describes some operating system dependencies that are specific to the ISC DHCP server (which runs on a variety of operating systems).

H.1 Choosing a DHCP Server

The ISC DHCP server and the Microsoft DHCP server are not the only servers available today. Indeed, several other DHCP servers exist that (although not as popular as the ISC and Microsoft servers) are competently implemented and are just as useful. Following is a description of some of the advantages and disadvantages of the ISC and Microsoft servers. You can use this information to help you compare other DHCP servers as well.

H.1.1 Operating System Platforms

The first difference you are likely to notice between the ISC and Microsoft DHCP servers is that the latter comes as part of the Windows NT Server package, and it runs only on Windows NT Server. The ISC DHCP server, on the other hand, runs on many UNIX and UNIX-like systems, but it does not currently run on Windows NT (although a port is in progress and may be available by the time this book is published). However, the ISC DHCP server comes with source code. So, in theory, it *can* run on almost any system. Table

H.1 shows some of the systems on which the ISC DHCP server was configured and tested.

Thus, if you run an NT-only site, you have at least one compelling reason to run the Windows NT DHCP server. If you run a UNIX-only site, or a site in which you run central computing services from UNIX machines, this may be a good reason to choose the ISC DHCP server.

The DHCP protocol requires that the server know on what network interface a packet arrives and determine on what interface a packet is sent. On operating systems that cannot provide this capability, the server cannot operate correctly if more than one network interface is installed.

On some operating systems, the network Application Programming Interface (API) that enables the server to communicate on more than one network interface at a time requires the application to perform link-layer packet framing. The ISC DHCP server supports link-layer framing for FDDI and Ethernet, but not for token ring. Finally, an unresolved bug exists in the network implementation on some versions of Digital UNIX that prevents the server from working correctly on FDDI networks.

Table H.1 shows a list of operating systems on which the two servers run, as well as network hardware and configurations they support.

TABLE H.1   OPERATING SYSTEMS FOR THE MICROSOFT DHCP AND ISC DHCP SERVERS

Microsoft DHCP Server	ISC DHCP Server	Multiple Interfaces	Token Ring	FDDI
Windows NT Server		X	X	X
	NetBSD	X		X
	Linux 2.0 kernels	X	X	X
	Linux >2.0 kernels	X		X
	Solaris	X		X
	MacOS X	X		X
	FreeBSD	X		X
	BSD/OS	X		X
	Digital UNIX	X	X	
	AIX		X	X
	IRIX		X	X
	SunOS		X	X
	Ultrix	X		X

H.1.2 User Interface

Another difference between the ISC DHCP server and the Microsoft DHCP server is that the ISC DHCP server is configured through a human-readable text file, which you can edit either with a text editor, with automated shell scripts, or with both. The Microsoft DHCP server is controlled entirely through a graphical user interface (GUI), which enables you to view and update the server configuration in a convenient hierarchical format, but prevents you from modifying the server configuration with any sort of automated script.

This can actually be a key difference between the two servers. For a simple installation, it may be much easier to configure the DHCP server using a GUI. For a more complicated installation—or for an installation in which you are trying to do things that weren't envisioned by the people who designed the GUI—being able to directly modify the server configuration with a program can be a big help.

H.1.3 Database

The Microsoft and ISC DHCP servers use different database formats. The Microsoft database is a binary database, which only Microsoft applications can read. The database format is not documented, and the Windows NT 4.0 distribution does not include a utility to dump the contents of the database into a human-readable form or to load data into the database.

The ISC DHCP server keeps its entire database in memory for quick access, and stores a log of all transactions on disk. The log is a human-readable text file, and the last entry in the file for any given IP address represents the current state of that lease. This database format has some major advantages: When the database is loaded into memory, references and updates to it are quick. Because the on-disk log is stored in a human-readable format, and because the format is documented, it's easy to directly examine the database to determine the state of a particular lease. Writing shell or PERL scripts to modify the database automatically is also very easy.

The disadvantage of the log-structured database is that the DHCP server must parse the entire file when it starts up before it can begin answering requests, whereas the Microsoft DHCP server's binary file enables it to begin responding to requests almost immediately after startup. Depending on the speed of the DHCP server machine's processor, it might take a site with 50,000 active leases several minutes to load the lease database.

H.1.4 Support for BOOTP Clients

Some DHCP servers only support DHCP clients — for example, some versions of the Microsoft DHCP server do not support BOOTP clients. For sites that still have BOOTP clients deployed and want to serve both DHCP and BOOTP clients using the same server, the ISC DHCP server is a better choice.

Serving both BOOTP and DHCP from the same server makes sense for the following reason. Because the BOOTP and DHCP protocols use UDP port 67 and share the same relay agent infrastructure, you need two separate server machines to run both a DHCP and a BOOTP server. Also, DHCP/BOOTP relay agents must be configured to send all packets to both DHCP and BOOTP servers because relay agents generally don't know the difference between DHCP and BOOTP packets. In addition to generating an unwanted load on both servers, this may also double the amount of traffic the relay agent generates.

> **Note**
>
> The DHCP server in Windows 2000 provides support for BOOTP clients, although at the time of this writing it is not clear exactly how that support compares to the BOOTP client support in the ISC DHCP server. If you require both NT and BOOTP service, this may be an option worth considering.

H.2 ISC DHCP Server Operating System Dependencies

Because the ISC DHCP server runs on such a wide variety of different operating systems, quite a few system dependencies are specific to these operating systems, as you see in the following section.

H.2.1 Problems with the 255.255.255.255 Broadcast Address

On almost every operating system in which the ISC DHCP distribution uses the BSD socket API to send and receive packets on the network, a bug exists in the API that prevents it from correctly sending packets to the 255.255.255.255 broadcast address. Instead, the kernel uses the local subnet broadcast address. For example, on a subnet with a subnet mask of 255.255.255.0 and a network number of 10.100.17.0, the kernel substitutes the address 10.100.17.255 if the DHCP server specifies an IP destination address of 255.255.255.255.

This substitution of a different broadcast address is a problem because the DHCP protocol specifies that if the DHCP server is to broadcast a response to the DHCP client, it must broadcast the response to the 255.255.255.255 broadcast address. Because the client doesn't know what network it is on, it has no way of knowing whether 10.100.17.255 is a host IP address or the broadcast address for the subnet. Many DHCP clients ignore this, but unfortunately the Microsoft DHCP client does not. As a result, the server receives DHCPDISCOVER messages from the Microsoft client and broadcasts responses, but the Microsoft client never hears the responses. Thus, it continues broadcasting DHCPDISCOVER messages until it gives up and tells the user it can't configure the network.

Fortunately, on most such operating systems, you can get around this problem by installing a host route to the 255.255.255.255 address. You can also avoid this problem in other ways, as described in the following sections under the operating systems on which the solutions were tried. However, if one solution does not work, you may want to try the suggested solution for another operating system instead.

Linux Difficulties

A variety of different problems can occur with DHCP distribution, depending on the version of the Linux kernel you are using. These difficulties are discussed in the order of the version of the operating system in which the problems occur, starting from the most recent version, Linux 2.2.

To use the ISC DHCP distribution with a Linux version 2.1 or later kernel, you must have version 2.0b1p18 or later of the ISC DHCP distribution. In addition, you must configure raw packet and Linux packet filter support into your Linux kernel. If you do not, you get one of a variety of errors when you first start the DHCP server, indicating that it can't create a socket or bind to it. The error message indicates that you must set CONFIG_FILTER=y and CONFIG_PACKET=y in your Linux kernel configuration file and rebuild the kernel.

Also, in current versions of the kernel, you must configure these capabilities into the kernel; they do not load automatically if you configure them as loadable modules. You can force the modules to load on system startup, but it's probably more reliable to just link them into the kernel that you start up.

Although several users reported this error message and claimed they installed everything correctly, in reality they either forgot to install the configuration parameters before they built the kernel, forgot to install the new kernel, or didn't succeed in getting the modules to load.

Some older versions of the Linux kernel (2.0.33 and later, until 2.1) provide the capability to use multiple network interfaces with the BSD socket API. This is actually preferable to the Linux packet filter/raw packet API in many ways, but on some kernels, it is necessary to configure a route to the broadcast address for this to work. On Linux, the process for adding a route to the broadcast address varies depending on the version of the Linux netutils package you are using. Example H.1 shows the easiest method, which works on more recent versions of netutils.

EXAMPLE H.1

```
% route add -host 255.255.255.255 dev eth0
```

If you are using more than one network interface, you must add the route to the broadcast address on all interfaces. Older versions of netutils do not accept an address of 255.255.255.255 on the command line because, as a signed 32-bit number, its value is -1; and this is the same as the error code returned by the inet_aton() function if it can't convert the address, and so the route command assumes the address is bad. To work around this, add an entry to your /etc/hosts file for the all-ones IP address, as shown in Example H.2.

EXAMPLE H.2

```
255.255.255.255 all-ones
```

Now specify the hostname you used as the destination for the route command, as shown in Example H.3.

EXAMPLE H.3

```
% route add -host all-ones dev eth0
```

On some older versions of netutils, even this doesn't work. You can try the command shown in Example H.4. It may work, but you should upgrade your version of netutils if you can. This is a *very* old version of netutils.

EXAMPLE H.4

```
% route add -net 255.255.255.0 dev eth0
```

Some versions of the Linux 2.1 kernel have a configuration parameter that you can turn on and off to indicate whether the kernel should enable processes to act as BOOTP agents. If this feature is not enabled, the DHCP server cannot run. If you have trouble getting the server to work on a Linux 2.1 kernel, you may need to enable this, as shown in Example H.5.

EXAMPLE H.5

```
% echo 1 >/proc/sys/net/ipv4/ip_boot_agent
```

Versions of the Linux kernel prior to 2.0.33 do not support DHCP service on more than one network interface. Even if you do not have more than one network interface, you should upgrade your Linux kernel before running DHCP; later kernels are known to work better with DHCP service in general.

HP-UX Difficulties

HP-UX has the broadcast address bug described earlier and can support only a single network interface. On some versions of HP-UX, it may be possible to use the route commands suggested in the section on Linux. If these don't work, another method that is known to work on some versions of HP-UX is to modify the /etc/rc.config.d/netconf file, as shown in Example H.6. (You must modify this to suit your configuration; see the HP documentation for more information.)

EXAMPLE H.6

```
INTERFACE_NAME[0]=lan0
IP_ADDRESS[0]=1.1.1.1
SUBNET_MASK[0]=255.255.255.0
BROADCAST_ADDRESS[0]="255.255.255.255"
LANCONFIG_ARGS[0]="ether"
DHCP_ENABLE[0]=0
```

Ultrix Difficulties

Ultrix uses the Ultrix Packet Filter API. For this to work, the *pfilt* device must be configured into the Ultrix kernel and be present in /dev. If you type man packetfilter, you get some information on how to configure your kernel for the packet filter (if it isn't already configured) and how to make an entry for it in /dev.

Solaris Difficulties

Multiple interface support on Solaris seems to be stable as of 2.0b1pl27. However, some problems were reported using the DLPI API with some network interface cards. If the DHCP server starts up with no errors but never seems to receive any packets, you may have this problem. If you have only one network interface, you can modify the includes/site.h file by adding #define USE_SOCKETS, and then type make clean; make. The DHCP server that this builds uses the sockets API instead of DLPI. Except for the restriction that the sockets API can be used with only one network interface on Solaris, no known problems exist on Solaris when using this API.

APPENDIX I

Glossary

/n   Indicates a subnet mask or *prefix length* of *n* bits (see *subnet mask*).

6bone   An experimental network testbed for IPv6.

address classes   The definitions of the network number and host identifier component of IP addresses. Class A, B, and C addresses define unicast addresses, class D addresses are used for multicast, and class E addresses are reserved for future use.

address pool   A set of IP addresses available for assignment by a DHCP server to clients on a specific network segment.

Address Resolution Protocol (ARP)   A protocol used by TCP/IP hosts to resolve an IP address into a hardware address.

application layer   The component of the TCP/IP protocol models that includes specific protocols used by application programs.

ARP cache timeout   Defines the lifetime for entries in the ARP cache.

authentication   In DHCP, the process of reliably identifying a DHCP client or server to other DHCP participants, and of guaranteeing the integrity of DHCP messages.

automatic allocation   Assignment of a IP address with an infinite lease to a client by a DHCP server (see *dynamic allocation*).

bootfile   A file containing additional information needed by a computer using TCP/IP. For example, a *bootfile* may contain the operating system code for a computer with no local disk storage.

Bootstrap Protocol (BOOTP)   A protocol that provides configuration information to network devices through the network and, thus, eliminates the need for the system administrator to manually configure each network device. BOOTP is a predecessor of DHCP.

bridge   A device that connects two network media, which appear to the attached computers to be a single network segment.

broadcast   A technique for delivering a network message to more than one destination. Many hardware technologies include the capability to broadcast a frame to all the devices attached to a network segment.

broadcast flag   A bit in the `flags` field of a DHCP message that controls the use of broadcast when sending messages to a DHCP client.

cable modem network   A networking technology that uses the coaxial cable infrastructure used by cable TV to provide network connections to residences at speeds up to several megabits per second.

class A, B, C address   The three classes of IP addresses used for unicast messages; see Chapter 4, "Configuring TCP/IP Stacks," for the formats of these addresses.

client   An application, computer, or other device that uses services provided by other applications or computers, usually through a network.

client identifier   A value chosen by a client to be used as its identifier by DHCP servers, rather than the client's hardware address.

client–server model   A paradigm for organizing distributed systems in which applications contact a server to perform application-specific functions.

collisions   In DHCP, the use of the same client identifier by different DHCP clients.

colon hexadecimal or colon hex   A textual representation of IPv6 IP addresses in which groups of 16 bits are written in hexadecimal notation, separated by colons.

data link layer   The component of the TCP/IP protocol model that is responsible for delivering an IP datagram across a network segment to the next hop on the path to the datagram's destination.

datagram An IP protocol message.

default router, default route A router used as the next hop to the destination when there is no specific route in the IP routing table; some implementations specify default routers as *default route* entries in the routing table.

dentist's office Used as a shorthand or example of a small office with a local network (origin unknown).

DHC Working Group The *Dynamic Host Configuration* Working Group of the IETF, which is responsible for the development of DHCP.

DHCP See *Dynamic Host Configuration Protocol*.

DHCP client A computer or other device that uses DHCP to obtain configuration parameters.

DHCP client port UDP port 68, reserved for transmission of messages to DHCP and BOOTP clients.

DHCP option A specific configuration parameter, carried in the `variable-format` section of a DHCP message.

DHCP server An application program or computer that provides configuration parameters to DHCP clients.

DHCP server port UDP port 67, reserved for DHCP and BOOTP transmission of messages to DHCP servers.

DHCPACK message Transmitted by a DHCP server to a client to confirm the use of the parameters requested by the client in a DHCPREQUEST message.

dhcpd.conf (file) The configuration file that controls the operation of the ISC DHCP server.

dhcpd.leases (file) The file in which the ISC DHCP server records information about leases on addresses assigned to DHCP clients.

DHCPINFORM message Used by a DHCP client that doesn't need an IP address to obtain other configuration parameters.

DHCPNAK message Transmitted by a DHCP server to a client to inform the client that it cannot use the parameters requested by the client in a DHCPREQUEST message.

DHCPRELEASE message Transmitted by a DHCP client to a server to explicitly terminate the lease on the client's IP address prior to the expiration of the lease.

DHCPREQUEST message   Used by a DHCP client to request initial configuration parameters, to confirm the validity of an address already assigned to the client, and to obtain an extension on the lease for an address assigned to the client.

DHCPv6   A version of DHCP for IPv6.

Domain Name System (DNS)   A service for translating names for Internet hosts into IP addresses.

dotted decimal   A notation for IP addresses in which each byte of the address is written as a decimal number, separated by periods ("dots").

dynamic allocation   Assignment of a IP address to a DHCP client for a finite period of time; the duration of the assignment is known as a *lease*.

Dynamic Host Configuration Protocol (DHCP)   A protocol that automates the process of configuring network hosts by allowing hosts to obtain IP addresses and configuration parameters through the network; DHCP eliminates the need for manual configuration of hosts and manual assignment of IP addresses by network administrators.

encapsulation   The technique of carrying data within a protocol message; for example, an IP datagram is encapsulated as the data area in an Ethernet frame.

Ethernet   A network technology that carries data at 10 Mbps across a shared medium.

Ethernet encapsulation   The specific format for transmitting an IP datagram in an Ethernet frame; in DHCP, either Ethernet version 2 (RFC894) or IEEE 802.3 (RFC1042) encapsulation.

EUI-64 identifier   A 64-bit unique identifier defined by IEEE. Assignment of EUI-64 identifiers is managed by the IEEE Registration Authority.

expression   In the `/etc/dhcp.conf` file, a mathematical statement whose value is derived from constants in the expression and by values extracted from the DHCP packet as specified in the expression; the value obtained from evaluating an expression is either true or false.

failover protocol   A protocol used between DHCP servers that allows a secondary DHCP server to provide service to DHCP clients when the primary server fails.

File Transfer Protocol (FTP)   A service that includes an application layer protocol for transferring files between computers.

finite state machine   A technique for describing the behavior of a system as a set of states, transitions between states, and outputs.

firewall   A device situated between an organization's network and the Internet that filters IP traffic to limit forwarding of unwanted IP datagrams.

fixed-format section   The part of a DHCP message that has the same format in every message; the fixed-format section is divided into several fields.

frame   A packet transmitted across network hardware.

hardware address   The unique identifier for a network interface on a network segment; a frame usually includes the hardware addresses of both the destination and source network interfaces.

hashed message authentication code   A technique for generating a message authentication code (MAC) based on a keyed message digest generator (see *MD5, MAC*).

hexadecimal   Base 16 representation for integers.

host   Any networked device that does not act like a router; that is, does not forward IP datagrams.

Host Requirements documents (RFC1121, RFC1122, RFC1127)   A summary and analysis of all the protocols in the TCP/IP suite.

host table   A file containing a list of hosts and their hardware addresses and DNS names.

hotelling   The temporary use of offices by staff on a daily basis.

HyperText Markup Language (HTML)   A system of tags used to define the appearance of a document.

HyperText Transfer Protocol (HTTP)   A protocol used to transmit documents, usually specified in HTML, for example, between World Wide Web servers and browsers.

interface identifier   A 64-bit value that can be generated from an interface link-layer address; used in IPv6 addresses (RFC2343).

internet   Any set of network segments connected by routers over which hosts use TCP/IP.

Internet   The global collection of public and private networks using TCP/IP.

Internet Control Message Protocol (ICMP)   A part of the TCP/IP suite that provides error reporting and information functions.

Internet Draft   A preliminary protocol specification published by the IETF for review and comment by the Internet community.

Internet Engineering Steering Group (IESG)   Guides the operation of the IETF and sets the status of Internet protocols.

Internet Engineering Task Force (IETF)   Organization for the evolution of the Internet, and development and coordination of new Internet protocols.

internet layer   The component of the TCP/IP model that is responsible for end–to–end delivery of protocol messages between computers.

Internet Protocol (IP)   The protocol in the TCP/IP suite that implements the internet layer.

Internet Relay Chat (IRC)   A service for real-time messaging among groups of network users.

Internet Software Consortium (ISC)   A nonprofit organization that produces reference implementations of TCP/IP protocols and services, including DHCP and DNS.

intranet   A private internet, usually within a single organization.

IP   See *Internet Protocol*.

IP address   A 32-bit number assigned to a network interface that uniquely identifies the computer and specifies the network segment to which the computer is connected.

IP datagram   The basic message unit for data delivered by IP.

IP IP address translation (IPNAT)   See *IP address translation (NAT)*.

IPng (IP next generation)   See *IPv6*.

IPv6 (IP version 6)   A new version of IP under development by the IETF.

ISC DHCP client   A freely available implementation of a DHCP client produced by ISC.

ISC DHCP relay agent   A freely available implementation of a DHCP relay agent produced by ISC.

ISC DHCP server   A freely available implementation of a DHCP server produced by ISC.

lease Period of time over which a DHCP client may use its assigned IP address.

Lightweight Directory Access Protocol (LDAP) A protocol used to access directory information from an X.500 directory.

limited broadcast IP address The IP address used for broadcast by hosts on a network segment; usually 255.255.255.255, but some legacy devices use 0.0.0.0.

link-layer address See *hardware address.*

Linux An operating system modeled after UNIX for which source code is freely available.

magic cookie or cookie A well-known number; in DHCP, a 32-bit number that identifies the format of the options in the variable-format section of a DHCP message.

management information base (MIB) A data structure consisting of named objects shared by SNMP agents and managers; a MIB gives agents and managers a common naming scheme for values to be managed through SNMP.

maximum transfer unit (MTU) The largest frame that can be accepted by a network segment.

message digest algorithm 5 (MD5) An algorithm for generating a message digest based on a secret key.

media access control (MAC) address See *hardware address.*

message authentication code (MAC) A value computed from the contents of an authenticated message that cannot be forged; the recipient uses the MAC to confirm that the contents of the message were not changed.

mobile device A networked computer or other device that can be moved among different network segments.

multicast A technique for delivering a datagram to multiple destinations by transmitting a single copy of the datagram across any network segment.

NetWare A protocol suite and set of network services developed by Novell.

NetWare Directory Service (NDS) A hierarchical naming or directory service for NetWare.

NetWare/IP A version of the NetWare protocol suite that uses IP for datagram transport.

IP address See *IP address*.

IP address translation (NAT) A technique for rewriting the IP addresses in IP datagrams; often used to convert internal, private addresses (for example, from network 10.0.0.0) to external addresses that can be routed through the Internet. A *NAT box* or *NAT* is a device attached to an internal network that provides NAT service.

network analyzer A device that receives all frames from the network segment to which it is attached and displays the contents of the frames in a variety of formats; sometimes called a *packet sniffer* after the name of a widely used commercial network analyzer.

Network Basic Input/Output System (NetBIOS) A protocol suite originally developed by IBM and now widely used among computers using the Windows operating systems.

Network File System (NFS) An open-standard protocol originally developed by Sun Microsystems for the exchange of file contents through a network.

Network Information Service (NIS), Network Information Service+ (NIS+) A directory service included with Sun Microsystems' Solaris operating system.

network interface card (NIC) Connects a computer or other device to a network.

Network News Transport Protocol (NNTP) An application protocol for transmission of data, used by the Network News (`netnews`) service.

network segment A distinct physical network; all computers connected to a network segment can transmit directly to each other.

Network Time Protocol (NTP) An application protocol for coordination of internal clocks among networked computers.

octet An 8-bit data item; usually synonymous with *byte*.

Open Shortest Path First (OSPF) A routing protocol based on a link-state algorithm.

option A configuration parameter carried in the `variable-format` section of a DHCP message; each option includes an *option code* that identifies the option, a *length*, and the *option data*.

options or `variable-format` section Carries DHCP options, whose length is variable and whose contents and format depend on the option type.

overlay or shared segment   See *shared network.*

packet   A generic name for a protocol message; may be used as a synonym for a hardware frame, an IP datagram, or a TCP segment.

path maximum transfer unit (PMTU)   The largest IP datagram that can be transmitted without fragmentation along the path between two computers; in IPv4, used to control the size of TCP segments to avoid fragmentation.

physical layer or hardware layer   The component of the TCP/IP protocol model that delivers data encoded in a physical representation, such as electrical current, radio waves, or light.

ping   An application that uses ICMP Echo Request/Echo Reply messages to determine if two computers can exchange network messages.

Point to Point Protocol (PPP)   A protocol used for transmission of IP datagrams across point-to-point networks such as telephone modem connections.

Post Office Protocol (POP)   A protocol used to access the contents of a mailbox on a mail server; for example, used by a desktop computer to access mail messages on an organization's mail server.

prefix length   Gives the number of bits in the network identifier portion (prefix) of a IP address; the notation /n indicates a prefix of n bits.

proxy ARP   A use of ARP in which a device answers an ARP request for an IP address not assigned to it.

relay agent   Forwards DHCP messages from clients to servers, allowing centrally located DHCP servers to provide DHCP service for clients on several network segments.

remote access server (RAS)   A device that provides network access to remote devices connected through, for example, a dialup connection or a tunnel.

renumbering   The process of assigning new IP addresses to all the hosts in a network.

Request for Comments (RFC)   A document in the series of documents published by the RFC Editor that pertains to the Internet and Internet protocols. The RFCs include protocol specifications, status reports on Internet protocols, and other reports about Internet-related topics.

reservation   An entry in a DHCP server database that manually assigns a specific address to a DHCP client (see *dynamic allocation*).

reserved addresses   IP addresses reserved for DHCP clients.

resource record (RR)   An entry in DNS that holds DNS data.

Reverse Address Resolution Protocol (RARP)/Dynamic RARP (DRARP)   A TCP/IP host uses RARP to find its IP address from a static database based on its hardware address; DRARP allows a new host to be registered in the address database automatically.

RFC   See *Request for Comments*.

router   A network device with more than one network interface that forwards IP datagrams between network segments.

router discovery   A mechanism (part of ICMP) through which TCP/IP hosts can find routers connected to the same network segment.

Routing Information Protocol (RIP)   A routing protocol based on a vector-distance algorithm.

routing table   A table that contains the addresses of routers to which IP datagrams are to be forwarded for delivery.

RR   *See resource record.*

scope   In the Microsoft DHCP server, a collection of IP addresses and associated parameter values to be assigned to DHCP clients; more generally, the range of influence of an option declaration or variable.

Service Location Protocol (SLP)   A dynamic directory for identifying and locating network services; can provide flexible and dynamic configuration of services also provided through DHCP options.

shared network   A network segment that was assigned two or more IP subnets.

shell script   A program written in a UNIX command interpreter language such as sh or csh.

Simple Mail Transport Protocol (SMTP)   A protocol used to deliver electronic mail messages.

source routing   A technique in which the source specifies the path for an IP datagram to its destination, rather than making routing decisions in routers.

state transition diagram   A graphical representation of the states and transitions that describe the behavior of a finite state machine.

static route   A fixed routing table entry that is not obtained through a routing protocol.

static (or fixed) allocation   Preconfigured assignment of IP address and configuration parameters to a DHCP client, usually in the DHCP server configuration file.

StreetTalk   A directory service included with Banyan Vines.

subnet   A set of IP addresses that share a common network number, defined either by the class of the IP address or by a subnet mask.

subnet declaration   In the ISC DHCP server configuration file, the definition of an IP subnet for which the server should manage address assignments.

subnet mask   A 32-bit number that identifies which bits of the address make up the subnet address and which are used as the host address.

subnetting   A technique for dividing Class A, B, or C addresses into smaller groups of IP addresses or *subnets* that more closely match the addressing requirements for network segments (RFC950, RFC1878, RFC1519).

superscope   In the Microsoft DHCP server, a network segment that was assigned more than one IP subnet.

T1   The time at which a DHCP client begins to attempt to extend the lease on its IP address from the DHCP server that originally assigned the address.

T2   The time at which a DHCP client begins to attempt to extend the lease on its assigned IP address from any available DHCP server.

TCP keepalive   A technique for maintaining a TCP connection by periodically transmitting bytes that are not part of the data in the TCP connection.

TCP/IP   The suite of computer communication protocols used in the Internet; the name comes from the two most important protocols in the suite, TCP and IP (see *Transmission Control Protocol* and *Internet Protocol*).

TCP/IP stack   An implementation of the TCP/IP protocol suite.

time to live (TTL)   Limits the lifetime of an IP datagram in an internet. Initially set to a positive integer and decremented by routers; if the TTL goes to zero, the datagram is discarded.

trailers   Two computers that negotiate to use *trailers* put the headers of TCP/IP messages at the end of each message rather than at the front (RFC893).

transaction ID A 32-bit identification number used to match DHCP response messages with DHCP request messages.

Transmission Control Protocol (TCP) Provides reliable, connection-oriented delivery of arbitrarily long messages or streams of data.

Trivial File Transfer Protocol (TFTP) A simple application protocol built on UDP for copying files between networked computers.

UCS Transformation Format (UTF-8) An encoding that represents 7-bit ASCII values in a single byte, and then uses multibyte values to represent other characters from the Unicode Standard.

unicast Delivery of a protocol message to a single destination computer; *unicast* describes the normal delivery of IP datagrams.

Uniform Resource Locator (URL) A syntactic notation for identifying network objects that includes an access protocol, as well as the location and name of the object.

Universal Character Set (UCS) Defines encodings for the characters from most of the writing systems in existence today.

Universal Time Coordinated (UTC) (formerly Greenwich Mean Time) The time of day at the Prime Meridian, which does not follow any seasonal adjustments to local time.

User Datagram Protocol (UDP) Provides best-effort, connectionless delivery of discrete messages; the protocol used to carry DHCP messages.

valid lifetime In IPv6, defines the time through which an address may be used.

variable-format section The portion of a DHCP message in which options are carried.

virtual hosting Provides for multiple copies of a service—for example, multiple World Wide Web servers—through a single physical interface by assigning more than one IP address to the interface.

Windows Internet Naming System (WINS) Provides dynamic NetBIOS to IP address name registration and resolution.

X.500   A directory system, originally part of the OSI protocol suite, now widely used with TCP/IP.

X Window System   A windowing system that can be used for remote graphical displays.

Index

Symbols

N

P-Q

The *Macmillan Technology Series* is a comprehensive and authoritative set of guides to the most important computing standards of today. Each title in this series is aimed at bringing computing professionals closer to the scientists and engineers behind the technological implementations that will change tomorrow's innovations in computing.

Currently available titles in the *Macmillan Technology Series* include:

Supporting Service Level Agreements on IP Networks, **by Dinesh Verma (ISBN: 1-57870-146-5)**

This essential guide provides ISP managers and engineers practical insight into the procedures required to fulfill their SLAs, and it describes methods and techniques that businesses can use to ensure that the requirements of their service level agreements are met.

Differentiated Services for the Internet, **by Kalevi Kilkki (ISBN: 1-57870-132-5)**

One of the few technologies that will enable networks to handle traffic to meet the demands of particular applications, Differentiated Services is currently being standardized by the IETF. This book offers network architects, engineers, and managers of Internet and other packet networks critical insight into this new technology.

Gigabit Ethernet Networking, **by David G. Cunningham, Ph.D. and William G. Lane, Ph.D. (ISBN: 1-57870-062-0)**

Written by key contributors to the Gigabit Ethernet standard, this book offers critical information to enable network engineers and architects to make cost-effective decisions about how to design and implement their particular network to meet current traffic loads, and to ensure scalability with future growth.

DSL: Simulation Techniques and Standards Development for Digital Subscriber Line Systems, **by Walter Chen (ISBN: 1-57870-017-5)**

With low-level coverage of xDSL technologies, this book is ideal for computing professionals who are looking for new high-speed communications technology, who must understand the dynamics of xDSL communications to create compliant applications, or who simply want to better understand this new wave of technology.

ADSL/VDSL Principles, **by Dr. Dennis J. Rauschmayer (ISBN: 1-57870-015-9)**

ADSL/VDSL Principles provides the communications and networking engineer with practical explanations, technical detail, and in-depth insight needed to fully implement ADSL and VDSL. Topics that are essential to the successful implementation of these technologies are covered.

LDAP: Programming Directory-Enabled Applications with Lightweight Directory Access Protocol, **by Tim Howes and Mark Smith (ISBN: 1-57870-000-0)**

If you design or program software for network computing or are interested in directory services, *LDAP* is an essential resource to help you understand the LDAP API, learn how to write LDAP programs, understand how to LDAP-enable an existing application, and learn how to use a set of command-line LDAP tools to search and update directory information.

Upcoming titles in the *Macmillan Technology Series* include:

Virtual Private Networks, **by David Bovee (ISBN: 1-57870-120-1)**

Directory Enabled Networking, **by John Strassner (ISBN: 1-57870-140-6)**

Understanding the Public-Key Infrastructure, **by Carlisle Adams and Steve Lloyd (ISBN: 1-57870-166-x)**

SNMP Agents, **by Bob Natale (ISBN: 1-57870-110-4)**

Intrusion Detection, **by Rebecca Gurley Bace (ISBN: 1-57870-185-6)**